Integrating Macs with Your PC Network

Ken Maki

John Wiley & Sons, Inc.
New York • Chichester • Brisbane • Toronto • Singapore

Trademarks

Designations used by companies to distinguish their products are often claimed as trademarks. In all instances where John Wiley & Sons, Inc. is aware of a claim, the product names appear in initial capital or all capital letters. Readers, however, should contact the appropriate companies for more complete information regarding trademarks and registration.

This text is printed on acid-free paper.

Associate Publisher: Katherine Schowalter
Editor: Tim Ryan
Managing Editor: Frank Grazioli
Editorial Production & Design: Electric Ink, Ltd.

Copyright © 1994 by John Wiley & Sons, Inc.

All rights reserved. Published simultaneously in Canada.

This publication is designed to provide accurate and authoritative information in regard to the subject matter covered. It is sold with the understanding that the publisher is not engaged in rendering professional service. If expert assistance is required, the services of a competent professional person should be sought. FROM A DECLARATION OF PRINCIPLES JOINTLY ADOPTED BY A COMMITTEE OF THE AMERICAN BAR ASSOCIATION AND A COMMITTEE OF PUBLISHERS.

Reproduction or translation of any part of this work beyond that permitted by section 107 or 108 of the 1976 United States Copyright Act without the permission of the copyright owner is unlawful. Requests for permission or further information should be addressed to the Permission Department, John Wiley & Sons, Inc.

Library of Congress Cataloging-in-Publication Data:

Maki, Ken.
    Integrating Macs with your PC network / by Ken Maki.
       p.   cm.
    Includes index.
    ISBN 0-471-30505-7 (paper)
    1. Local area networks (Computer networks)   2. Macintosh (Computer)
3. IBM-compatible computers.   I. Title.
TK5105.7.M337   1994
004.6'8—dc20   93-49414

Printed in the United States of America
10 9 8 7 6 5 4 3 2 1

This book is dedicated to Arturo Arias.

Without your classes none of my books would have been written. I cannot begin to express my gratitude.

Natura creans et non creata.
—M. Bakhtin

Acknowledgments

There is no way that a book can proceed from the idea to the finished product without a lot of help from a lot of people. And this list of people always ends up being listed in a section called "acknowledgments." Hence, rather than breaking from tradition, I'll also enter my thanks and heartfelt gratitude to those who were instrumental and influential in the creation of this book.

First of all, thanks go to Tim Ryan of John Wiley and Sons. He is a good editor who undoubtedly suffered because of the scheduling problems I caused. And although he is too kind to tell me I'm a pain, I know that I can be and appreciate his patience and support. Frank Grazioli, also at Wiley, is responsible for this book's being printed. For the copy editing and production staff at Electric Ink, Karl Barndt and Lydia Ievins: you have my condolences, you did a great job. Thanks one and all.

Many vendors and their tech support staff helped me when I had questions about how something operates. The following are public relations and technical people without whom this book could not have been started, listed along with their respective companies:

- Rose Kearsley—*Novell*
- Joanne Anderson, Carl Foote, Rob Vazzana, and Tim Blake—*Banyan Systems*
- Katherian Morgan—*Miramar Systems*
- Cory Maloy—*Dayna Communications*
- Bob Olliver and Keri Walker—*Apple Computer*
- Stacy Lemire—*Microsoft*

Acknowledgments

- Joe Stunkard—*Artisoft*
- Freda Cook—*Aldus*
- Kathy Mandle—*Adobe Systems*

I would also like to extend a special thanks to Asanté Technologies for providing some of the equipment that made this book possible. Without their support and networking cards and hubs, it would have been more difficult to network all of the different computers used.

Unfortunately, I know that I have forgotten or missed some people or companies in this list. I received some help from almost every company listed in the book, and I have not intentionally left anyone out. Please do not feel slighted if your name is not mentioned; you do have my deepest gratitude.

Finally, there are those who had to put up with my frantic schedule, long hours, and neglect. This list includes my clients and my family; neither saw enough of me during this book's writing. If it were not for my wife, Chris, keeping the fabric of our home together as the book was written, I'm not sure it would have been finished. Thanks, honey.

Contents

Introduction — xv

CHAPTER 1

The Macintosh Invasion — 1

Introduction — 1
Macintosh Networking Basics — 3
   AppleTalk and AppleShare   3
   Macintosh Protocols and Terminology   4
   AppleTalk System Architecture   9
Macintosh Networking Options — 13
   System 7 File Sharing   14
   AppleShare File Servers   15
   AppleTalk LaserWriters   18
Several Approaches You Can Take to Solve Your Needs — 19
   File Exchanges   19
   E-mail   21
   Running Applications   22
   Groupware   24
Conclusion — 25

CHAPTER 2

Macintosh Networking — 27

Introduction — 27

Contents

The Macintosh Operating System   28
   The System Folder   29
   Macintosh Disk Basics   46
   Macintosh File Structures   50

The Mac's Networking Software   54
   Macintosh System Networking Elements   54
   Installing Macintosh Networking Software   58
   System Versions and Networking Concerns   63

Macintosh Networking   64
   Accessing an AppleShare File Server   65
   Access Privileges Security   67
   Inheritance   76
   Basic Network Trouble-shooting   77

Macintosh Networks   79
   Network Cabling and Adapters (Bus Sizes, Comparative Speeds, and Compatibility Issues)   80
   Routers   85

Conclusion   86

Chapter 3
SneakerNet and Other Simple Connections   87

Introduction   87
Exchanging Floppy Disks   88
   Floppy Disk Drives   89
   On the Mac Side of Things   89
   Attaching Drives to the SCSI Bus   90
   DOS on the Other Side   91
   Making the Floppy Connection   92
   Apple File Exchange   93
   Translating MS-DOS Files with Apple File Exchange   95
   Desktop Mounting Utilities   97
   Assigning Extensions to Macintosh Applications   109
   MS-DOS-to-Mac or Mac-to-MS-DOS Utility Programs   116
   Ideas   119

Conclusion   120

Chapter 4

Using a LANtastic Macintosh Gateway — 123

Introduction — 123
Description of LANtastic for Macintosh — 124
Basic Requirements — 127
   The Gateway Machine — 127
   Macintosh Requirements — 130
   Planning the Physical Network — 130
Setting Up the Gateway — 133
   The Gateway's LANtastic Configuration — 134
Installing the LANtastic for Macintosh Software — 136
   Configuring LANtastic for Macintosh — 138
Using the Gateway — 161
The Gateway from a Macintosh Point of View — 164
Trouble-shooting LANtastic for Macintosh — 169
   Configuration Errors — 170
   Server Crashes and System File Problems — 170
   Memory or Buffer Problems — 171
   Printer Problems — 172
Conclusion — 172

Chapter 5

Connecting Your Macintosh to a Novell Server — 175

Introduction — 175
Just the Facts Please (Various Server Configurations) — 176
   Macintosh Network Cards — 177
NetWare as an AppleTalk Router — 179
   Preparing Your Novell Server for the Mac Invasion — 180
A Brief Look at ATCON — 186
   The Macintosh NetWare Utilities — 187
   Using the NetWare Macintosh Utilities — 190
   Making Sense of the Novell AppleTalk Printing Services — 200
   Accessing a Novell Server with Third-Party Software — 219
Conclusion — 221

CONTENTS

CHAPTER 6

Banyan VINES   223

Introduction   223
VINES and the Macintosh   224
    AppleTalk on the VINES Server   224
    Combined Networks   225
    Mapping Your Network   230
    AppleTalk Ports   237
AppleTalk on VINES   240
    Installing the VINES Macintosh Option   240
    Configuration   241
    Restarting AppleTalk   247
    StreetTalk and STDA   250
    DOS Extension Mapping   251
    Guest Login   253
VINES on the Mac   254
    Testing the Connection the First Time   254
    The VINES Extension   255
    The VINES Utilities   257
    Using a Macintosh Internet Router   268
    Intelligent Messaging or VINES Mail   269
AppleTalk PostScript Printers   269
    Creating   270
Trouble-shooting   276
    Known Problems   276
    Port Status   279
Conclusion   281

CHAPTER 7

Microsoft LAN Manager   283

Introduction   283
LAN Manager Services for the Macintosh   284
LAN Manager Services for Macintosh Installation   287
    Your Server's Requirements   287
    Planning the Network   288
    Installing LAN Manager Services for Macintosh   288

LAN Manager Services for Macintosh Administration 294
 Sharing and Modifying Macintosh Volumes 295
 Access Rights 297
 Allowing Guest Logins 299
 Extension Mapping 300
 Stopping and Restarting Services for Macintosh 301
 Using the MACADMIN Program from an
  OS/2 Workstation 302
AppleTalk Printers 302
 Macintosh Printer Access Only 303
 Using LAN Manager as a Print Server 305
 Connecting the Printer to the Server 309
Trouble-shooting 310
 Sharing a CD-ROM 310
 User Access Problems 310
 Administrator and Server Problems 311
 Macintosh File Problems 313
Conclusion 314

CHAPTER 8

Mac-centric Networks 317

Introduction 317
Alternatives to PC Network Operating Systems 318
 PhoneNET Talk 318
 Personal MacLAN 319
 CoActive Connector for DOS/Windows 321
 LANtastic for Macintosh Windows Gateway 323
Using Your Mac as an MS-DOS Machine 323
 A Hardware Macintosh/MS-DOS Machine 324
 Emulation Software 326
 RunPC 329
 Timbuktu 329
Network Utilities 331
 Network Mapping 332
 Traffic Analyzers 335
 Packet Analyzers 338
 Network Management 339

    System and Software Management 341
    Security 343
    Remote Connections 344
    Apple Remote Access 345
Conclusion   349

CHAPTER 9
Cross-Platform Applications   351

Introduction   351
Cross-Platform Software   352
E-mail   353
    QuickMail 355
    cc:Mail 357
    DaVinci eMail 358
    Microsoft Mail 359
Word Processing   360
    Microsoft Word 361
    WordPerfect 364
    Using Other Macintosh Word Processors 365
Spreadsheets   366
    Microsoft Excel 367
    Lotus 123 367
    WingZ 368
    Using Other Spreadsheets 368
Desktop Publishing and Graphics   369
    Aldus 370
    Altsys 372
    Adobe 372
    Quark 375
    Frame Technologies 375
    Microsoft 376
    Deneba Systems 376
    Using Other Graphic Packages 376
Databases   377
    Microsoft Corporation 378
    Blyth Software 378

    Claris Corporation   379
    Novell   379

Workgroup Applications   380
    Lotus Notes   381
    WordPerfect Office   382
    Microsoft Office   382

Integrated Applications   383
    Microsoft Works   383
    WordPerfect Works   384
    ClarisWorks   384

Conclusion   384

CHAPTER 10

Network Trouble-shooting   387

Introduction   387

Trouble-shooting Overview   388
    Tools You'll Need   389
    Identifying the Symptoms   398
    Basic Techniques   403
    Physical Link and Network Problems   406
    Application Problems   407
    Support Resources   409

Conclusion   411

INDEX   413

Introduction

When I first started consulting, I was a Mac-only consultant. It only took a few months for me to realize that I would have to contend with MS-DOS computers. First I was asked to transfer data from Macs to PCs and from PCs to Macs, and then someone asked me to network the two platforms. At that time, networking the two platforms was possible only with software that no longer exists, or through the use of very expensive and complicted gateways. Fortunately, now that I've realized that I can't live in an all-Macintosh world, the manufacturers of PC network operating systems have discovered that they can no longer ignore the Macintosh world.

Every major network operating system now supports the Macintosh, and network administratiors are discovering that they must support this upstart machine. And with the addition of the Macintosh, they have to learn new neworking protocols and a completely new operating system.

You can't add a Mac to your network just by connecting it and turning it on. You must modify the network operating system software. Before you can share files, you have to implement new procedures, and often purchase compatible software, just to name a couple of the issues involved. The world of cross-platform networking is in its adolesence; it will take a few years before it reaches maturity.

Who Needs This Book?

Until cross-platform maturity is reached it will usually be up to the consultants and network administrators to make the two platforms work together. You may not be a consultant or network administrator—you might be someone in a small office who has the added responsibility of taking care of your company's computers. Or maybe you can't afford a consultant.

Whatever your situation, this book is written for anyone who has to deal with the Macintosh in an environment that is predominantly PC-based. I've tried to look at the problem from the perspective of a systems administrator who already has an installed network, but little to no Macintosh experience. The book can also be used by those familiar with the Mac who need to know what software and utilities can be used to network Macs and PCs. Finally, it can be used by anyone who needs to know the issues involved with cross-platform connectivity.

How Will This Book Help You?

This book will help anyone with Macintosh and PC cross-platform concerns by telling you about the basics of Macintosh networking and the integration of the Mac with Novell, Banyan VINES, Microsoft Lan Manager, and Artisoft LANtastic networks. You will also find chapters on Macintosh network trouble-shooting, Mac-to-PC utilities that are not network-dependent, and applications that are cross-platform-compatible.

Basically, this is book is meant as a general cross-platform primer for people who are not really experienced with the Macintosh. But even if you do know the Mac, you should find information that will help you with cross-platform issues. Browse through the book and see if it will meet your needs. The topics covered in the book are:

Chapter 1: The Macintosh Invasion

This chapter offers a basic overview of the Macintosh's networking capabilities, a description of the AppleTalk networking protocol, and some of the issues involved in Macintosh and PC cross-platform networking.

Chapter 2: The Anatomy of a Macintosh Network

This chapter discusses Macintosh System 7 networking and describes the essential system components required for network-

Introduction

ing the Macintosh in any AppleTalk environment. If you have limited experience with the Mac, this chapter is intended to help you get up to speed and make you look like a hero.

Chapter 3: SneakerNet and Other Simple Connections

Here you'll learn about all of the ways you can exchange files between a PC and a Macintosh without a network. This chapter discusses utilities for using PC disks on a Mac or using Mac disks on a PC.

The next four chapters cover specific network operating systems and their implementations of the AppleTalk networking protocol. Each chapter describes how to set up the server or gateway and install the Macintosh software, as well as highlighting the most common problems you'll encounter. Although no chapter is a substitute for the manual, each of these chapters can make the installation process easier. They provide a concise and detailed guide by consolidating a lot of information in one place, since it is often scattered across several manuals. Also, you will that find each chapter can get you up and running with a minimum of frustration. Each provides a short trouble-shooting section specific to the NOS it discusses.

Chapter 4: Using a LANtastic Macintosh Gateway

If you need to add Macintosh support to your LANtastic network, this is the chapter you'll need. It covers everything you need to know for setting up a LANtastic gateway and making the connections between your PCs, Macs, and AppleTalk laser printers.

Chapter 5: Connecting Your Macs to a Novell Network

Here you have a short but complete installation guide for providing Macintosh connectivity for your Novell network. It will guide you through installing the Novell for Macintosh software, and through providing printing services to AppleTalk laser printers for both PCs and Macs. For simply setting up Macintosh connectivity, this chapter is perfect.

Chapter 6: Banyan VINES

If you have a VINES network, this chapter will help you by detailing how to install, set up, and administer the network with Macintosh connectivity. All of the essential topics are covered, including topologies, tunneling, StreetTalk, and connecting AppleTalk printers.

Chapter 7: Microsoft Lan Manager

This chapter discusses Microsoft's Lan Manager and its Macintosh implementation. The chapter provides an overview, then describes the installation, administration, and trouble-shooting of a Lan Manager network with Macintosh integration.

Chapter 8: Expanding Your Horizons

Integrating a Mac into your PC network may not be the answer you are looking for. You might want to connect a PC to your Macintosh network, run MS-DOS software on your Mac, or even control a PC from your Mac. This chapter discusses some of the software that will allow you to perform these tasks and more. Also covered in this chapter are the Macintosh utilities that provide for Macintosh security, remote access, and other networking utilities to help you administer a Macintosh Network.

Chapter 9: Cross-Platform Applications

Once you have your Macs and PCs talking to each other, you'll want to know what software you can use so you have a minimum of problems. This chapter covers almost all of the software that is cross-platform-compatible. You will find short descriptions of word processing, spreadsheet, database, E-mail, and other applications that work in both environments. With this chapter, you can find the software that will work on both platforms, and thus keep your headaches to a minimum.

Chapter 10: Network Trouble-shooting

This is the chapter you need when you have networking headaches. Hopefully, it will act as an aspirin, providing you with immediate relief for your Macintosh networking woes. It is not an advanced network trouble-shooting guide, but just an aspirin or a quick bandage. It is Macintosh-specific and should point you in the proper direction for fixing your network problem, especially if it is a software problem.

How to Use This Book

You will get the most value from this book by reading the chapters that address your particular concerns. You can use this book if you need help with any of the following:

- Transferring data from PCs to Macs
- Transferring data from Macs to PCs
- Cross-platform networking
- A basic Macintosh networking primer
- Almost any Macintosh-to-PC cross-platform issue

Until the day comes when Macs and PCs interoperate seamlessly, there will be cross-platform issues that need to be addressed. This book will help you sort out the issues, and it will get you started in the Macintosh and PC cross-platform world. As the need to exchange data between the platforms increases, books like this one will become an essential part of your library.

Contacting the Author

The author can be contacted at any of the following E-mail addresses:

CompuServe	76120,2755
AT&T Mail	!kmaki
AppleLink	KMAKI
Internet	kmaki@netcom.com

The Macintosh Invasion

Introduction

When you are adding a Macintosh to your network, it is possible that you will view the Mac as an interloper, imposing itself into your nice, stable computing environment, and destined to cause no end of problems. However daunting the task may seem, it is really not as bad as you might imagine. Actually, connecting a Mac is easier than you might think.

The networks that provide for Macintosh connectivity are harder to set up on a PC than on a Macintosh, because Macintosh connections are mostly "plug and play." This means that you set up the PC network to accept the Macintosh, then plug the Mac into the network and go to work. Now, you are probably saying that this attitude is an oversimplification of the situation, but it really isn't.

The Macintosh's hardware and operating system hide all of the really messy details you're used to futzing with when setting up PCs. You do not have to worry about IRQs, DMAs, or memory addresses as you install Macintosh networking hardware. Software installation is just a matter of inserting the proper floppy disk, selecting the type of software installation you want to perform, and letting the Mac do the rest. Very rarely will you have a problem with a Macintosh's software installation, and usually, if you do, the problem will be due to a some system software conflict that is easy to fix.

Of course, you still have to be concerned with general networking issues that are applicable to all computers, such as proper cabling, network addresses (depending on the type of network you're using), and sometimes protocol issues. But even these problems will seem trivial if you've ever spent hours trying to get a couple of PCs to talk to each other and had to create the network from the ground up. The first PC network I installed was a LANtastic network. Artisoft, the manufacturer, had gone to great lengths to make sure the installation is as simple as possible. Yet it took me several hours to make it work right. Part of the problem was familiarizing myself with LANtastic. But the bulk of my problems were not software- but hardware-related issues. I had to figure out what memory addresses the network cards were using, resolve DMA (Dynamic Memory Access) settings, and extend memory exclusions for both DOS and Windows. After those were figured out, I then had to make sure the cabling was correct and all of the connections worked. Then I got to learn how to configure the servers and shared network resources. It was indeed a learning experience.

Compared to LANtastic or any PC networking solution, Macintosh networking is like buying a preassembled toy at Christmas instead of one you have to assemble yourself. If you take two brand-new Macs out of their boxes and connect them with the proper cable, you will have both Macs networked and sharing files in less than five minutes. Everything the Macs need to communicate with each other is built into the system and ready to go, regardless of the wiring protocol.

If you want to use the Macs in a LocalTalk, PhoneNET, or Ethernet environment, all you have to do is connect the cables, turn on the networking software, create an access list, and you've got a LAN (Local Area Network). Macintosh networking is really that simple. And the good news for anyone who is integrating Macintoshes into a PC network is that connecting the Mac is still that simple. This is because Apple has managed to convince the manufacturers of PC network operating systems to support Apple's networking standard, AppleTalk.

The Macintosh Invasion 3

However, just because the actual mechanics of integrating a Macintosh into a PC network have been simplified, it does not follow that you will not have to do any planning or that the PC side of things will be easy. And after you have the Mac attached, you will be confronted by issues of application compatibility, E-mail systems, security, and all of the other networking problems you encounter in your existing environment.

This chapter explains the tasks you'll face as you integrate PCs and Macs on a common network. You will also find a discussion on Macintosh networking terms and general concepts. If you do not understand the Macintosh's networking capabilities and how the Mac handles data, you will have problems when you integrate one into your existing system. So even though this chapter may seem to be elementary, it contains information that will make your networking life easier.

Macintosh Networking Basics

Before diving into a technical discussion of using a Mac on the networks discussed in this book, let's look at a few Macintosh networking terms and the Mac's native networking capabilities. With this knowledge, you will have the foundation you need to plan your network by knowing what you can and can't do with the Macs. You will also be alerted to some security issues you might want to consider. This section will cover basic networking capabilities and Macintosh terminology.

AppleTalk and AppleShare

To use a Macintosh on a PC network without adding software to the Mac, your PC networking platform must support and provide AppleTalk as part of, or as an add-on option for, the network operating system (NOS). The AppleTalk system architecture is a set of networking protocols used by all Macintoshes to access networked resources. This book covers only Macintosh/PC networking solutions that use AppleTalk for their servers. Often, this networking protocol is referred to as the AppleTalk Filing Protocol (AFP), or as an AppleTalk option.

The AppleTalk option and Macintosh support for the networks discussed in this book are add-on options that you will have to purchase. Each of these network operating systems creates a router or gateway connection that links the Macintosh and PCs. With any of these solutions, you will be creating either an internet that has the native NOS and an AppleTalk network, or a single network that uses AFP as part of its protocol, allowing the Macintosh to access the network's file servers. The minimum functionality you can expect from any of these internets is:

- Macintosh access to the PC file servers and the sharing of data between the two platforms.
- PC and Macintosh access to Apple LaserWriters on the Macintosh network. (You may need to install an additional router.)
- Limited network administration capabilities from the Macintosh.

These basic capabilities provide you with the foundation needed to use a Mac with your PC network. Once your network supports AppleTalk, you can begin to work on cross-platform compatibility by providing services such as E-mail, groupware applications, and server-based database applications that will be accessible to both your PC and Macintosh users.

What you will not be able to do with any of the NOSs discussed in this book is have PC access to Macintosh AppleShare volumes. (See the next section for a discussion of AppleShare.) If you need to have access to an AppleShare file server from a PC, you will find this topic covered in Chapter 8. Another area where you will run into challenges is if you want to provide remote access to your network for other Macintoshes. It is not impossible, but you will have to use Macintosh-specific tools to make it happen.

The day has not yet arrived where it is possible to have complete and seamless integration between Macintosh and PC networks. That day is coming, and may even be in the near future. But for now, you will have to learn about the Macintosh and piece together your own solution.

Macintosh Protocols and Terminology

As with all different computer systems, the Mac has a language all its own. You will probably find that the terms most used in the Macintosh networking manual are *AppleTalk* and *AppleTalk Filing Protocol*. The problem with Macintosh networking terminology is its lack of specificity. When compared to the detailed explanations you will find in the manuals for your NOS, the Macintosh implementations will all of a sudden appear fuzzy and incomplete.

This is because the Macintosh operating system handles the entire networking interface at a level the users—and even the network administrator—rarely, if ever, see. If you are used to setting up PC workstations, you know that you have to load the protocol stack and network card drivers, bind the cards to the stack, and allocate memory buffers, in addition to any number of other configuration tasks. When you set up a Macintosh and prepare it to access your network, you will see none of the nuts and bolts you need to set up a PC. The seamlessness of the Mac's networking software has a direct impact on how someone talks about Macintosh networking. For example, someone who is familiar with only Macintosh networking has no idea what binding is or why it is important. Even though binding does take place at a Macintosh OS level, the Mac user is never aware of this process. All a user sees when connecting to a file server or a networked printer is the name of the network resource and a couple of buttons that complete the process of connecting the computer to the shared resource.

Because all of this fuzziness can be a bit confusing, we need to establish a few of the conventions that will be used throughout this book.

- The term *AppleTalk* will be used to describe the Macintosh protocol and network in general, regardless of the data link mechanism or physical link (that is, the type of network that is being used, whether it is LocalTalk, Ethernet, or Token Ring).

- The term *AppleTalk Filing Protocol (AFP)*, when used as a descriptor, means that a Macintosh connects to a file server in the same manner as it would to an AppleShare file server. (You will find the real definition of *AFP* in the AppleTalk System Architecture section.)

- If the type of physical link is important, it will be discussed with the proper terminology, like *PhoneNET*, *Ethernet*, or *Token Ring*. Otherwise, the discussion is applicable regardless of the data link mechanism. From the Mac's point of view, the physical link only affects the speed of the network. Otherwise, the Mac really couldn't care less.

The rest of this section will be used to define Macintosh networking terms you will run across. Some of these terms are used routinely; others are provided for your information.

AppleShare

AppleShare is Apple's file server application. All Macintoshes that are running System 7.0 or greater can have a local version of AppleShare installed. Although you might see or hear about a file server being an AppleShare file server, the only real AppleShare file servers are those created by the AppleShare program or the Macintosh System 7 operating system.

AppleTalk

AppleTalk is a set of protocols that provide for Macintosh networking. See the section on AppleTalk System Architecture.

EtherTalk

EtherTalk is Apple's implementation of AFP for the Ethernet wiring standard. If you are using a standard Ethernet network, whether it is 10BaseT, Coaxial, or ThickNet, the protocol used by all Macs is the same.

EtherTalk is the Ethernet driver used by the Macintosh that allows the Mac to use AppleTalk on an Ethernet network. To use EtherTalk, the Macintosh must have an Ethernet card or a built-in Ethernet interface. EtherTalk works on any of the current Ethernet cabling standards.

TokenTalk

TokenTalk is the Token Ring driver used by the Macintosh that allows the Mac to use AppleTalk on a Token Ring network. To use TokenTalk, the Macintosh must have a Token Ring card.

AppleTalk Phase 1

AppleTalk Phase 1 is the original implementation of AppleTalk, and is now called Phase 1 so it can be distinguished from AppleTalk Phase 2. AppleTalk Phase 1 uses a single network address. If the version number of AppleTalk on the Macintosh is less than version 53, then the Macintosh is using AppleTalk Phase 1.

The Macintosh Invasion

AppleTalk Phase 2

AppleTalk Phase 2 is the implementation of AppleTalk that allows a Macintosh to work on an extended network. It is the implementation of the parts of the IEEE 802.2 and 802.3 protocols that allow AppleTalk networks to use an address range number or extended addressing rather than a single address number. AppleTalk Phase 2 gives the Macintosh the ability to coexist with PC Ethernet networks, since the same standard is used for all Ethernet cards.

AppleTalk Phase 2 is AppleTalk version 53 or higher. The Macintosh LX (Lisa), Macintosh 128, Macintosh 512, and Macintosh 512E cannot use AppleTalk Phase 2.

AppleTalk Remote Access

AppleTalk Remote Access is Apple's telebridge software. It lets a Macintosh connect to and access an AppleTalk network via a modem or ISDN connection.

LocalTalk

AppleTalk is Apple's physical link or cabling system. LocalTalk runs at 230.4 kbs and uses a single strand of twisted-pair wiring with a special adapter. A LocalTalk network is always constructed using a daisy chain topology. (See Fig. 1.1.)

Guest Account

A guest account is a special access account that can be enabled on AppleShare file servers. It allows anyone to log into the file server and access files that have been granted guest access. This feature is also implemented on some NOSs that provide AppleTalk access.

Figure 1.1
A LocalTalk network

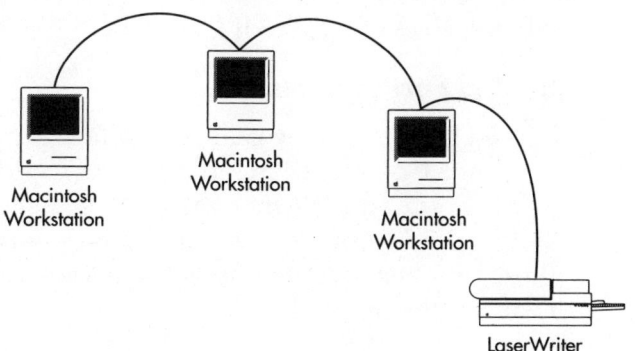

Figure 1.2

A PhoneNET system using a star topology

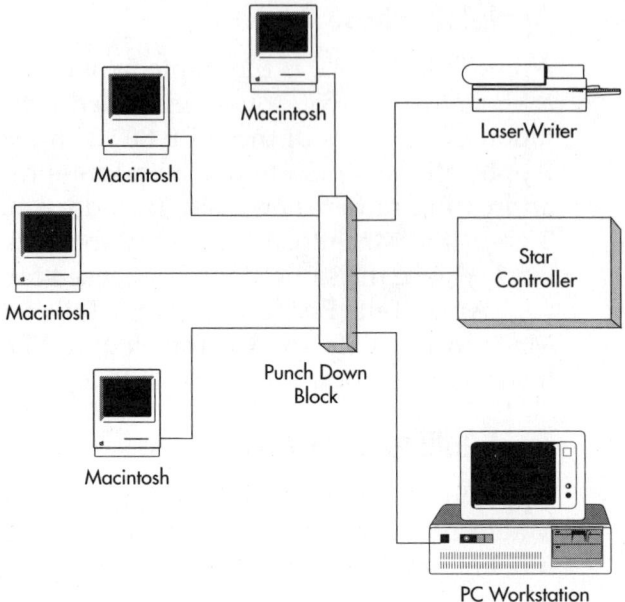

PhoneNET

PhoneNET is a physical link scheme, developed and patented by Farallon Computing, that is similar to LocalTalk. PhoneNET uses standard telephone twisted-pair cabling and RJ11 connectors with a special PhoneNET connector. A PhoneNET system uses either a daisy chain or a star topology. (See Fig. 1.2.)

Registered User

A registered user is a user who has been defined on an AppleShare file server as having specific access rights. All of the Network Operating Systems discussed in this book enable you to define registered users, although some of them will not allow for guest access.

Seeded Port or Router

A seed port or router is an AppleTalk port (usually on the server) or router that must have the network address numbers and zone information entered manually. Once a seed port or router has its assigned address numbers and zone information, it will broadcast those numbers over the network, allowing other AppleTalk devices to access the network.

Zone

For AppleTalk Phase 2 on an Ethernet or Token Ring network, a zone is a grouping of shared resources. A zone is usually established by the network administrator to segment a network and define separate functions, departments, or networks. AppleTalk Phase 2 does not require the elements of a zone to be part of the same physical network if you are using an Ethernet or Token Ring network.

For AppleTalk Phase 1 or a non-extended network like LocalTalk or PhoneNET, a zone defines the physical network. (See Fig. 1.3.)

AppleTalk System Architecture

One of the terms bandied about so far has been *AppleTalk*. AppleTalk is the Macintosh's native networking architecture, and it has been built into every Macintosh ever made. AppleTalk is not a specific protocol, but a number of layered protocols. As a whole, it is called the *AppleTalk System Architecture*. As mentioned in the introduction to this section, *AppleTalk* is the generic name used to

Figure 1.3
A Macintosh internet with zones

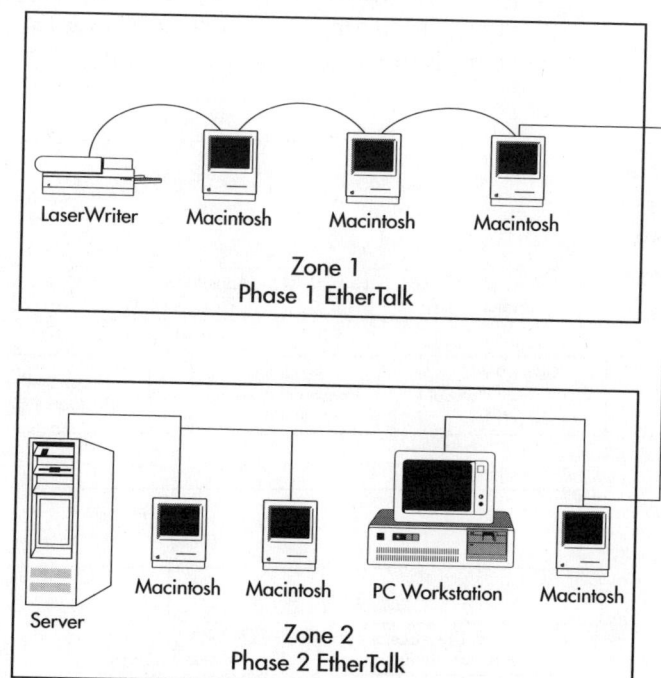

refer to this system architecture. Although in most cases you will not need to know what is happening or what protocols are being used, many of the AppleTalk protocols will be listed here anyway.

Apple developed the AppleTalk system architecture in such a fashion that it can be implemented on any computing platform. This is why the networks discussed in this book all use AppleTalk to provide for Macintosh networking. It is easier to tap into the abilities built into every Macintosh than to write software that will make a Mac run the native protocol of the file server. Any of the AppleTalk protocol functions can be addressed individually by Macintosh programs, and for that reason, you will want to be aware of these protocols and their functions. Usually, programs and the Macintosh System access only the parts of the AppleTalk system that are needed. This means that you may run across capabilities that are available in a pure Macintosh networking environment but are not present with your particular network.

This section provides only a general overview of the AppleTalk System Architecture. A description of the entire AppleTalk structure would only be useful to you if you are a programmer, so if you need this information, you can find it in the *Inside Macintosh* series published by Addison-Wesley.

Figure 1.4 shows the basic structure of the AppleTalk system architecture, including its layers and how they interact. This figure is a basic map of the device drivers only.

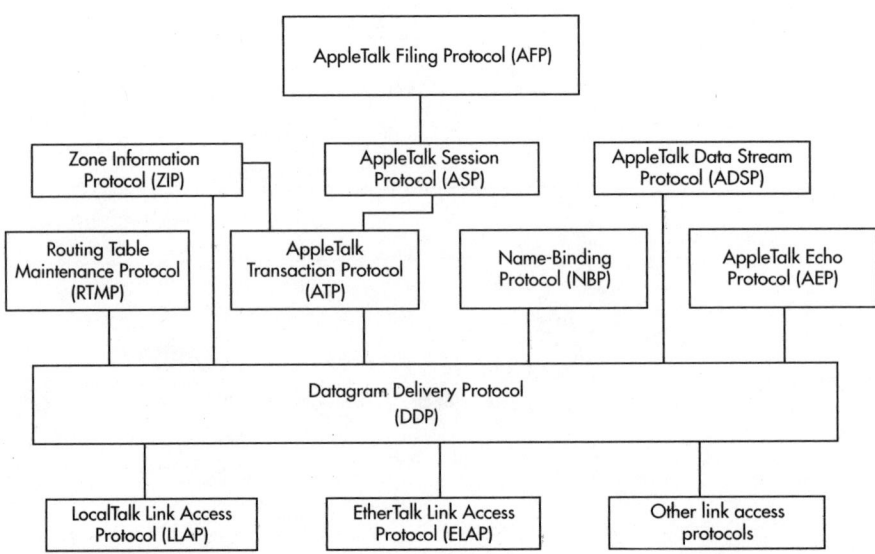

Figure 1.4
The AppleTalk system architecture

AppleTalk Data Stream Protocol (ADSP)

The AppleTalk Data Stream Protocol is a symmetrical protocol that provides a pipeline between two computers on the network with a full-duplex data stream. It is used by programs like Claris's FileMaker Pro database program to connect two computers on an AppleTalk network without using an intermediate file server. In this situation, one Mac functions as a database server, and the other accesses the database only as a client.

ADSP can be used for terminal emulation, telephone communications, and other applications that send a continuous data stream between two machines. This is one of the more common protocols used by Macintosh programs. However, not all network operating systems implement this protocol, which means that Macintosh programs that use a ADSP pipeline on a native Macintosh network will not necessarily communicate when using a PC- or UNIX-based network as a bridge. However, any two Macs on the same physical network will be able to use ADSP if their programs support it.

AppleTalk Session Protocol (ASP)

The AppleTalk Session Protocol is the protocol that controls all network sessions between a file server and a workstation. The connection between the server and the workstation is a one-way connection: the workstation sends commands and the file server responds.

AppleTalk File Protocol (AFP)

You will see the term *AppleTalk File Protocol* used throughout this book. AFP provides the client interface for server access between a computer and a file server. AFP works in conjunction with ASP to provide access to the file server. AFP can be implemented on any PC, provided that it has the proper software, so the PC can access an AppleShare file server.

None of the PC NOSs discussed in this book implements AFP for PC workstations, so the PC workstations will not be able to access any server as an AFP client. However, if AFP software (like Farallon's PhoneNET Talk) were installed on a PC, rather than the normal client software for whatever NOS you are using, the PC with the AFP software could access the file server as if it were a Macintosh, with all of the same capabilities as Macintosh client.

AppleTalk Transaction Protocol (ATP)

The AppleTalk Transaction Protocol is used to make sure data delivery over the network retains its integrity. It is a *transaction-based protocol* that is used by the Macintosh AppleTalk Manager. Macintosh programs can use ATP to transmit data over a network or internet. ATP operates like all data transaction protocols: data is sent, received, and checked, and confirmation of receipt is sent. If a data packet is not received, ATP requests retransmission.

AppleTalk Echo Protocol (AEP)

The AppleTalk Echo Protocol is a client-based protocol that listens for packets sent by another node on the network and then echoes the packets back to the transmitting machine. It is primarily used to see whether a specific device is available on the network.

Datagram Delivery Protocol (DDP)

The Datagram Delivery Protocol provides for the delivery of data on an AppleTalk network or internet. DDP is the part of AppleTalk that creates the packets that are sent over the network. Each DDP packet contains the packet's address in the form of the socket number, node ID, and network number.

DDP is a socket-to-socket delivery mechanism. Any computer on an AppleTalk network can have multiple sockets, so DDP allows for the seamless functioning of multiple network-dependent applications. It also allows file server access from any individual machine using AppleTalk.

Name-Binding Protocol (NBP)

The Name-Binding Protocol binds a device or workstation to the network by entering the network address and name of each device into a table. Each device that is available to other network devices is entered into this table, and the device's entry in the table determines its availability. If a device is not entered in the table, it is not available.

The *internet address* in the table contains the socket number, node ID, and network number. The name is composed of the object, type, and zone. The object and type are assigned by the device, and the zone is the logical grouping that contains the device.

NBP is the mechanism that provides one network device with the network address of any other network-visible device. This is done by mapping the client name to the internet address, which is then used by DDP to send and receive data.

Routing Table Maintenance Protocol (RTMP)

The Routing Table Maintenance Protocol consists of two parts, and is used by routers on an AppleTalk internet to forward data packets to the proper network address. The router uses the part called a *routing table* to determine the shortest possible path to get the packet to its destination. Any other device or workstation on the network uses an *RTMP Stub*. DDP uses an RTMP Stub to determine a device's network address and communicate that information to the router.

Zone Information Protocol (ZIP)

The acronym for the Zone Information Protocol is very apropos. ZIP maintains a table that contains information about all networks and zone names. This is very much like a postal ZIP code directory, where each code is a zone. The only difference is that a zone on an AppleTalk Phase 2 network is a logical determination, so elements of a single zone can reside in various networks.

Link Access Protocol

The Link Access Protocol is the protocol that provides access between a physical network and a computer. There is a different LAP for each type of network cabling. The LAP resides on the computer being connected to the network. The following is a list of the three LAPs provided with Macintosh System 7:

- EtherTalk Link Access Protocol
- LocalTalk Link Access Protocol (LLAP)
- TokenTalk Link Access Protocol

The LAP is also called an *AppleTalk connection file*. If you are using a physical link other than one of the ones listed above, the manufacturer of the network interface card will have to provide the AppleTalk connection file.

Macintosh Networking Options

When you connect Macs to a PC network, you are taking advantage of the software and hardware that are already built into the

Mac. Because of this, you are usually not disabling any of the capabilities already present in the Mac. All you are doing is providing the Macs with access to data and network resources that were not previously available.

The Macintosh connection brings the ability for PC workstations on the network to access Apple LaserWriters. Otherwise, the Macintosh connection is one-sided: the Macs get to access all of the network's resources, while the PCs, even if the NOS provides a router, will get only a printer without access to any AppleShare file servers.

Any programs that use the NOS, like Novell Network Loadable Modules or NLMs, will only run on PCs. The same applies to any applications that use the NetBios protocol and/or the NetBEUI interface: they will not be accessible to the Macs unless you go to some extra lengths.

The rest of this section will discuss some of the networking options you have in a Macintosh environment. As stated before, you will lose none of these options when providing Macintosh support to your network. The topics covered in the rest of this section are Macintosh System 7 file sharing, AppleShare file servers, and printing to Apple LaserWriters. This section is not an operation guide, but is intended to give you an overview of the Macintosh's capabilities.

Instructions on setting up, configuring, and using the Macintosh's networking capabilities can be found in Chapter 2.

System 7 File Sharing

In System 7, Apple has provided basic peer-to-peer networking capabilities, so any Macintosh that can run System 7 can also double as an AppleShare file server. This means that the software to access an AppleShare file server is also built into the Mac OS. So it is possible to have your Macs communicating independently of your primary network.

If your Macs are running System 6.0.X, you can install the AppleShare workstation software, and they too will be able to access a networked System 7 machine or a regular AppleShare file server. You will need the AppleShare workstation software for your Macs so they can access the file server from your NOS. The AppleShare workstation software will not be provided with the AppleTalk option you purchase for your network, since it is already included in Version 6.0.X or 7.X of the Macintosh System software.

A System 7 file server can have only 10 clients logged into it. Also, depending on the type of Macintosh being used, there can be a nominal to a severe performance penalty when it is acting as a file server. A low-end Mac like a Mac Plus or Classic will not fare well when working as a file server, the intermediate Macs with 68030 CPUs and 32-bit data bus architecture will have a medium performance penalty, and 68040 based machines will hardly notice shared access unless it gets too heavy.

When you use System 7's file sharing, each Mac user who is going to make files available can also set access rights for the different volumes, defining the users and groups who have access to the shared files. The user also fully controls when and how the Mac's files will be available. These security precautions are good, but as a result, Mac users who know their system will also know more about system security than you will as a PC user, which means that you will have to make sure you've taken proper precautions with your Server. Otherwise, Mac users could gain access you don't want them to have.

It is possible to disable System 7 file sharing if you don't want your Mac users creating their own independent network. One of the main reasons that you would want to disable System 7 file sharing is that it will put an additional load on the network, and you will lose bandwidth to the Macs if they are operating independently. Of course, you might also have your own security reasons, depending on your environment and how you want your people to work. What you won't be able to control on your Macintosh networks are those occasions when your Mac users decide that they want to play a company-wide network game using all of the Macs.

AppleShare File Servers

In a sense, any server that can be accessed by a Mac is an AppleShare file server. However, AppleShare is Apple's trademarked name for its file server software. Any server software that can be accessed by a Mac is often called an *AppleShare-compliant* file server. Throughout this book, *AppleShare* will be used specifically to indicate an AppleShare file server or a shared System 7 volume. Any server that a Mac can access will be referred to as an *AppleTalk File Protocol-compliant* or *AFP-compliant* server.

Apple makes AppleShare 4.0, which can be used on any Macintosh to turn it into a dedicated file and print server.

AppleShare 4.0 should be used on 68030 Macintosh with a 32-bit architecture as a minimum. If you are going be using the server to access large multi-user database applications, then you will want to look at a Mac with a 68040 CPU or one of the Workgroup Servers. The maximum number of users that can connect to an AppleShare 4.0 server is 120, with 5 networked printer queues.

Also available from Apple are three dedicated file servers called:

- Apple Workgroup Server 60
- Apple Workgroup Server 80
- Apple Workgroup Server 95

Each of these Workgroup Servers is a 68040-based machine that uses either AppleShare 4.0 or AppleShare Pro. The Workgroup Servers 60 and 80 use System 7 and AppleShare 4.0. The Workgroup Server 95 uses A/UX 3.0.1 and AppleShare Pro.

The Apple Workgroup Servers are intended for use in a Macintosh environment, where speed and performance are key issues—that is, in multi-user databases or workgroups where many people need to access large graphic files. The group's needs will determine which Workgroup Server should be installed.

The advantages that Workgroup Servers offer over AppleShare 4.0 are speed and performance. The Workgroup Servers are optimized models of current Macintoshes. AppleShare 4.0 on a WorkGroup Server runs at three to four times the speed of AppleShare 3.01 (Apple's older version of AppleShare), and AppleShare Pro runs at three to four times the speed of AppleShare 4.0. Table 1.1 lists the Workgroup Servers, their versions of AppleShare, the number of concurrent users, and the Macintosh models they are based on.

Apple did not make these servers to compete with the NOSs discussed in this book. They are intended for workgroups that use

Table 1.1 Workgroup Servers

Apple Workgroup Server	AppleShare version	Concurrent users	Macintosh Model
Apple Workgroup Server 60	AppleShare 4.0	20	Centris 600
Apple Workgroup Server 80	AppleShare 4.0	30	Quadra 800
Apple Workgroup Server 95	AppleShare Pro	50	Quadra 950

The Macintosh Invasion

primarily Macintosh computers, as stated above. Also, a good dedicated 486 or Pentium-based server will provide performance that is better than the Workgroup Server 95 in many circumstances, at the same time allowing for better cross-platform connectivity.

Mac users will not be able to tell the difference between an AppleShare file server and an NOS with AppleTalk when they are working, except that the icon for a volume from an NOS will be different from the AppleShare icon. In Figure 1.5, you can see the two file servers available to a Macintosh on the network as the user would see them before logging on. The file servers you see in the figure are:

- **SMC_Server**—The main file server on a Banyan VINES NOS
- **Systems Management Server**—An AppleShare file server

When a file server is mounted on a Macintosh, it will have an icon that positions itself on the right-hand side of the screen, like those in Figure 1.6.

In the figure, the mounted volumes are:

- Home Base—System 7 File Sharing
- VITAL_DATA—A Novell volume

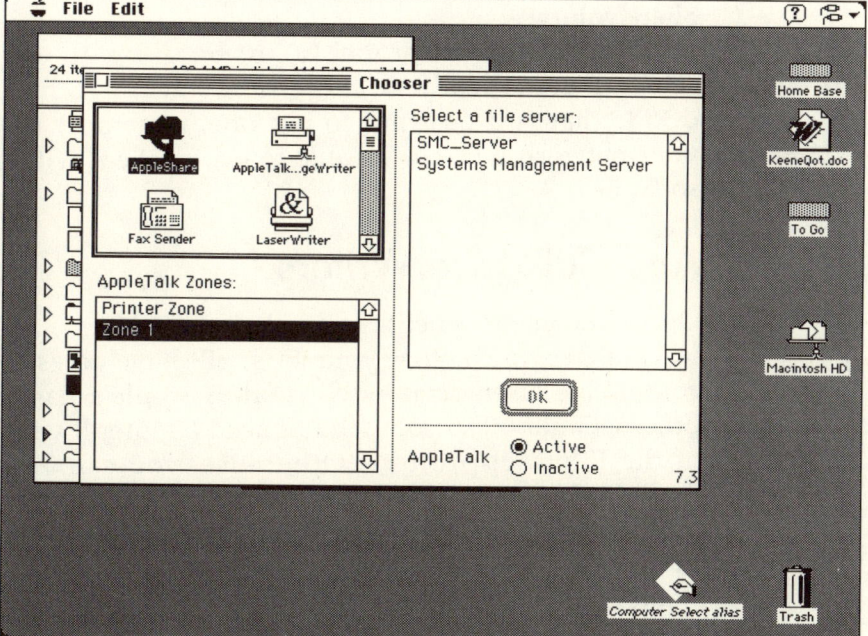

Figure 1.5
File servers available on a Mac

Figure 1.6

Mounted file server volumes

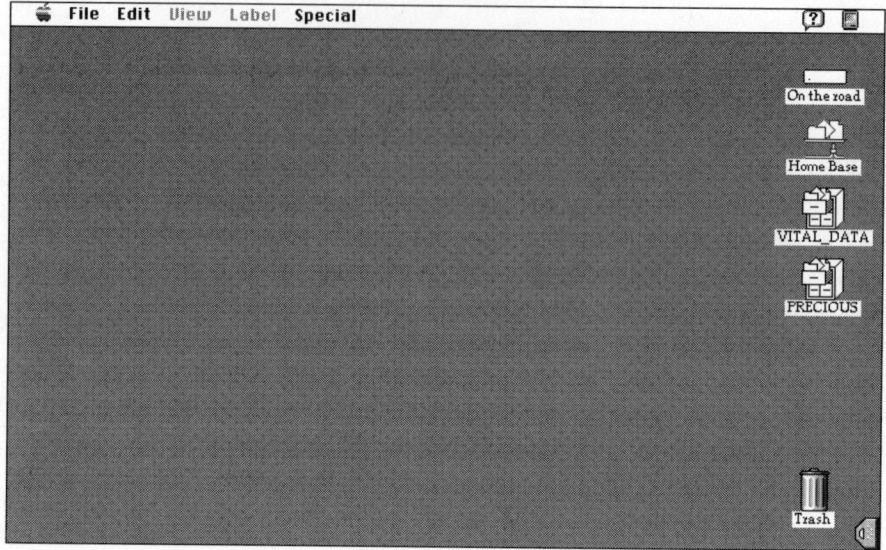

- PRECIOUS—A Novell volume

When a volume is mounted on a Macintosh, it will have an icon that identifies the type of server software being used. Notice that volumes 2 and 3 have the same icon because they are both Novell volumes, while volume 1 displays the icon for an AppleShare volume.

Since you will probably not be using an AppleShare file server, there is really no more to say about them. If you should decide that you do want to use one, remember that the PCs on your network will not be able to access them without additional software.

AppleTalk LaserWriters

One of the major benefits you will notice when you add AppleTalk to your network is that your PCs will have access to AppleTalk-compatible laser printers. Several of Apple's LaserWriters have Ethernet built in, so you will not need a router if you are using one of the Ethernet printers. Otherwise, you can either install an AppleTalk card in the server and use its routing capabilities to access an AppleTalk printer, or install a software router on one of the Macintoshes like Farallon's LocalPath or Apple's Internet Router so the PCs can access the printer. Almost all AppleTalk-compatible printers use PostScript, which can make them a very useful tool. Connecting the printers to your network and making them accessible to the PC is a subject that is covered in the discussion of each NOS. Sometimes this task can be a challenge, but it is not impossible.

Several Approaches You Can Take to Solve Your Needs

There are many ways to use a Macintosh when it is connected to a PC network. You can use the Macintosh and provide it with all of the capabilities of any PC on the network, you can isolate the Mac and use the network only for transferring files, or you can provide it with capabilities that fall somewhere between the two extremes. Whatever you are planning to do, you should know what you want to do before you purchase any additional network options or other software.

Ideally, you should have a plan that includes where the Mac is going to be placed, what network protocols you will use, and the capabilities that the Mac will have. The main limitation you will have when using a Mac on a PC-based network is that on many networks, such as a Novell or Banyan VINES network, you need a PC to access the file server(s) for maintenance or as a system administrator. Otherwise, you can do almost anything with a Macintosh that you would normally do with a PC, and usually more easily.

In this section we'll briefly discuss some of the possibilities for any networked Macintosh, like E-mail, cross-platform software, security issues, and groupware. Some network operating systems also have their own additions to these overall capabilities, but those will be covered in the discussions of the individual NOSs.

File Exchanges

One of the major reasons for adding AppleTalk to any network is so you can share files between your Macs and PCs. Because you will be dealing with two different types of computing platforms, there are some issues you need to consider when using the same files on both platforms. This section will look at a couple of those issues. You will also find more information on Macintosh file structures in Chapter 2.

Sharing Files

As software becomes more sophisticated, more and more programs will automatically have file formats that are seamlessly compatible across various platforms. If you are using programs that do not already have cross-platform compatibility, there are utilities that you can use to convert files from one format to another. Chapter 3 discusses some of these utilities.

The easiest way to avoid problems is to use programs that are cross-platform-compatible. Most major manufacturers are writing their software so that the files are compatible with the same application, whether you are using Mac, DOS, or Windows. Chapter 9 discusses most of the applications available that offer cross-platform file compatibility.

Another issue you will be faced with when working with shared Macintosh and PC files is that of file names. Every AppleTalk option allows the Macintosh user to use 32-character file names on the file server. But DOS recognizes only an 8-character name with a 3-letter extension. Most NOSs have an automatic work-around to handle this potential problem. What happens is that the Macintosh name is automatically truncated, and an extension is either applied according to the document's type or taken from the continuation of the Macintosh file name. How the file names are handled depends on the NOS, and will be discussed in the appropriate chapter.

Extension Mapping

The Macintosh can tell what application made which file because it assigns a type and a creator code to each file. These codes are kept intact when the files are placed on an AppleTalk file server. But the DOS files that are on the server are associated with the application that created them by their extensions. So when a Mac accesses a DOS file, the user has to know what application created the file and use an application on the Mac that can read the DOS file, or else the server has to assign the file creator and type codes.

The preferable choice is to have the NOS automatically assign the type and creator codes, so that all the Mac user has to do is open the file, which will then automatically launch the correct application. This process is called *extension mapping*, and it is a feature that can make life a lot easier.

You will have to train your Mac users to use DOS names for their files. Believe me, this will not be an easy task. One of the reasons people like the Mac is that they are not constrained by the (in their opinion) archaic file-naming conventions found in DOS. But if you are persistent, they will adjust.

Whatever happens, you will probably have to compromise with the Mac users, or just lay down the law and force them to use DOS names on the server. If you use both Mac and DOS names on your server, you will end up with something that looks like the screen in Figure 1.7.

As you can see, it can turn into quite a mess. If there are some files that the Mac users are not going to be sharing with DOS users, you should configure your server so that the Mac users have their own volume or directories for file storage where they do not have to worry about using DOS naming conventions.

E-mail

Chances are very good that you will want everyone on your network to communicate using E-mail, if you have a network of any size. However, the task of setting up a cross-platform-compatible E-mail system could prove to be troublesome. To simplify the task,

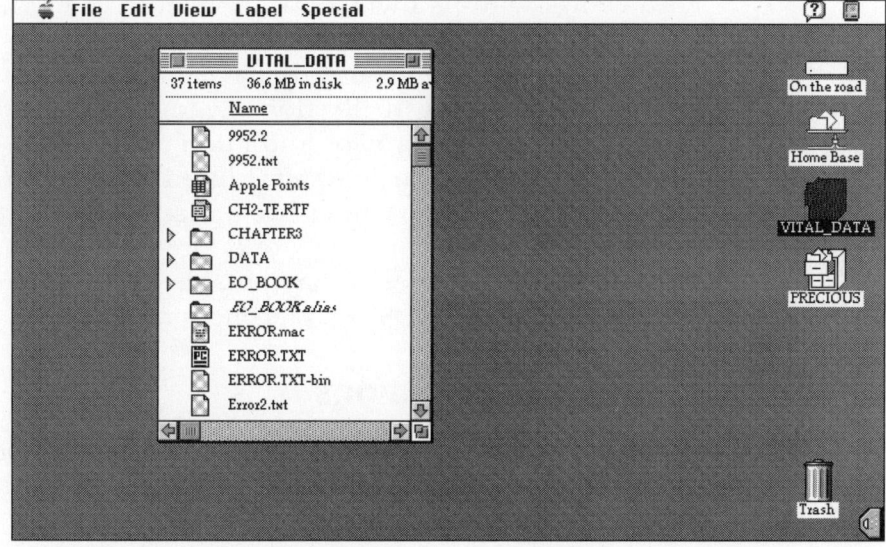

Figure 1.7
DOS and Mac names on the file server as seen from a Mac

you should use an E-mail system that supports both Macintoshes and PCs. Otherwise, you will be faced with the problems of establishing E-mail gateways.

If you end up using E-mail gateways, you will encounter problems when sending data files from one system to another, because most gateways cannot handle file conversions. You will encounter problems where the E-mail system will want to convert files or fail to recognize Macintosh file structures, and in general you will find that your hair has gotten thinner during the process of setting up the E-mail system.

These really ugly E-mail problems exceed the scope of this book, so other than a warning, I'm going to follow my own advice and avoid this pain. Instead, we'll look at the available E-mail packages that support both Macintosh and PC computers. These packages are:

- QuickMail (Quick Mail will only work if your PCs have AppleTalk access)
- cc:Mail
- DaVinci e-mail
- Microsoft Mail
- WordPerfect Office

Any one of the above packages will enable your E-mail system to send files and messages between Macintoshes and PCs. Each comes with its own set of problems. The basic features of these packages will be discussed in Chapter 9.

Since you probably already have an E-mail system, you will be thinking that you really don't want to change just because you're adding a Mac or two. And I don't blame you. So if you are not using one of the mail systems listed above, you will have to see whether the manufacturer has a Macintosh interface that you can use. Also, since most networks provide some form of rudimentary mail system, you may be able to use the native E-mail that comes with the NOS you're using for the PCs.

Running Applications

Under most circumstances, you will not be running Macintosh applications directly off of a networked file server. The reason for this is that the applications will run too slowly. Also, there are very few applications that can run off of a file server on a Macintosh and a PC concurrently. Novell is the only company that currently has any network modules that can service both a Macintosh and a PC. The NLMs (NetWare Loadable Modules) offer a glimpse of what will come, where Macs and PCs will be able to access simultaneously the same programs running on a file server, but that day is not here yet.

In most cases, you will have to be content to use your file servers as repositories for your clients' files, and let them access the data files while running the appropriate application from their local Macintoshes. And in some cases, it will probably be advantageous to have the Mac users copy the data files they want to use to a local hard drive before working on the files. This is especially true if the data file is a large graphic or page layout file. The exception to this is when the Mac user is using a database application that is shared among several users. And even in this case, the application should be run from the local hard drive while the data files are accessed via the network.

If you are tempted to run a networked application over a network, be prepared for some serious speed degradation. This is especially true if you're used to running DOS applications over the network and are satisfied with their speed. The Macintosh cannot run a networked application, even when using Ethernet or Token Ring, at the same speed as a DOS application. Even networked Windows applications can run faster than Mac programs. So don't say you haven't been warned.

Data Security

Each network discussed in this book has its own built-in security system. The NOS you are using will determine how you plan your network security. Chapter 2 contains a detailed discussion about Macintosh networking, and you will want to review that chapter as part of the network planing stage. Every network discussed in this book provides security at the NOS level, so you do not have to be too concerned about weaknesses you may perceive in the AppleTalk layer of your network.

The primary weakness is the Mac's ability to save a password after a volume has been mounted. At any point after a networked volume is mounted, a user can go to the Chooser (the utility that the Mac uses to access networked devices) and tell the Mac to mount a networked volume automatically while at the same time saving the password. The next time the Mac is started, it will mount the network volume as part of the Mac's boot sequence. The most effective way to keep this from being a problem is to require that users change their passwords after a predetermined amount of time, or to disable this option if possible.

Another security concern you will have involves some of the native capabilities built into all new Macintoshes. Every new Macintosh, when it is first unpacked, can act as a file server for other Macintoshes, letting them link to it and run programs on it. These capabilities are part of System 7. These capabilities are very similar to the file-sharing and networking capabilities of Windows for Workgroups.

But if you do not want your Mac users taking up network bandwidth and generally clogging your network's arteries, you will have to take some steps to remove the System 7 file-sharing capabilities. Be warned, however: any determined person with a set of the Macintosh System disks can easily restore the file-sharing capabilities, which means that you may want to keep a closer eye on the Macs to make sure they are configured the way you, the network administrator, want them.

It will be hard to keep people from making their own private networks if they are determined. If you anticipate this as a possible problem, install a device that will lock the floppy disk drive. This will prevent anyone from starting the Macintosh with a floppy disk, installing software, or copying software or files. And actually, this would probably be a good idea as a matter of practice, since die-hard Mac users love to add all kinds of TSR-type software to their Macs, and often customize them beyond belief.

Groupware

There is a new type of software that has been emerging over the last year or so, called *groupware*. Groupware applications are programs used to coordinate workgroups and allow people to work on projects directly on the network. Some of the groupware programs that are now available are very large server-based applications that keep track of schedules and projects, provide E-mail services, and handle all of the files associated with a project. Other groupware applications are small and fulfill a single purpose, such as scheduling.

The two major groupware applications available that have both Macintosh and PC compatibility are WordPerfect Office and

Lotus Notes. Each of these applications has its own requirements, and each one approaches the tasks of scheduling and project management differently. WordPerfect Office is a lot like an E-mail system on steroids, while Lotus Notes can be used to create a complete work environment. If you are already using groupware and you want your Macintosh users to participate, you should check with the software's publisher to make sure you can use it with your Macs. Since groupware is a new category of software, there will be more applications available as time goes on. Right now, you will find that you are limited to the two major groupware applications (Lotus Notes and WordPerfect Office) that have full cross-platform support. But applications like Microsoft Mail & Schedule could also fall into the groupware category.

You will find more detailed information about groupware, E-mail, and cross-platform-compatible applications in Chapter 9.

Conclusion

This chapter is an overview of Macintosh networking and some of the issues you will be confronted with when you add Macintoshes to your Network. By reading this chapter, you have started the process of gathering the information you will need to administer AppleTalk on your network. You should now be able to identify the major problems you might face, and have a good grasp of the possibilities, as well. Networking Macs is really not difficult, it is just time-consuming to learn a new platform. Hopefully, this chapter will help you keep the disruption caused by the Macintosh interlopers to a minimum.

Macintosh Networking

Introduction

The purpose of this chapter is provide you with an operational guide to the Macintosh OS and System 7 networking. Macintosh networking is fundamentally the same as PC networking (insofar as you achieve the same results), but the way Macintosh networking is implemented by a user is where the similarity ends. It is possible to make comparisons between a Mac and a PC on a hardware or system level. But the differences are such that you'll have to get used to and know the Mac OS well enough to perform some basic trouble-shooting, set up configurations, and know where the software tools live before you can really integrate your Macs into your networking environment.

To speed you on your way, this chapter will provide a brief overview of the Macintosh System and the System elements needed for networking. It will also show you how to use System 7 networking and provide a discussion about Macintosh networks and their capabilities. Whenever possible, I'll draw comparisons between the MS-DOS and the Macintosh OS. This will make it easier for you to remember the various system elements and their functions.

Once again, the information you'll find in this chapter is introductory in nature. Although there will be a lot of procedural steps for performing necessary tasks, none of the information will go into the depth it deserves. If you need more in-depth information, you'll have to seek out other resources. You should be familiar with the Macintosh's System 7 Reference Manual; even though it is very basic, you will find information in it that is not covered here. Also, if you browse in the local computer book store, you'll find several good books about the Mac.

The Macintosh Operating System

Like all computers, the Macintosh has an operating system. You should not be deceived by the Mac's friendly interface (if you think it's friendly) or its apparent simplicity. There is a tendency to underestimate the Macintosh's complexity. If you assume that the Mac OS is simple because of the user interface, you will get bitten by the Mac and not know what to do.

First of all, the Macintosh operating system is simply called the *System*. With each incarnation, it becomes increasingly complex. Five years ago, the System fit on two 800K floppy disks, and the version number was System 6.0.3. Today, the version of the System released with Apple's new AV machines is number 7.1, and it has 13 high-density disks.

As you can see from the number of floppy disks, the system rivals OS/2 or Windows in its overall complexity. If you, as a system administrator, do not understand the basics of the Macintosh System, you can get into trouble rapidly. To help you stay out of trouble, this section will look at the Macintosh System, disk drives, and file structure. With what is provided in this section and the next, you will have the basic information you need to set up a Macintosh workstation, as well as the knowledge you'll need for doing basic trouble-shooting.

This section assumes that you know basic Macintosh operations. You should know what icons, menus, and other basics are and how they function. You should also know how to select and open files, as well as how to run programs. Also, basic text-editing skills are required. If you are unfamiliar with basic Macintosh operations, you should go through the tutorials and manuals that came with your Macintosh. If you're already familiar with the Mac and don't need the information in this section, you might what to browse through the rest of the chapter. If you know the information that is being presented, then you can go on to other chapters that interest you. However, I hope that this section and the rest of the chapter contain something that you do not already know.

The System Folder

The software heart and soul of every Macintosh is contained in a folder (*directory*, in DOS parlance) called the *System folder*. If someone has been playing with the Mac you're looking at, the folder may be renamed to any name conceivable. But generally it will be called *System folder*.

Another way to recognize the System folder is by its icon. The System folder for all Macintosh Systems from version 6.0.5 on has an icon that looks like Figure 2.1.

Inside the System folder, you will find all of the files that make the Macintosh run. In principle, the System folder is like the DOS or DOS and Windows directory on a PC. The System file is like the DOS SYS.IO file that runs the machine. However, the Mac requires two files to operate. These are called *System* and *Finder*. If either of these files is missing or damaged, the Mac will not work. Figure 2.2 shows the inside of a System folder. This is a plain System 7 folder with no additions or modifications.

Figure 2.1
The Macintosh System folder icon

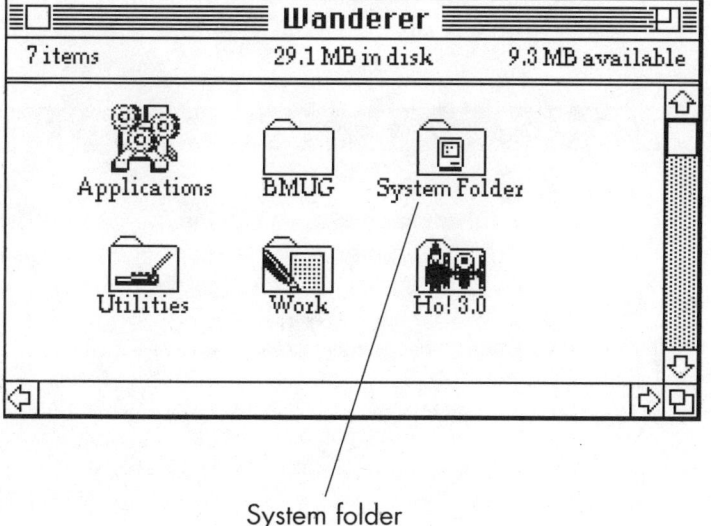

System folder

Figure 2.2

Inside the System folder

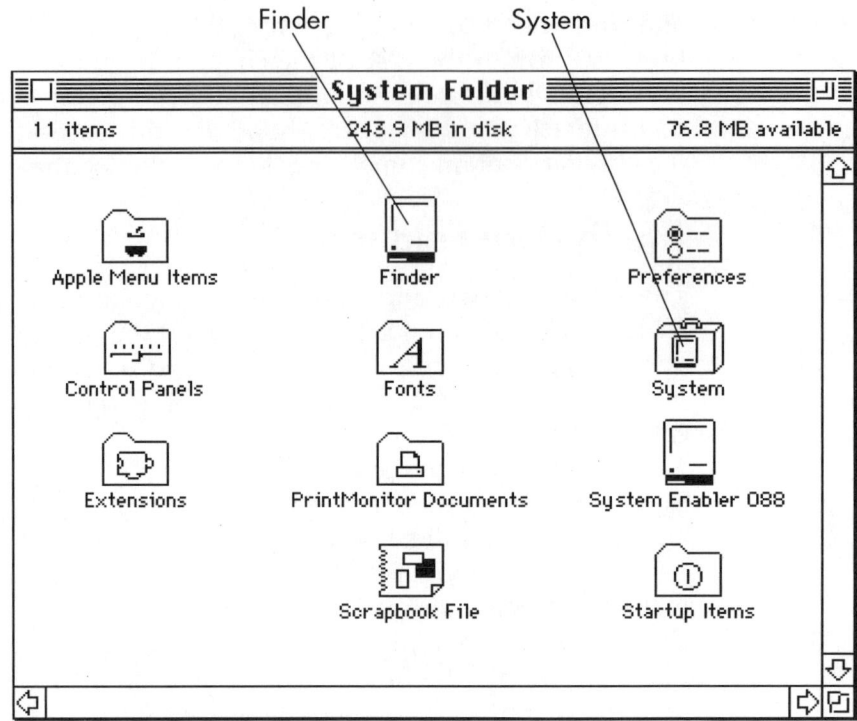

Most of the elements you see in Figure 2.2 are described in the section on System Elements. Usually, you will not have to go into the System folder. Most software for the Mac installs automatically any files that need to live in the System folder. If you have to de-install an application, there is a very easy way to do so; this technique is described in the Mac's Networking Software section

Note

There are several common elements to the Macintosh System folder in either System 6.0.X or System 7. However, the arrangement of these elements is different depending on which System version you're looking at.

System 6.0.X is mentioned because there are a lot of Macs out there that are running System 6.0.X, so you will need to be aware of some of these differences. However, this discussion will concentrate on System 7.X; references to System 6.0.X will be made only to the explain essential aspects of System 6.0.X.

Macintosh Networking

of this chapter. So long as Apple's installer software is used to install the software, you will be able to de-install software using the same instructions for de-installing networking software.

In the rest of this section, you'll find a brief discussion about the differences and similarities between a Macintosh and an MS-DOS or Windows machine. Then each of the System elements and types of system software will be discussed. The section will conclude with a brief set of warnings regarding the Macintosh System.

What You Won't Find

In principle, all computers are the same. They perform the same tasks, and the way they work is based on a set of principles that remain the same from one system to the next. What is different from one system to the next is the implementation of these basic tasks and the way the user interacts with the computer. Also, this means that the computer's configuration can vary widely. For these reasons, there are several things you can find on DOS machines that you cannot find on Macs. Knowing what these differences from the beginning will help you when you approach the Mac, because you will not be wasting time looking for files that do not exist. Beyond that understanding, the differences can help you make the mental shift you need to interact easily with the Mac.

Quite often, someone who is using a Mac and comes from an MS-DOS background gets frustrated and confused because the two machines are so different. To keep this level of confusion to a minimum, the first step you need to take has an element of Zen: you need to forget most of what you know and start with a frame of mind that is clear. Get rid of your expectations and keep in mind the following differences:

- The programs contained in the DOS directory are (almost all) included as functions of the Macintosh's Finder. You will not find a copy program like XCOPY.COM on the Mac.

- There are no editable configuration files on a Macintosh: you will not find an AUTOEXEC.BAT, CONFIG.SYS, WIN.INI, or SYSTEM.INI file, or anything like them, on a Mac.

- The Mac uses a graphic interface and there is no way to issue commands from a prompt, unless you are a programmer and have a debugger installed on the Mac.

- There is no debugger program that comes as part of the Mac's System software. Although there is a debugger in ROM, you will have to search far and wide to find instructions on using it. So for the time being, forget it.

- The Macintosh does not have the 640K memory limitation of DOS, and you do not have to worry about managing memory in the same way. There is no such thing an extended or expanded memory, nor does the Mac have an HMA to worry about. Either the Mac will have memory or it won't. All installed memory in a Mac is automatically configured by the System at start-up. The System will take the memory it needs and the rest will be available to applications.

The above is just a beginning. There are many more differences that you will discover as you work and get familiar with the Macs. Examples are SCSI (Small Computer Standard Interface) hard disks in every Mac, auto-configuring built-in video, and all of the drivers for the hardware devices built into the Mac's ROM (Read-Only Memory). So you will not have to configure device drivers or any of the other messy details you will find on a DOS system.

If you compare a Mac to a Windows system, you will find some similarities. For one, they both use a Graphic User Interface, which consists of icons, menus, windows, and the ability to run multiple applications simultaneously. Most Windows applications install automatically like the Macs, but de-installation is a real mess. In either a Mac or a Windows system, you can find program files in a variety of places. But application files on the Mac are easy to find and remove if you want to de-install a program, whereas finding all of the files for a Windows program can be very much like looking for a needle in a haystack—not to mention editing all of the .INI files afterward.

However, the best way to see these differences is to look at the system elements and see how the Mac works.

System Elements

Inside the System folder you'll find a variety of elements. The elements in this section are the ones you'll find on a Macintosh Quadra 660AV or 840AV. At the moment, these are the two newest Macintoshes on the market, and they have some System elements that are not found on other Macintosh Systems. However, anyone can install the latest system on a Mac and have these System elements.

The System version being discussed here is System 7.1. All of the important aspects of the System's components will be covered, but the information here is not 100% complete. What this section contains is the essential information you'll need to know about these System elements. If you need more information, you'll have to check out a good Mac book, like the *Inside Macintosh* series by Addison-Wesley. Also, a lot of information can be obtained from Apple's on-line service, AppleLink.

The System

The Macintosh System is similar in function to the DOS IO.SYS file. It is the one file required by any Macintosh. The disk that contains the System file running the Macintosh is the one in the upper right-hand corner of the screen, as shown in Figure 2.3.

The System file is usually configured by the Installer to work with a specific Macintosh. In some cases it will be configured to work with all Macs, but because of the System Enablers and number of different Macs, a System configured to work with all Macs will become a rarity. Included in the System is the code needed to make the Mac work at its most basic level. The System works in conjunction with the Mac's ROM and contains patches, drivers,

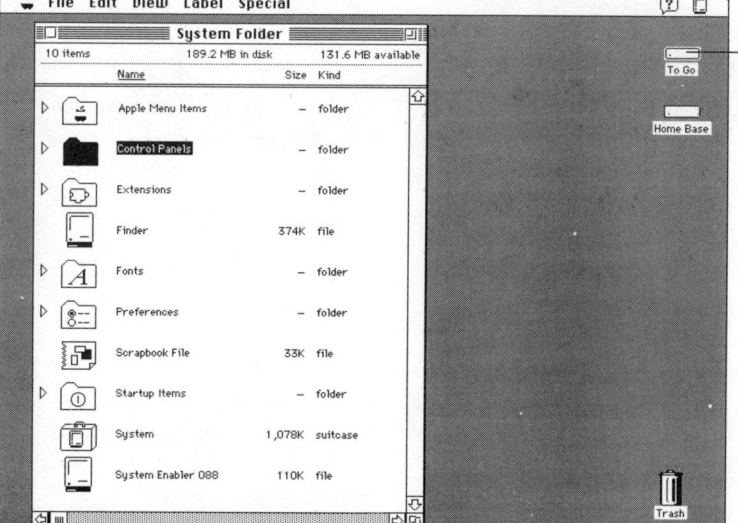

Figure 2.3
The drive controlling the Macintosh

Drive that contains System

keyboard layouts, and sounds. Also included in the System are all of the system level messages you'll see, error messages, icons, and other pieces of code needed to operate the Mac. However, a System by itself will not run a Macintosh; there must be an accompanying program. Usually the accompanying program will either be an Installer or the Macintosh Finder. The accompanying program will launch as the Mac is booted and will create your interface with the Mac. In this sense, the accompanying program is like the COMMAND.COM file on an MS-DOS boot disk.

The Finder

Finder

As mentioned above, the Finder is an application. It creates the Desktop (the gray area of the Macintosh Screen), displays the drive icons, allows for file management, and displays the Menu commands in the Menu bar. In short, it is the primary interface to the Macintosh, and is like a combination of Windows' Program and File Managers. The Macintosh terms *Finder* and *Desktop* are usually used interchangeably. So don't get confused if you hear people talking about the Desktop—they mean the Finder.

Each version of the System has its own version of the Finder, but the version numbers only correspond with System version 7.1. All other versions of the Macintosh system have Finder version numbers that are different from the System version. An example is System 6.0.7, which has Finder version 6.1.7. So do not move the Finder around without making sure it is matched properly with the System. The easiest way to match the System to the Finder is to perform a Get Info on the System and Finder that are on the Macintosh System installer disks.

To perform a Get Info, follow these steps:

1. Select the item you want information on—in this case, the System.
2. Select the "Get Info" command from the Finder's File menu

   or

   use the ⌘-I keyboard combination.

When you perform the Get Info command, you will see a window like the ones in Figure 2.4.

This procedure will provide you with information on any Macintosh file.

MACINTOSH NETWORKING   35

Figure 2.4

The Info window for System 6.0.7

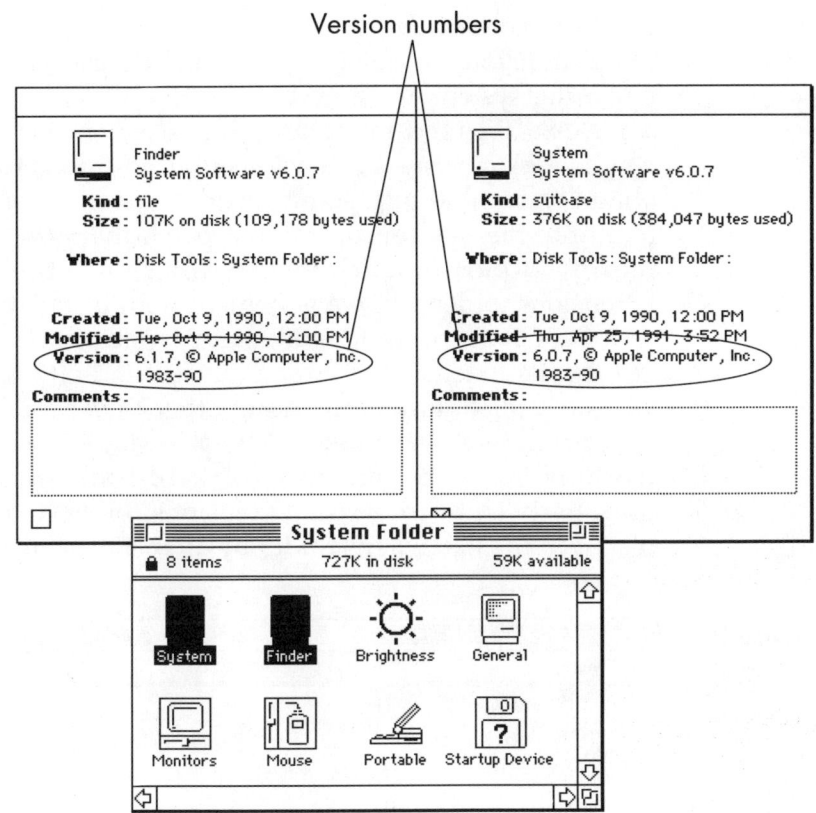

Next to the System file, the Finder is the most important file on a Mac. Without it, the Mac won't run, unless the System has been specifically configured to run a program other than the Finder.

System Enablers

All of the newer Macintoshes—the Centris, Quadra 800 and 840AV, and some of the PowerBooks—use a System Enabler. The System Enabler is a system component of System 7.1. Apple developed the Enabler so it would not have to rewrite the system for each new model of Macintosh that is released.

Each model of the Macintosh that uses an Enabler has a different version of it. At the moment, there are 10 System Enablers, each for a different Macintosh. So be sure you have the correct Enabler: otherwise, the Mac will not work.

The Extensions Folder

The Extensions folder is where all extensions to the Macintosh operating system are stored. An extension is the equivalent of an MS-DOS TSR (Terminate and Stay Resident) program. Another way to look at system extensions is as additions to the Mac's operating system that add some form of system level operability not built into the System file, or that patch the System file to provide improved performance. Figure 2.5 shows the contents of the Extensions folder when a general system installation is performed on a Centris 660AV or Quadra 840AV Macintosh.

In the Extensions folder, you will find all of the network drivers needed for any networking other than basic AppleTalk. (The networking software needed by the Mac is covered in the Networking Software section.) You will find Apple software and third-party software in the Extensions folder. Usually, software is placed in the Extensions folder by an installer program.

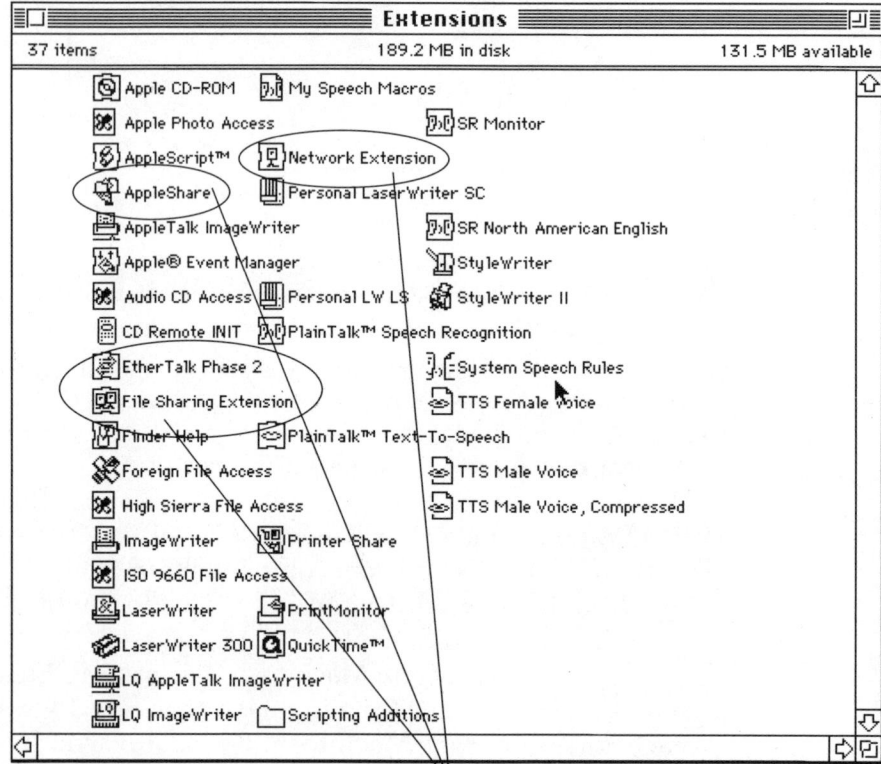

Figure 2.5
The contents of the Extensions folder

If your Mac develops problems or will not completely boot, 80% of the time the problem will be a system extension that is conflicting with the System, the hardware, or another system extension. To see whether the problems you are experiencing are related to a system extension, hold down the **Shift** key as the Mac boots to disable all of the system extensions. (More trouble-shooting techniques can be found in the Trouble-shooting chapter.)

If you are working with Macintoshes that are using System 6.0.X, you will not find an Extensions folder. In older versions of the System; the system extensions are called *Inits*, and they are stored loose inside the System folder. There is no easy way to shut them all off without an extension manager, other than removing them. They are called *system startup documents* when you perform a Get Info on the file.

In general, your Macs (if you have control of their configurations) should have only the extensions required for their operation. Shareware, freeware, and other third-party extensions should be kept to a minimum, if they are installed at all. This means that you will have to spend a little time learning which system extensions are essential to your operations. If you see one that is not required, find out where it came from and what it does. If it is not needed to run the Mac, delete it.

> **Note**
>
> One of the biggest headaches you'll have is people installing fun extensions and control panel devices onto your networked Macs. There is a tendency for Mac users to trick out their systems in all kinds of interesting ways. It is easy to do and adds personality to the machines.
>
> Unfortunately, this free-spirited behavior is difficult to control, and it can result in problems if you are responsible for maintaining all of the individual systems as well as the network. To keep your life bearable, you might want to create a policy that restricts the installation of any software until you have had a chance to check it out. Also, the spreading of viruses is reason enough for this type of policy—I'm sure that you don't let your PC users install just anything they think would be neat, and there is no reason to treat the Macs any differently.

Control Panels Folder

The Control Panels folder contains small programs that are used to set environmental options on the Macintosh. The programs found in the Control Panels folder are called either *control panels* or *Cdevs*. "Cdev" stands for "Control Panel Device," which is the type code for the software that lives in the Control Panels folder. (Type codes are discussed in the Macintosh File Structure section.)

Figure 2.6 shows the contents of the Control Panels folder for a System 7.1 installation.

Most control panels share some of the attributes of system extensions, insofar as they load into memory during the boot process and can cause some of the problems discussed above. However, they differ in that they are used to set the PRAM (Parameter RAM) settings, which are the Mac's equivalent to the environmental settings of the CONFIG.SYS and AUTOEXEC.BAT files in MS-DOS. Many of the Mac's system-level utilities like macro programs, program launchers, and others are also implemented as control panels. The Macintosh's control panels are very much like the Control Panel in Windows.

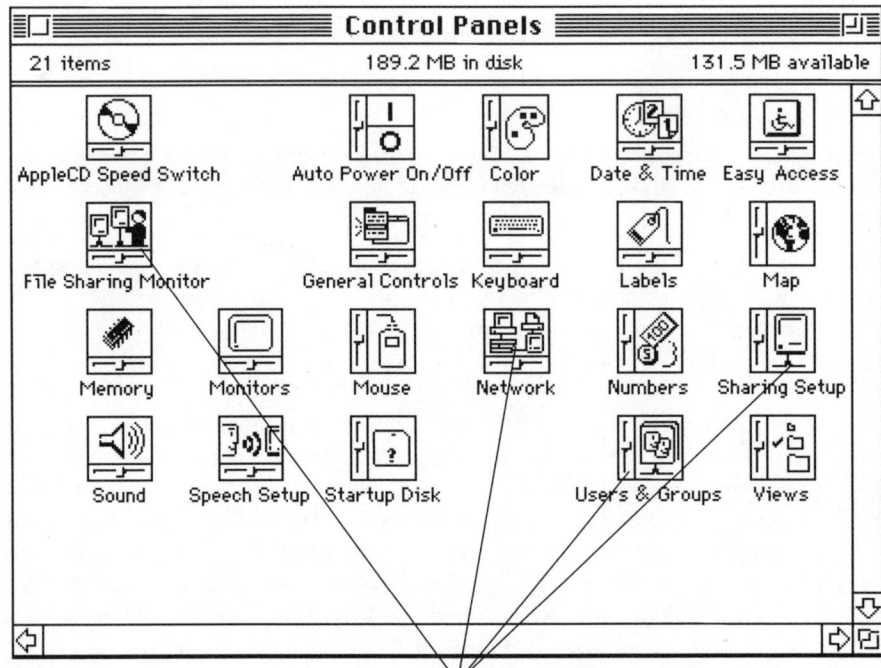

Figure 2.6 The Control Panels folder

In System 6.0.X, the implementation of control panel devices is the same as that of system extensions, except that the means of accessing the control panels is a little different. The other difference is the loading order: in System 7.X, the Macintosh loads the system extensions and then all of the control panels, loading each set in alphabetical order; System 6.0.X loads the Inits (system extensions) and control panels together in alphabetical order.

The Preferences Folder

The Preferences folder contains files that are automatically created by system-level utilities and Macintosh applications. Officially, every program is supposed to check the Preferences folder, as it loads, for its Preferences file (if it has one), and if the file is missing, it should create a new one. Not all programs will recreate the Preferences file, although this inability is becoming increasingly rare.

When the Preferences files become important is when one gets corrupted. There are times when everything will appear to work correctly, except that you are not getting the results you want. When this happens, you should remove the Preferences file for the offending function or application, reboot, and see if the problem goes away. After doing this, be sure to reconfigure the function's or application's preferences using the application, or with the appropriate utility or Control panel.

Figure 2.7 shows the contents of the Preferences folder.

As you can see in Figure 2.7, preferences for the Macintosh's System 7 file sharing are kept in a folder inside the Preferences folder; the Users & Groups data file is also a networking component. On Macs using System 6.0.X, Preferences files aren't as neatly controlled. Some will be found loose in the System folder, some will be kept in a Preferences folder, and others will be put into folders created by an application. So in this sense, System 6.0.X can be a bit more troublesome.

Startup Items Folder

The Startup Items folder is where an application or its alias is placed so that the application will automatically launch when the Mac starts. This folder provides the same function as placing a execution line in the AUTOEXEC.BAT on an MS-DOS system. It is also like entering an application in the Load or Run line of the WIN.INI file when you're running Windows.

Figure 2.7

The Preferences folder contents for System 7.1

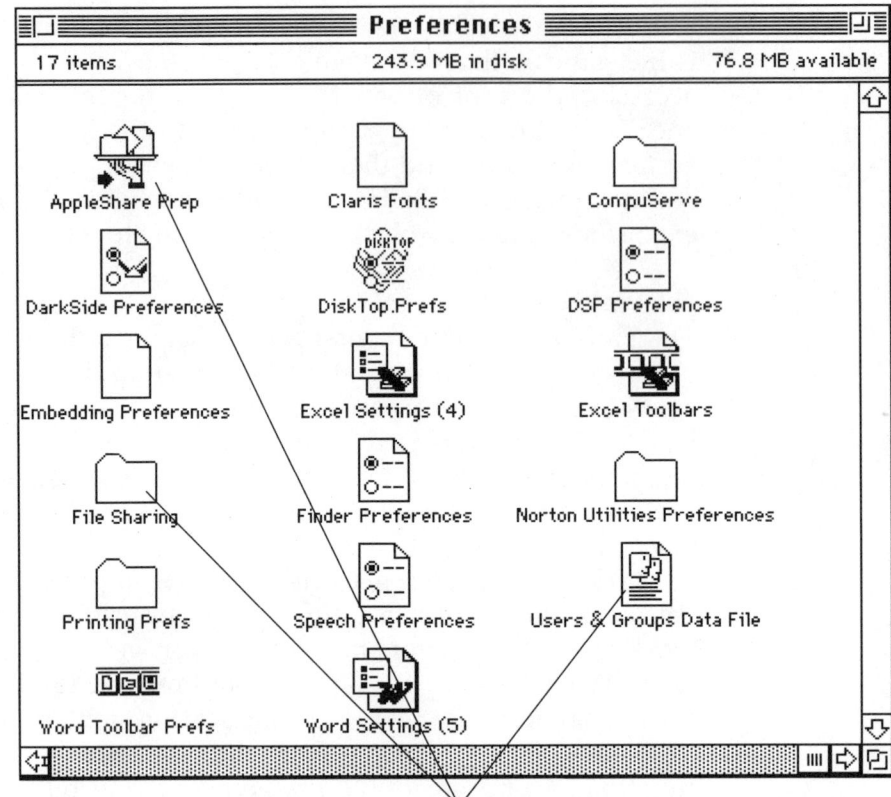

Network preferences—files and folders

Apple Menu Items Folder

The Apple Menu Items folder is used to provide access to applications, documents, or folders—or to aliases for any of these items—so they are easily accessible at all times. When the System is first installed, you will have a few small applications called *Desk Accessories* in the Apple Menu Items folder (see Fig. 2.8).

The Apple Menu Items folder is also new with System 7.X. If you are using a Macintosh with 6.0.X, Desk Accessories that are accessed from the Apple menu (see Fig. 2.9) are installed into the System file using a utility called Font/DA Mover. This utility is included on the Macintosh System Tools disks that came with the Mac. With System 7, Apple did away with this utility and declared Desk Accessories to be an outmoded type of application. Now any program that used to be a Desk Accessory is nothing more than a small application that can be stored and run from any location on the hard drive.

MACINTOSH NETWORKING

Figure 2.8
The Apple Menu Items folder

Control Panels alias

Figure 2.9
The Apple menu's contents

 Fonts Folder
The Fonts folder is a folder that contains all of the typefaces and printer fonts used the Macintosh's System. Whenever you install a new font, it will be stored in the Fonts folder (see Fig. 2.10). The Fonts folder is a System 7.1 implementation.

Figure 2.10

The contents of the Fonts folder

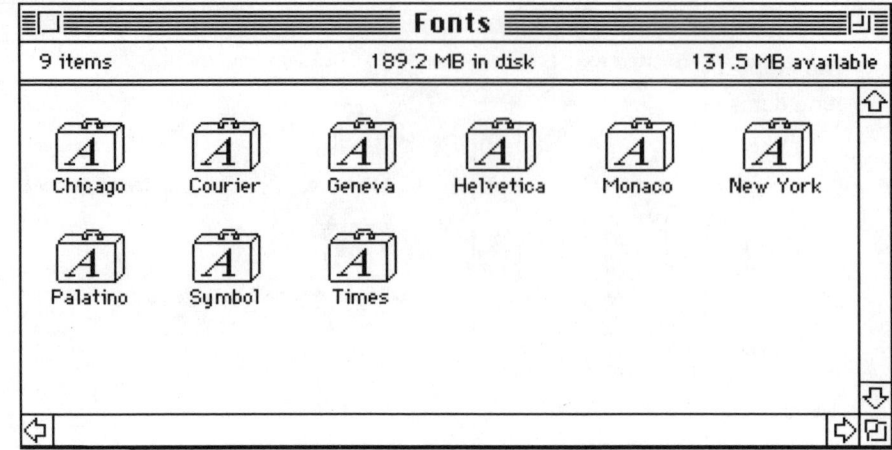

Typefaces are stored in files called *suitcases*; you can open them to view their contents. In Figure 2.11, you will see the contents of the Times suitcase. You can open a font suitcase by double-clicking on it.

Figure 2.11

The Times font suitcase while open

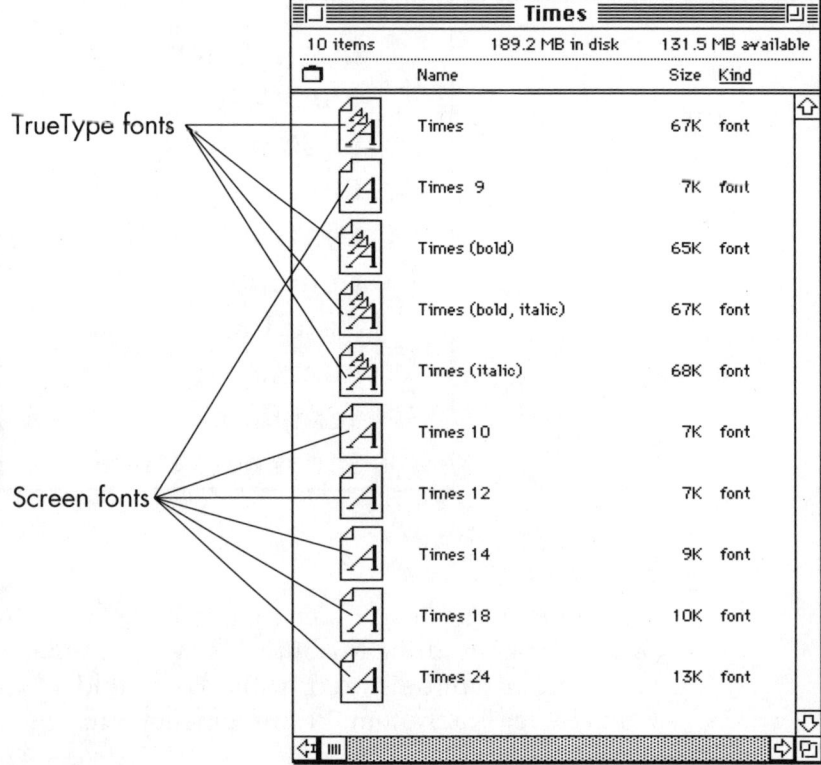

In the open suitcase, you will see two different types of fonts. One is a TrueType typeface (the icon with the three As), and the other is a standard pre-sized typeface (the icon with the single A).

The machine's overall font configuration will depend on how the Mac is being used. Because there are such a large number of fonts and typefaces available, it is not always practical to keep fonts in the Fonts folder. Often, people use a font utility like SuitCase from Symantec to open and close a specific set of fonts. Any fonts in the Fonts folder are available to any Macintosh application.

In System 6.0.X, the typefaces were stored in the System file and placed there using the Font/DA Mover utility. However, there are also font management utilities that were used with System 6.0.X. In System 7.0 or 7.0.1, the fonts are still stored in the System file, but you do not need the Font/DA Mover utility to install the fonts. You can open the System file in System 7.X by double-clicking on its icon. The Font folder is new with System 7.1.

If you are using downloadable PostScript fonts, the printer fonts need to be stored in the Fonts folder with the typeface suitcase. If the typeface suitcase and PostScript font are not together, the font will not be sent to the printer. This is usually true of font management utilities that allow you to access typefaces of fonts from other locations on the hard disk. The one alternative to storing the printer font on the Macintosh is to have a hard disk attached to the printer that contains all of the printer fonts used by your workgroup(s).

PrintMonitor Documents Folder

The PrintMonitor Documents folder is created in the System folder the first time you print while using the Print Monitor to spool the printed document. If you have a problem with printing a particular document, and it has been spooled, you may have to go into the PrintMonitor Documents folder and delete the spooled file before printing again.

System Caveats

This is a short section about general system concerns. The information in this section is intended to keep you from making mistakes that could cause you heartache and frustration. All of these suggestions and warnings are general in nature and not necessarily network-related. But if you cannot use the Mac reliably, it does not matter what's happening on the network.

The section heads below provide a list of the topics covered.

Multiple System Folders

It is possible to place multiple System folders onto a Macintosh hard drive. This is not as serious a problem with System 7.X as it is with System 6.0.X. However, even when using System 7.X, you should exercise caution if you intentionally install more than one System folder.

The reason this is not a good practice is that you may have difficulty determining which System is running the Macintosh. You could have two System folders that have different drivers and capabilities, and the result could be that the Macintosh does not behave as you think it should because it is being controlled by a System folder you are unaware of.

If you are using System 6.0.X, multiple System folders are definitely undesirable. If you have multiple systems on a System 6.0.X Mac, you could have problems that range from erratic behavior to a Mac that cannot boot. If you are using System 6.0.5 or later, the active System folder will have an icon like the one in Figure 2.12.

Figure 2.12

The active System folder

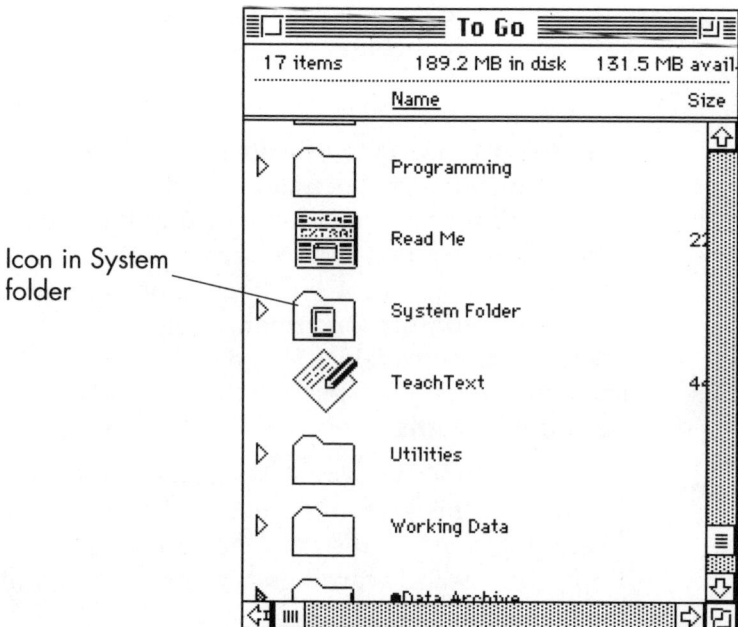

Icon in System folder

Multiple systems usually get dragged onto a hard drive when people install software from a floppy disk that also contains a System folder, and they copy the entire diskette onto the drive. It can also happen when you have two or more hard drives attached to a Mac, where each hard drive has a System folder and someone has copied the System folder from one drive onto another by accident.

To find duplicate System folders, you will have to use a search utility, like the Find command from the File menu in the Finder (System 7.X) or the Find File Desk Accessory (System 6.0.X). If you need to delete a duplicate System folder and it is the duplicate that is controlling the Mac, you will have to boot the Mac using a floppy disk or another hard drive (use the Startup Disk Control Panel), then delete the offending folder when it is not controlling the Mac and reboot.

Another problem with having multiple Systems on a hard disk occurs when the System is copied to the hard disk. Whenever a System is copied onto the hard disk, it rewrites parts of the hard drive's boot blocks. You can usually tell the Mac to use the new System when it boots from a particular drive.

In general, just avoid multiple System folders. If you really want to use two System configurations on the same Mac, attach a second hard drive and install the alternate System on the second hard drive.

Automatic Creation of System Support Folders

When you are using System 7.X—especially if you are trying to troubleshoot a Mac and boot from a disk that has only the System and Finder (and an Enabler if you need it)—the System will automatically create the Extensions, Control Panels, Fonts (7.1 only), Startup Items, Apple Menu Items, and Preferences folders if they do not exist already. This is not a critical note, but something that is nice to know.

System Disk Space Requirements

The amount of disk space that the Macintosh System can occupy ranges from 1.1M to over 20M. The 1.1M System is found on the floppy disk that comes with every Macintosh, the Disk Tools disk, while System folders larger than 20M can be found on a Mac that has been completely tricked out. Usually, your average System folder will run about 15M after adding some utilities, fonts, and application preferences. A standard installation on a Macintosh

Quadra 840AV will use 13.5M before adding any extra utilities or fonts.

Macintosh Disk Basics

Because the hard disk is the most important component of a system other than the CPU, you need to know something about maintaining your Macintosh hard disk and managing some of its quirks. This section, albeit brief, will discuss the most important aspects of Macintosh disk installation and maintenance.

Macintosh Disk Drives

Every Macintosh sold today comes with a hard drive and a floppy drive, and many have a CD-ROM option. The floppy drive is a 1.44M high-density drive, although older SEs and Macintosh Pluses have an 800K double-density drive.

When dealing with floppy drives, you'll run across two problems. One is when the drive is actually broken and needs to be replaced, and the other is when the drive is just dirty and needs to be cleaned. On the Macintosh IIcx, IIci, and Quadra 700 models, you'll find that the fan sits behind the floppy drive and causes the drive to act as a vacuum cleaner. These drives get incredibly dusty and need to be cleaned on a regular basis. Otherwise, they will fail, seeming broken when they are only dirty.

Other than dirt, the single biggest cause for a broken floppy is forcing a disk into or out of the drive. If a disk gets stuck, you should be very careful when trying to remove it. If it does not come out, take it to a technician. Often, if the operation is performed properly, the disk can be removed and the patient will live. When you insert a disk, some Macs will grab it just before it is completely inserted into the drive slot. Do not impede this process. Soon, however, Apple will be changing the type of floppy drives it uses, and the drives will not grab the disk as it is being inserted—so this, too, is something you need to watch for. Finally, do not slam floppy disks into a Macintosh drive: be gentle and insert the disks slowly.

Every Macintosh hard drive is a SCSI drive; depending on the Macintosh model, the hard drive can be internal or external. Regardless, the standard rules for SCSI implementation apply, so you can have ID numbers from 0 to 7. The Macintosh is always SCSI ID 7. All internal Apple drives are originally set to SCSI ID 0.

If you add a NuBus SCSI adapter to a Macs with a NuBus slot, you can double the number of SCSI devices connected to it. The Quadra 900 and 950 each have a second internal SCSI interface. An internal CD-ROM in a Mac is SCSI ID 3.

When connecting SCSI devices to the Mac, make sure you are using good shielded cables and following the standard rules of SCSI implementation. SCSI trouble-shooting goes beyond the scope of this book, but you might want to pick up a book that covers Macintosh trouble-shooting, because trouble-shooting SCSI problems has become known as a fine art in the Mac world. And if you're not sure of what you're doing, you'll drive yourself crazy.

Hard Disk Utility Software

There are two types of software that you will use on a Mac hard drive. One is formatting software, and the other is some type of disk protection and recovery utility. Both types of software are really necessary for smooth and trouble-free Mac operations.

The formatting software that comes as a part of the Macintosh operating system will only work on Apple drives. So if you have an extra SCSI drive kicking about that you want to put into a Mac, you will have to purchase formatting software before you can use it. If you purchase a third-party drive for the Mac, it will usually come with its own formatting software.

Likewise, some type of hard disk utility software for protecting and recovering crashed drives usually becomes a necessity at some point. You are better off getting one now rather than waiting until you are in a crisis situation. Macintosh hard disks do crash, people do accidentally delete files, and the Macintosh operating system has no utilities to help you. Just because DOS 5 and 6 have some of these utilities doesn't mean you can expect to find them on a Mac. They are available only as third-party software.

The rest of this section will discuss each of these types of software in a little more depth.

Formatting Software

Every Macintosh comes with a disk that is called Disk Tools. This floppy contains the Apple HD SC Setup software, which is Apple's hard disk formatting software. As mentioned above, this software only works on Apple brand hard drives. Although you can make it work with non-Apple drives, you would have to hack the HD SC

Setup, and that is really a violation of Apple's licensing agreement.

So if you are installing additional hard drives, you need to make sure that the formatting software comes with the drive. Usually, this is not a problem, unless you are building the drive yourself by purchasing a bare drive and putting it into the Mac or an external case. If you are doing this, then you need to purchase formatting software.

There are several companies that make formatting software for the Mac. One of the best is a company called FWB in San Francisco, California. They make a package called the Hard Disk Toolkit that will format any type of SCSI drive and give you optimum performance. The following is a list of available formatting software:

- **Hard Disk Toolkit**—FWB
- **RapidTrak**—Insignia Solutions
- **SCSI Director**—Transoft
- **FormatterOne**—Software Architects

When formatting a Macintosh hard disk, you need to make sure that the software you're using is System 7-compatible—older formatters are not. Also, if you have a disk drive that was used on a Mac with System 6.0.X, you will have to update the drive's driver to use it on a Mac with System 7.X. Every Macintosh hard disk has a driver that is placed on the drive by the formatter. If the driver gets corrupted, the drive will not operate properly. Also, each drive contains a set of boot blocks and a Macintosh Desktop file. All of these are critical to the drive's operation. Once again, I'll have to refer you to other sources for information on Macintosh hard drives if you want to know more.

Another bit of information about Mac drives will probably be familiar to you. This is the block allocation size. The same principles that apply to MS-DOS drives apply to Macintosh drives. The larger the partition, the more blocks are allocated to each file. So if you are using a partition that is 1 Gig in size, your file allocation size will be about 25K, which means that you can end up wasting a lot of disk space if you are using small files on a large hard drive. To go along with this, the Mac's Finder can comfortably handle about 15,000 files. If you find that you have more than 15,000 files, you may notice erratic behavior when copying files. Try to keep the number of files below this number. If necessary, repartition the hard drive so it is smaller and spread the files over a couple of volumes.

Also, try to keep some spare space on your Mac drives. You should keep anywhere from 5M to 10% of the total drive space free. That way, you will be sure to have some room for temporary files, which can get quite large with some applications.

Two more things you should remember are fragmentation and in-use sectors. Fragmentation can slow down a drive's speed on a Mac drive, just like it can on an MS-DOS drive. So you will want to check for this problem from time to time and use a disk optimizer. And in-use sectors are a condition that exists for both Mac drives and DOS drives. The problem with in-use sectors is that Apple does not provide a utility like CHKDSK.EXE for freeing them up—once again, you'll have to use third-party software like that described in the next section.

Disk Utility Software

As mentioned several times above, you should have a disk utility package on each of the Macs in your network. If you use this software just once to recover a crashed drive, it will have paid for itself. And if you are using a number of Macs, you will use the software. All of these packages have the same basic features, from disk and file recovery to disk repair and drive optimization. The most popular Macintosh packages are made by the same people who do DOS disk utility packages: Symantec's Peter Norton and Central Point Software.

If I were asked which I think is best, I would have to say that Central Point's MacTools is better than Norton Utilities, but I reserve the right to change my mind as these two companies continue to battle it out. The current version of MacTools will do a better job of recovering a crashed disk drive, but that could change with Norton's next release.

Regardless of which package you choose, each of these utilities will create a backup directory for your Mac drives that could save you a lot of time—especially since the Macintosh does not automatically create a backup directory like the second DOS FAT you'll find on MS-DOS formatted drives. You need one of these packages for this reason alone, no matter what optimization, backup, and other disk enhancing utilities they provide.

Viruses

For several years, Macintoshes have been plagued by viruses, just like other computer systems. There are nowhere near as many Macintosh viruses as MS-DOS viruses, but they do exist and they can be just as dangerous. For this reason, you should also have virus protection software installed on each networked Mac. The following is a list of some of the anti-virus software available for the Mac:

- **Central Point Anti-Virus**—Central Point Software
- **MacTools**—Central Point Software
- **Virex**—Datawatch
- **LanProtect**—Intel
- **AntiToxin**—Mainstay
- **Symantec AntiVirus for Macintosh**—Symantec

Any of these utilities should provide the protection you need. Like MS-DOS viruses, most Macintosh viruses are transferred from machine to machine via floppy disk. The viruses usually live in the System, Desktop, or application files on Mac disks, rather than in the boot blocks like on MS-DOS disks. Regardless of where they live, they can cause trouble ranging from random system problems to the destruction of data on the hard disk. Now you've been warned.

Macintosh File Structures

The Macintosh uses a file structure that consists of two parts. One of these parts is the resource fork, and the other is the data fork. How these structures are supposed to be used is described in the *Inside Macintosh* series published by Addison-Wesley. You should be aware that these data structures exist.

But what will be of more concern to you as a network administrator is how the Macintosh keeps track of a file's creator. In the DOS world, a file's type is determined by its file name extension. This is even true in the Windows environment. However, the Mac uses a completely different method for keeping track of a file's application.

Every Macintosh file is assigned two codes: a type code and a creator code. The creator code identifies the application that created the file, while the type code is used to classify the file format. Thus, a file type of APPL is a user-executable application, while a TEXT type means that the file is an ASCII data document. The Desktop file, which is a pair of invisible files that are on every Macintosh disk, associates the proper icon with a file and assists in linking data files and applications. This all becomes important to you when you start storing Macintosh files on non-Macintosh disk drives like your file server.

The creator and type codes are what enable the Macintosh to launch a file when you double-click on the file, so if the associations between the creator and type are lost (or non-existent, in the case of a DOS file), then the Mac cannot launch the proper application from the file. For DOS users, this is not much of a problem, but Mac users will go nuts if they have to open every file from inside the application. So most networking environments that provide AppleTalk support also provide Macintosh name support as part of the AppleTalk implementation. This is great, because files created on the Mac retain their attributes when placed on the server.

The problem now gets passed onto MS-DOS and Windows users who have to access the same files. Here the problem is the file name itself: most Macintosh users will be hard-pressed to use a file name with eight characters and a three-letter extension. Your problem as the Administrator will be to try to keep everything straight.

Some of the network operating systems discussed in this book will provide mapping functions that associate the Macintosh applications to MS-DOS files based on the file's extension. Some also, based on the Mac's file type, display the proper extension to DOS users. However, the implementation of these capabilities is not the same for each NOS, so you will probably have to work with your Mac users and teach them how to open MS-DOS files with Macintosh applications if the Macintosh file mapping is not available.

To open an MS-DOS file with a Macintosh program:

1. Launch the Mac application.
2. Select "Open" from the application's File menu.

3. Select the file type you want to open (if the application has this feature).
4. Select the MS-DOS file to open.

In most cases, the file type for the DOS file will be TEXT as far as the Mac is concerned, and most applications will be able to open text files. Once the application starts to open the file, the application will convert into a readable format as it opens. This, of course, assumes that the Mac application can perform file translations.

An example of this process is provided by Microsoft Word. When a DOS or Windows Word file is opened by Microsoft Word for the Mac, Word will recognize the text file as being readable. When Word starts to open the file, it checks the file's format. If the file is not a Macintosh file, Word compares it to Word's translators. If the file format matches one of the translator formats, Word can convert and open the file. However, some Mac applications cannot read a text file, and therefore cannot recognize the MS-DOS file from the application's Open dialog box. When this happens, you will have to do one of two things: you can either convert the file using a file conversion utility, or—if you know that the file is in a format that the Mac program can read—you can just change the file type from TEXT to one the application can read.

In most cases, it will probably be easiest to use a conversion utility. If you provide your Mac users with the utility, then they can perform the conversion without bothering you. The package that has works best for this type of data processing is called MacLink Plus and is published by DataViz.

Otherwise, changing the type code is not difficult—you just need a utility that will enable you to access the type codes. One program that works well is DiskTop, from PrairieSoft. With Disk-Top, you will be able to change the file's type and creator codes quickly. Figure 2.13 shows DiskTop's view of a hard disk, so that the Type and Creator files are visible. The selected document is a Word for Windows file on the Mac. Notice that the type code is TEXT and the creator is ????.

If this file is double-clicked, the Mac will not be able to launch an application, because there is no application associated with the file. Changing the association would require that the creator code be changed. Figure 2.14 shows the DiskTop Info dialog window where you can edit both the creator and type codes for a file.

MACINTOSH NETWORKING

Figure 2.13

A display of a Mac hard drive using DiskTop (a Word for Windows file is highlighted)

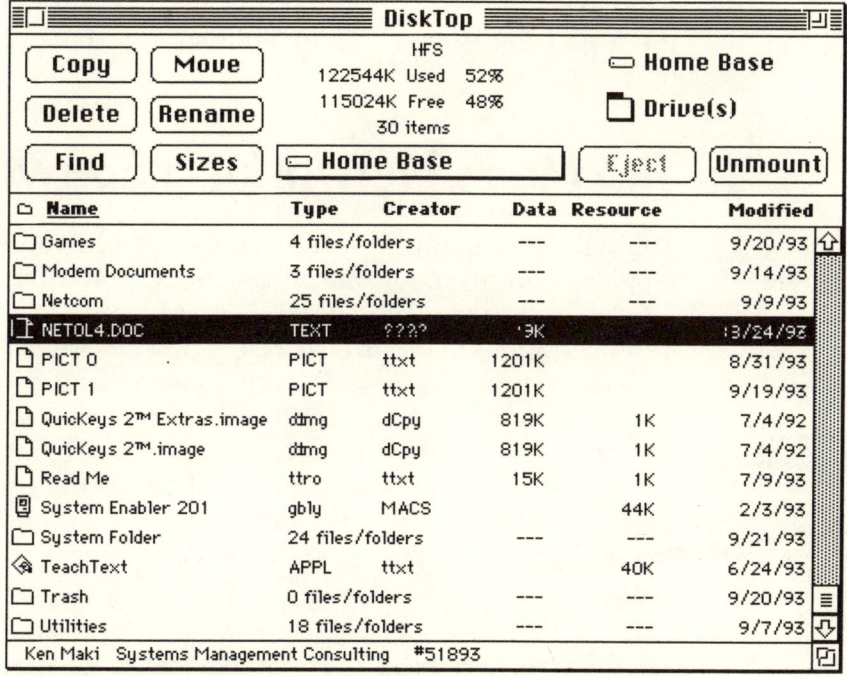

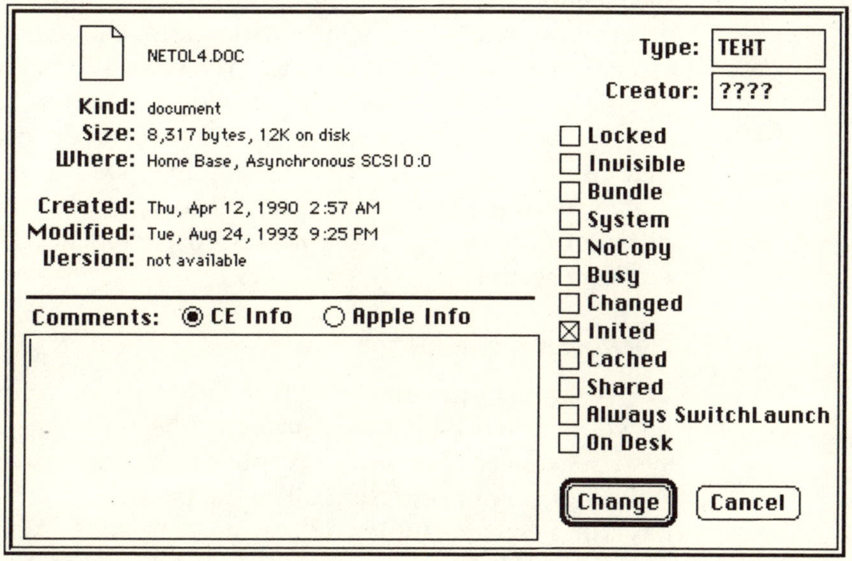

Figure 2.14

DiskTop's Info window

An example of when you would want to use this technique to change a creator code is when an MS-DOS application creates a TIFF file but your Mac graphics package will only recognize files that have a PICT or TIFF type code. In this case, you would change the type code from TEXT to TIFF so the Mac application could open the file.

The Mac's Networking Software

The network operating systems discussed in this book use the AppleTalk protocol for Macintosh connections. The only NOS-specific software you will have to install on a Mac is the NOS's administration, mail, or chat utility. Otherwise, NOS software all depends on the Macintosh's native networking capabilities. All of the networking software you'll need for your Mac is included with the Macintosh operating system: you just install the appropriate System features. This section will look at the System elements needed for Macintosh networking, the installation of the networking software, and the different networking concerns you'll have with System 7.X and 6.0.X.

Macintosh System Networking Elements

A Macintosh has to have several System software elements installed before you can use it as a workstation. The specific networking extensions, Control Panels, and Preferences files you need will be listed in this section, along with descriptions of their functions.

Each of these System elements is installed with the Installer that comes on the Macintosh System disks, received with your Mac or with the disks you received to upgrade your Mac OS. The different utilities and software are discussed in the System 7 Networking section.

Networking Extensions

The networking extensions in the Extensions folder will depend on your networking configuration. The following list of network system extensions are all of Apple's network-related system extensions, but do not represent all of the possible extensions you could have in a System folder. If you need to use a Mac as a software router, you'll have additional system extensions. Some of the NOSs will also have an additional utility extensions. But for basic networking, you will need only what comes with the Macintosh system, regardless of what NOS you're using with your Mac.

Macintosh Networking

A/Rose
This is Apple's TokenTalk card driver. It allows the Mac to use Apple's TokenTalk networking card.

AppleShare
The Mac uses the AppleShare extension to connect to an AppleShare file server. This extension is critical for Macintosh networking, because it is the component that allows the Macintosh to log into an AppleShare file server. The AppleShare extension is what is called an *Rdev* or *Chooser Device*, which is the same type of file as all of the Mac's printer drivers. All Rdevs, when properly installed, present the user with another choice when opening the Macintosh's Chooser. Without the AppleShare extension, the Macintosh cannot connect to an AppleShare or AFP file server.

EtherTalk
This is Apple's Phase 1 Ethernet driver. It is close to being obsolete and does not support the extended addressing capabilities of EtherTalk Phase 2. But if you are using a Phase 1 or non-extended Ethernet network, you will need to use this extension rather than the current Phase 2 EtherTalk Extension. This driver is activated from the Network control panel.

EtherTalk Phase 2
The EtherTalk Phase 2 is the Ethernet driver that allows the Mac to take advantage of a Phase 2 Ethernet network. The Ethernet Phase 2 network supports extended addressing and allows for multiple and virtual zones. The NOS you're using will give you a choice regarding what Ethernet Phase you want to use. However, it should correspond to the Phase you're using on your network. This driver is activated from the Network control panel.

EtherTalk Prep
EtherTalk Prep is an extension that prepares the Mac to use EtherTalk. This extension is automatically installed if it is needed.

File Sharing Extension
The File Sharing extension allows Macs to use System 7 file sharing. This file is used in conjunction with other system extensions and elements. It is basically a driver, and controls the Sharing Setup control panel. If the file sharing does not start up or the file

sharing section of the control panel is not present, the File Sharing extension is corrupted or not installed.

Network Extension
The Network extension works in conjunction with the File Sharing extension. It also controls the File Sharing control panel.

TokenTalk Prep Extension
The TokenTalk Prep extension is the file that prepares a TokenTalk card for use with the Macintosh.

TokenTalk Extension
The TokenTalk extension is the driver that allows the Mac to access a TokenTalk network. The TokenTalk extension supports the same extended network features found in EtherTalk Phase 2.

Networking Control Panels

The Macintosh's networking software is accessed and configured through various control panels. The network-related control panels you will be using are listed in this section.

File Sharing Monitor Control Panel
The File Sharing Monitor is used to monitor file sharing on a System 7 Mac that is also acting as a file server. It shows which items are shared, who the connected users are, and the amount of sharing activity. You can also use the File Sharing Monitor to disconnect users.

Network Control Panel
The Network control panel is used to choose what type of network the Mac is going to use. It is only installed if the Macintosh has Ethernet or Token Ring capabilities. A Mac using LocalTalk or PhoneNET will not have the Network control panel installed. The Network control panel also displays the version of EtherTalk, TokenTalk, LocalTalk, and AppleTalk being used on the Mac.

Sharing Setup Control Panel
The Sharing Setup control panel is used to establish the Macintosh's network identity, turn on the file-sharing capabilities, and initialize a feature called *program linking*. Program linking allows a Macintosh to exchange data with programs on the linked Mac. This is a feature that is only of interest to other Mac users.

Macintosh Networking 57

Users & Groups

Users & Groups Control Panel

The Users & Groups control panel is used to define who has access to the shared items on a Macintosh that is acting as a System 7 file server and what type of access they have. By creating individual users, you control who can access the System file server. The Groups function lets you combine different users into workgroups so you have full control over who has access to what information.

Networking Preferences Files

The Networking preferences files are files that maintain your network's configuration. They are stored in the Networking folder. If a Networking preferences file gets damaged or accidentally deleted, you will have to reconfigure the Macintosh's networking setup. This section lists the various preferences files used and created by the Mac's networking software.

AppleShare Prep

The AppleShare Prep file maintains a list of the volumes that have been selected to mount at boot time. It stores the location of the server volume and its zone. This information is kept in a *boot volume list* and accessed by the Chooser when the AppleShare option is selected.

File Sharing Folder

The File Sharing Folder is used to store the access rights for shared drives that are read-only, like CD-ROM disks. If you have a CD-ROM and are going to share it, the access information for the drive will be kept in the File Sharing folder.

Users & Groups Data File

The Users & Groups data file is where all of the data created by the Users & Groups control panel is stored. If this file is removed or damaged, the users and groups that were defined will be lost and you will have to recreate them.

Chooser

The Chooser

There is only one network item that finds its way to the Apple Menu Items folder when the System is installed. This is the Chooser. The Chooser is the application that lets you access printers, serial device drivers, and the network. From the Chooser, you will be able to select the zone you want to access and any networked printers or AppleShare file servers in the selected zone. Once everything for the network is configured, your users will probably use the Chooser only to access the file server and printers.

Installing Macintosh Networking Software

The Macintosh's System software is installed with an installer application. When you install Macintosh networking software, you should always use the Installer. The reason for using the Installer is that it does more than move the proper System elements from the floppy disks to their location in the System folder. The Installer also checks the Macintosh's hardware configuration and existing software, updates old software, and installs what are called *resources* into the System file, like adding ROM patches that are needed, while at the same time saving System configurations. If you try to install software by copying the various System elements to their proper folders, there is a very good chance the System will not have some of the resource code it needs to go along with the networking elements.

When you update or install a Mac's operating system, you need to find the entire set of Macintosh System disks. The number of disks you'll use depends on the System version you're installing. If you're using System 6.0.X, the System Tools disks will not have any of the TokenTalk or EtherTalk drivers you might need. This is because Macs that use System 6.0.8 do not have Ethernet or Token Ring capabilities without the installation of an Apple or third-party card, which comes with the necessary networking drivers and an installer.

When you are using System 7.X, all of the network drivers you need for an Ethernet or Token Ring network are included with the set of installation disks. This is because some of the newer Macintoshes have built-in Ethernet capabilities. The TokenTalk drivers are included in case you are upgrading a Mac with a TokenTalk card. As of yet, there are no Macs that have built-in Token Ring adapters.

The following steps are for installing System 7.X. Installing System 6.0.X is very similar except that there are fewer options.

To install the Mac's networking software:

1. Shut down the Mac you're going to install the System software on.

2. Insert the Install 1 or Install Me First disk into the floppy drive.

MACINTOSH NETWORKING

3. Restart the Macintosh.
4. When the Macintosh boots, the Installer will automatically launch, and you will see a dialog window like the one in Figure 2.15.
5. Click on the OK button or press the **Enter** key.
6. You will see a screen like the one in Figure 2.16. The button that says Install in the figure could also say Easy Install.

Figure 2.15
The Installer Welcome screen

Figure 2.16
The Easy Install screen

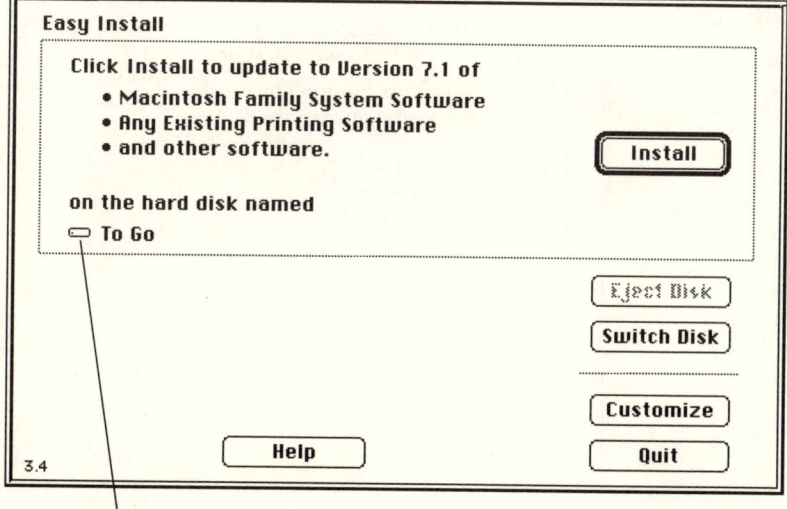

Selected hard drive

CHAPTER 2

At this point, the Installer has interrogated the Macintosh and knows what type of Mac it is, what network cards it uses, and its current System software configuration. If there is a System folder on the selected hard drive (see Fig. 2.16), the Installer will automatically select the same elements to be installed as those that already exist on the hard drive. So if you are installing new system software because you want to add networking capabilities, you'll have to perform a custom installation. The customized installation will allow you to install selected parts of the Mac's system. Otherwise, if there is no System folder on the target drive, selecting the Install or Easy Install button will install the System software for the Macintosh, all possible printer drivers, networking software, and any additional software that will work on the Macintosh.

To customize an installation, follow steps 1 through 6 above, and then do the following:

1. Click on the Customize button You will see a dialog window like the one in Figure 2.17.

2. Select the System features you want to install from the selection window. To select multiple features, hold down the **Shift** key while clicking on the items you want to select.

3. Double-check your selections. They are listed below the selection window, as shown in Figure 2.18.

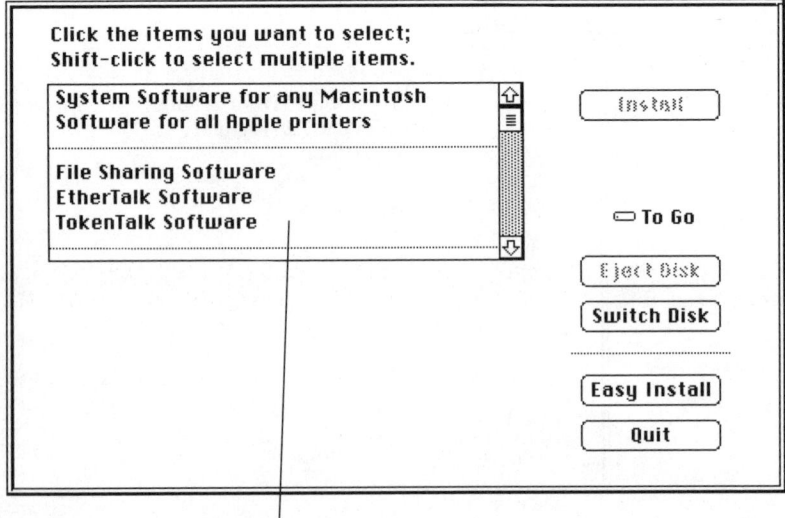

Figure 2.17
The custom installation screen

Selection window

Macintosh Networking

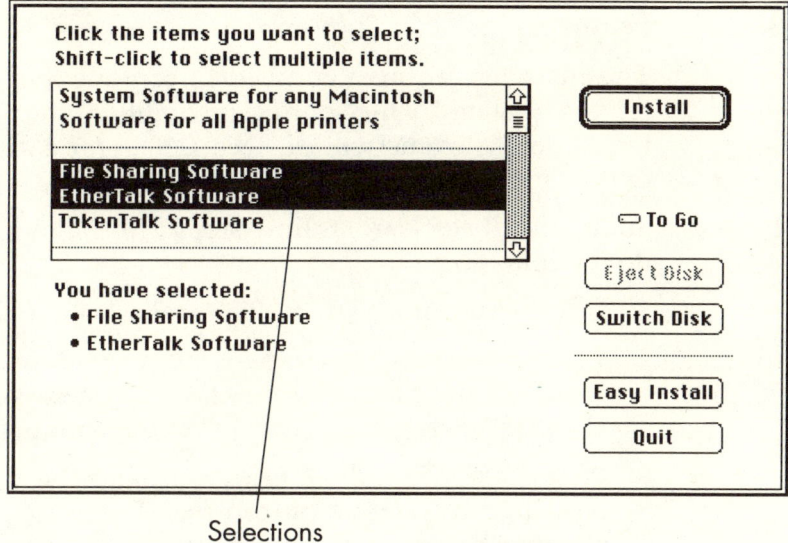

Figure 2.18
Selecting specific System features

4. Click on the Install button. The installation will commence and you will be prompted for the correct System disks.

5. After the installation is complete, you will be asked whether you want to perform an installation on any other hard disks. If you decline the offer, the Installer will prompt you to quit and restart the Mac.

At this point, the installation will be complete. If you are using an Installer for a special networking card, you can run the Installer while the Mac is operating from its hard disk. The Installer will automatically close any running applications and then install the networking software. You will have all of the options discussed above. You will have to restart the Mac if you performed the installation on the hard disk that is controlling the Mac.

> **Note**
>
> With System 7.X, when you perform a standard installation, the AppleShare software needed for connecting to an AppleShare file server is automatically installed. However, when installing System 6.0.X, you will have to perform a custom installation and select the AppleShare Workstation installation in addition to the other System features you want.

Removing Installed Software

The Installer can also be used to remove System software. To remove System 7's file-sharing capabilities, you will need the System disks that came with the Macintosh (or a set of System disks of the same version currently running on the Mac).

To de-install software, follow steps 1 through 6 above, and then do the following:

1. Select "Customize" from the Installer's main dialog window.

2. From the Customize dialog window, you can select which elements of the Macintosh operating system you will install or de-install. Select "File Sharing" in the window on the left.

3. Now hold down the **Option** key, and the Install button will turn into a Remove button (see Fig. 2.19). Clicking on the Remove button will remove all the System file sharing software from the selected hard drive.

4. If the Macintosh has multiple hard drives, you will be given the opportunity to repeat the process for the different drives. Perform steps 1 to 3 for each hard drive you want to use the Remove function on.

When you de-install the Mac's file sharing capabilities, you will leave intact the Mac's ability to operate as a workstation. The

Figure 2.19
The Remove option

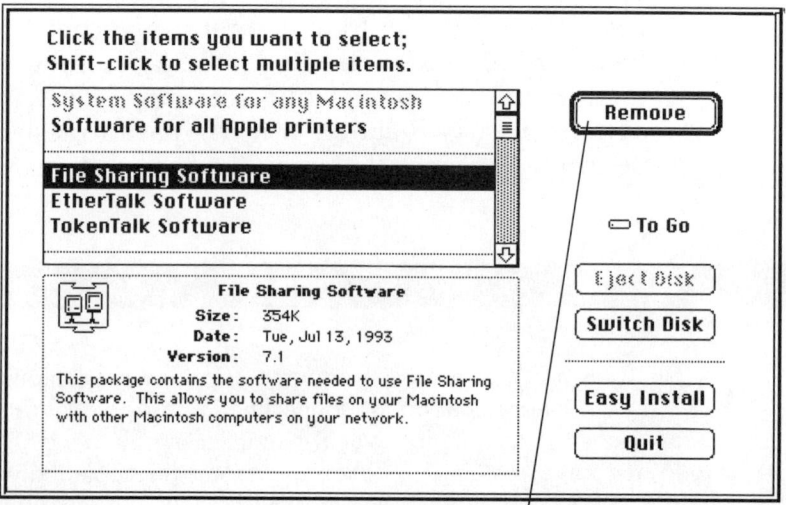

Remove button

reason for disabling the file sharing abilities of your Macs is to keep your Mac users from creating their own network that is out of your control.

System Versions and Networking Concerns

As mentioned several times in the preceding sections, there are differences between Macintosh System 7.X and System 6.0.X networking capabilities. The primary difference is that a Mac running System 6 does not have the ability to be used as a file server. The peer-to-peer networking capabilities are a feature of System 7.X.

It is possible to implement peer-to-peer network services for System 6, but you will have to use third-party software like DataClub from Novell. You could also use Tops for the Macintosh if you can find an old version (Tops is no longer available since Sun Select stopped supporting it). With either System version, you can access an AppleShare file server. Your primary concern will be the version of AppleTalk that is being used on the Macintosh. If your network is an Ethernet network and you want to run EtherTalk Phase 2, you will have to make sure you are using AppleTalk version 53 or higher. Otherwise, you do not have Phase 2 capabilities. This also applies to TokenTalk.

Since Phase 2 capabilities are only available with high-speed network protocols, you can check the version of AppleTalk from the Network control panel.

To check the version of AppleTalk:

1. Open the Network control panel.
2. The AppleTalk version is listed under the EtherTalk or TokenTalk version numbers. (See Fig. 2.20.)

The current version of AppleTalk is 58.03. However, you can have varying AppleTalk version numbers on various Macs without experiencing networking problems. What you will have to watch out for if you have Macs running different System versions, though, is the version of the LaserWriter driver.

If you are printing to a PostScript laser printer and have different versions of the LaserWriter driver (it lives in the Extensions folder), the laser printer will want to be re-initialized each time a Mac prints to it using a different version of the LaserWriter driver. This will be a problem if you are using Macs that have System 7.X and 6.0.X on the same network. If you have to use both System

Figure 2.20

The Network control panel

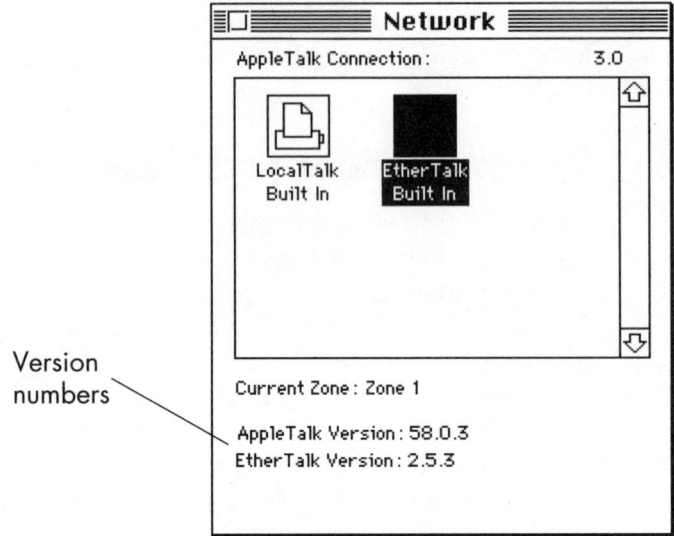

Version numbers

versions on your network, you can avoid this problem in one of two ways. You can run System 6.0.8 on the System 6 Macs, or you can install the LaserWriter drivers from System 7.X on any Mac running System 6.0.5 or greater. The drawback to using System 6.0.8 is that it could cause some erratic System errors on any Mac that pre-dates the Macintosh IIsi or Classic. If you are using System 6.0.5 on one of the older Macs, you can perform a custom installation selecting only the LaserWriter software. Regardless of how you install the System 7 LaserWriter driver, you must have the same version running on all Macs.

Macintosh Networking

Since this book is about connecting Macs to PC networks, the process of setting up and using System 7 file sharing will not be discussed. If you need to use this Macintosh feature, I refer you to your System 7 manuals or to the manuals that came with your Mac. The preceding sections are intended to familiarize you with the Macintosh operating system so that you will have an idea of how it is constructed and what its various elements are.

This section, on the other hand, will discuss general networking concepts that are Macintosh-specific and apply to any AFP- or AppleShare-compliant server. Although some information has already been presented regarding this subject, there is still more

Macintosh Networking

that you need to know. This section will cover accessing an AppleShare file server, security, and some basic trouble-shooting for Macintosh networks.

Accessing an AppleShare File Server

The process of accessing a Macintosh file server is fairly basic.

To access an AppleShare file server:

1. Open the Chooser from the Apple menu (see Fig. 2.21).
2. Select the AppleShare icon in the Chooser's selection window.
3. Select the zone that contains your file server.
4. Select from the available file servers the one you wish to use.
5. Click on the OK button.
6. Enter the user name and password, as shown in Figure 2.22.
7. Click on the OK button.
8. Select the server volume you want to mount (see Fig. 2.23).
9. Click OK.

If you want the server volume to be mounted every time the Mac boots, check the box next to the server volume name. You will

Figure 2.21

The Chooser with AppleShare and zone selected

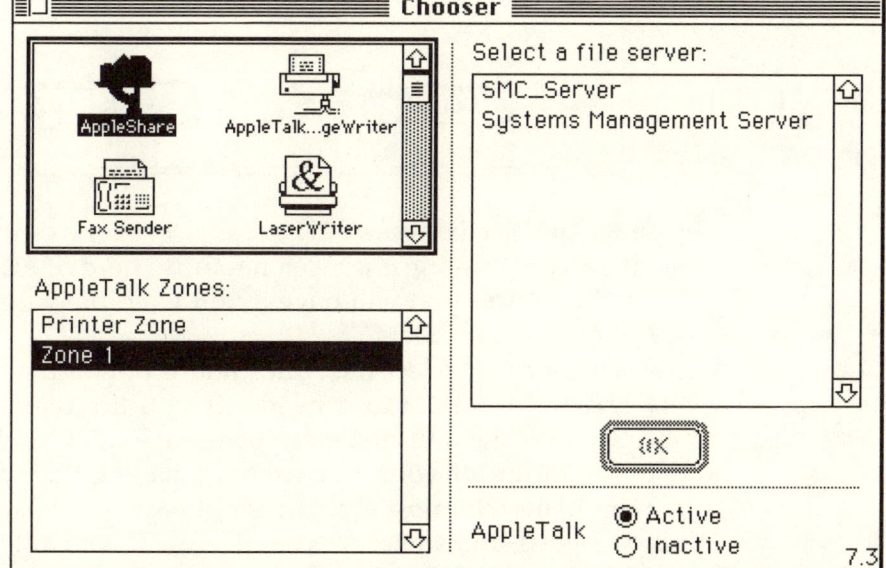

Figure 2.22
Entering the user name and password

> **Connect to the file server "Systems Management Server" as:**
> ○ Guest
> ⦿ Registered User
>
> Name: `Rasputin`
> Password: `••••••` (Two-way Scrambled)
>
> [Cancel] [Set Password] [OK]
> v7.1

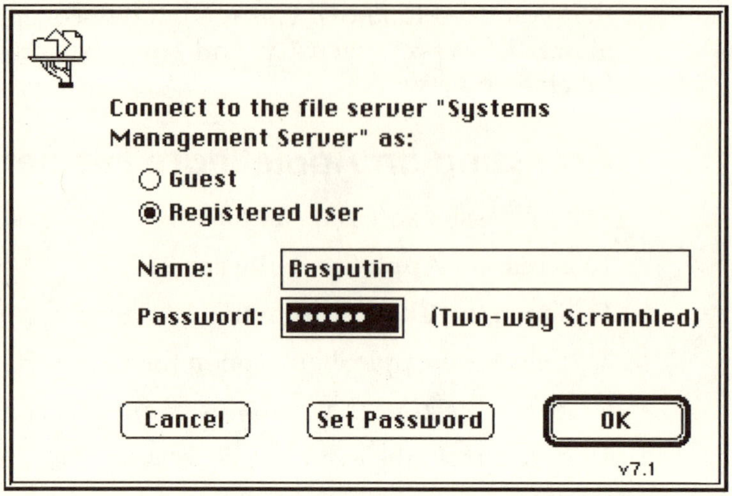

Figure 2.23
Selecting the server volume

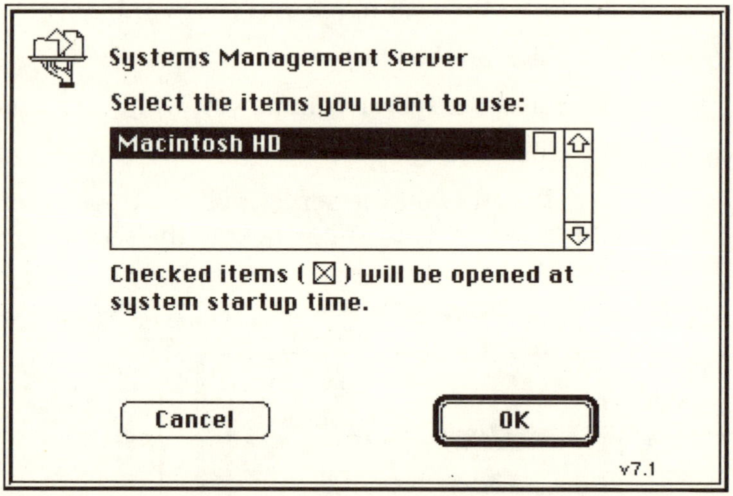

> **Systems Management Server**
> Select the items you want to use:
>
> | Macintosh HD | ☐ |
>
> Checked items (☒) will be opened at system startup time.
>
> [Cancel] [OK]
> v7.1

be given a choice between saving the user name or the user name and password; saving the user name is the default. Figure 2.24 shows the choices you will have if you want the volume mounted every time the Mac boots.

Whether you select the Auto-mount option depends on your network environment and needs. If you are using a NOS like VINES, where the user name can be quite long, you might want to make life easier for your Mac users by having their Macs remember their names. In most cases, it is not wise to save both the name and password, and sometimes the NOS will not allow it anyway. If

Figure 2.24

Selecting the Auto-mount option

you save both the name and password, then anyone who boots the Mac will have access the files on the server.

Once a server volume is mounted, you can unmount it by dragging the server volume icon to the trash. This same procedure will unmount any Macintosh drive except the boot drive.

Access Privileges Security

Security is an issue with all network operating systems. AppleShare security has been been criticized as being too lax. With AppleShare file servers, you will have a different or additional set of security options from your normal PC environment. Depending on your NOS, you might have two sets of security options: one dealing with PC files and the other pertaining to Macintosh files. Regardless of how a NOS deals with its access privileges, an AppleShare volume provides for a specific set of security options. The two major security options you will have are the users you allow to log in and the access rights you assign to specific folders (directories) for each user. Also, most NOSs do not fully implement the security options you would find on one of Apple's AppleShare file servers.

This section will look at the different access privileges you can assign in an AppleShare environment. Remember, the example being used here is Apple's AppleShare file server, which means that the NOS you're using may use different terminology or provide for these functions in different ways. Depending on your needs, you can provide access to a whole volume or to directories on a volume. When you provide for access to directories on a volume, the directories will be visible in the Chooser as individual volumes. You can assign different access privileges for each volume, making it available to a specific user or group of users. Also, within the volume you can define who has access to a specific directory and what type of access they have. Figure 2.25 shows the window used to assign access privileges for a folder (directory) that will appear as a volume.

Although this is example is done using System 7 file sharing, the choices are the same as those from a standard AppleShare file server. In Figure 2.25 you will see that you can assign an owner and a user/group. The owner of the volume or directory is the person who can change the access privileges to a volume or folder. So if you make a user the owner of a volume, that user has the ability to change access privileges to the volume. If you do not want a user to have this ability, you should never make the user an owner of a volume.

Once a volume is mounted, whenever a directory is created, it belongs to the creating user. To change the access rights, all the user has to do is select the folder and execute the "Sharing..." command from the Finder's File menu to get an Access Privileges window like the one in Figure 2.26.

Figure 2.25

An Access Privileges window

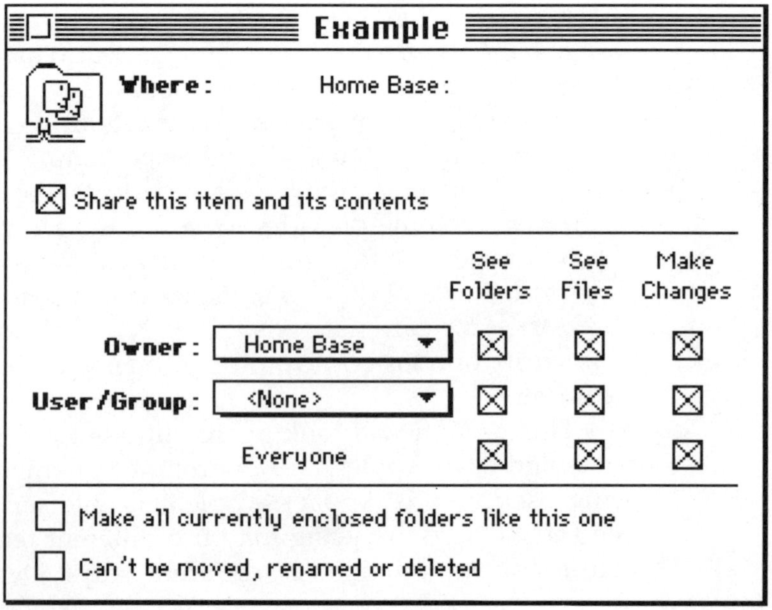

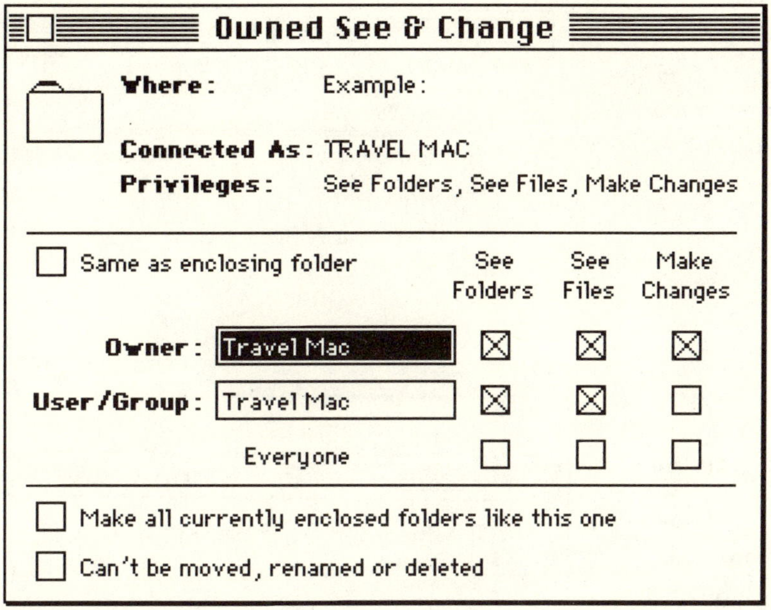

Figure 2.26

Access rights for a folder on an AppleShare file server, as seen from the user's Mac

```
╔══════════════ Owned See & Change ══════════════╗
│                                                │
│  📁   Where:      Example:                     │
│                                                │
│       Connected As: TRAVEL MAC                 │
│       Privileges:   See Folders, See Files, Make Changes │
│  ────────────────────────────────────────────  │
│                                  See    See   Make    │
│  ☐ Same as enclosing folder     Folders Files Changes │
│                                                │
│       Owner:    [Travel Mac]      ☒     ☒     ☒      │
│  User/Group:    [Travel Mac]      ☒     ☒     ☐      │
│                  Everyone         ☐     ☐     ☐      │
│                                                │
│  ☐ Make all currently enclosed folders like this one │
│  ☐ Can't be moved, renamed or deleted          │
╚════════════════════════════════════════════════╝
```

The owner of a folder can change any folder within the owned folder. So if Alice owns a folder and Joe then creates a folder within Alice's folder, Alice automatically owns the folder. Alice can change the privileges to Joe's folder by checking the "Make all currently enclosed folders like this one" box. And if Alice so chooses, she can even deny Joe access to his folder.

These abilities will vary depending on the NOS you use, because each one can implement these options in different ways, but you need to be aware of the possibilities, because the inheritance rights for AppleShare volumes are the same regardless of the NOS. When viewing a shared volume on a Mac, you can tell whether the Mac you're using is the owner by the appearance of the folder's icon. Figure 2.27 shows a mounted volume where only one folder is owned by the workstation—this folder is the one called "Owned—See and Change."

Using the access rights settings, you can provide a user with full access to a directory or volume or totally lock them out, or anything in between. Figure 2.28 and Table 2.1 show the access privileges that would allow everyone on the network to access the volume or folder.

By changing the access rights, you can create directories that are combinations of the possible access rights. Whenever you grant full access rights to everyone, then the rights you've set for

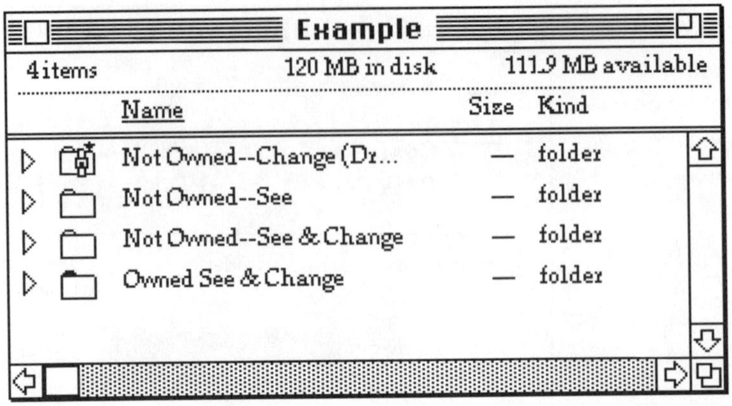

Figure 2.27
A folder owned by the workstation

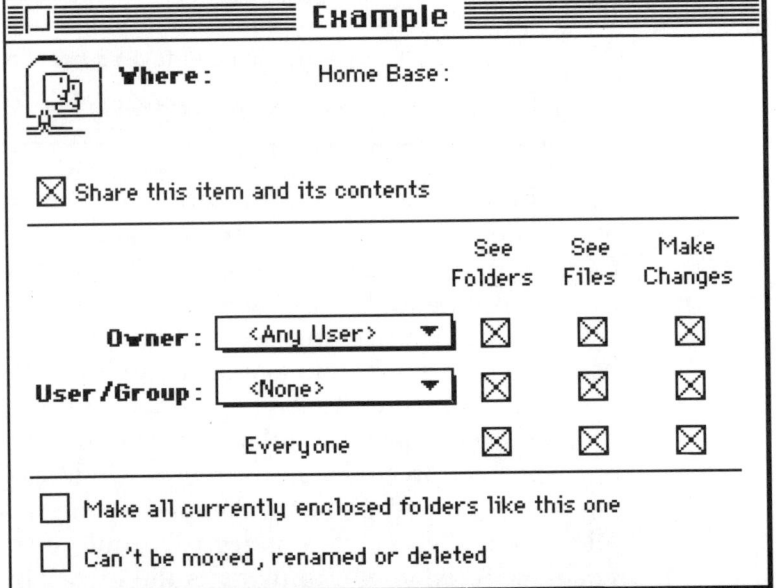

Figure 2.28
A folder owned by anyone

Table 2.1	Access privilege settings for unlimited network access			
Owner/User	See Folders	See Files	Make Changes	Comments
Owner	X	X	X	Grants the owner full access
User/Group	X	X	X	Grants the registered user or group full access
Everyone	X	X	X	Grants everyone full access

the owner and user do not matter; the owner and user automatically inherit the rights granted to everyone. So if you are restricting access, you must disable the access privileges for everyone. Also, if you disable all of the access rights for everyone on a volume or on a directory that will be mounted as a volume, you will be disabling the guest log-in ability as well. Then only the user or group member assigned to the volume will be able to mount it; to everyone else it will be grayed out when viewed in the Chooser. Figure 2.29 shows a server volume with five folders, each of which has different access rights.

The folder named "Locked out" has had all accesses to the current user denied. The access settings for this folder are displayed in Table 2.2.

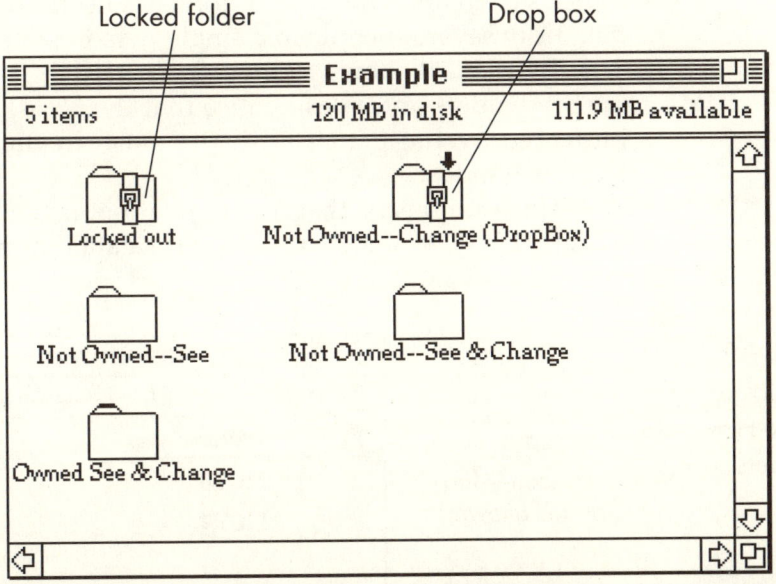

Figure 2.29

A server volume with five folders

Table 2.2	Access privilege settings for "Locked out" folder			
Owner/User	See Folders	See Files	Make Changes	Comments
Owner	X	X	X	Grants the owner full access
User/Group				Denies the registered user or group access
Everyone				Denies everyone access

For this type of folder to be effective, the volume must have access rights that can be changed only by the administrator. If the volume is owned by the user or everyone (both of which are possible with AppleShare), then the registered user or even a guest can change the access privileges to the entire volume. These settings will also work for a directory that you want the user to mount as a volume, and that no one else has access to. However, a better strategy would be to keep the administrator's name in the Owner box and the user's name in the User/Group Name space.

In Figure 2.29, there is another folder that is called "Not Owned—Change (Drop Box)." This folder is not owned by the user—the user does not have either See Folders or Files access, but can Make Changes. This type of folder is called a *drop box*: the user can copy files and folders to the folder, but cannot see or access the folder's contents. This type of folder is useful for passing sensitive data from several people to a single person who needs to see it.

Figure 2.30 shows a directory where the user's access rights are See Folders and Files. Notice that the access privileges are also indicated by the pencil with the slash in the Label line of the folder's window.

This icon means that the user cannot make any changes to the folder. This type of folder is good for data that needs to be accessi-

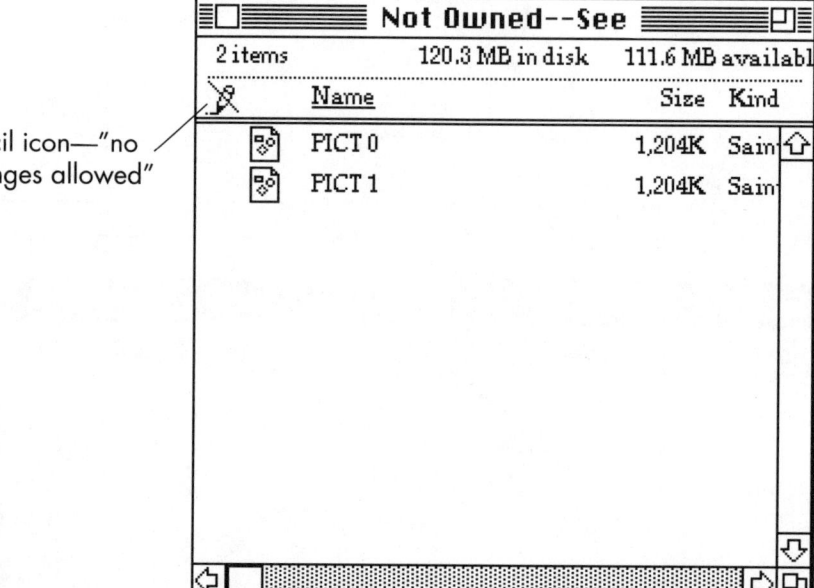

Figure 2.30
A folder with See Files and Folders access

Pencil icon—"no changes allowed"

MACINTOSH NETWORKING

Table 2.3 Access privilege settings for a read-only folder

Owner/User	See Folders	See Files	Make Changes	Comments
Owner	X	X	X	Grants the owner full access
User/Group	X	X		Allows the registered user or group read-only access
Everyone				Denies everyone access

ble, but to which you do not wish changes made. A user can copy any file or folder from this folder to a local hard drive, but cannot add to or change any document on the server. The access settings for this folder are shown in Table 2.3.

Figure 2.31 shows yet another option. In this case, files cannot be seen, but folders can, and changes can also be made to the folder.

Both files and folders can be added. This folder will work just like the drop box where files are concerned: they can be placed into the directory, but then they cannot seen or accessed by the

Figure 2.31
A folder with write access—files are not visible

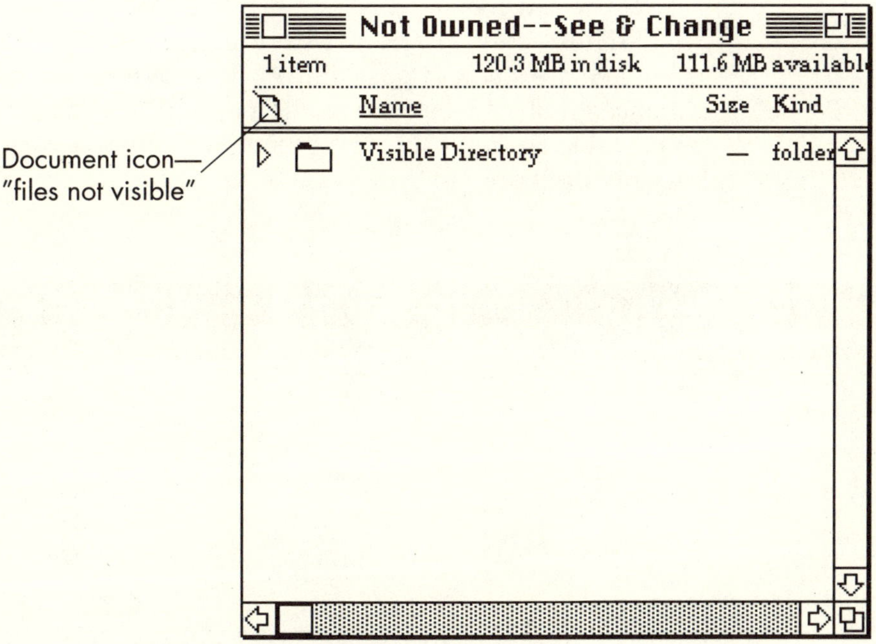

Document icon—"files not visible"

Table 2.4 Access privilege settings for a folder with "invisible" files inside

Owner/User	See Folders	See Files	Make Changes	Comments
Owner	X	X	X	Grants the owner full access
User/Group	X		X	Allows the registered user or group read-only access
Everyone				Denies everyone access

user. In this case, you see a document icon with a slash through it in the label line of the window. This icon means that either files or folders are not visible. Table 2.4 shows the access settings for this folder.

If you want the user to see files but not see folders, you would set the access to "none" for See Folders and check the See Files box instead. If you have settings like those in Table 2.5, you will see both the pencil and document icons with slashes through them in the item line of the window, as shown in Figure 2.32.

The final option you'll have is to not see folders or make changes while the files are still visible. When a folder or volume has this type of access, you will see a folder that looks like Figure 2.33. The settings for this type of access are displayed in Table 2.6.

These combinations provide you with the basis for all of AppleShare's access possibilities. To provide you with a quick reference, Table 2.7 lists all of the possibilities for access privileges. This table assumes that the owner has full access rights; the rights listed apply only to the User/Group setting.

Table 2.5 Access privilege settings for a folder with read-only folders inside

Owner/User	See Folders	See Files	Make Changes	Comments
Owner	X	X	X	Grants the owner full access
User/Group	X			Allows the registered user or group read-only access
Everyone				Denies everyone access

Figure 2.32
Rights set to See Folders only — Pencil and document icons

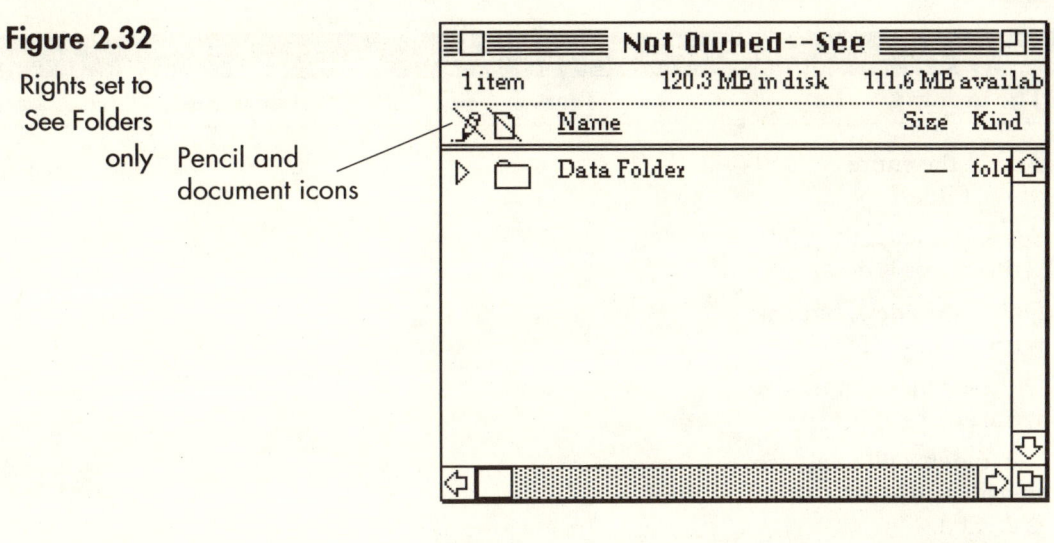

Figure 2.33
Files are visible, but folders are invisible and write access is denied — Pencil and document icons

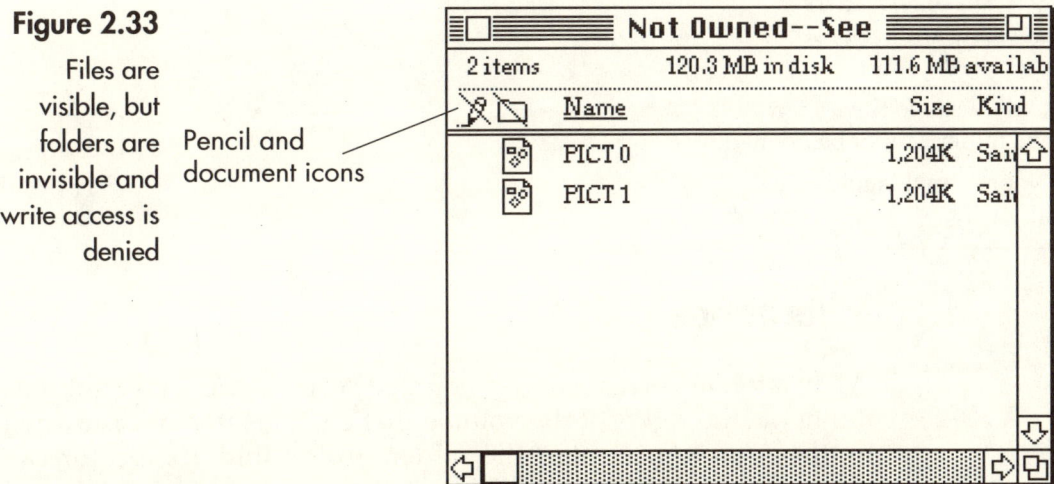

Table 2.6	Access privilege settings for a folder with read-only files inside			
Owner/User	See Folders	See Files	Make Changes	Comments
Owner	X	X	X	Grants the owner full access
User/Group		X		Allows the registered user or group read-only access
Everyone				Denies everyone access

Table 2.7 Access privilege description

The user can	See Folders	See Files	MakeChanges	Icon
Access the entire contents of the folder.	•	•	•	None
See folders and files, but write access is denied.	•	•		
Only see folders, but has write access to folder.	•		•	
Only see files, but has write access.		•	•	
See folders only; files are invisible and write access is denied.	•			
See files only; folders are invisible and write access is denied.		•		
Only write to the folder; the folder cannot be opened.			•	
Not access this folder in any way.				

Inheritance

When a folder is created on a mounted AppleShare server volume, it inherits the rights of the volume that contains it, but it is owned by the user who created the folder. So the folder's creator can change the access rights. This can create some confusion if someone assumes that everyone will be able to view a folder when the directory it was created in has limited access rights.

To avoid this type of problem, you should—except in special circumstances—grant everyone full access at the root level of any server volume. (Remember, a server volume can be a directory and not the entire hard drive.) Then, if you want to restrict access to specific directories, you can do so. This strategy lets all of the users share data, but still provides security for folders that contain sensitive data.

Now for the rub: the above describes Apple's AppleShare file servers. Because an NOS provides an AppleShare volume, it does not follow that the inheritance rights or rules are the same as Apple's implementation. Some NOSs, in their implementation of AppleShare have set the inheritance rules so that the owner of the volume maintains ownership for all items created or stored on the volume unless intentionally changed by the administrator. However, once a user owns a directory, that user can then change the access rights as described above, with the "Sharing..." command from the File menu.

Basic Network Trouble-shooting

Here we're going to look at the problems you could have connecting to a file server from a Macintosh where the fix for the problem is strictly Macintosh-related. Because there are several elements to the Mac's networking capabilities, it is easy for one of the control panels or the Chooser settings to be incorrect. This will result in an inability to access the network.

Usually, your first indication of a problem will be when you go to the Chooser and cannot see a file server or a printer when clicking on the AppleShare or LaserWriter icons. Another indication is if you do not see any zones. When this happens, the first thing to check is the AppleTalk setting in the Chooser. Figure 2.34 shows the Chooser and the AppleTalk settings.

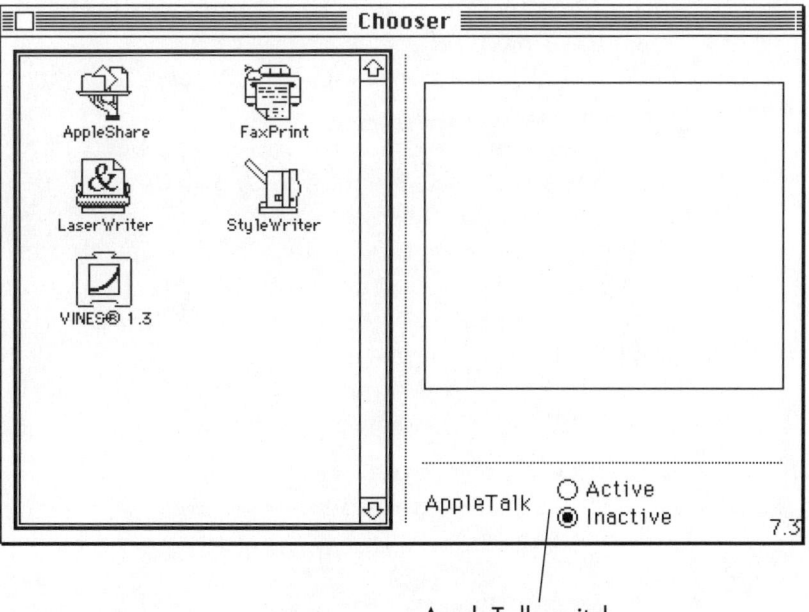

Figure 2.34
The Chooser

If the AppleTalk setting is inactive, you will have no network access. So this is the first item to check. What happens next will depend on other network settings. If AppleTalk is active and you are still do not have network access, and you are using Ethernet or Token Ring, you should check the Network control panel. If you are not using a high-speed network, but relying on LocalTalk or PhoneNET talk, either you are physically disconnected from the network or the network services are down.

From the Network control panel, you need to make sure the correct network is selected. If, when you try to access the Network control panel, you receive an error message that says that there is a network error or that AppleTalk is turned off, you need to return to the Chooser and double-check your settings. You can also experience an error when accessing the Network control panel if there is a problem with your network interface connector. However, if you get the Network control panel open, reset the Mac to use the high-speed network option.

If, when accessing the Ethernet or Token Ring network, you receive a network error, then there is a problem with the network interface hardware: it is not connected, malfunctioning, or somehow disabled. The problem will depend on the type of network interface you're using and whether it requires additional software. If the network interface is a SCSI device, there will be an additional extension that is the driver for the SCSI device. You will have to make sure this extension is not missing or disabled. The same applies to the Token Ring drivers and any third-party Ethernet drivers you might be using.

Once all of these options have been checked, you should probably begin to suspect your hardware. But before you do, re-install the Mac's System software. Your problem could be the result of a corrupted System or System element. Also, it would probably be a good idea to perform a function called *zapping the PRAM*. The PRAM holds the Mac's configuration settings, somewhat like the CMOS settings of a PC. If you follow the steps below, the PRAM settings will be returned to their defaults. However, you will have to reconfigure the network settings. (This procedure is for System 7.X.)

To reconfigure your network settings:

1. Shut down the Macintosh.
2. Restart the Mac.

3. Immediately and simultaneously press and hold the ⌘, **Option**, **P**, and **R** keys.

4. Continue to hold the key combination down until the Macintosh restarts.

5. If the Mac does not restart, then you pressed the keys down too late or released them too soon.

If you are using System 6.0.X, the process for zapping the PRAM is as follows:

1. Hold down the **Option** key while selecting the Control Panels desk accessory.

2. As the Control Panels desk accessory opens, the Mac will beep, indicating that the PRAM has been zapped.

3. Restart the Macintosh. The PRAM effects will not take place until the Mac is restarted.

This section covers the basics of Mac network trouble-shooting. If you continue to have trouble, you should trouble-shoot the network cabling. From here on out, you are probably familiar with these trouble-shooting techniques, so they will not be covered here.

Macintosh Networks

Because of Apple's foresight in providing for networking capabilities from the beginning, creating a physical network has never been a real problem. Beyond the mess of installing wire and making sure you have the correct cabling adapter, little else is needed for basic connectivity. Although the LocalTalk standard is slow, it works, and it works well. However, making the jump to cross-platform connectivity has been a problem for a long time, and has been truly addressed in only the last couple of years. Now it is possible to include a Mac in either an Ethernet or Token Ring network at nominal cost for the hardware. Depending on the NOS you're using, the cost of adding an AppleShare network option may be less than adding a Macintosh AppleShare server and more efficient for cross-platform shops.

This section will address the issue of Macintosh cabling by talking about what is available for network adapters, Macintosh capabilities, and some of the topologies you might consider. The purpose of this section is to provide you with the information you need to decide how to wire your Macs and integrate them into your existing network. All of the networks discussed in this book have router and/or gateway capabilities. This means that each of the networks can use a LocalTalk adapter card of some type. The card will let the Macintoshes connected to it access the file server and other network services, while at the same time the PC will be able to access PostScript printers connected to the Macs using the same AppleTalk adapter. For some NOSs, these services will be restricted to the server that contains the AppleTalk card, and for others with true routing capabilities, the network resources from the AppleTalk card will be network-wide. These capabilities will be discussed in the chapter that covers each NOS.

Network Cabling and Adapters (Bus Sizes, Comparative Speeds, and Compatibility Issues)

Besides using LocalTalk and a PC adapter card in your server, you can use Ethernet or Token Ring. For either Ethernet or Token Ring you can drop a Mac into your existing network, then install the AppleShare option to your NOS without any additional concerns. Whatever your choice may be for network cabling, you can treat the Mac just like any PC on your network.

The Macs can plug into the same hub or MAU, or be daisy-chained on the ThinNet or ThickNet cable right with the PCs. A couple of years ago this was not possible. You would have had to have a separate Mac network that connected via a gateway to the PC network, if the jump was possible at all. Usually it was messy and almost more trouble than it was worth. So more important than how the Macs will fit in your network is what you need to add to the Mac so you can connect it. The rest of this section will look at LocalTalk configurations, along with Ethernet and Token Ring adapters. Here you will learn what type of adapter to use with which Mac.

LocalTalk and PhoneNET

By now you're probably sick to death of hearing about LocalTalk and PhoneNET. But chances are fairly good that you will end up using some type of router, either a server-based router or a software router, to get access to a LocalTalk PostScript printer. Although new PostScript laser printers are now being provided with a built-in Ethernet port, there are millions of serviceable printers that do not have built-in Ethernet. Also, it is less expensive to use LocalTalk or PhoneNET for Macs when speed is not an issue, you only want an E-mail connection, and file sharing is at a minimum.

LocalTalk and PhoneNET both operate at 230 kbs (kilobytes per second), which, although slow, does get the job done. This speed is too slow for multi-user databases and the transferring of large files. But even with these limitations, it is very versatile and stable.

LocalTalk and PhoneNET talk use different cabling, and even though they can be inter-mixed, it is usually easier to use one cabling standard or the other. LocalTalk is harder to implement unless the Macs are in close proximity and running a cable from one Mac to another can be done safely and unobtrusively. LocalTalk cabling comes in predetermined lengths and uses special connectors to connect cables when more length is needed, so it is cumbersome and more difficult to use.

PhoneNET connectors allow you to use standard phone wire, even existing phone wire in the walls. PhoneNET uses two of the four wires in your twisted-pair phone line, and an RJ11 plug to attach the wire to the connector. A network done with PhoneNET connectors can be done in a daisy-chain configuration, a backbone, an active star, or a passive star configuration. Both of the star configurations use a telephone punchdown block as the terminus for the network wires.

Figure 2.35 shows the four basic topologies available for PhoneNET.

On both the active and passive star configurations, you can have several devices connected a single port on the punchdown block in a daisy chain. This is called a *branch*. Table 2.8 provides you with the basic length and number of network nodes you can have for each of the different LocalTalk or PhoneNET topologies.

With PhoneNET connectors, you'll need to terminate the ends of each daisy chain, backbone, or branch. The terminators come with the PhoneNET connection boxes.

A star controller will speed up network access; it can also be connected to other star controllers. Each star controller would have its own zone and you would have an internet of Macs. One

Figure 2.35
Four PhoneNET topologies

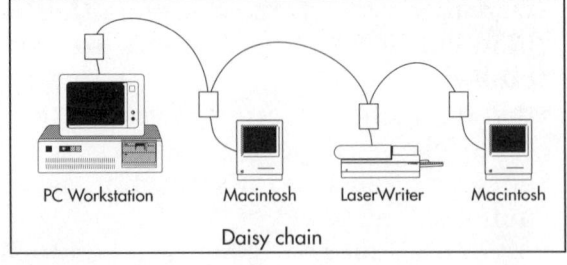

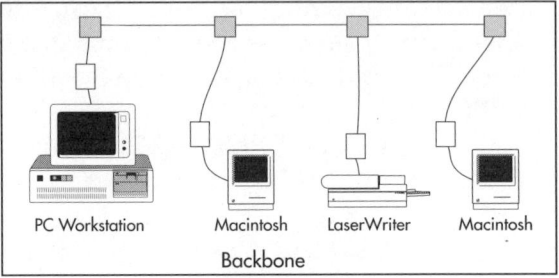

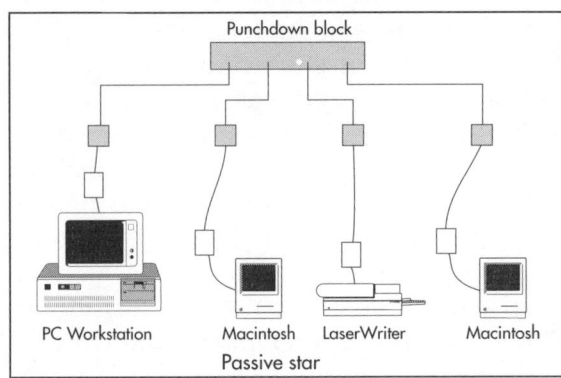

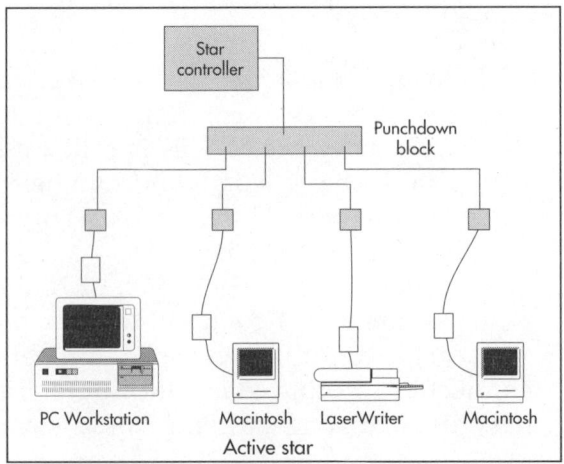

Table 2.8 AppleTalk adapters and topologies

Adapter	Topology	Nodes	Maximum Length	Comments
LocalTalk	daisy chain	32	1000 feet	LocalTalk connectors are self terminating.
PhoneNET	daisy chain	24	1800 feet	Need terminator at each end of daisy chain.
PhoneNET	backbone	32	4500 feet	Termination is installed at each end of the backbone.
PhoneNET	passive star	32	4500 feet or 4 branches of 1125 feet	Branches are connected to a punchdown block. Each branch can also be a backbone.
PhoneNET	active star	48	12 Ports which can support 4 branches, each with lengths up to 3000 feet total length per port	Branches are connected to a punchdown block. Each branch can also be a backbone.

final way of using the PhoneNET system is to have an Ethernet backbone with hardware routers connecting each PhoneNET network to the backbone, also creating an internet.

However, chances are slim that you're even contemplating a low-speed network of the complexity alluded to here. So this concludes your brief introduction to LocalTalk and PhoneNET. You have enough information to get started.

Ethernet

You can use Ethernet with any Mac from the Macintosh Plus on. The Ethernet connection is made in one of three ways with the Macintosh. Either the Mac either has a slot into which a card can be installed, the Mac has Ethernet built in as a connection off the motherboard, or you can use a SCSI-to-Ethernet adapter. Of course, the adapter is dependent on the model of Macintosh. For every Mac that has a slot, someone manufactures an Ethernet card, and for those that do not have slots, you can use an Ethernet-to-SCSI adapter.

You can also use whatever type of Ethernet cable you want: 10BaseT, ThinNet, or ThickNet. With the proper adapter, a Mac can fit seamlessly into any network. And if you wish, you can even get an adapter that will connect to an AppleTalk laser printer so you don't need to use a router. Table 2.9 shows the different types of adapters and their corresponding Macs.

So as you can see, any Macintosh you'll run into in a business environment today can be connected to an Ethernet network and some of Apple's laser printers.

Token Ring

Connecting to a Token Ring network is just as easy as connecting to an Ethernet network, except that you'll have to purchase an adapter. Also, there is no SCSI-to-Token Ring adapter that I'm aware of, so any slotless Mac is out of the loop, so to speak. But any Mac with a slot can be connected to a Token Ring network. Most of the Token Ring cards available will run at 4 or 16 Mbps, but some are only 4 Mbps. So you will have to make sure the card runs at the speed you need.

Installing Macintosh Cards

Unlike the PC, when you install a card into a Macintosh with a slot, you don't need to worry about DMAs, IRQs, or memory addresses. The Macintosh automatically takes care of all of these

Table 2.9 Ethernet adapters for Macintosh computers

Adapter	Mac Models	Comments
SCSI to Ethernet	Plus, Classic, Classic II, Portable, all PowerBooks except the PowerBook Duo with a Duo Dock	The SCSI adapter requires a driver, which should be provided by the manufacturer. The SCSI adapters follow all of the SCSI rules.
Adapter Card	SE, SE/30, Color Classic, LC, LCII, LCIII, II, IIx, IIcx, IIsi, IIci, IIfx, Centris 610, Centris 650	The type of card depends on the type of slot in the Mac.
Built-in	Centris 610, Centris 650, Centris 660, all Quadras, LaserWriter IIg, LaserWriter Pro 630	The built-in Ethernet requires an AUI (Autonomous Unit Interface or Attachment Unit Interface) connector.

details for you. So the installation process is one of opening the Mac, installing the card, closing the Mac, and installing any needed driver software. Really, it's that simple.

Other Cabling Standards

If you want to use one of newer high-speed cabling protocols, you'll probably have to wait a bit. Whenever a new standard is announced, it takes a while for it trickle down to the Mac. Right now there are two vendors making NuBus FDDI boards, and they're both very expensive, pushing the $1,750 to $2,000 range. And 100Base cards have not really been announced yet, but someone somewhere is working on them. However, there are some high-speed hubs available. So if a hub will accelerate your Ethernet network, it will accelerate your Macs and PC together. But these really are high-end products and not likely be become common in most businesses for a couple of years, at least.

If you are using either OmniNet or G/Net, you can get cards for the Mac. Each of these proprietary networks goes beyond the scope of this book, but I thought I would mention them since this is not common knowledge—or maybe it is, if you're using one of these networks.

Routers

The last subjects to discuss are gateways and routers. You may not need to worry about a router with the networks discussed in this book, but you might want to know what is possible. Your choices will be to use the routing capabilities of your server and NOS, a software router on the Macs, or a hardware router. This last section will look quickly at routers.

For the most part, routers are used to make connections between AppleTalk and TCP/IP, UNIX, DEC Pathworks, or VAX terminals. This is in addition to the uses for a router already discussed. You can get a router to make the jump from AppleTalk to any of these other protocols. However, before you do, you should consider that you may have what you need already.

If you are running one of these protocols with one of the NOSs discussed in this book, then you will have the NOS router or gateway capabilities when you purchase the AppleShare option for the NOS.

Since this book is really about connecting Macs to PC networks, all of these other protocols really fall outside of its scope.

The NOS routers for the networks discussed in this book should be able to handle TCP/IP to AppleTalk without a problem. Also, you can install TCP/IP on a Mac without too much trouble using Wollongong's products. You might not need to use an AppleShare option if you can get by with TCP/IP alone. And regardless of the abilities of the NOS, you can always purchase a hardware router that will deal with these other protocols.

What you will probably need is a software router that will make the Ethernet to LocalTalk jump on a Macintosh so that your PC users will have access to the printers, as I've already said. If you need this type of network service, all you need is the Apple Internet Router or Farallon's LocalPath. Either of these will work, creating an additional zone that will contain the printer and any Macs that are not on Ethernet.

To use the software router, all you need is a Mac that is using both Ethernet (or Token Ring) and LocalTalk (or PhoneNET). Once the router software is installed, you can have it assign the zones automatically. Then all of your Mac users will have access to the internet, and the PCs will be able to print to the AppleTalk printers. This type of implementation will be discussed for each NOS as we go along.

Conclusion

From this chapter you should have all the information you need to plan your Macintosh integration. You know what software, hardware, and cabling the Mac needs. You probably know more about Mac networks than you wanted, but at least you're prepared. Now you should be ready to look at the specific network that you're going to be using.

SneakerNet and Other Simple Connections

Introduction

This chapter is more than just a novelty chapter, because it lays the foundation necessary for exchanging data between your PCs and a Macintosh. This chapter provides you with information you can use regardless of how you exchange data, whether you are exchanging disks or transferring data over a network such as a Novell, VINES, or Pathways network. Using a Macintosh with your PC network is more than adding another machine to the network: it is also knowing what to do with the data once you have the Mac. So this chapter will address the simplest methods of combining PCs and Macintoshes, as well as some data-exchange fundamentals.

Integrating a Macintosh with your PC computers does not always necessitate adding the Macintosh to your network. If all you need to do is exchange a few data files between your PCs and a Mac, your task will be greatly simplified. All you have to do is learn how to exchage floppy disks between the two different types of computers. To help you learn how to exchange data between your PCs and a Mac, this chapter will cover the following topics:

- Exchanging floppy disks
- Utility programs

In the Exchanging Floppy Disks section, you will learn how to seamlessly exchange PC disks with a Macintosh. That is how this chapter derived the name "SneakerNet." Although exchanging disks does not constitute a network in the strict sense of the word, running from one machine to another has been dubbed "SneakerNet" because if you are doing a lot of disk swapping, you will probably need a pair of Nikes or Reeboks.

The other section of this chapter will concentrate on the different software utilities, peripherals, and tips for exchanging data between your PC and Mac. The topics of discussion include data compression, translation, and other cross-program compatibility issues. A sample scenario involves sending a 40M file from a PC in Washington, D.C. to a Mac in Seattle, Washington.

Exchanging Floppy Disks

Several years ago, Apple took the initative for making sure that the Macintosh could easily share its data with MS-DOS machines. The way Apple accomplished this was by providing every Mac manufactured since the SE/30 with a high-density 3.5-inch floppy disk drive that could read both Macintosh and PC formatted disks. In addition to the SuperDrive, Apple also sells a 5.25-inch drive that can be installed in any Macintosh that has a NuBus slot. This 5.25-inch drive is DOS-compatible but needs the Apple File Exchange utility in order to access an MS-DOS disk.

Next, Apple provided the software necessary for the infomation to be exchanged between the two different types of disks. And finally, third-party manufactures have taken up the call to produce hardware peripherals and software utilities that enable the Mac to read and write PC Disks. Some of the utilites even provide translation capablilites. The software has gotten so sophisticated that now a 3.5-inch PC disk can be used on a Macintosh as if it were a native Macintosh disk.

This section will look at all of the hardware requirements and most of the software utilities necessary for the seamless (or almost seamless) exchange of floppy disks between the two computing platforms.

Floppy Disk Drives

When Apple first provided the Mac with the ability to read a floppy disk formatted for a PC, most PCs did not have 3.5-inch drives, and Macs did not have 5.25-inch floppy drives. But there are, and always have been, remedies for this problem. This is not the issue it once was, since most new PCs come with 3.5-inch disk drives. But before getting into the actual steps of exchanging disks, let's cover the hardware requirements.

Every Macintosh sold since the spring of 1989 has had a floppy disk drive capable of reading a high-density (1.44M) or low-density (760K) floppy disk formatted for use in an MS-DOS machine. Apple has dubbed this drive the "SuperDrive." The problem at the time was that most PCs did not have 3.5-inch drives. So to help speed things along, Apple also provided a 5.25-inch floppy drive for the Macinstosh II. But all of this was done before there was much concern about exchanging data between PCs and Macs.

Now, however, the need to exchange data is much more immediate. To use a floppy disk as the transfer medium, you need to have either a 3.5-inch drive in your PC or a 5.25-inch floppy drive attached to your Mac. Let's take a look at some of the different hardware configurations you can use.

On the Mac Side of Things

Since all Macs manufactured since the spring of '89 have a Super-Drive, you need an additional drive for any earlier Mac. The Macs that will need an additional drive are the Mac Plus and the SE. For either of these models, you can purchase a floppy drive that can read PC disks. It attaches to the Macintosh's SCSI (Small Computer Standard Interface) port (see Fig. 3.1). One company also produces a floppy drive that can be attached to the external drive port.

There are three different types of drives you can purchase to attach to a Mac that will format and read PC 3.5-inch diskettes. One type is a standard 3.5-inch drive that is attached to the floppy drive port. Drives that connect to the floppy port can only be

CHAPTER 3

Figure 3.1

The back view of a Macintosh SE

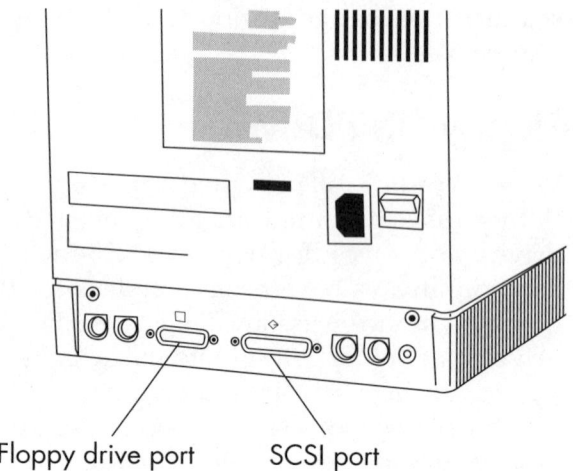

Floppy drive port SCSI port

attached to the Macs with a floppy disk port. Any floppy drive attached to a floppy port will be recognized as a standard Macintosh floppy. The next type is a SCSI 3.5-inch floppy drive. These come in two flavors: a standard floppy drive, or a 20M optical floppy drive. The latter can read both 20M floptical disks and MS-DOS or Macintosh 3.5-inch floppy diskettes in either high or low densities. The final type of disk drive is a 5.25-inch floppy drive that attaches to Mac's SCSI port.

Attaching Drives to the SCSI Bus

Apple chose the Small Computer Standard Interface (SCSI) as the means for attaching most peripherals to a Macintosh. The SCSI port is more than a high-speed data transfer port, it is an industry standard for connecting peripheral devices and their controllers to the microprocessor in the host computer. The SCSI interface is based on a standard established by the American National Standards Institute and by the computer industry as an whole.

Since most PCs do not have SCSI adapters (at least, not yet), you may need more information about attaching a SCSI drive to a Macintosh. A drive that connects to a Macintosh SCSI port can be used on any Macintosh (unless you have a SCSI port on one of your PCs and driver software that recognizes the drive). When attaching a drive to the SCSI port, you need to keep the following rules in mind:

- All SCSI devices are numbered from 0 to 7. The Mac's internal drive is normally set to ID 0, and the Macintosh itself always uses ID number 7. Any SCSI device attached to a Macintosh must have a unique SCSI ID number. In other words, no two devices in a Macintosh SCSI chain can have the same ID number.

- The SCSI bus must be terminated at the beginning and end of the SCSI chain. A SCSI chain is the designation for the actual order in which the devices are connected. All SCSI devices are connected in serial. (See Fig. 3.2.)

If your ID numbers are all unique (0 thru 6 with no duplicates) and the chain is terminated at the first and last device, not including the Macintosh (unless you are using a Macintosh Quadra), your added floppy drive should work without any problems.

Once you have the drive attached to the SCSI bus, you will probably have to install software that will let the Mac communicate with the drive. The PC-disk-compatible drive will come with any necessary software. However, several of the generic disk utilities discussed later in this chapter will let a SCSI floppy drive read a PC diskette.

DOS on the Other Side

If you want to use PC disks on a Mac and do not have a 3.5-inch drive, the easiest solution to the problem is to install a 3.5-inch drive in your PC. Installing the floppy drive is easy, and the drives are inexpensive. If you are using an older AT or PC class machine

Figure 3.2
A Macintosh SCSI chain

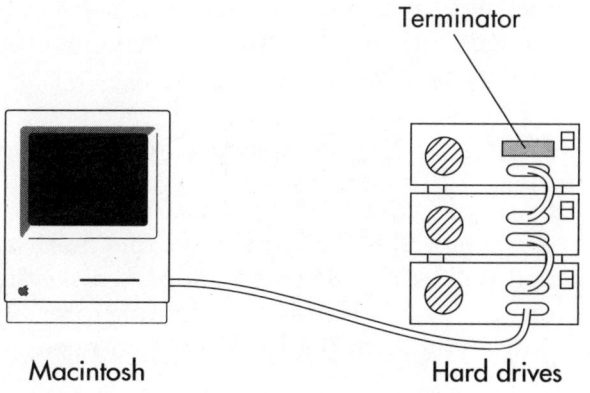

(note that this is different from the generic description of PC for personal computer), you will only be able to install a 760K 3.5-inch floppy drive. This is not necessarily bad, it just means that your data transfers have to take place within 760K of data space.

If you are adding a drive to an older MS-DOS machine, you may also have to upgrade the machine's BIOS (Basic I/O System, also called ROM BIOS) in order for it to recognize the 3.5-inch floppy drive. In a PC class machine, this can be difficult, since BIOS upgrades can be hard to find.

In an AT class system, getting a BIOS upgrade should not be too difficult. You can get a BIOS upgrade from the manufacturer. If you have a generic clone rather than a brand-name MS-DOS machine (or if the manufacture has gone out of business), you can get a BIOS made by another manufacturer. In all modern MS-DOS machines—those with a 386SX CPU or better—the BIOS and floppy controller card should support a 3.5-inch drive without any trouble.

The process of installing the drive, however, is another story. If you are technically adept and comfortable inside your computer, you can read the instructions that came with your 3.5-inch drive and your disk controller and install the floppy drive yourself. If you are squeamish about playing inside your computer, or if the instructions that came with the drive or disk controller seem like gibberish, you will probably want a professional service person to install the drive for you.

Because there are so many different configurations possible, from drive cabling to jumper settings and various combinations thereof, this is not the appropriate place to tell you how to upgrade your MS-DOS machine. You can either pick up one of the several good books available about upgrading your MS-DOS machine or take it into the shop. If you have a high frustration tolerance level and the time, do it yourself; otherwise, have it done professionally.

Making the Floppy Connection

Once you have a Mac with a SuperDrive and a PC with a 3.5-inch drive, or a SCSI 5.25-inch drive on your Mac, you still need software that will let the Mac read your PC disks. In the case of the 5.25-inch drive on a Macintosh, the manufacturer of the drive will have provided you with the software you need. You can use some of the other software that is available, as well, but check out the software first to make sure it will work with your 5.25-inch Mac drive.

The software utilities that are available for the Mac are:

- Apple File Exchange
- PC Exchange
- DOS Mounter
- AccessPC

Each of these utilities enables your Mac to read an MS-DOS disk. PC Exchange, DOS Mounter, and AccessPC are functionally identical: they mount an MS-DOS disk on the Macintosh's desktop. The Apple File Exchange utility is an application that lets your Mac read an MS-DOS diskette. Since the desktop MS-DOS disk mounters all operate on the same principles, a discussion of their shared attributes will precede a quick look at each utility.

Other utilities that will be discussed enable your MS-DOS machine to read a Macintosh disk. They work with floppy disks, removable media hard disks, and Macintosh partitions on hard drives.

Apple File Exchange

Apple's File Exchange utility is distributed as part of Apple's System software. It was originally introduced with the SuperDrive. Apple File Exchange can be found in the Apple Utilities folder on the Tidbits disk of Apple's System 7.1 and 7.0 System disks. If you are only going to be transferring a few files between your MS-DOS machine and a Mac, this is the only utility you really need. With the Apple File Exchange Utility, you can transfer files, read, and format MS-DOS disks on your Macintosh.

To use Apple's File Exchange to read and transfer files from an MS-DOS disk:

1. Open File Exchange by double-clicking on the Apple File Exchange icon.

2. After the application launches, you will see a screen like the one in Figure 3.3.

3. On the left-hand side, you can see the directories (folders) on the Macintosh hard disk. The right side is blank until you select the drive button or insert a floppy disk. If you try to read

Figure 3.3

Apple File Exchange's main window before you insert an MS-DOS disk

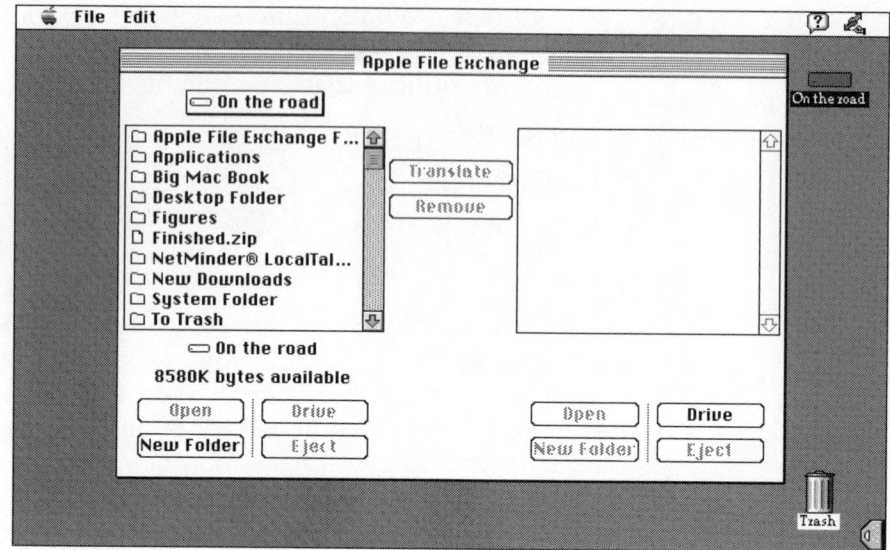

an MS-DOS floppy disk before running the File Exchange utility, the Mac will ask you whether you want to format the disk. If you format the disk, you will destroy any data on it and turn it into a Macintosh diskette.

4. Insert the MS-DOS floppy disk.

5. The files and directories on the MS-DOS floppy will appear in the right-hand file window.

6. Select the file you want to transfer by clicking on it with the mouse. When the file is selected, the Translate and Remove buttons between the two directory windows will become selectable (see Fig. 3.4).

7. Select the directory where you want to place the file you are transferring by double-clicking on it.

8. Set the translation options by selecting the MS-DOS to Mac menu that appears after step 7. You can see your choices in Figure 3.5.

9. Press the Translate button. The MS-DOS file will be translated if any options were selected, and copied to the selected directory on the Macintosh.

SneakerNet and Other Simple Connections

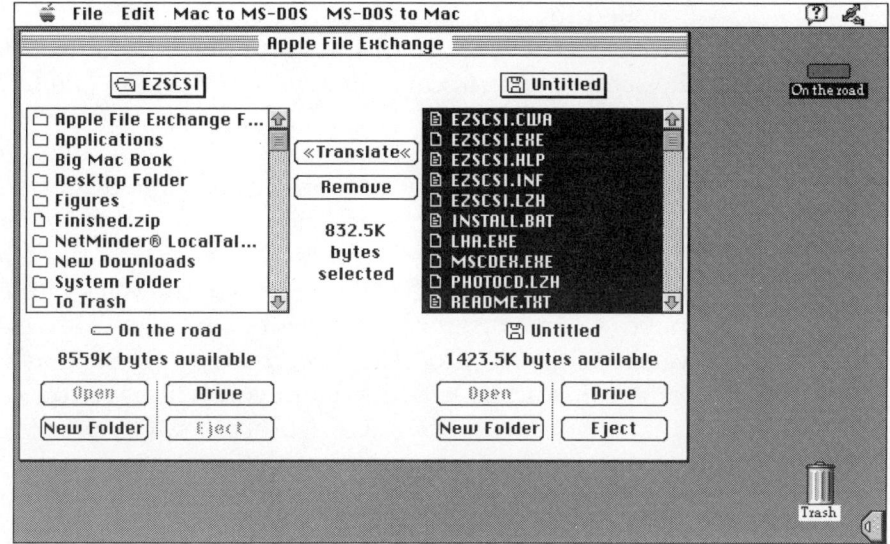

Figure 3.4
Selecting the files to transfer after inserting an MS-DOS Disk

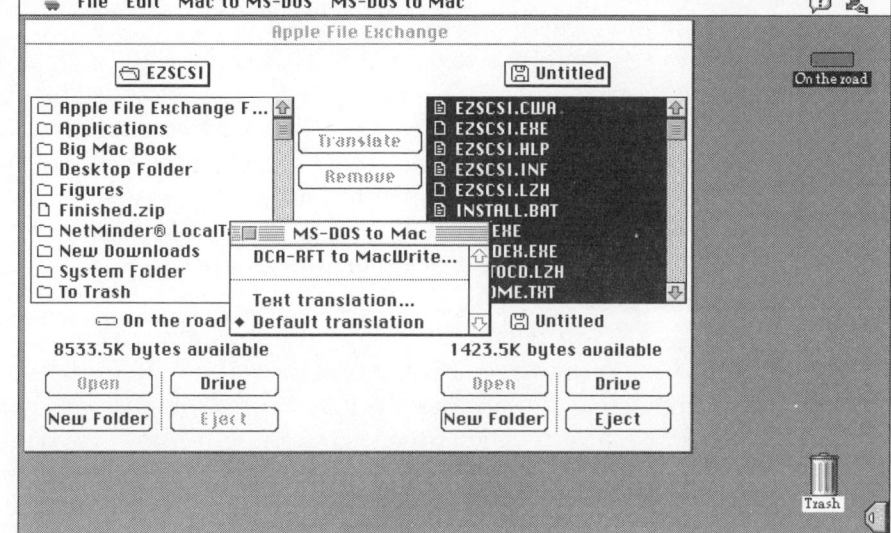

Figure 3.5
File translation options for MS-DOS-to-Mac file transfer

Translating MS-DOS Files with Apple File Exchange

If you need to convert or translate a file, you have three options with Apple's File Exchange utility. One is the DCA-RFT to MacWrite option, and the second is the Text Translation option. In order to use the third option, Other Translation, you need to have installed the translators prior to starting the Apple File Exchange utility. Translators are installed by placing the translation file into the same folder (or directory) with the Apple File Exchange utility. Translators that will work with the Apple File Exchange utility are available as commerical products—MacLink Plus, for example—and a few can be obtained from your Apple dealer.

The DCA-RFT to MacWrite translation option is only for files that have been saved in a DCA or RFT format. Selecting this option will convert the file into a Claris MacWrite format, which most Macintosh word processors can read. However, almost all Macintosh word processors can read an RFT file as well, and only some can read a DCA file. Here you will have to experiment as to what works with your word processor. Chapter 9 lists all of the word processors that are cross-platform-compatible.

Files that are cross-platform-compatible, such as a Microsoft Word for Windows file for which you will use a compatible Macintosh program, do not require translation. You should select the Default Translation option, which is a binary translation and will not alter the file format in any way.

Translating text or ASCII files is a good idea, because MS-DOS machines use a text file format that is different from the Mac's. All MS-DOS text files have a carriage return (CR) and a line feed (LF) at the end of each line. Macintoshes, on the other hand, use just a carriage return to end a line of text. If you do not translate a text file, you will have a file that looks like Figure 3.6. Each of the little squares at the beginning of the lines is a line feed character.

If you need to massage the files after they are on the Macintosh, you can use at word processor that will find and replace ASCII characters and remove the line feeds. By being creative, you can also reformat a text document by removing both carriage returns and line feeds so the text file will line-wrap. If you experiment, you will be able to reformat a text file for a nicer presentation.

When copying Macintosh files to your MS-DOS disk, just follow the above steps in reverse, moving the files from the Macintosh disk to the MS-DOS disk. Instead of using the MS-DOS to Mac menu for translating, you will select your translation options from the Mac to MS-DOS menu. Otherwise, the process is the same. If you have Macintosh files that are readable by your DOS applications, use the Default Translation option. The only other detail you need to be concerned with is the name of the file.

Figure 3.6

An MS-DOS text file on a Mac that has not been converted

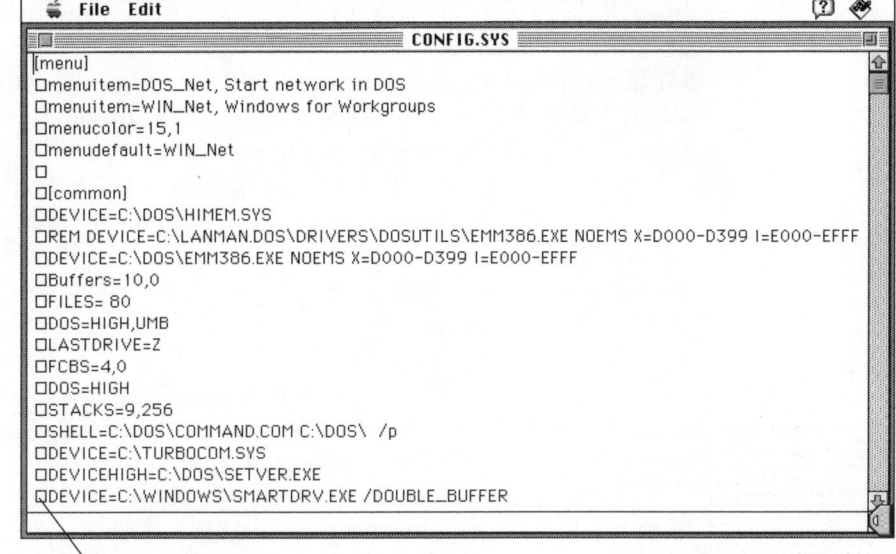

Line feed character

Macintosh files can have up to 32 characters in their names, while DOS files can only have 8 characters plus a 3-character extension. So you will have to rename the Macintosh file and give it the proper extension. If you are transferring a Microsoft Excel file named "Sales Report" to your MS-DOS machine, you will have to rename it to something like "SALESRPT.XLS". Otherwise, Apple File Exchange will automatically rename it for you with a name like "SALES_RE.POR".

Desktop Mounting Utilities

There are three utilities avaliable for the Mac that will mount an MS-DOS disk on the Macintosh Desktop. They are PC Exchange by Apple, DOS Mounter by Dayna Communications, and AccessPC by Insignia Solutions. All of these products work on the same principles.

They are all control panel devices (Cdevs), accessed from the Control Panels folder under the Apple menu in System 7.0 or better, or from the Control Panel desk accessory if the Mac is using System 6.0.X. Each utility lets the Mac recognize your MS-DOS disk as if it were a Macintosh disk, while acknowledging that the disk is an MS-DOS disk.

All three utilities allow you to copy files from an MS-DOS disk to the Mac or from the Mac to your MS-DOS disk. An MS-DOS disk that is mounted on the desktop with one of these utilities is treated by the Macintosh as if it were a native Macintosh disk. Each utility gives your MS-DOS disk a unique Desktop icon.

When you copy a file to or from the MS-DOS disk, the file is copied without any type of translation. This means that you will have the best results if you are using cross-platform applications that create files that do not need translating. If the file format is same for both the MS-DOS and Macintosh applications, or if the Macintosh application can translate the MS-DOS file, the Mac will operate as if the file were a native Macintosh file. Otherwise, you will have to translate the file before it can be read by the Macintosh's program. (Translation utilities will be discussed in the last section of this chapter.)

Finally, each utility allows you to map or assign DOS extensions to specific Macintosh applications. The mapping capability lets you launch the application specified by double-clicking on the icon of the MS-DOS file.

Because the files on the MS-DOS disk are treated as Macintosh files, you have to watch your file names (depending on the utiltity). Otherwise, you will have very strange names when you look at the disk from an MS-DOS machine. (See Fig. 3.7.)

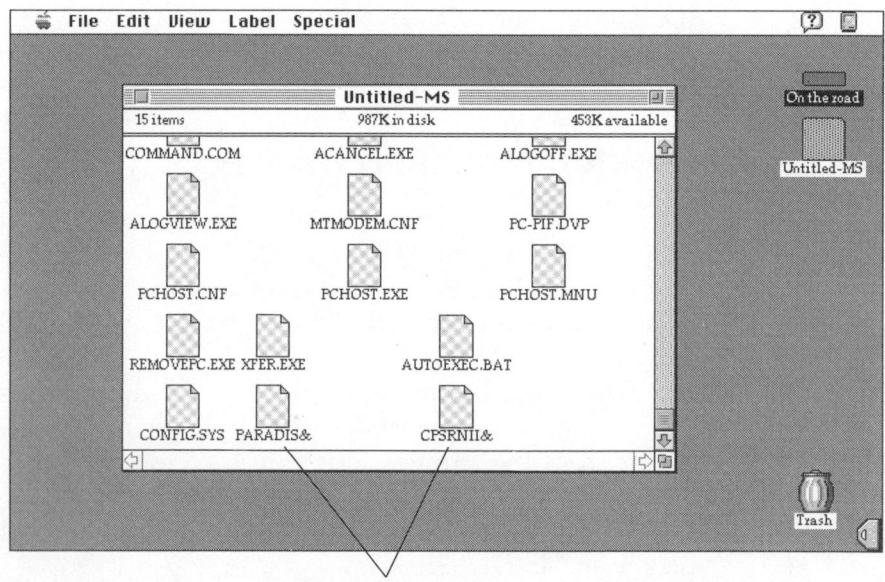

Figure 3.7
An MS-DOS disk mounted on a Mac with Macintosh and MS-DOS names

Macintosh file names

Figure 3.8

A Mac disk with MS-DOS files from a desktop utility and Apple File Exchange

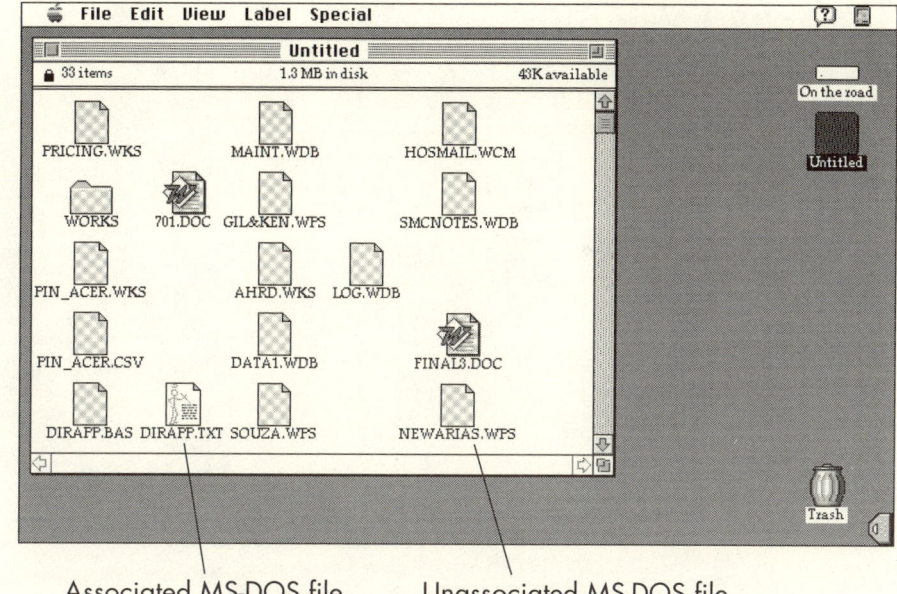

Associated MS-DOS file   Unassociated MS-DOS file

You have to change the name of a file copied onto the MS-DOS disk into a name recognizable by an MS-DOS machine. You also have to add the file's extension so the application that uses the file will recognize it. These utilities also provide a Macintosh file icon to any file that has the proper mapped extension (see Fig. 3.8).

These utilities work with all floppy disk sizes—provided, of course, that you have the appropiate hardware. A couple of them also work with removable media hard drives and optical drives that have DOS partitions. These utilities make it possible for you to share files between MS-DOS machines and Macs without a network. They are also handy even if you do have a network, since putting a file on a floppy will always work even if the network is down.

PC Exchange

PC Exchange is Apple's MS-DOS disk mounting utility. Its Control Panel icon appears in Figure 3.9. You can tell if the Macintosh is running PC Exchange because the Desktop icon will look like the one in Figure 3.10.

With PC Exchange and the appropiate drive, you can read and format 1.44M or 760K 3.5-inch and 1.2M and 360K 5.25-inch floppy disks—in other words, all of the possible floppy configurations for a standard MS-DOS machine. PC Exchange works with

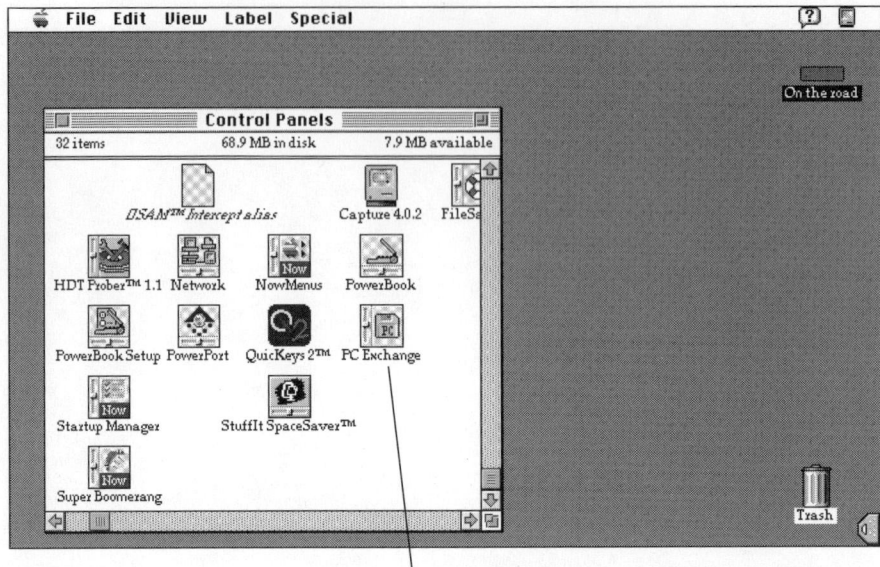

Figure 3.9

The Apple's PC Exchange icon

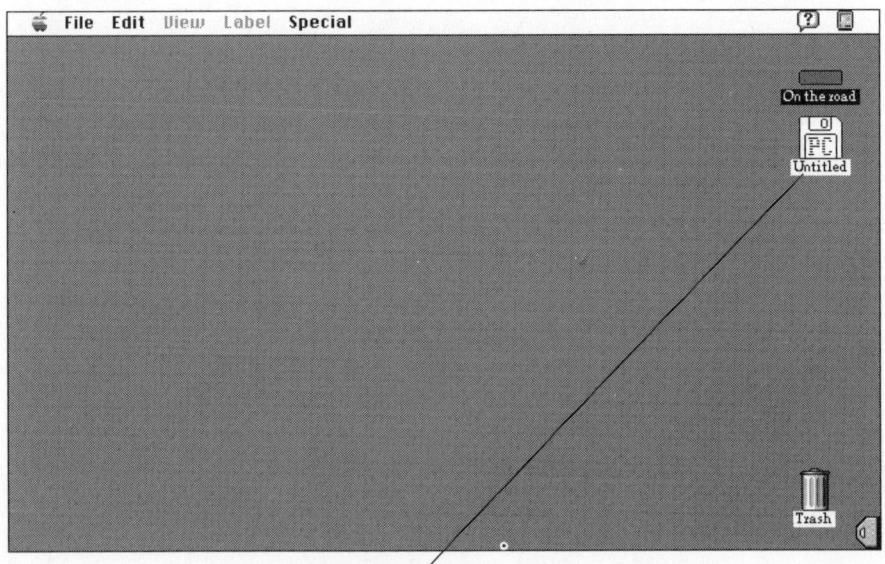

Figure 3.10

The Apple's PC Exchange Desktop icon

any Macintosh running System 7.0 or later that has an Apple SuperDrive or an external Macintosh-compatible 3.5 or 5.25-inch floppy drive. Unfortunately, PC Exchange has the fewest capabilites of all the DOS mounting utilities and works only with

Figure 3.11

PC Exchange's control panel

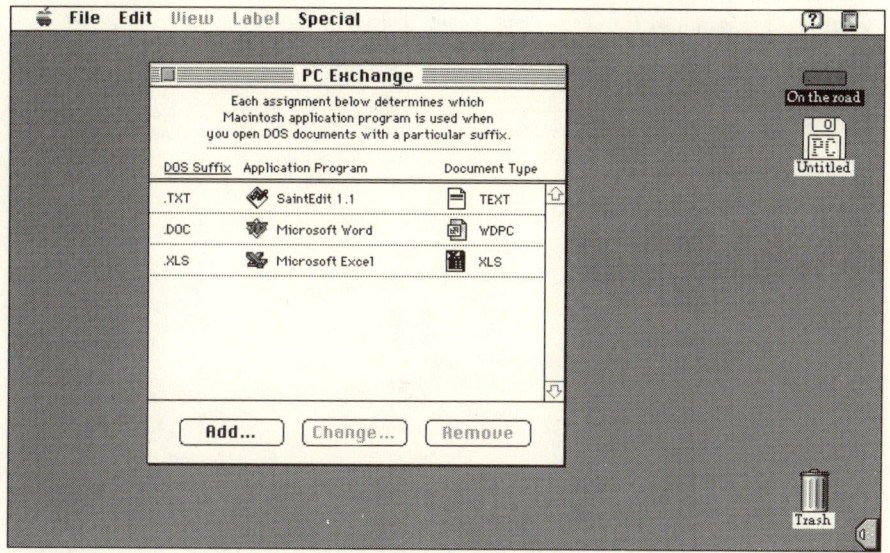

floppy disks. So if you need support for SyQuest, Bernoulli, or optical disks, you will need a different utility.

Figure 3.11 shows the PC Exchange control panel. You can see that any DOS file with the .DOC extension is automatically assigned to Microsoft Word, while an .XLS extension is assigned to Microsoft Excel. Although Figure 3.11 shows the default assignments, you can assign an extension to any application and add it to the list in the control panel.

DOS Mounter Plus

Of all the Macintosh desktop mounting utilities, DOS Mounter Plus by Dayna Communications is the most unique. In addition to mounting MS-DOS floppy disks, DOS Mounter will also mount a Novell Netware volume. DOS Mounter requires a Macintosh with a SuperDrive, a Dayna SCSI 5.25-inch floppy drive, or another third-party SCSI floppy drive. DOS Mounter does not support Apple's 5.25-inch disk drive. The DOS Mounter Control Panel icon appears in Figure 3.12.

At one time (in the very recent past), this capability was part of Dayna's Net Mounter, while DOS Mounter was strictly for mounting removable media disks, including floppies. Now Dayna has combined both utilities into one product. Figure 3.13 shows the icon DOS Mounter creates on the Macintosh's Desktop.

Figure 3.12

The DOS Mounter icon

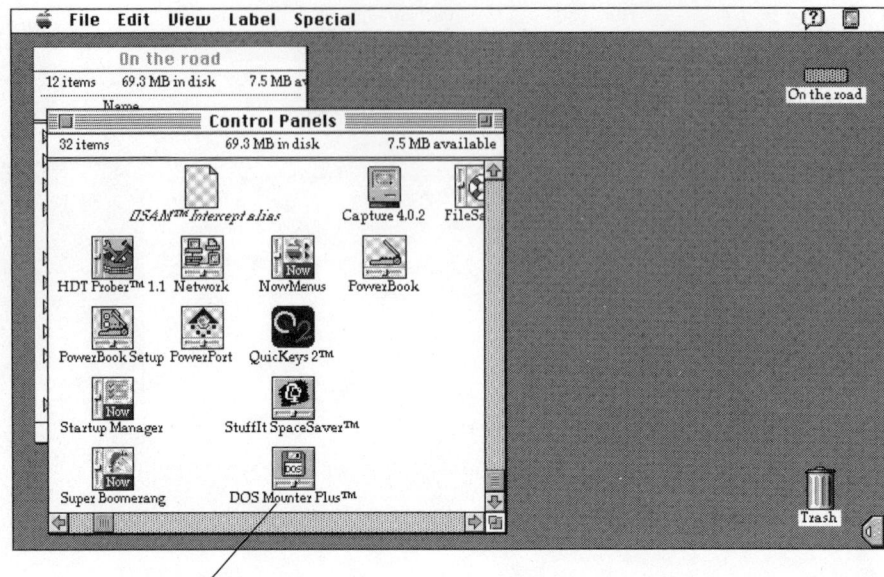

DOS Mounter icon

Figure 3.13

Dayna's DOS Mounter Desktop icon

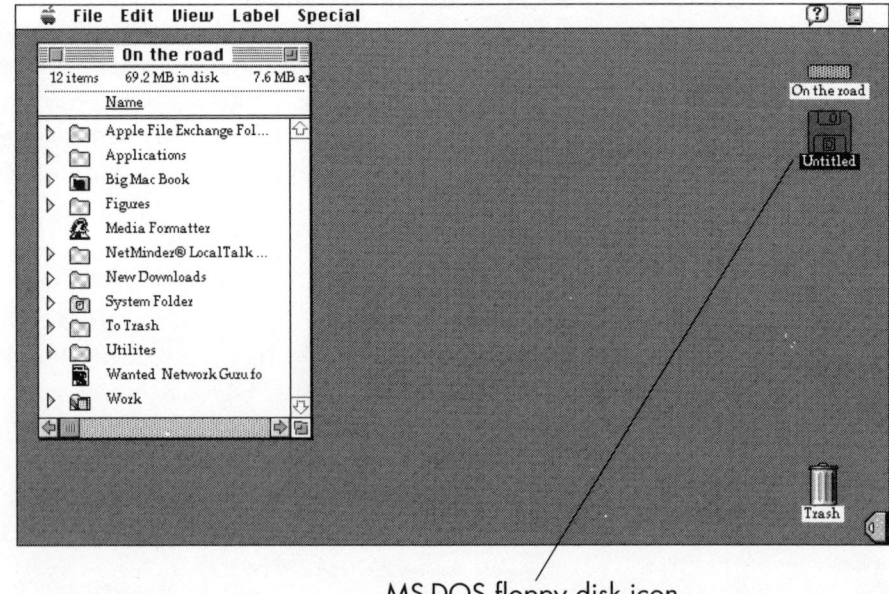

MS-DOS floppy disk icon

DOS Mounter does not allow Macintosh file names on MS-DOS disks. If you copy a Macintosh file to an MS-DOS disk mounted with DOS Mounter, you will get a file name like the one

SneakerNet and Other Simple Connections

Figure 3.14

An MS-DOS disk mounted on a Mac with DOS Mounter

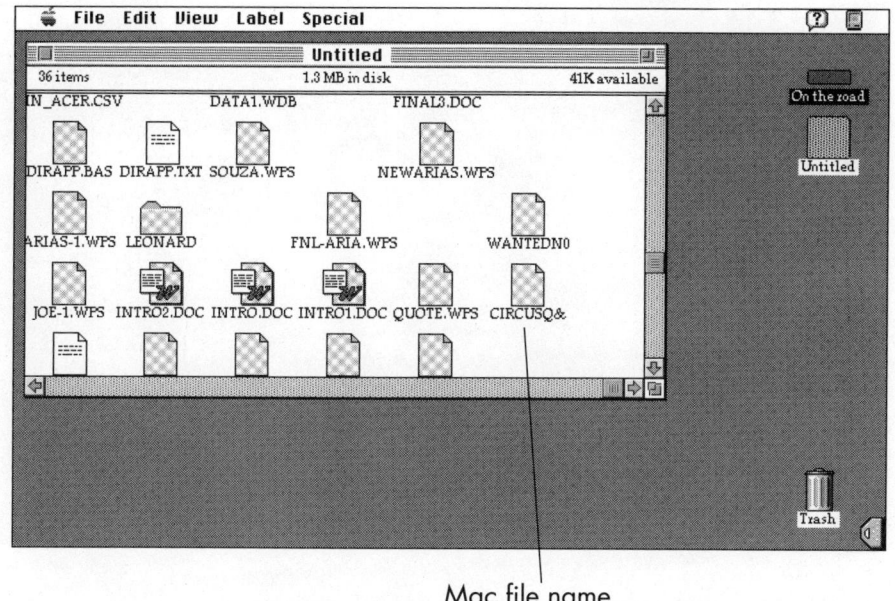

Mac file name

in Figure 3.14. Compare this figure to Figure 3.7. You will see that DOS Mounter treats file names in the same manner as the Apple File Exchange utility.

Just like PC Exchange, the DOS Mounter control panel is used to link DOS extensions and Macintosh applications. Figure 3.15 shows DOS Mounter's control panel and the extension assignment for Microsoft Excel. However, DOS Mounter also allows you to disable it, either by checking the Disable check box and rebooting the Mac or by holding down the **Option** key when you insert a disk. This can be helpful if you want to use the Apple File Exhange utility or some other application that does not like DOS mounting utilities.

AccessPC

AccessPC is published by Insignia Solutions. Insignia Solutions also makes a series of MS-DOS emulators that run on the Mac, and a utility that allows a Windows machine to read Macintosh floppy disks. (The MS-DOS emulators will be discussed in Chapter 9.) AccessPC, even though it is a standalone utility, is made with the emulators in mind and has some additional features.

One of the additional features is the ability to mount a virtual MS-DOS hard disk created by Insignia's line of SoftPC emulators. AccessPC also comes with a removable hard disk driver called

Figure 3.15

The DOS Mounter control panel

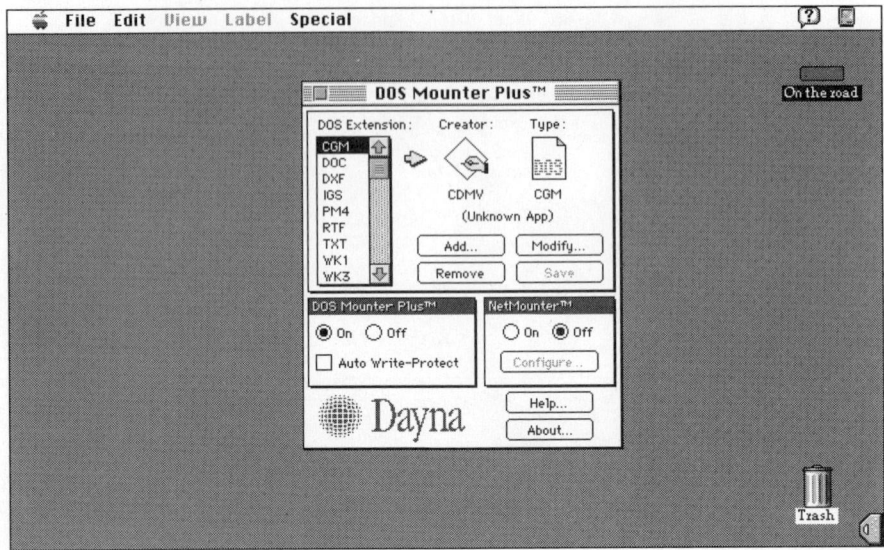

MULTI-DRIVER and a hard disk formatter called Media Formatter. The MULTI-DRIVER is needed if you are going to use MS-DOS removable media hard disks on your Macintosh. The AccessPC Control Panel icon is shown in Figure 3.16, while the AccessPC Desktop icon appears in Figure 3.17.

Figure 3.16

The AccessPC icon

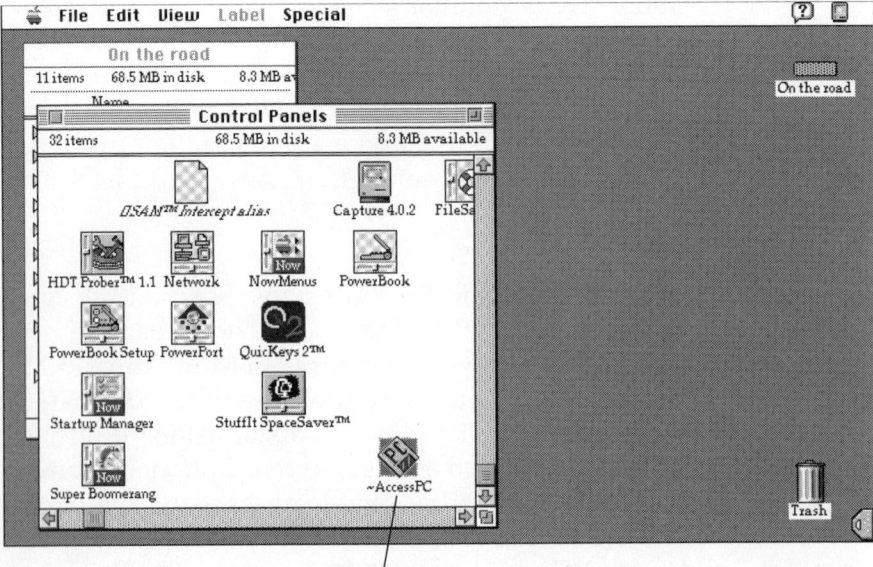

AccessPC icon

SneakerNet and Other Simple Connections

Figure 3.17
The AccessPC Desktop icon

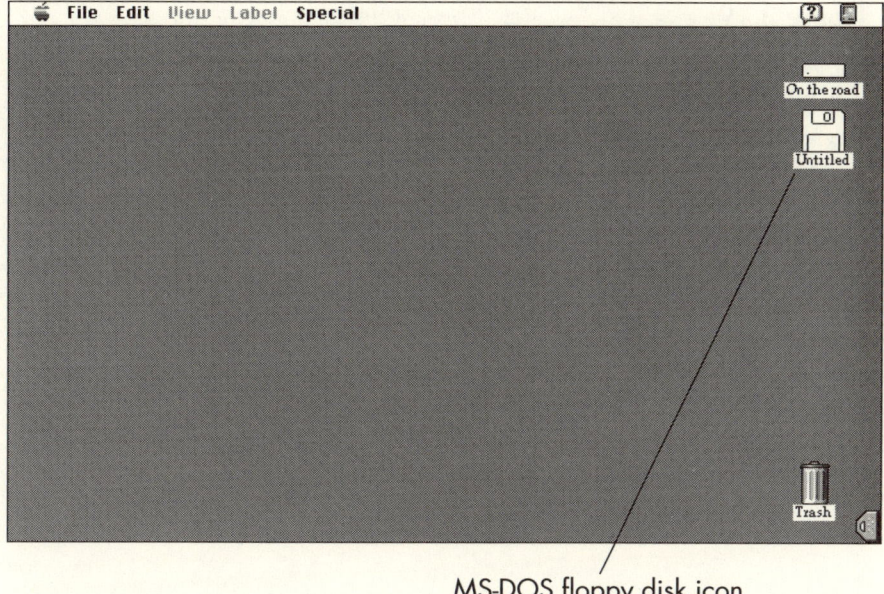

MS-DOS floppy disk icon

Again, a control panel is used to configure this DOS disk Desktop utility (see Fig. 3.18). The AccessPC control panel has the usual section for assigning extensions to Macintosh applications, plus a couple of extra features.

Like DOS Mounter, AccessPC converts Macintosh file names so that they are recognizable by an MS-DOS machine. In Figure

Figure 3.18
AccessPC's control panel

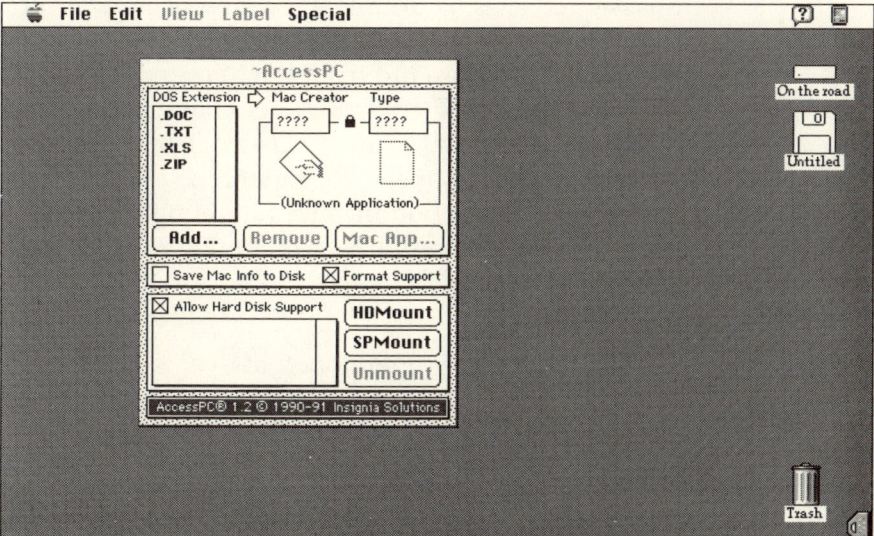

Figure 3.19
An MS-DOS disk mounted on a Mac with AccessPC

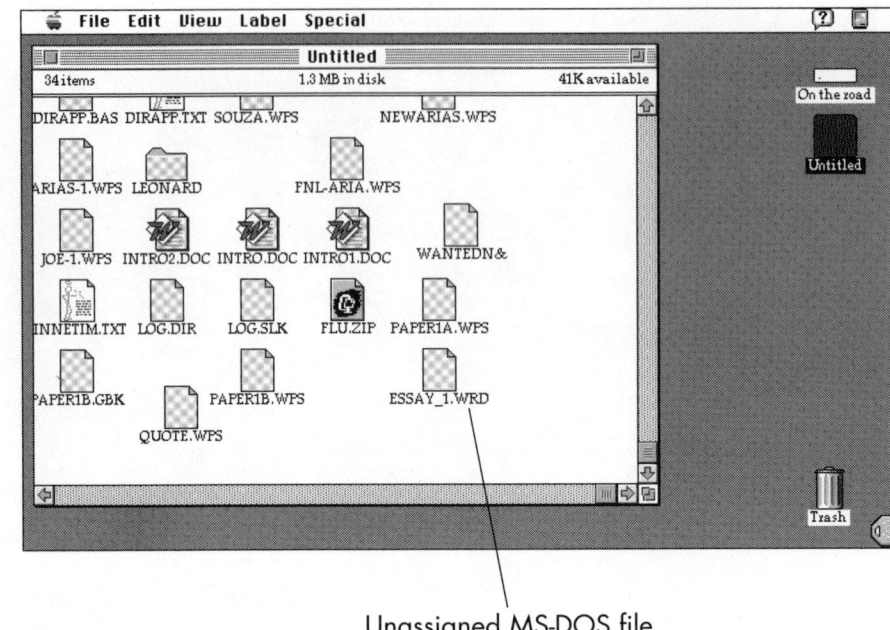

Unassigned MS-DOS file

3.18, the .DOC extension is assigned to Microsoft Word. Figure 3.19 shows an MS-DOS disk mounted by AccessPC. In Figure 3.19, you will notice that the extensions that are not assigned have generic Macintosh document icons. In order for the unassigned files to have an icon that indicates that they are PC files, you need to have some version of Insignia's SoftPC installed. However, the unassigned files, if double-clicked, will launch the SoftPC emulator. To use an unassigned file with a Mac application, you have to use the Open command from the Mac application's File menu.

The AccessPC control panel contains additional options, the SPMount and HDMount buttons. The SPMount button in the AccessPC control panel is for mounting a SoftPC hard disk partition, and the HDMount button is for mounting an MS-DOS partition on a removable media hard drive (this option requires MULTI-DRIVER).

MULTI-DRIVER

MULTI-DRIVER, as mentioned above, is a removable-media hard-drive driver. Usually, when a Macintosh boots, the hard-disk drivers are read from the Mac's hard disks and loaded into memory. However, if you want to use an MS-DOS disk with your Mac, the MS-DOS disk does not have a Macintosh driver. Consequently, the Mac

Figure 3.20

The MULTI-DRIVER icon

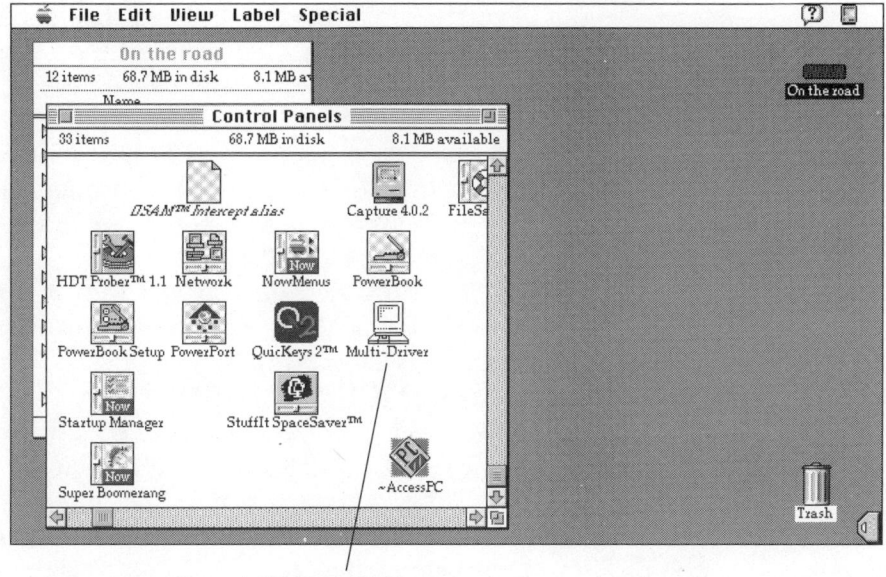

MULTI-DRIVER icon

cannot read the MS-DOS disk without some help. Enter MULTI-DRIVER. (See the MULTI-DRIVER Control Panel icon in Figure 3.20.)

Figure 3.21 shows MULTI-DRIVER's control panel. MULTI-DRIVER works with Syquest and Ricoh removable media hard drives, Sony and Ricoh magneto-optical drives, and any hard drive formatted with Media Formatter.

Figure 3.21

The MULTI-DRIVER control panel

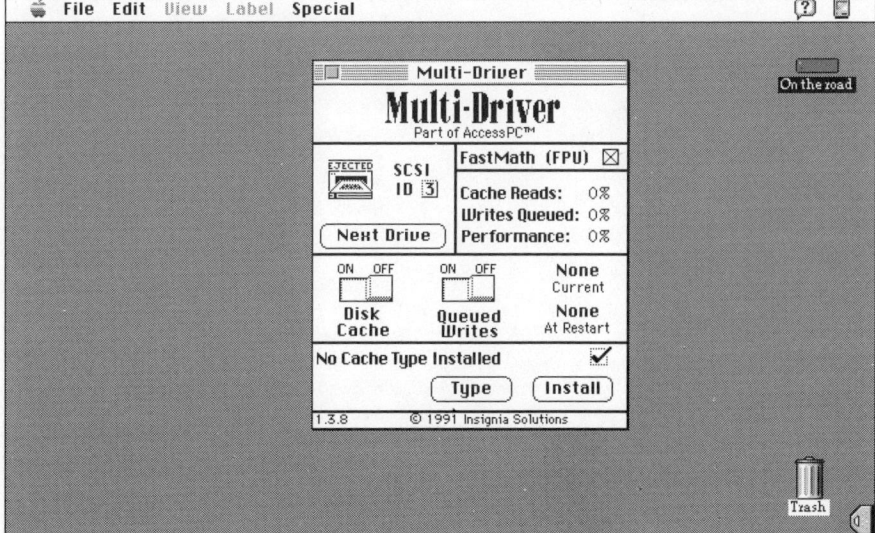

Media Formatter is a Macintosh hard disk formatting utility. However, it does not create an MS-DOS partition. Only a Mac hard disk formatted with Media Formatter is cacheable with MULTI-DRIVER or an MS-DOS removable disk. The caching capabilities are nice, but not essential to using MULTI-DRIVER. Just make sure MULTI-DRIVER is in your Control Panels folder, which is found inside your System folder under System 7, or loose in the System folder if you are using System 6.0.X.

What MULTI-DRIVER does best is mount the removable media MS-DOS disk just like AccessPC mounts an MS-DOS floppy. Figure 3.22 shows an MS-DOS SyQuest cartridge mounted on a Macintosh using MULTI-DRIVER.

Because MULTI-DRIVER works in conjunction with AccessPC, your MS-DOS hard disk will be handled just like an MS-DOS floppy. All of your extension assignments will be used, and any Macintosh file you copy to the MS-DOS disk will have its name truncated to eight characters.

MULTI-DRIVER is useful, maybe even invaluable, if you need to share large data files or large quanities of data between the MS-DOS and Mac platforms. Another way MULTI-DRIVER can be helpful is if you are using a database application that has compatible files on either platform (there are many programs with this capa-

Figure 3.22

An MS-DOS disk mounted on a Mac with AccessPC and MULTI-DRIVER

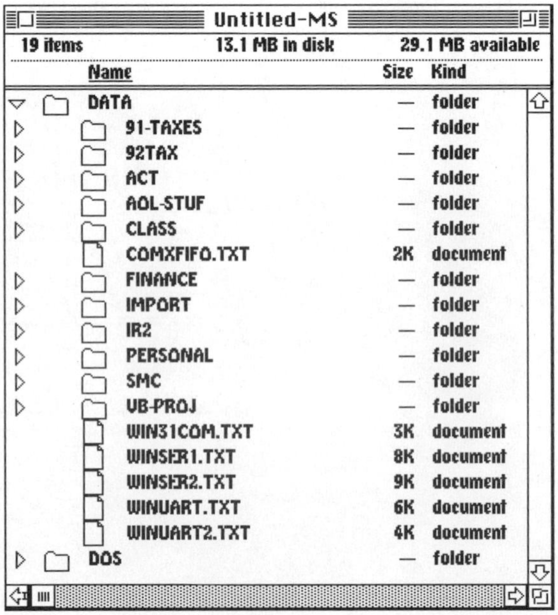

Name	Size	Kind
DATA	—	folder
91-TAXES	—	folder
92TAX	—	folder
ACT	—	folder
AOL-STUF	—	folder
CLASS	—	folder
COMXFIFO.TXT	2K	document
FINANCE	—	folder
IMPORT	—	folder
IR2	—	folder
PERSONAL	—	folder
SMC	—	folder
UB-PROJ	—	folder
WIN31COM.TXT	3K	document
WINSER1.TXT	8K	document
WINSER2.TXT	9K	document
WINUART.TXT	6K	document
WINUART2.TXT	4K	document
DOS	—	folder

Untitled-MS — 19 items — 13.1 MB in disk — 29.1 MB available

SNEAKERNET AND OTHER SIMPLE CONNECTIONS

bility) and you need to use the data on different machines that are not in the same location. MULTI-DRIVER is also a means of moving large quantities of data from one site to another without having to be concerned about the type of computer at the receiving end.

Assigning Extensions to Macintosh Applications

Each of the above MS-DOS disk mounters has the ability to assign a DOS extension to a Macintosh application. The procedure for accomplishing this is the same with each utility. The basic procedure is as follows:

- Select the Add button from any of the control panels.
- You will be presented with a dialog box, similar to the one in Figure 3.23, where you insert the DOS extension.
- After adding the extension, you must assign the Macintosh application by clicking on the Mac App button in AccessPC and the Applications button in DOS Mounter. (See Fig. 3.24.)
- If you are using PC Exchange, the actions of adding an extension and assigning the application are done from a single dialog window, shown in Figure 3.25.

Figure 3.23

The Add Extension dialog window from AccessPC

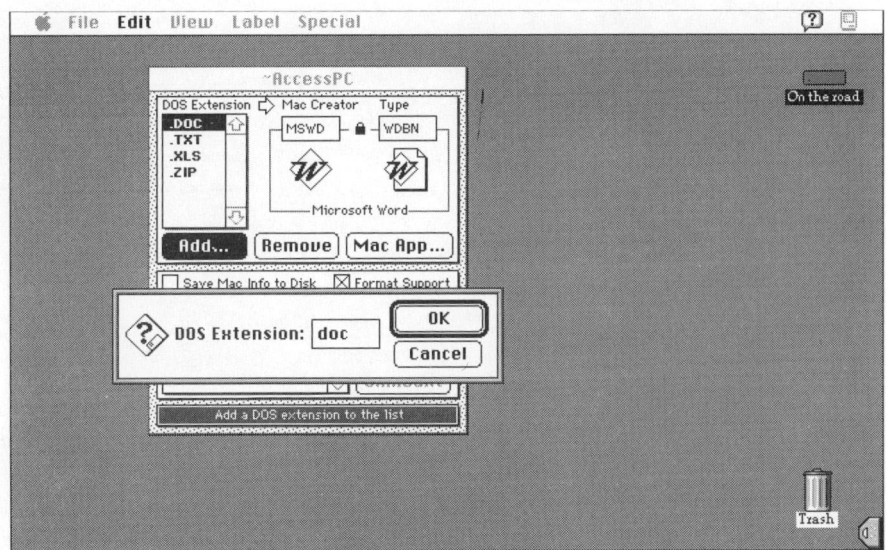

Figure 3.24

The Assign Application dialog window from AccessPC

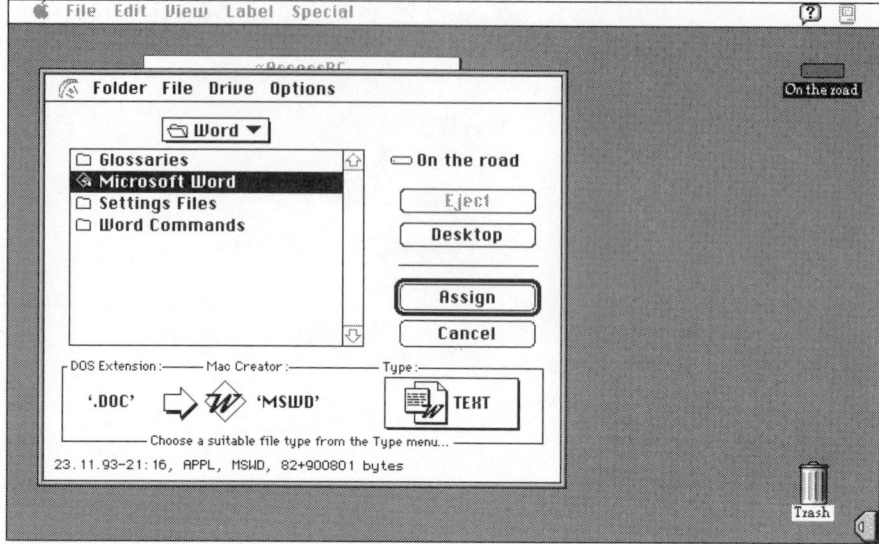

Figure 3.25

The Extension and Application Mapping dialog window from PC Exchange

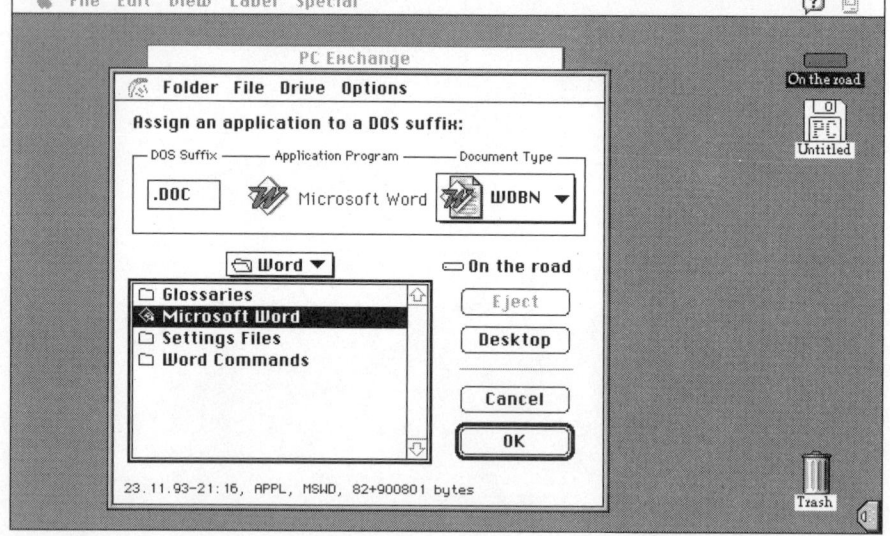

- To assign applications, you have to navigate your way to the desired application using the standard Macintosh Open dialog box.

- After selecting the application, you will also have to select the type of document you want opened. Many Macintosh applications can open a variety of file formats. Microsoft

Figure 3.26

Assigning a Microsoft text file specification with PC Exchange

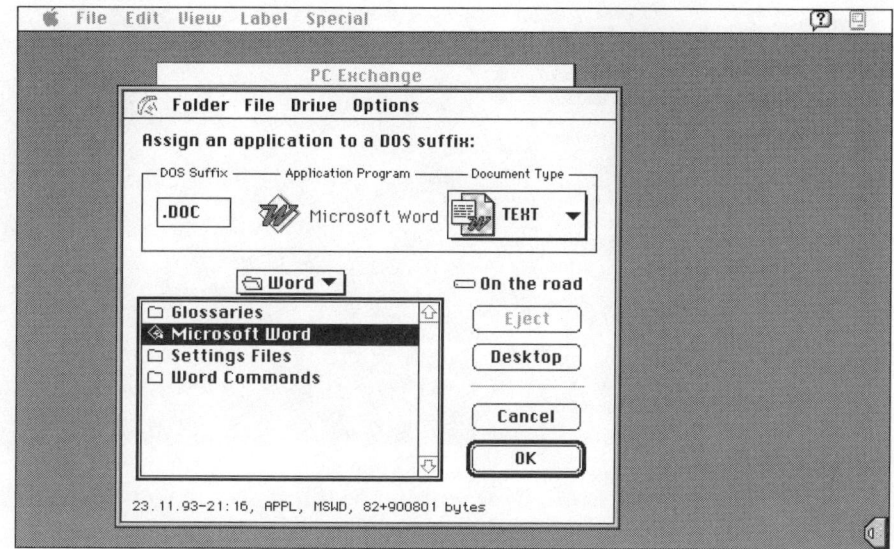

Word can open text, Microsoft Word for Windows, Word for DOS, DCA, and RTF files, to name a few. Often, the different types of files are represented by different icons. So if you select the Word Text icon for text files (see Fig. 3.26), you will be telling the mounting utility that you want to run Word and open a text file.

It is important to remember that you can make any assignment you want. If you have WordPerfect for the Mac and need to convert a Microsoft Word for Windows document, it is possible to have WordPerfect start when you double-click on a file with the .DOC extension. All of these utilities give you total control over your MS-DOS files in a Macintosh environment.

Mac-To-DOS

Mac-To-DOS is an MS-DOS utility written by Peripheral Land for reading, formatting, and writing a Macintosh floppy disk (see Fig. 3.27). Although Mac-To-DOS is not at all sophisticated, it is very effective for the task at hand. In addition to working with floppy disk drives, it will also work with any Peripheral Land removable media drive, including their optical drives.

Using Mac-To-DOS is easy: it recognizes your 1.44M 3.5-inch drive and will automatically use it unless you have more than one

Figure 3.27

Mac-To-DOS opening screen

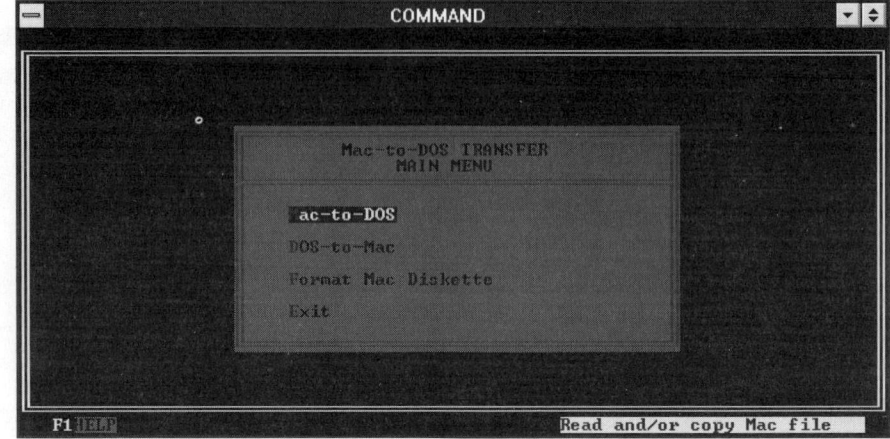

drive installed. To copy a Macintosh file to your MS-DOS machine, follow these steps:

- Start the program by navigating to your Mactodos directory (the default set-up by the Install program) and typing **mactodos**.
- After a brief opening screen, you will be presented with the opening screen shown in Figure 3.27.
- Insert the Macintosh disk into your 3.5-inch floppy drive.
- Select the Mac-To-DOS option and press **Enter**.
- Mac-To-DOS will automatically scan your floppy and display the disk's tree structure and any files stored at the root level of your floppy disk (see Fig. 3.28).

Figure 3.28

Opening view of a Mac disk in Mac-To-DOS

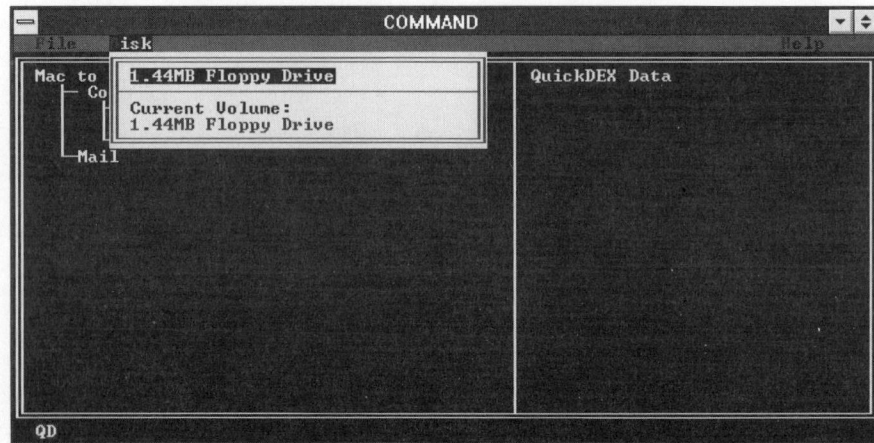

Figure 3.29

Mac-To-DOS disk selection menu

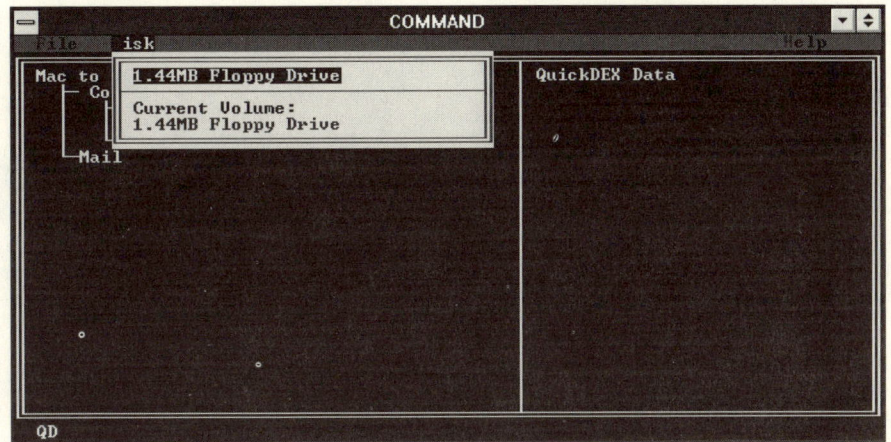

- If you are using more than one Mac-To-DOS-compatible drive, you can select the proper disk from the Disk menu (see Fig. 3.29).

- You can only transfer files from one directory at a time, so you have to select the directory level you want by using the cursor keys. As you select the different directories, the files in each directory will be displayed on the right-hand side of the screen (see Fig. 3.30).

- Once you have selected the directory that contains your files, press **Enter**. You will be presented with a listing of all of the files in the directory (see Fig. 3.31).

Figure 3.30

Selecting a directory

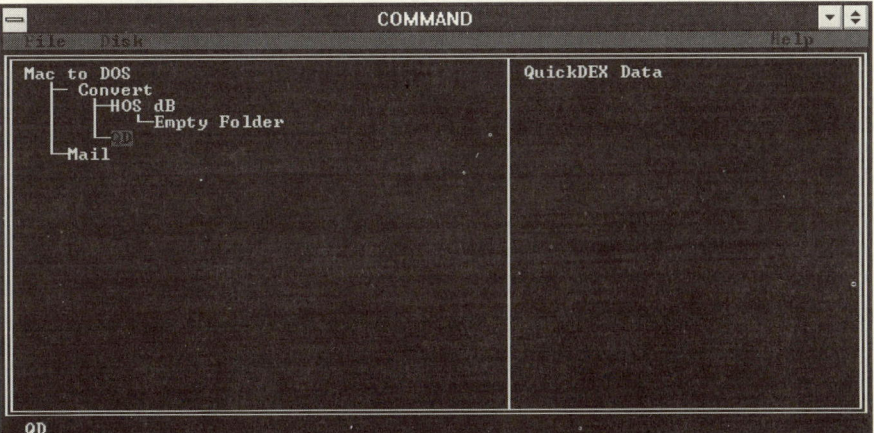

Figure 3.31

Mac-To-DOS file selection screen

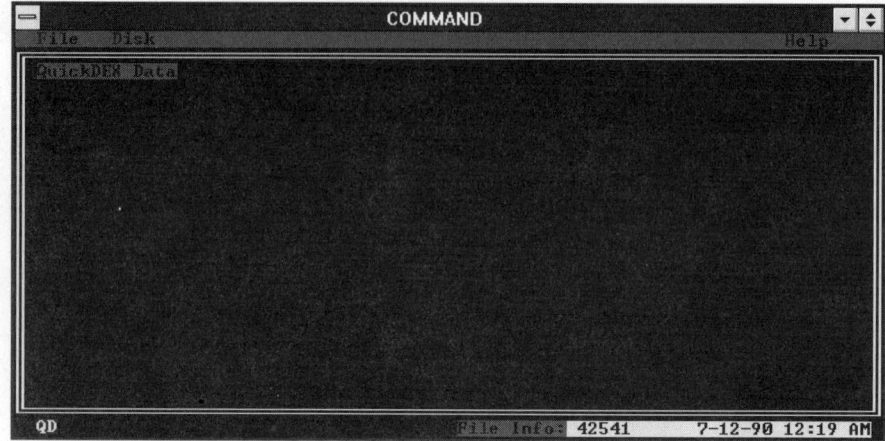

Figure 3.32

File manipulation menu

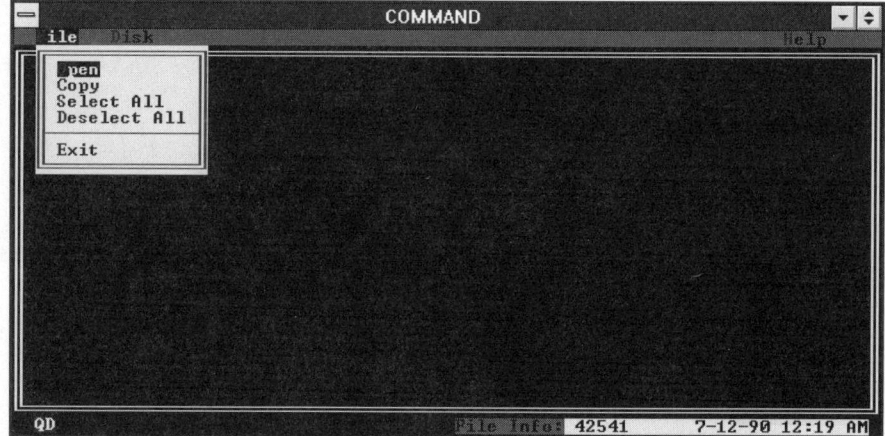

- Using the File menu (see Fig. 3.32), you can Open, Copy, Select All or Deselect All of the files in the window.

- Opening a file will display its contents in a new window. The Copy option will copy the selected file(s). You can select files by highlighting them with the cursor and pressing the spacebar, or with the Select All command from the File menu. Figure 3.33 shows a selected, or *tagged*, file. Tagged files appear with diamonds next to them.

- After selecting your files, press **F** to drop down the File menu and select Copy. Across the bottom of the screen, you will be asked to enter the path name for the file's destination. Enter your path name and press the **Enter** key.

SneakerNet and Other Simple Connections

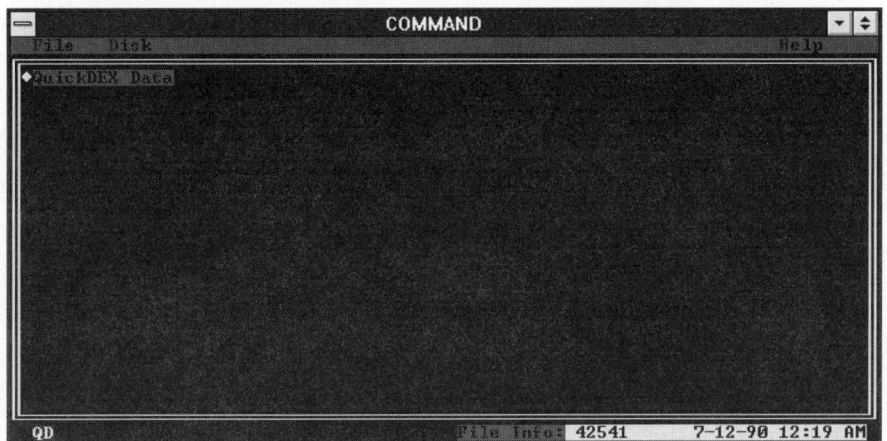

Figure 3.33
File selected for copying

- Mac-To-DOS will then copy each file to the directory you selected, truncating the Macintosh file names to MS-DOS names and applying the extension .MAC to each file. Figure 3.34 shows how the Macintosh names were truncated; the copied files are on the right-hand side of the screen.

To copy an MS-DOS file to a Macintosh disk, use the above procedure, but select the Dos-to-Mac option from the opening menu. When a DOS file is copied to a Mac disk, you will be given an opportunity to name the file and give it a Macintosh name. What you will not be able to do is assign any attributes to the file, so when it is seen on a Macintosh it will have a generic document icon (a blank page-shaped icon with a folded upper right corner).

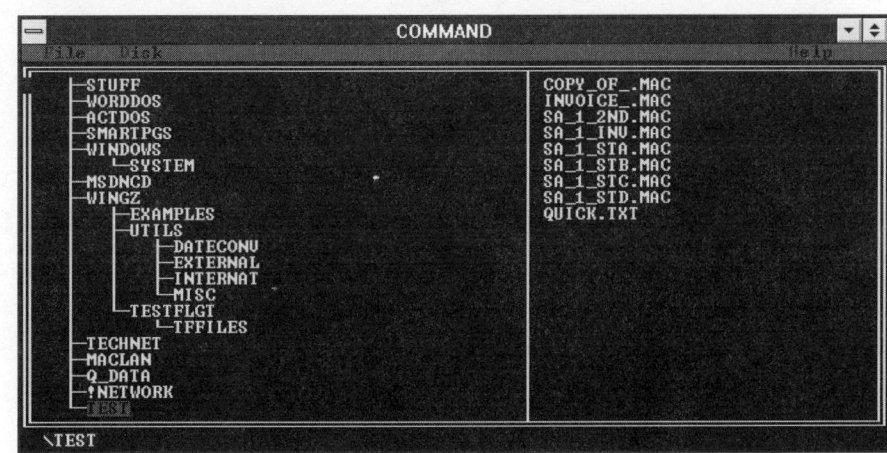

Figure 3.34
Truncated Macintosh names. The copied files are on the right-hand side of the screen.

There is nothing sophisticated about Mac-To-DOS. It is a simple utility that gets the job done. If your needs are such that you only have to copy a few files every once in a while from a Mac, then this utility could be your answer. In one sense, it is the truest implementation of SneakerNet.

MacDisk for Windows and DOS

Another Macintosh disk-reading utility you might find interesting is one published by Insignia Solutions. Insignia publishes an MS-DOS and Microsoft Windows counterpart to Access PC called MacDisk. The MacDisk a utility is a TSR (Terminate and Stay Resident) program, requiring 57K of memory, that lets a PC use a Macintosh high-density (1.44M) diskette.

MacDisk automatically maps Macintosh files by changing the file's name into a unique DOS file name and adding the proper extension. It is different from the other utilities that read Mac disks, because you do not have to run a special progam to access the files. Instead, the disk is mounted on the PC as a native PC disk. Since the automatic name conversion could make it difficult to find a specific file, Insignia also supplies a utility that lets you see the Macintosh file name. With MacDisk, you will have full access to the Macintosh disk. Besides reading the files, MacDisk lets you copy, delete, write, and format the Macintosh floppy disk.

The biggest probem you'll have with MacDisk is the amount of memory it uses. If you are already tight on memory, you may have to choose which TSR is more important. The Windows version of MacDisk should be easier to use, because Windows can load utilities without using precious DOS or high memory. If you choose to use MacDisk, you have another tool for Macintosh-to-MS-DOS connectivity, especially if you're a PC user who needs to read Macintosh disks without having to purchase a Mac.

MS-DOS-to-Mac or Mac-to-MS-DOS Utility Programs

Using a floppy disk utility is not the only way to get files from a Mac to the PC or vice versa. There are also several packages you can use to make serial connections between the two platforms for the purpose of exchanging files. And if the need should arise, you can also get one of the file translation utilities that make it possible

SneakerNet and Other Simple Connections

to use almost any Macintosh file on a PC or any PC file on a Macintosh.

This section will look briefly at the following progams:

- MacLink Plus by Dataviz
- Run PC by Argosy
- LapLink Mac by Traveling Software

Each of these programs can be used to move files directly from a PC to a Macintosh using a serial connection or modem. The advantage they offer is the ability to transfer large amounts of data—files that will not fit on floppies—from one machine to another.

Also, at the end of this section, you will find a section called Ideas. In this section, you will find a couple of ideas that might solve your probems if you have large data files that need to be transferred and do not have the benefit of a high-speed data link that goes cross-country, or if you routinely have to move files large data files from one platform to the other and do not have a network.

These discussions are going to be short, and are meant to provide you with an overview of the possiblities. It's just not possible to explain how to use every program on the market in one book, and this chapter is actually a digression, anyway. But this information may help you solve a particular problem without installing a network.

MacLink Plus

MacLink Plus, by DataViz, is a file translation utility that runs on the Macintosh. There is also a PC version called MacLink Plus/PC; this program is part of MacLink Plus. With these two programs, you can transfer files from a Mac to a PC, or from a PC to a Mac, using either a serial connection or a modem.

In addition to transfering the files, you also have the opportunity to translate the files at the time of transfer. So you could send a WordStar file from your PC to the Macintosh while simultaneously translating it into a Macintosh Microsoft Word file. This process of one-step file transfer and translation is very handy and saves you time.

If you want, you can translate the file on the Macintosh before or after you send to or from the PC with MacLink. The Macintosh portion of the MacLink Plus is a standalone application that will translate almost any Macintosh file into a PC file—or, of course, a PC file into a Macintosh file. The PC and Windows portion of MacLink, however, is not a standalone program: it will work only when connected to a Macintosh.

The translators that are provided with MacLink can also be used with the Claris XTND translation system. The Claris XTND translation system lets programs use translators to read and import files that are in formats other the program's native file format. Almost all of the Claris programs use this system, as do many other Macintosh programs. All of the MacLink Translators can be used with the Apple File Exchange program.

MacLink comes with Apple's PC Exchange utility for mounting MS-DOS disks on a Macintosh. So, in one package you have a solution that can translate a file created by almost any program on one platform into a format that is usable on the other platform. MacLink also provides you with MS-DOS access via floppy disk, direct serial connection, and modem. These capabilites make MacLink one of the most valuable programs for routine file exchange between Macs and PCs.

Run PC and Software Bridge

Run PC is an odd little program. It is written by Argosy Software. Run PC lets you control an MS-DOS machine from a Macintosh. With Run PC, you can sit at a Macintosh and control a PC running DOS, via a serial connection, over a modem, or over a network. Run PC also lets you transfer files from the Mac to the PC and from the PC to the Mac.

In addition to the PC remote control application, the Run PC package comes with a file translator and a MS-DOS disk-mounter utility for the Macintosh. Other features of Run PC include the ability to control one PC from another, compatibility with Symantec's pcAnywhere, and the abilty to use printers connected to MS-DOS or a Macintosh.

LapLink Mac

LapLink Mac from Traveling Software is one of the most efficient Macintosh PC file-transfer utilities you can use. It offers both direct serial and modem support for transferring files. As a bonus, LapLink Mac will also work between two Macs using a direct serial connection or modem, or via a SCSI connection if you are using a Macintosh laptop or notebook computer.

When using LapLink to connect to a PC, you have full access to the entire hard drive of the remote machine from the host machine. With this utility, you can control the file transfers from either the Mac or the PC. LapLink provides a basic binary file transfer, so unless you are transferring text files, you will not have any type of file translation. Any files transferred will retain their native format. If you need to translate the files before you use them, you will need a translation utility, as well.

Ideas

If you have a database with files that need to be accessed by both a Macintosh and an MS-DOS or Windows database application, without the benefit of a network, you could have a problem on your hands. Some of the progams that might require the transfer of these large files are FileMaker, FoxBase, Dbase files, or even large graphic files created by programs that have cross-platform counterparts.

How do you get 10, 20, 30 or more megabytes of data from one machine to the other? This becomes even more of a problem if you have to send the files across the country. Using a modem for really large files could take several hours and cost a fortune in telephone charges. If something happens to the connection, you might have to start over again, unless you're using a file transfer protocol that will automatically restart a failed data transfer, like ZMODEM. In any case, using a modem is probably not your first choice, nor should it be.

Although the task may seem close to impossible, it is not. The best way to deal with the problem is to use a program like AccessPC or DOS Mounter. With either of these applications, you can mount an MS-DOS formatted disk using some type of removable media. As mentioned above, you can use either of these progams with rewriteable or magnetooptical disk drives, which are available in sizes up to 1 Gig. These utilites also work with SyQuest and Bernoulli drives.

There is way to achieve the same result using a backup program. FastBack Plus, by Symantec, uses a data file that has the same structure on both a Mac and a PC. This offers you a way to back up and compress large data files from one platform and send them to someone who is using a different platform.

This scenerio could go something like this: You have a very large FileMaker database on your Windows machine, and you're in Washington, D.C. You're collaborating with someone in Seattle who needs to use your database. What do you do? The database is 75M and you only have a 44M SyQuest drive. The time it would take to trim the size of the database to fit on the SyQuest would put you behind schedule. And even when the database is compressed using PKZIP, it will not fit on one SyQuest disk. You're already late, and there are thousands of dollars at stake.

Do you kiss the job goodbye? Not likely. But before you ship your entire computer to Seattle, you might want to get Fastback Plus for the PC. At the same time, have your Seattle counterpart get Fastback Plus for the Mac and one of the MS-DOS disk-mounting utilites mentioned above. (Make sure it can be used with removable media hard drives.)

Format your SyQuest disks—you'll need two of them. Back up the database file onto the disks. Fastback will split your file, letting you use two disks. Now you send the disks to your Seattle counterpart. S/he then uses FastbackPlus on the Mac and restores the files. Since FastBack uses the same datafile structure on either platform, you're home free.

This will work even if you don't have a SyQuest. You can accomplish the same task using floppy disks, too—it just takes a bit longer.

Another way to get files from one machine to another is to zip the files on the PC and then send them to a Mac user. The Mac user can then use a Macintosh utility called Stuffit Deluxe to unzip the files. All you have to do is make sure that the PC can read Macintosh floppies, or that the Mac can read PC floppies.

Conclusion

This chapter, although it does not talk about networks, should provide you with a nutshell manual for getting files from the Mac to a PC or from a PC to a Mac. There are enough programs and techniques discussed here that you should be able to get your files from one machine to the other with minimal problems.

It can sometimes be frustrating to transfer your files and make them work on a foreign platform, but it is not impossible. If all you're trying to do is get your files from the Mac to the PC or vice versa, you've got all you need right here. Some of the programs discussed here are handy even if you're using a cross-platform network.

Using a LANtastic Macintosh Gateway

Introduction

The LANtastic networking operating system, made by Artisoft, is a MS-DOS peer-to-peer networking system that also provides Macintosh connectivity. Since LANtastic is normally used in small to medium-sized businesses, it does not really compete with the high-end client/server network operating systems discussed in this book. But that does not mean that there is not a need for Macs even in small to medium-sized businesses.

LANtastic is not a high-end network, and it does not have some of the features you'll find with LAN Manager, VINES, or Novell, but it does provide a solid solution for its target audience. A year ago, LANtastic had almost 100% of the peer-to-peer networking market. Although that market margin has shrunk, due to Windows for Workgroups and Novel Lite, it still has an installed base of 300,000 networks. Some of these installations will undoubtedly want to network Macs to their PCs, so if you are in a situation where you need to share files and have a LANtastic network, this chapter is for you. This chapter will describe the set-up, configuration, and management of LANtastic for Macintosh.

Description of LANtastic for Macintosh

LANtastic for Macintosh is an add-on product that is sold separately from the LANtastic NOS. LANtastic for Macintosh is an AppleTalk gateway between LANtastic and your Macintoshes. With LANtastic for Macintosh, you can use a Macintosh to access any PC file server on the LANtastic network or any shared PostScript printers. You can also share AppleTalk printers with your PCs. LANtastic does not provide physical link routing capabilities or multiple adapter support for the Macintosh to LANtastic gateway.

LANtastic for Mac is a combination of products licensed by Artisoft from Farallon and Miramar that, when combined, will let a dedicated PC appear as an AppleShare file and printer server to your networked Macs. Farallon provides the AFP protocol support for the PC network adapter, and Miramar supplies the AFP server software. Both of these products have been modified and optimized by Artisoft so you have a single product that provides you with Macintosh connectivity.

Also included in the LANtastic for Macintosh software package is an administration program for the Mac. With the LAN MAC Manager, you can administer your users and groups from a Macintosh, rather than the gateway server console. This program is simple and easy to use.

Your basic network will consist of the LANtastic network(s) and the Macintosh network(s) connected by the gateway into an internet. Figure 4.1 shows two possible topologies for a LANtastic network.

When you use LANtastic for Macintosh, your biggest problem will be how to configure the physical link. This is because LANtastic for Macintosh lacks routing capabilities. You cannot install a LocalTalk card into the gateway and access a Macintosh EtherTalk network from the gateway. Instead, you'll have to use a router on the Macintosh. Likewise, you will not be able to access the mail and other network resources available to the PC LANtastic users from your Macintosh workstations. For an E-mail solution, you'll have to use a third-party cross-platform E-mail system, where the post office files are stored on a PC server that is available to the Macs as well as the PCs.

And although these are limitations to the LANtastic NOS, they are not insurmountable problems, nor should they cause you

Using a LANtastic Macintosh Gateway

Figure 4.1
Two LANtastic for Macintosh networks

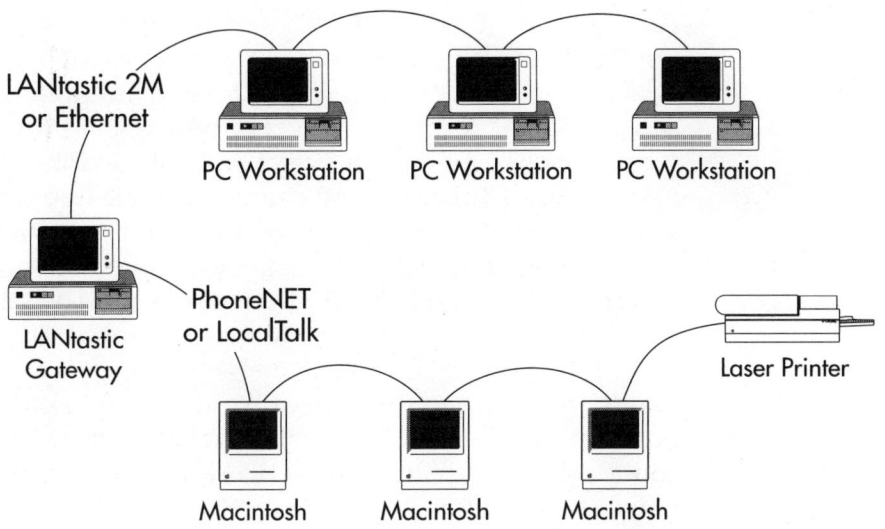

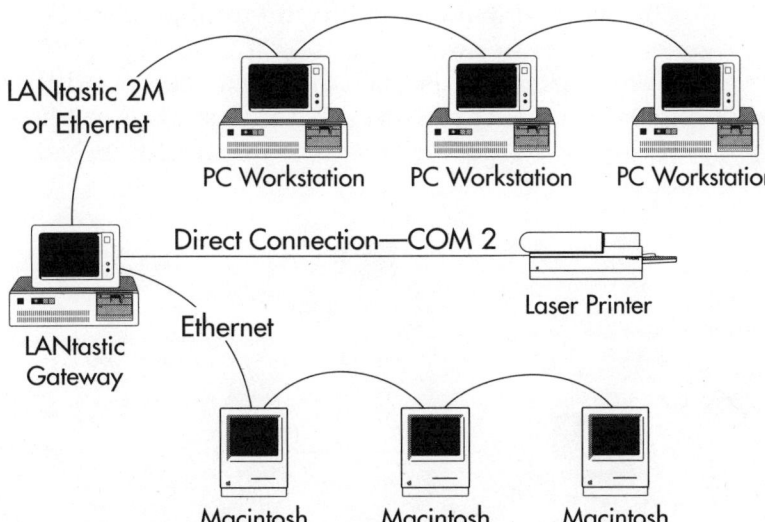

to switch NOSs. You will just have to be a bit more creative in planning your network. The first configuration in Figure 4.1 shows one solution, where Ethernet is being used to connect the Macs to the Gateway, and a Macintosh software router is being used to connect a Macintosh LocalTalk network. The second configuration shows the Macs all using LocalTalk and being connected directly to the gateway machine without a router. In either configuration, the Macs can all access PC file servers, and the PCs have access to the AppleTalk laser printers.

In each case, the gateway can have multiple adapter cards to service the LANtastic network, but only one for the Macintosh network. That one can be Ethernet, LocalTalk, or Token Ring. If you are using 10BaseT Ethernet, you can use a single hub for both the Macintoshes and the LANtastic network. In this situation, you actually have two separate networks using the same hub, but it does work. Figure 4.2 shows how this configuration would be set up.

What you will have to watch is network traffic. If you have a lot of traffic on the LANtastic network, you may experience some bandwidth degradation, because the network will be carrying both AppleTalk and LANtastic packets, which means that they could collide and slow the network down. However, for a small network (8 to 12 machines total), this would work just fine. If you have a larger network, you should try to keep the two networks separate, with the PCs and Macs on their own dedicated networks. This will just make your life and trouble-shooting easier.

The most important thing to remember when using LANtastic for Macintosh is that it is not a router and there is no way to make it one. You will have to depend on a Macintosh software router like Apple's InterNet Router for physical link routing.

Figure 4.2

A 10BaseT network for both Macs and PCs

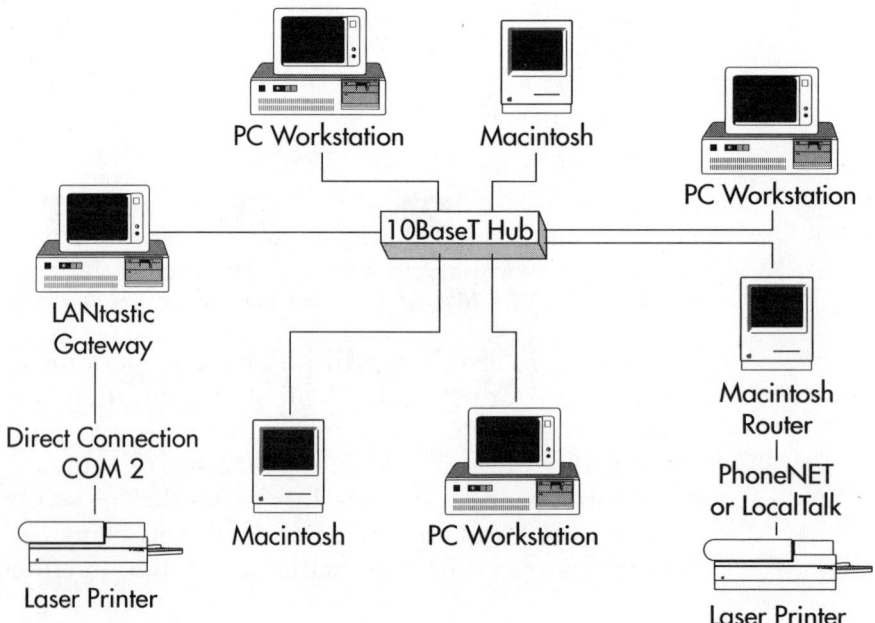

However, even if you were to use one of the higher end networks, you could easily end up using a Macintosh software router, so you are not seriously limited by LANtastic's not having this feature, although it would be nice if Artisoft added it.

Next, the LANtastic gateway software does not allow Macs to communicate directly with PCs on a LANtastic network. All PC-to-Macintosh connections are made at the gateway server. To have access to a networked PC drive, the networked drive has to be logged into the gateway machine and the drive has to be available as a networked resource. AppleTalk network packets do not get passed through the LANtastic network like they do with the NOSs covered in this book. The two networks are basically incompatible; this is why the LANtastic for Macintosh is a gateway.

Basic Requirements

Before you can add the LANtastic for Macintosh gateway to your network, you have to have the proper equipment and software. Primarily, you need a dedicated PC to act as the gateway, the LANtastic NOS, and the LANtastic for Macintosh software option. The LANtastic for Macintosh software can be purchased with or without Farallon's PhoneNET card. In this section, you will find what you need to set up a LANtastic for Macintosh gateway. We'll look at the hardware requirements for the gateway machine and your Macs.

The Gateway Machine

As I've already mentioned, you need a dedicated PC to serve as the LANtastic for Macintosh gateway server. This machine can be an IBM or compatible XT class PC with at least 640K RAM. You can also use an 80286, 386, or 486 machine as the gateway server. I would recommend a 286 with 1M of RAM as a minimum machine, and even better would be a 386SX with 1M.

The reason for recommending a 386SX over the 286 is that you can load some of the networking software in the UMB (Upper Memory Block) memory areas on a 386SX, which will leave your lower or conventional memory free for the gateway software. LANtastic for Macintosh needs at least 450K of conventional memory to run after you've loaded the LANtastic NOS.

What PC you use will also depend on what type of network you're using. If you're using Ethernet, you will want the processing power and speed of a 386SX at a minimum, especially if you're using Ethernet for the Macs. If you plan on using LocalTalk for the Macintosh connection, there is no reason not to use that 286 in the closet unless you plan on using Ethernet on the PC side of things. Then, the 286 could be a bit slow. But the Macs on LocalTalk won't blink at the 286 because LocalTalk is slow enough that a faster machine might even be wasted on the Macs. And if the gateway server is going to be used as a central file server, servicing a lot of machines and running Ethernet, you will want to consider using a 386DX or 486 PC just for the processing speed they offer.

The PC also has to have a hard disk, MS-DOS 3.1 or higher, and you will need the LANtastic NOS version 4.0 or higher, or the LANtastic Windows version 4.1 or higher. You will have to use a network adapter for the LANtastic portion of the network that is compatible with your existing network. And finally, you'll need an AppleTalk network adapter card. The AppleTalk compatible cards you can use are:

- Farallon PhoneNET Card PC (ISA or MicroChannel)
- Daystar LocalTalk (ISA or MicroChannel)
- Dayna DL2000 (ISA)
- Dayna DL2 (MicroChannel)
- 3Com EtherLink II (3C503 or 3C503TP) or compatible adapter
- IBM Token-Ring Network PC adapter or adapter II
- IBM Token-Ring Network 4,16,/4 adapter (Micro Channel) or adapter II

For any of these cards, if you can find a compatible card by another manufacturer—a card that will use drivers developed specifically for these cards—you are welcome to use it. However, if you have problems, be forewarned: Artisoft tech support will blame any trouble you might have on the network card. So you might as well get the real McCoy to begin with.

In the same vein, you must use cabling that is approved by Artisoft. If you do not use cabling that is approved for use with an Artisoft product. you will find their tech support department to be reluctant with their assistance. So you will have to convince them that your cabling is OK or tell them that you are using approved cabling. The 10BaseT cabling that Artisoft supports is:

- Artisoft UTP (Unshielded Twisted Pair)
- AT&T 1041A
- Belden 1455 A
- Belden Plenum 1457 A

The hardware platform you choose will depend on what type of network configuration you have. However, I would not be comfortable recommending anything less than an a 386SX in most cases. You might find Table 4.1 helpful.

These recommendations are my own. All Artisoft says is that you need a minimum of an XT-class IBM PC with at least 640K RAM. They do recommend that you use a 286, 386, or 486 machine.

For the gateway server to be completely prepared, it will have to be connected to your LANtastic PC network. This means that you will have the proper cabling and adapter card already connected to the gateway PC. To prepare your gateway PC for Macintosh access, you will have to install one of the AppleTalk-compatible network cards listed above and connect the cabling to

Table 4.1 Network configurations and hardware platforms

PC Network Protocol	Macintosh Network Protocol	Minimum Gateway Machine	Gateway Function
2M LANtastic	LocalTalk	286 12 Mhz	Macintosh gateway and print server
2M LANtastic	LocalTalk	386SX 16 Mhz 1M RAM	Macintosh gateway, print server, and file server.
Ethernet or Token Ring	LocalTalk	386SX 16 Mhz 1M RAM	Macintosh gateway, print server, and/or file server.
Ethernet or Token Ring	Ethernet or Token Ring	386DX 25 Mhz 1M RAM	Macintosh gateway, print server, and/or file server.
Ethernet or Token Ring	Ethernet or Token Ring	486SX 25 Mhz 1M RAM	Macintosh gateway, print server, and central file server.

your Macintosh network. When you install the AppleTalk adapter, remember to write down the card's memory address and its settings for DMA and IRQ. Once you have the gateway PC connected to both the LANtastic PC and the Macintosh networks, you're ready to start installing software.

Macintosh Requirements

The major Macintosh requirement you need to be concerned with is that you are using Phase 2 AppleTalk. LANtastic for Macintosh does not support Phase 1 AppleTalk. If you are not sure which phase of AppleTalk you're using, read Chapter 2. There you will find descriptions of the AppleTalk phases and learn how to determine what phase you've installed on your Mac.

In addition to the correct AppleTalk phase, you'll need to make sure your Macs have the necessary software for connecting to an AppleShare file server, namely the AppleShare system extension (INIT for System 6.0.X) and drivers for the type of network you're using. Basically, you need nothing more than Apple's standard Macintosh System software.

Planning the Physical Network

When planning your network, you will need to be concerned with which peer servers you're going to let the Macs connect to, which printers you're going to access, and which machines can access them. Since LANtastic is not a centralized or client/server-based network operating system, the access configurations can be more complicated.

LANtastic for Macintosh will let Macintosh users access any LANtastic server and any Macintosh-based AppleShare file servers (either System 7 file sharing or an AppleShare file server). The result of all of these capabilities is that you can have a centralized file server on the gateway, peer PC servers, and peer Macintosh servers, with each of these servers accessible to the Macs. Add to this any PostScript printers that are connected to the gateway, PC servers, and everything on the AppleTalk network, all accessible to either Macs or PCs, and you can have quite a zoo.

Figure 4.3 shows a network where there are several servers, printers, a gateway, and some Macs. When you look at the picture, you begin to get an idea of how complicated a LANtastic network can get and why careful planning is needed.

Using a LANtastic Macintosh Gateway

When you sit down to plan this network, you need to remember that all Macintosh access to any shared network resource occurs at the gateway. From the gateway, you specify how the Macs

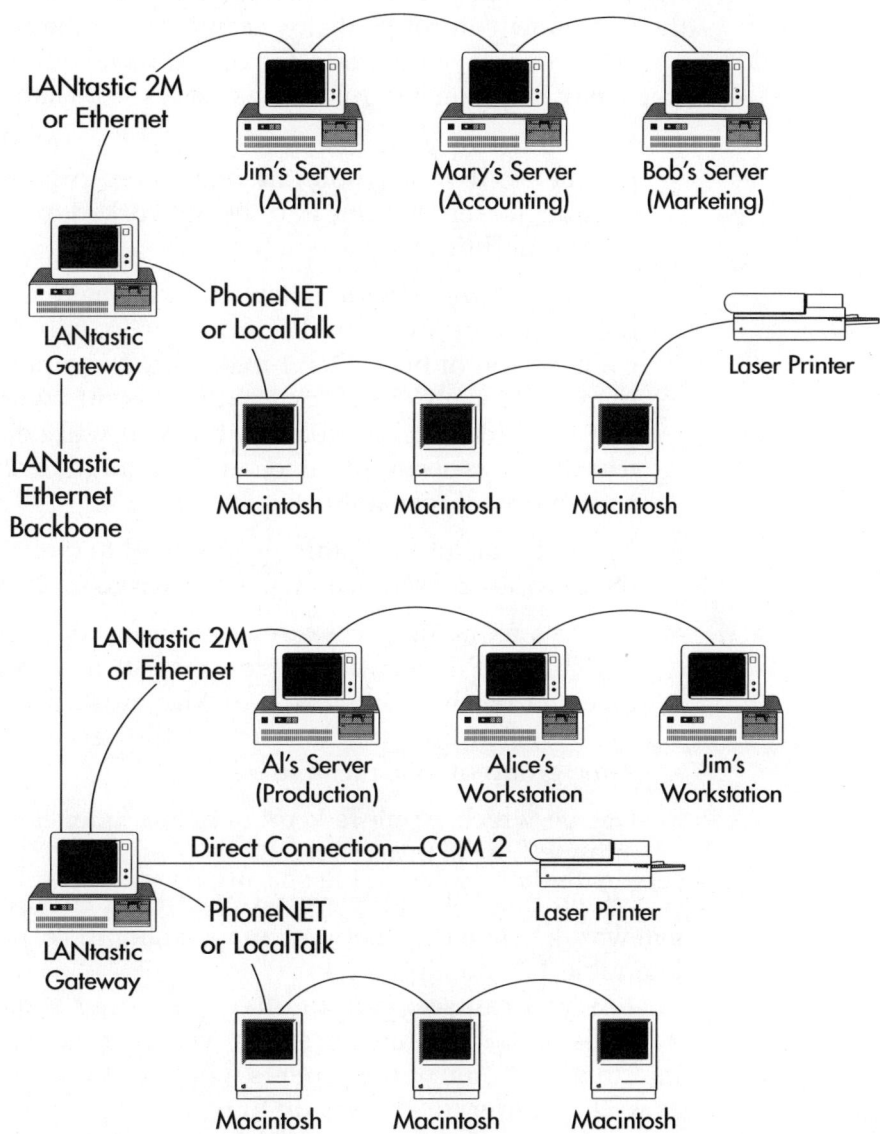

Figure 4.3
A complicated LANtastic network

By using two gateways, the Macs and PCs have access to all of the printers, both servers, and shared PC servers.

interact with the network by mounting the accessible servers, who has access to these servers, and the access privileges associated with each Macintosh user or group. All Macintosh access rights are separate from PC access rights, so you will have two sets of access rights to contend with. I'm making the assumption that you have the PCs under control, so that we can focus on the Macintoshes.

Before we even get into the actual installation, the following steps may help you control who has access to what:

1. Make a list of your LANtastic servers, networked PostScript printers, and your AppleTalk networked printers. On this list, include the server name and the networked drive path for each volume and printer.

2. For each server, decide if you want to make a Macintosh volume of the entire shared volume, of its sub-directories, or a combination of both. Don't make it too complex. It is possible to make Macintosh volumes with different owners and groups of a single LANtastic volume, but you will be creating a system that is very complicated, and you might overload the gateway machine's capabilities.

3. For each Macintosh volume you intend to create, make a list of the Macintosh users who will have access to the volume.

4. Create a name that will serve as a group name for each of the LANtastic PC-networked volumes. If any volumes will be accessed by the same group of Macintosh users, you can use the same group name for each of the servers that shares the same group of Macintosh users.

5. Decide which AppleTalk printers and queues you're going to allow PC users to access.

Keep this list handy; you'll need it when you configure the gateway. If you have a network map, it should correspond to a list, like Table 4.2 and Figure 4.4.

As you can see, you will have to mount some of the server volumes on both gateways so the Macs can access the necessary information. Some of the printers will have to service both servers, as well. In order for this set-up to work properly, each of the gateways also has to be a server. However, if you try to share a PC server volume on multiple gateways, you will have problems. You have to plan your workgroups so that volumes accessed by Macs are not shared by two gateways. The reason for this is that there

Table 4.2 User list for network map in Figure 4.4

LANtastic for Macintosh Gateway	LANtastic Servers & Networked Printers	Macintosh Volume & Path Name	Macintosh Users	Group Name
Admin Gateway	Jim's Server	Admin \\Admin	James June	Admin
	Admin II Printer	@Admin2PTR		
	Admin Printer	@AdminPTR		
Production Gateway	Bob's Server	Marketing \\Market	William George	Marketing
	Al's Server	Production \\Produce	Mary Anne Sally	Production
	Production Printer	@Prod		
	Admin Printer	@AdminPTR		

would otherwise be two sets of Macintosh-specific information files, one set on each server, and that information cannot be shared between the servers. With this information in hand, you're ready to set up the gateway.

Setting Up the Gateway

Now you should be ready to turn the gateway PC from an empty box into a cross-platform tool. The software installation process requires two steps, the installation of the LANtastic PC network software and then the installation of the LANtastic for Macintosh software. Since this book is about integrating Macs into your PC network, I'm assuming that your LANtastic network is up and running and that you are familiar with the installation and operation of the LANtastic PC networking software.

This is just another way of saying that you will not find installation instructions for a PC-based LANtastic network. What you will find is a discussion about how the LANtastic PC network should be configured (although the actual steps for configuring the PC software will be skipped), and about the installation and configuration of the LANtastic for Macintosh software. By the time you're finished with this section, you will have a functioning gateway.

CHAPTER 4

Figure 4.4

A network map

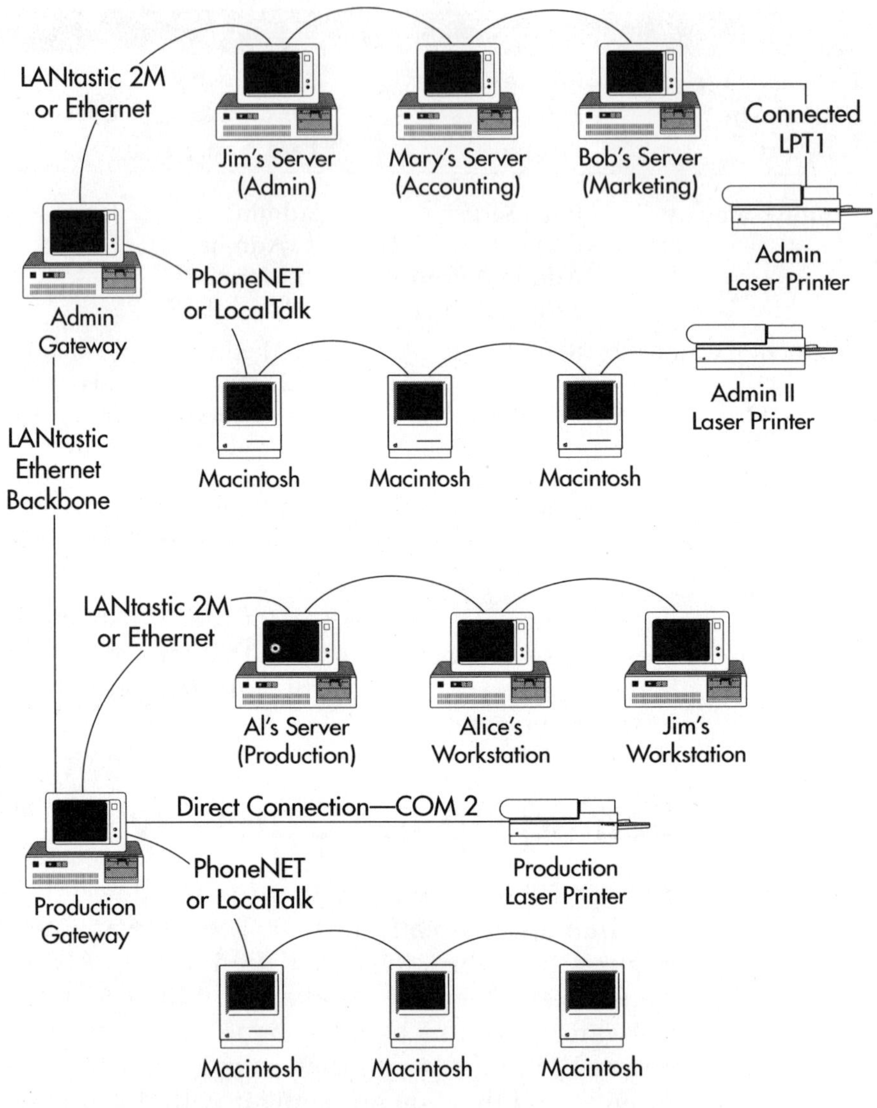

By using two gateways, the Macs and PCs have access to all of the printers, both servers, and shared PC servers.

The Gateway's LANtastic Configuration

Once you have the LANtastic PC network software installed on the gateway server, you will be ready to configure it for use with LANtastic for Macintosh. You can use the gateway as either a workstation or a server. However, using the gateway as workstation means that the gateway's hard drive(s) and printers will only be accessible to the Macintosh workstations. The Macs will still have access to other PC servers and printers on the network, but none of your PCs will have access to the gateway's resources.

If you set up the gateway as a server, you can use the hard drive to store E-mail post office files, a printer queue, and Macintosh or PC files. The only reason I can see for installing the LANtastic software as a workstation is if you need the memory used by the server software (which is not much) for the Macintosh software, because of the number of Macintosh users accessing the PC network, or, if you want to use the gateway as a dedicated Macintosh file and print server.

When you set up LANtastic, you should not run any TSR (Terminate and Stay Resident) programs—you will need all of the memory you can get. In the same vein, you should also optimize the server's memory if you are using DOS 5 or 6, where you have the ability to load programs into the Upper Memory Blocks (UMB). This will free some conventional memory, but you cannot load all of the workstation or server software high.

The following is a sample CONFIG.SYS file. These two files are designed to optimize memory, assuming that you are using MS-DOS 5 or 6. They represent a basic configuration.

- **CONFIG.SYS**

    ```
    DEVICE=C:\DOS\HIMEM.SYS
    DEVICE=C:\DOS\EMM386.EXE NOEMS
    DOS=HIGH,UMB
    FILES=100
    BUFFERS=50
    LASTDRIVE=Z
    FCBS=16,8
    STACKS=0,0
    ```

In this CONFIG.SYS file, you will notice that there is no disk cache. This is done to conserve memory. If you want to use a disk cache, use one that loads into and uses high memory. If you use conventional memory for the cache, you'll probably not have enough memory for LANtastic for Macintosh.

Your STARTNET.BAT file should look something like the following (line numbers appear here only for reference; they are not part of the file):

- **STARTNET.BAT**
    1. `SHARE /L:200 /F:4096`
    2. `LH AEX`
    3. `LH AILANBIO`
    4. `REDIR SERVER LOGINS=1`
    5. `LH SERVER`
    6. `NET LOGIN/WAIT \\SERVER SERVER`
    7. `NET LPT TIMEOUT 10`
    8. `NET QUEUE HALT \\SERVER LPT1`

This STARTNET.BAT file makes the gateway a server and a workstation. In the STARTNET.BAT file, there are three things you have to watch for. One is that you have to create an account on the server and log in with that name, as shown in line 6. The Share command must have a minimum of 200 for locks and 2096 for the Files setting; otherwise, LANtastic for Macintosh will not work. Finally, line 8 is required if you're using the gateway as a print spooler. The NET QUEUE HALT command allows the LANtastic printer queue to accept jobs but not offload them; it leaves this process to the LANtastic for Macintosh software.

When using the gateway as a server, install the LANtastic server software using the default server settings. You do not need to define any shared resources other than a printer, the volumes you want to share with PC users, and the user accounts for the PC users who will have access to the gateway. Figure 4.5 is an example of a basic resource configuration from LANtastic's NET_MGR program.

There is one important factor you will have to keep in mind when setting up the server. You will have to have 450K of free conventional memory, and even then, you can have problems running the LANtastic for Macintosh software. The moral of this story is to keep as much memory available as possible. Now we're ready to install the LANtastic for Macintosh software.

Installing the LANtastic for Macintosh Software

In this section we'll go through the steps for installing the software and look at some of the files that control LANtastic for Macintosh, primarily the LMSTART.BAT. The examples in this section will use

Figure 4.5

A sample resource configuration

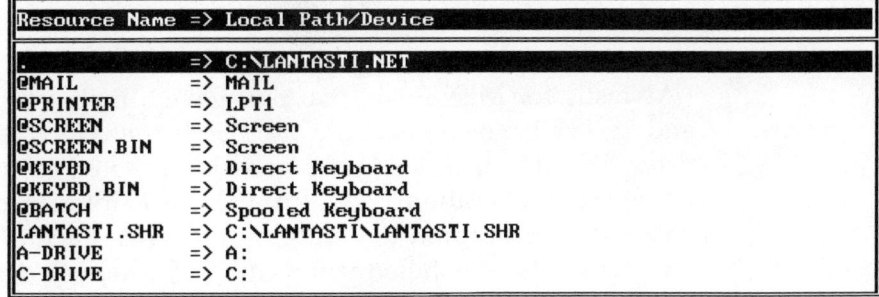

Farallon's PhoneNET PC card. You may be using a different adapter, so you will need to watch for—and I'll point out—the adapter-specific settings. In order for you to install LANtastic for Macintosh, the gateway machine must be operating as a server or workstation, and all of your LANtastic network settings should be configured and working.

Installing LANtastic for Macintosh is a very straightforward process. Put the installation diskette into the server's floppy drive and type **A:\INSTALLM**. This will start the installation program, which copies all of the LANtastic for Macintosh files and creates any needed directories. After you exit the Installer's splash screen and preliminary instructions, you will see the screen shown in Figure 4.6.

Perform the following steps:

1. Select or create the LANMAC directory.
2. Select your network adapter.

Figure 4.6

The installation set-up screen

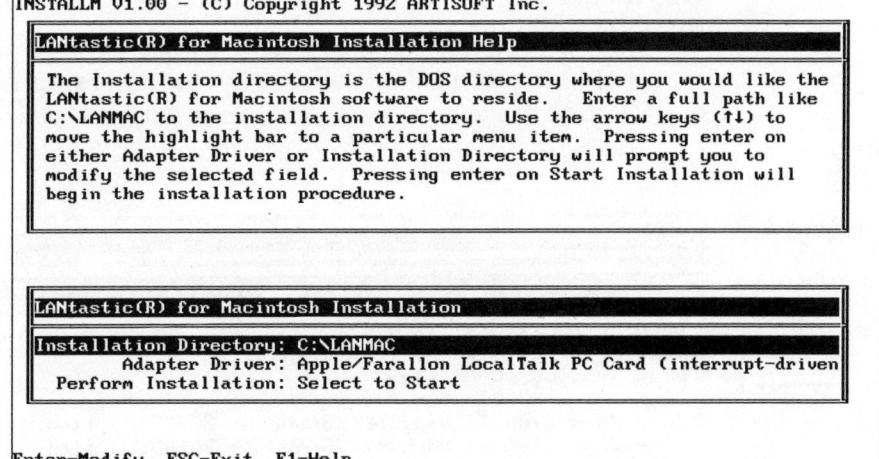

3. Start the installation process.

Although you can choose a network drive when installing LANtastic for Macintosh, you will have a more efficient gateway and server if you install the files onto the gateway's local hard drive. When you choose your network adapter, the default choice is the Apple/Farallon LocalTalk PC Card (interrupt-driven); you will not be prompted to configure the card. Each of the network adapter cards is installed using the card's factory default settings. If you are using different settings, you'll have to change them after installing the software.

To change either the path for the files or the adapter, you need to select the option and press the **Enter** key. You will be presented with a dialog box, where you can type in a new path or select an different network adapter card. Figure 4.7 shows the dialog box for selecting different network adapters.

Once you've selected the network card and path, the LANtastic for Macintosh program will copy all of the software to your drive and give you the option of starting the LANtastic for Macintosh administration program LMAC-MGR.EXE. I prefer to exit the installation program before starting LMAC-MGR, because the installer sometimes hangs when performing the switch and you will have to reboot the gateway machine. Once you've installed the software, your next task will be to configure the gateway.

Configuring LANtastic for Macintosh

Configuring the gateway machine consists of several steps, and which ones you perform will depend on the capabilities you wish to confer upon the server. These tasks are:

- Modify the NET.CFG file if you are using settings other than the factory default on your network adapter card.

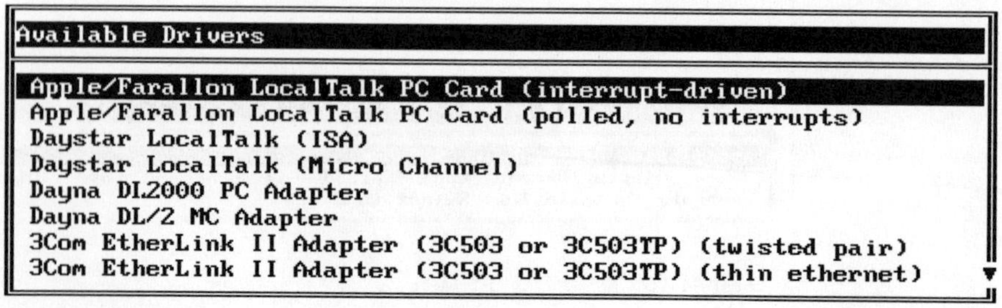

Figure 4.7
The Network Adapter Selection dialog box

```
Available Drivers
Apple/Farallon LocalTalk PC Card (interrupt-driven)
Apple/Farallon LocalTalk PC Card (polled, no interrupts)
Daystar LocalTalk (ISA)
Daystar LocalTalk (Micro Channel)
Dayna DL2000 PC Adapter
Dayna DL/2 MC Adapter
3Com EtherLink II Adapter (3C503 or 3C503TP) (twisted pair)
3Com EtherLink II Adapter (3C503 or 3C503TP) (thin ethernet)
```

- Check the file LMSTART.BAT.
- Run LMAC-MGR.EXE to configure the gateway's settings.

This section will go through each of these steps.

The NET.CFG File

The NET.CFG file contains the configuration information for the network adapter card—in this case, we're using a Farallon AppleTalk card. If you're using a different network adapter, you will have a configuration specific to the network card's drivers. The Farallon AppleTalk card is being used for our examples here because LANtastic for Macintosh can be purchased with the Farallon AppleTalk card. However, Ethernet and Token Ring cards also have a NET.CFG file.

When you run the INSTALLM program and select one of the Farallon cards as your network adapter, the NET.CFG file will be created and stored in the C:\LANMAC directory on the gateway server's drive. When the NET.CFG file is created, it is set up with the assumption that you are using the card with its factory default settings, so you may have to edit the NET.CFG file before you can run the gateway server software. The NET.CFG file is a text file and can be edited with any MS-DOS editor.

- **NET.CFG**

```
Link Support
  Buffers 10 603
  MemPool 6K
Protocol AppleTalk
  DEFAULT LTALK$ #1
Link Driver LTALK$
# Apple LocalTalk PC Card (polled, no
interrupts)
  DMA #1 1
  PORT #1 240 8
  Node Address 65
```

The NET.CFG file is divided into three sections: Link Support, Protocol AppleTalk, and Link Drivers. Each section has its own configuration settings. The sections can appear in any order, and the lines within a section can appear in any order. The file is presented above as it was written during the installation process. We'll look at each section and briefly discuss its contents.

Link Support

This section sets aside memory required to hold AppleTalk packets received on the network. The BUFFERS determine how many buffers are reserved and the size of those buffers.

Protocol AppleTalk

This section supplies the ODI (Open Data-Link Interface) protocol with the protocol stack information and determines which MILD (Multiple Interface Link Driver) will be used. The Default line binds the AppleTalk MILD to the network card.

Link Driver

This section contains all of the network card's configuration information. If you've changed the card from its defaults, you'll have to edit this section of the NET.CFG file. The different sections are:

- **INT**   The hardware interrupt line. If you're using the Polled Interrupt option, this line will be missing.
- **DMA**   The DMA channel used by the network card.
- **PORT**   Specifies the port address used by the card.
- **NODE ADDRESS**   This is the AppleTalk node address that will be assigned to the AppleTalk port. If you have a problem with AppleTalk address conflicts, you might want to remove this line. If you do, the MILD will choose its port number randomly. Otherwise, you can change the number to one that you know does not conflict with other AppleTalk nodes. (To find this information, you'll need an network utility like Inter•Poll, NetAtlas, or TrafficWatch.)

If you need more information about the NET.CFG file, check with LANtastic technical support. Usually the only section you will have to edit is the Link Drivers section. The other sections should be left alone unless you know what you are doing.

The LMSTART.BAT File

The LMSTART.BAT file is the batch file that loads the AppleTalk network drivers and starts the LANtastic for Macintosh server software LMSERVER.EXE.

- **STARTNET.BAT**

    LSL

Using a LANtastic Macintosh Gateway

```
REM PORT ADDRESS=240, INTERRUPT=POLLED, DMA=1
LTALKP  /NAME=LTALK$
ATALK
COMPAT
PAP_WS
PAP_SRV
LMSERVER
```

The LMSTART.BAT must be run from the C:\LANMAC directory or the directory containing your LANtastic for Macintosh files, even if the LANMAC directory is included on your path. Also, if you quit the LMSERVER application and want to restart the server, you have to run LMSERVER from the LANMAC directory. These requirements are because the LANtastic for Macintosh files reside in the LANMAC directory, and LMSERVER only looks in the current directory for the system files. Do not run the LMSERVER.EXE program until you have used the LMAC-MGR program, which creates LANtastic for Mac's system files.

Running the LMAC-MGR Program

Whenever you run LMAC-MGR, you *must* run it from the directory that contains all of your LANtastic for Macintosh files. If you run the program from another directory or the top level of your hard drive, your LANtastic for Macintosh files will be placed in the current directory and the gateway will not work properly. So the first step in running LMAC-MGR is to change the current directory to your LANtastic for Macintosh directory. (For our purposes, we'll use the default C:\LANMAC.)

The LANtastic for Macintosh administration program is used to configure the following:

- Server startup parameters
- *Individual account management
- *Group account management
- Volume (directory) management
- Printer management
- *File extension mappings
- Configuration password maintenance
- Manage system files

Each of the items above with an asterisk (*) can be performed from a Macintosh using the LAN MAC Manager program. If you would rather perform these tasks from the Mac, you can skip them here. Also, once you have the basic Macintosh volumes defined, you can use the LAN MAC Manager program to assign access privileges. For the time being, we're going to look at each of the items in the list from the LMAC-MGR program.

When you run LMAC-MGR, remember that you must do so from the directory that contains the LANtastic for Macintosh files. If you are performing maintenance, changing the gateway configuration, or adding volumes, you will have to exit the LMSERVER program before running LMAC-MGR. To run LMAC-MGR, type **LMAC-MGR** at the C:\LANMAC prompt. You will see the screen shown in Figure 4.8.

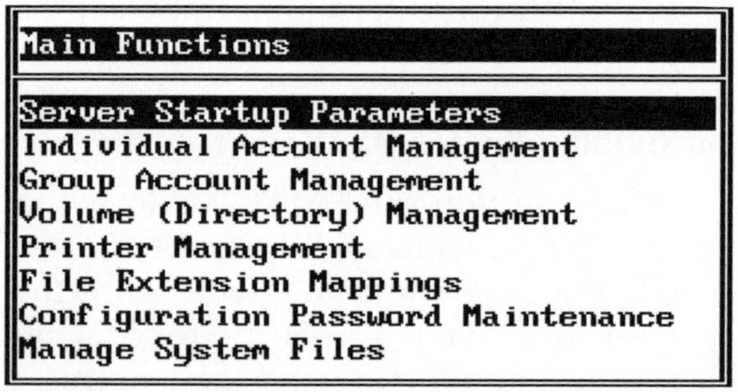

Figure 4.8
LMAC-MGR's main screen

```
Main Functions

Server Startup Parameters
Individual Account Management
Group Account Management
Volume (Directory) Management
Printer Management
File Extension Mappings
Configuration Password Maintenance
Manage System Files
```

Note

Although the LMAC-MGR options are presented in the order in which they appear in the program, after you are familiar with what each option does, you should set up up your server for the first time using the following options in the order listed here:

1. Group Account Management

2. Individual Account Management

3. Volume (Directory) Management

All of the other options can be used in any order. But when you are initially setting up your users and volumes, you may find this order easier to manage.

USING A LANTASTIC MACINTOSH GATEWAY

To select any of the options:

1. Use the cursor keys on your keyboard.
2. Highlight the desired option.
3. Press **Enter** to make the selection.

These steps are consistent throughout LMAC-MGR for selecting and modifying options and will not be repeated.

Server Startup Parameters

When you select the Server Startup Parameters, you will see a screen like the one in Figure 4.9.

From the Server Startup Parameters screen, you can edit or set any of the following options:

- **Server Name** This is the name that will be broadcast to your Macintosh users and seen from the Chooser when AppleShare is selected.

- **Description** A description for your convenience.

- **Guest Logins** Enable or disable guest Macintosh logins. The default is ENABLED. To prevent guest logins, change this entry to DISABLED.

- **Audit Trail** If you want an audit trail of your Macintosh users' activity, ENABLE this option. Its default is DISABLED. Your log files will be kept in a series of files called LOG.*.

- **Failed Login Retries** The default for this setting is NO LIMIT. If you want to disable a user's account automatically after a specific number of failed logins, enable this

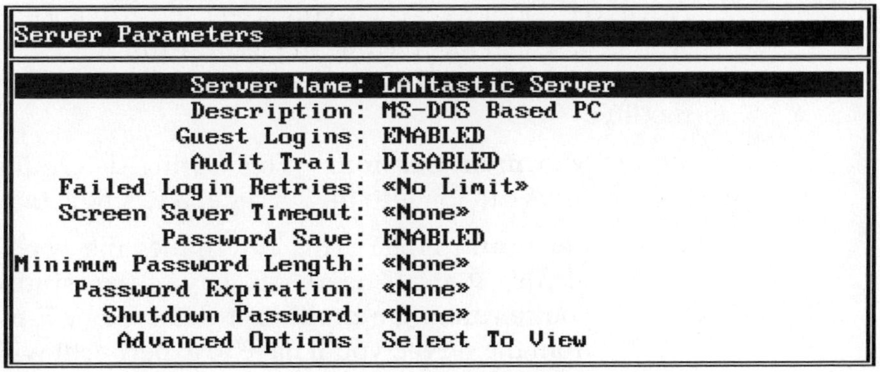

Figure 4.9
The Server Parameters screen

```
Server Parameters
            Server Name: LANtastic Server
            Description: MS-DOS Based PC
           Guest Logins: ENABLED
            Audit Trail: DISABLED
    Failed Login Retries: «No Limit»
    Screen Saver Timeout: «None»
          Password Save: ENABLED
  Minimum Password Length: «None»
     Password Expiration: «None»
       Shutdown Password: «None»
        Advanced Options: Select To View
```

option by specifying the number of unsuccessful login attempts that can be made. If an account gets disabled, you will have to reactivate the account with one of the administration programs.

- **Screen Saver Timeout**   With this setting, you specify the number of seconds before the screen saver turns on when the LMSERVER software is running. The default is NONE.

- **Password Save**   This option allows or disallows the Macintosh users' ability to have their passwords saved so they can reboot without having to enter a password. The default setting is ENABLED.

- **Minimum Password Length**   You can require that a Mac user use a password, and specify the minimum length of that password by entering the number of characters. The default setting for this option is NONE.

- **Password Expiration**   The number entered here is the number of days before a Mac user's password will expire. The default setting is NONE.

- **Shutdown Password**   This option allows you to specify a password for shutting down the LMSERVER program. Setting a password would mean that only those who know the password can shut it down. The default is NONE.

- **Advanced Options**   The Advanced Options are for specifying performance options that affect how the server runs. They are described below.

How you set any of the settings listed above will depend on your security requirements and personal preferences. The only settings that affect performance of the gateway server are the Advanced Options. When you select the Advanced Options, you will see a screen like the one in Figure 4.10.

In the Advanced Options, there are four settings you can modify:

- **Maximum Sessions**   This setting determines how many users can log into the server at any single time.

- **Maximum Files**   This determines the maximum number of files that all users can have open simultaneously. If you're running a multi-user database or E-mail post office from the server, you'll have to experiment with this setting.

Figure 4.10
The Advanced Options screen

```
Advanced Server Parameters

        Maximum Sessions: 10
           Maximum Files: 40
Maximum Byte Range Locks: 20
             Performance: High Performance
```

- **Maximum Byte Range Locks** This setting specifies the maximum number of file and/or record locks the server can perform simultaneously. If you're running a multi-user database from the server, you'll have to experiment with this setting.

- **Performance** This option opens the Server Parameters dialog box (see Fig. 4.11), which contains performance settings for the server. There are two predefined settings you can choose: High Users and High Performance. The other option is to select Custom, which allows you to specify the Performance settings.

These are the settings that you use to specify the following:

- **Read/Write Buffers** These are large input/output buffers that are used each time a user reads from or writes to the server. The number of buffers can be set from 2 to 999. When High Users is selected, this number is 4, and for High Performance it is 15.

Figure 4.11
The Server Parameters dialog box

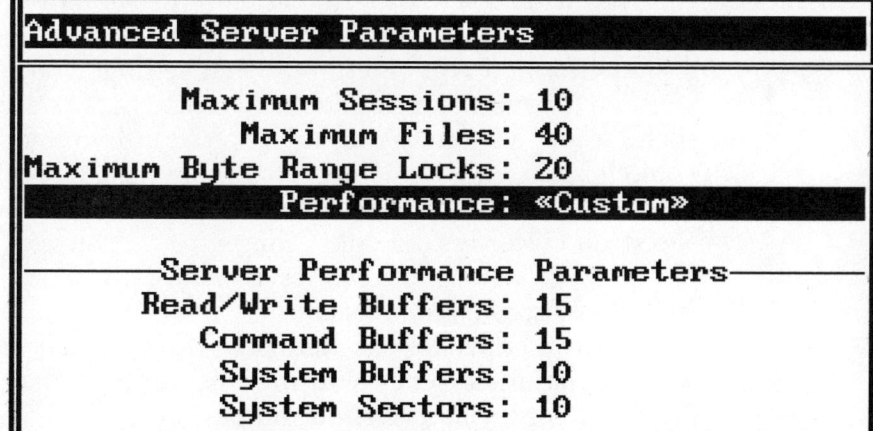

- **Command Buffers** The command buffers are used to process requests from users. Each time a user logs in, one command buffer is used. The maximum number of buffers is 999. You need to exercise some care with this setting. If it is too low, you will have users who cannot log in even though the maximum number of users has not been exceeded. Also, if you are using a program that logs into the server, like an E-mail package, you may have to allocate a buffer for each mail user in addition to those needed for each standard login.

- **System Buffers** The system buffers are used by LMSERVER to manage system files. Increasing this number can improve the gateway server's performance. The recommended setting is between 20 and 40, and the maximum number of system buffers is 50. The number of buffers and the next setting, size, determine how much memory you will need for LMSERVER to run. Remember, LMSERVER uses conventional memory, so you are limited by your available memory. If you've optimized your machine, you should have around 500K to run LMSERVER after all of your network adapters and the LANtastic PC network software have been loaded.

- **System Sectors** This setting determines the system buffers' size in Kilobytes. The range can be from 4 to 15. Artisoft recommends that you use from 8 to 12. Increasing the size of the system buffers will improve server performance but use more memory.

You will have to experiment with the Server Performance settings. How many users you have and the network tasks that need to be performed will determine what settings you use, and there are no hard and fast rules about what to choose. You will have to spend a few days tweaking the server until you get performance you're happy with. Remember that there will always be a trade-off between speed and the number of users: the more users, the less speed, and vice versa.

Individual Account Management
This is the area where you define your individual users and their basic capabilities. When you initially set up a user, you will be prompted for the user's name and password.

Once you've created a user, you can view the user's profile and assign or change the following:

- **Name** The user's login name
- **Password** The user's password
- **Privileges** There are three privileges that a user can have:
  1. **L (Login)** This privilege is automatically assigned to every user. If an account gets disabled and a user can't log in, this is the privilege that must be reassigned.
  2. **E (Every privilege)** A user who is given Every privilege will have full access to all of the files and folders created on a volume, regardless of the set AppleShare privileges. A user with this privilege can also change the access privileges to any directory by using the Sharing command from the Macintosh's File menu. Because the privilege applies to all volumes, it should only be granted to trusted users who are also responsible for administration tasks.
  3. **A (Administration)** This privilege is exactly what it appears to be. Users with the Administration privilege have the Every privilege, and they can also run the LAN MAC Manager program from their own Macs.
  4. **Main Group** With this option you set the default group to which a user belongs.
- **Groups** This is a list of the groups to which a user belongs.

If you have any questions about AppleShare access privileges, review Chapter 2.

To view a user's profile, select the user's name and press Enter. You will see a screen like the one in Figure 4.12.

Deleting a user is the same as deleting a group. To delete a user, see the Group Account Management section.

Group Account Management

Like the Individual Account Management option, this menu selection lets you manage your AppleShare groups.

To create a new group:

1. Press the **Insert** key.
2. Type a group name when requested.

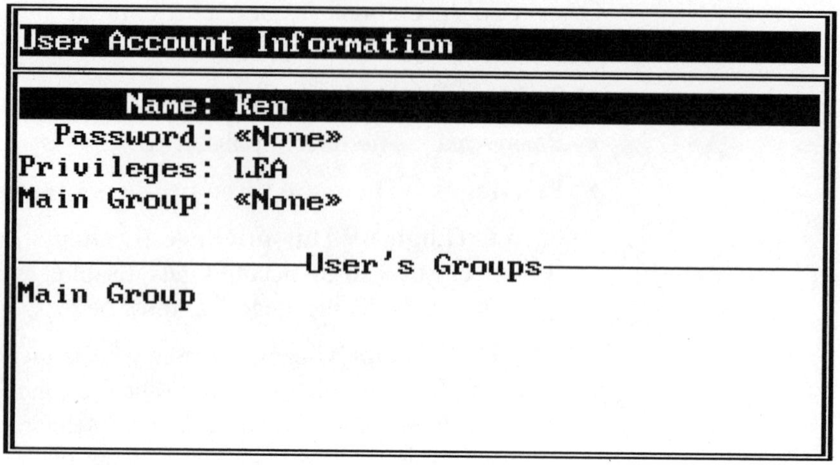

Figure 4.12

The User Account Information screen

```
┌─────────────────────────────────────────────┐
│ User Account Information                    │
├─────────────────────────────────────────────┤
│         Name: Ken                           │
│     Password: «None»                        │
│   Privileges: LEA                           │
│   Main Group: «None»                        │
│                                             │
│─────────────────User's Groups───────────────│
│ Main Group                                  │
│                                             │
│                                             │
└─────────────────────────────────────────────┘
```

3. Press the **Enter** key.

Once a group has been created, you can modify its name and members by selecting the group name and pressing the **Enter** key. When you modify a group, you can add or delete members and you can change its name. Figure 4.13 shows the Group Account Information dialog box.

To add a member:

1. Press the **Insert** key
2. You will see a list of the available members like the one in Figure 4.14.
3. Select the user to add.
4. Press the **Enter** key.

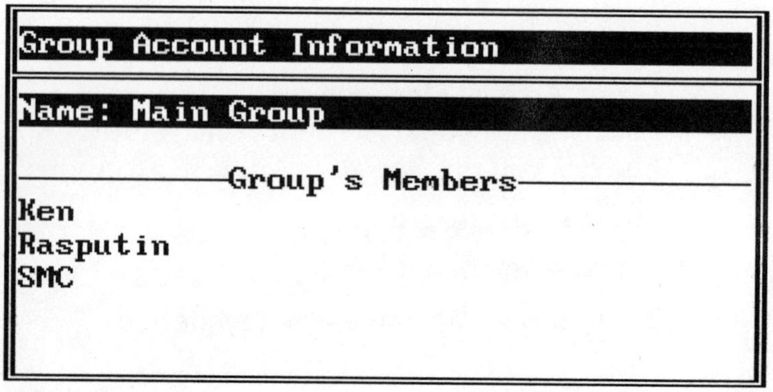

Figure 4.13

The Group Account Information dialog box

```
┌─────────────────────────────────────────────┐
│ Group Account Information                   │
├─────────────────────────────────────────────┤
│ Name: Main Group                            │
│                                             │
│─────────────────Group's Members─────────────│
│ Ken                                         │
│ Rasputin                                    │
│ SMC                                         │
│                                             │
└─────────────────────────────────────────────┘
```

Figure 4.14

The available users to add to a group

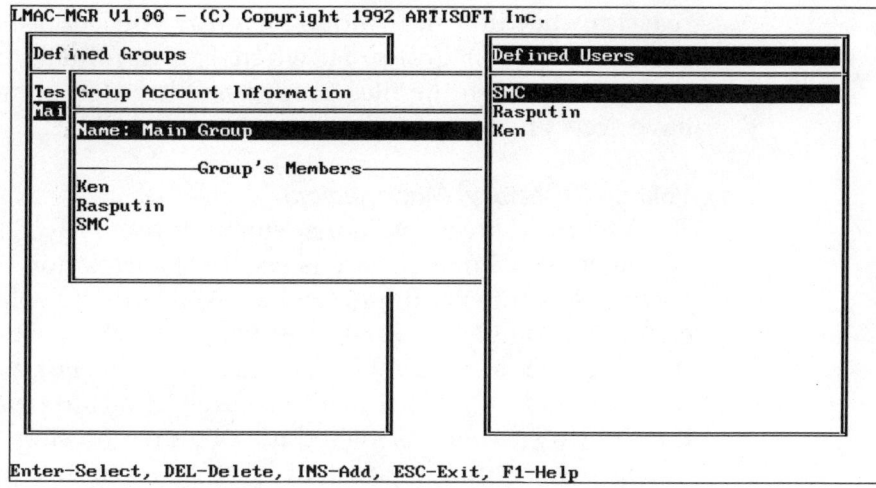

The selected user will be added to the group. Likewise, to delete a group member, select the user's name and press the **Delete** key.

When you delete a group or a user, you will be asked to reassign the ownership of the user's or group's files. You will be presented with a dialog box like the one in Figure 4.15, from which you need to make your selection.

When you delete a user, you will be asked to reassign the user's files to another user, the volume's default owner, or any Owner. Whenever you delete a user or group, you will have to

Figure 4.15

Reassigning folder privileges

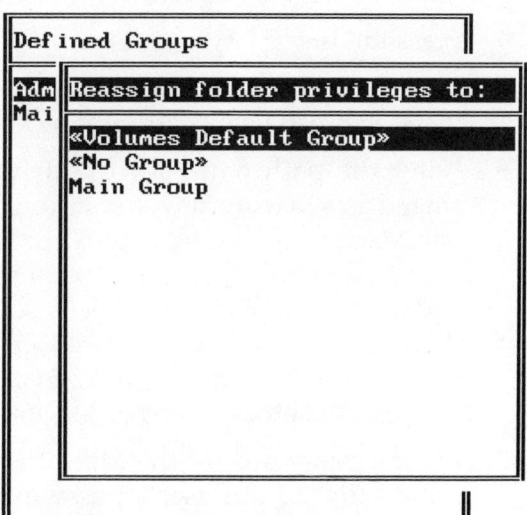

reassign the files and folders, even if you choose the volume's default owner or group. So when you terminate an account, be sure you reassign the files properly. Otherwise, some people may have access to data you don't want them to see.

Volume (Directory) Management

The Volume (Directory) Management option is used to set up your AppleShare volumes. There is no direct correlation between a networked Macintosh volume and a LANtastic PC volume until you create it using LMAC-MGR. Just because a PC is set up as a server does not mean a Mac will have access to it. For a Macintosh to have access to a LANtastic PC volume, it has to be a volume that the gateway server has logged into. Before you start to set up your Macintosh volumes, you will have to have mounted all of the drives to which your Macs are going to have access. When it comes to overall gateway performance, you have to be concerned with how the gateway performs as a LANtastic workstation and then as a gateway server.

Once your gateway server is configured, you can set up the Macintosh volumes.

To define a Macintosh volume:

1. Select the Volume (directory) Management option from the LMAC-MGR program.

2. Press **Enter**.

3. You will see a list of defined volumes.

4. Press the **Insert** key.

5. Type the volume name. This is the name that will be seen by the Macintosh users; it cannot be more than 32 characters.

6. Enter the path name for the drive or directory that will be shared as a Macintosh volume. You can define a sub-directory as one Macintosh volume and its parent directory as another Macintosh volume. This is not recommended, however, because LANtastic for Macintosh keeps separate system files for each directory, so if you have nested or recursive volumes, changes made to one volume will not be visible in another. The files will not have the proper icons or Macintosh names.

7. Enter a password for the Macintosh volume. This password is in addition to the user's password. If you enter a password,

Using a LANtastic Macintosh Gateway

your Macintosh users will have to know it before they can have access to the volume.

8. The volume will appear in the list of defined volumes.

Once you have a volume defined, you can select the volume name and press **Enter** to see the Volume Information dialog box (see Fig. 4.16).

In the Dialog Information dialog box, you have access to the following options or settings. To change an item, select it with the cursor keys and press the **Enter** key. The first set of options apply to all Macintosh users who are accessing a volume.

- **Name** This is the volume name that is broadcast on the AppleTalk network.
- **Read Only** Enabling this option makes the volume read-only. The default setting is NO.
- **Password** This is the password for the volume. If there is a password, every user who is going to access the volume must know it.

The Privileges settings that follow apply only to the files on the top level of the volume when it is created and any MS-DOS files placed on a volume. To make access rights apply to an entire volume, and to make that volume inaccessible to anyone other than the owner and/or an owing group member, you will have to set the volume access rights from the Folders/SubDirs (**F3**) screen. Setting access rights from the Folders/SubDirs window provides a higher

Figure 4.16

The Volume Information dialog box

```
Volume Information
         Path: C:/
   Total Bytes: 42366976
    Free Bytes: 33755136
         Name: Example
    Read Only: NO
     Password: **********
    Privileges: «Custom»
─────────────────Volume Privileges─────────────────
         Owner: Ken
         Group: «No Group»
  See Folders: 0--
     See Files: 0--
  Make Changes: 0--
```

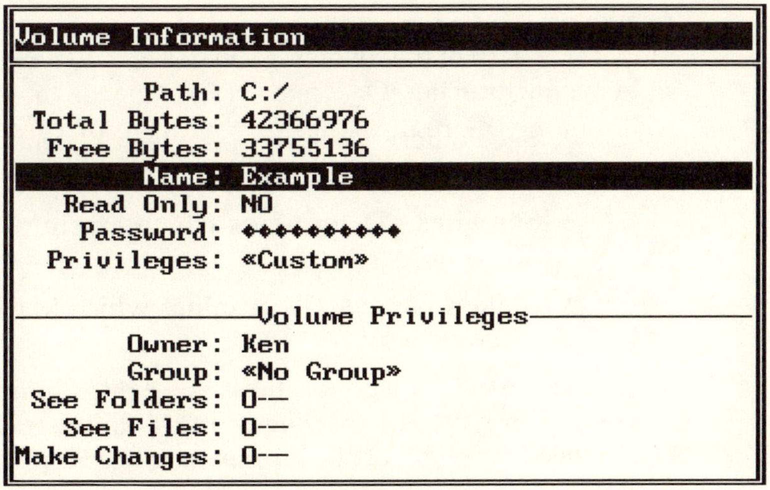

level of security because you can apply access privileges to sub-directories that differ from those of the volume itself. When access rights are initially assigned to a volume, they apply to the volume and any of the volume's sub-directories. Otherwise, the meaning of and the method for setting access privileges are the same for either section of the Volume (Directory) Management section.

- **Privileges** The default setting for the privileges is PARENT. PARENT means that the directory (if it is a directory that is being shared) has the same access rights as its parent directory or the drive. The other setting is CUSTOM, where you can specify the volume's access rights by setting the remaining access rights in this list.

- **Owner** The default owner is <<Any User>>. Unless you specify a specific owner, each folder created on a volume will be owned by any Mac user accessing the volume. Otherwise, only the assigned Macintosh user will have access.

- **Group** The default owner is <<Any Group>>. Unless you specify a specific group, each folder created on a volume will be accessible by any Macintosh user unless an individual owner is assigned. Otherwise, the directory will be accessible to the members of the group that has the assigned access.

For each of the listed categories you can specify the Owner (O), the Group (G), or Everyone (E). When you specify that an owner or group has access, the owner or group will be the one assigned in the Volume Information dialog box, as described above.

For each of the following categories, you assign the access rights by typing the letter (O, G, and/or E) while the category is selected.

- **See Folders** Determines which Macintosh user(s) can see folders.

- **See Files** Determines which Macintosh user(s) can see files.

- **Make Changes** Determines which Macintosh user(s) can make changes.

These access rights follow the AppleShare rules, except for users who have All privileges and Administration privileges. If you need a review of the AppleShare access privileges, see Chap-

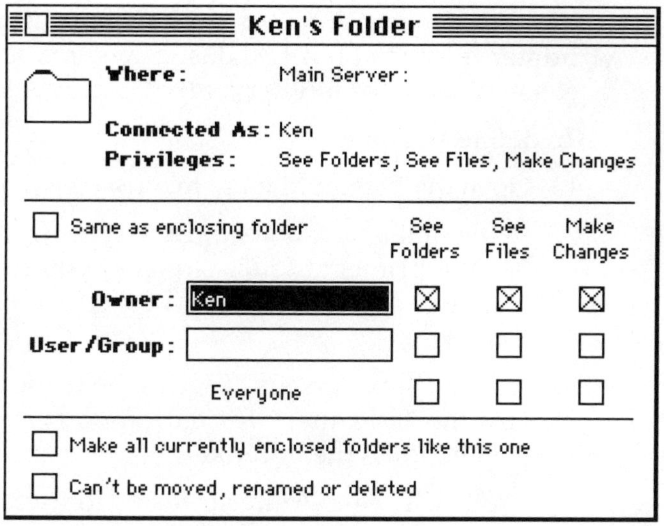

Using a LANtastic Macintosh Gateway

Figure 4.17
The Macintosh Sharing dialog box

```
┌─────────────── Ken's Folder ───────────────┐
│                                             │
│   📁   Where:        Main Server:          │
│                                             │
│        Connected As: Ken                    │
│        Privileges:   See Folders, See Files, Make Changes │
│   ─────────────────────────────────────────│
│                                  See   See   Make  │
│   ☐ Same as enclosing folder    Folders Files Changes│
│                                             │
│        Owner: [Ken        ]       ☒    ☒    ☒     │
│   User/Group: [           ]       ☐    ☐    ☐     │
│             Everyone              ☐    ☐    ☐     │
│   ─────────────────────────────────────────│
│   ☐ Make all currently enclosed folders like this one │
│   ☐ Can't be moved, renamed or deleted     │
└─────────────────────────────────────────────┘
```

ter 2. The above settings do correspond to the settings you see in the Macintosh's Sharing dialog box (Fig. 4.17); it just the format that is different.

Printer Management

The Printer Management section is where you will find all of the options you need to access a PostScript printer connected to a PC, or to make an AppleTalk PostScript printer available to MS-DOS machines. Figure 4.18 shows the Printer Management screen with one printer defined.

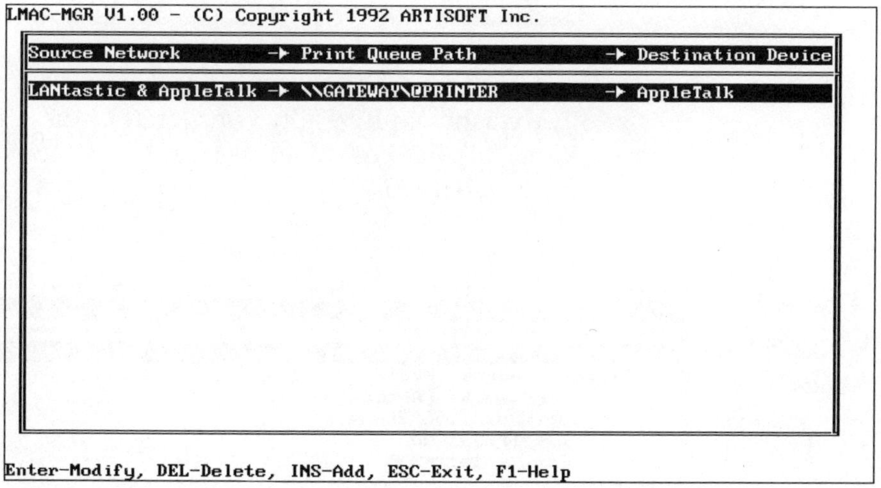

Figure 4.18
The Printer Management screen

```
LMAC-MGR V1.00 - (C) Copyright 1992 ARTISOFT Inc.
┌─────────────────────────────────────────────────────────────┐
│Source Network         → Print Queue Path    → Destination Device│
│LANtastic & AppleTalk  → \\GATEWAY\@PRINTER  → AppleTalk     │
│                                                             │
│                                                             │
│                                                             │
│                                                             │
│                                                             │
└─────────────────────────────────────────────────────────────┘
Enter-Modify, DEL-Delete, INS-Add, ESC-Exit, F1-Help
```

Before you define a printer, you must have defined a PC printer resource on a LANtastic server. The printer can be on the gateway server or any server that is available to the gateway.

To define a printer:

1. Open the Printer Management screen and press the **Insert** key.
2. In the dialog box that appears, type the name of the server that has the printer resource (queue) you're going to use. Use the "\\Server" path format when selecting the server. Press the **Enter** key.
3. A dialog box appears. Type in the name of the printer resource. Use the "@Printer" format when typing in the name of the printer. Press the **Enter** key.

You will see a Printer Information screen like the one in Figure 4.19.

Within the Printer information screen, you have the following options:

- **LANtastic Server** The server that contains the printer resource.
- **Server Resource** The name of the printer resourse.
- **Source Network** This option tells the gateway which computers have access to the printer. You can make the printer available to just the LANtastic network with the default setting, LANtastic, or to both LANtastic and AppleTalk devices with the setting LANtastic & AppleTalk.
- **Destination Device** The destination tells the gateway where the printer actually resides. It will either be connected to a LANtastic server (which is the default setting "LANtastic"), physically connected to the server, or on the AppleTalk network. Figure 4.20 shows the possible choices for the destination.

Figure 4.19
The Printer Information screen

```
Printer Information
       LANtastic Server: \\GATEWAY
       Server Resource: @PRINTER
        Source Network: LANtastic
    Destination Device: LANtastic
            LaserPrep: NO
            Font File: «None»
```

Using a LANtastic Macintosh Gateway

Figure 4.20

The Output Devices choice list

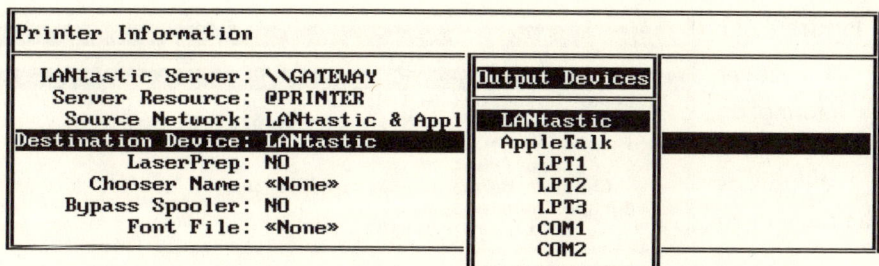

- **Laser Prep** This option has a default of NO. If you are going to bypass the print spooler, you should choose YES for this option. Selecting YES will send a laser prep file to the printer every time the spooler is used to initialize the printer.

- **Font File** This option is available only if your destination is a LANtastic server. The font file contains the list of printer-resident PostScript fonts. The list of supported printers can be found in the LANtastic for Macintosh manual in Appendix B.

  All standard Apple LaserWriters and most PostScript laser printers are supported. However, if you do not find your printer listed, you can create your own font file by modifying one of the existing font files. The font file is a text file.

Configuring Printer Access It makes no sense to define a printer that has LANtastic as both a destination and a source. The purpose of the Printer Management section is either to make an AppleTalk printer available to the LANtastic network or to make a LANtastic printer available to the AppleTalk Network. So either the Source Network or the Destination Device option should have AppleTalk as one of the settings.

One of the configurations you might use is LANtastic & AppleTalk as the Source Network and LANtastic as the destination. If the printer destination is LANtastic, the Printer Information window will change and look like Figure 4.21.

In the expanded Printer Information window, you will see an additional setting called Chooser Name. The Chooser name is what the Macintosh users will see when they select a printer using the Macintosh's Chooser. If you use a configuration like the one in Figure 4.21, all print jobs will be spooled to the server that controls the printer before they are printed.

Figure 4.21

The Printer Information window with LANtastic as the destination

```
Printer Information
     LANtastic Server: \\GATEWAY
      Server Resource: @PRINTER
       Source Network: LANtastic & AppleTalk
   Destination Device: LANtastic
            LaserPrep: NO
         Chooser Name: Lantastic Printer
       Bypass Spooler: NO
            Font File: STAND35.FNT
```

Your other option is to access a printer that is on the AppleTalk network. In this case, you would have a Printer Information screen that looks like the one in Figure 4.22.

In Figure 4.22, you will see that the Font File option is gone and that you have two additional settings:

- **Printer Name**   The printer name is the name of the printer as it is seen from the Macintosh Chooser. You must enter the name exactly as it is seen from the Mac. Remember that some printers have an extra space at the end of their names.

- **Printer Zone**   The printer zone should be the name of the zone that contains the printer if you're using an internet router on the Macintosh network. Otherwise, the default zone will not have a name. If you do not have a Macintosh internet and the zone name is left blank, some printers will still work. However, others require an asterisk (*) for the zone name. If you enter an asterisk (*) it should work with all printers. The asterisk (*) is AppleTalk's default zone designation.

With the configuration in Figure 4.22, the gateway will remove the printer's name from the network and broadcast only the Chooser name that is entered in the Printer Information screen.

Figure 4.22

The Printer Information screen configured with AppleTalk as the destination

```
Printer Information
     LANtastic Server: \\GATEWAY
      Server Resource: @PRINTER
       Source Network: LANtastic & AppleTalk
   Destination Device: AppleTalk
            LaserPrep: NO
         Chooser Name: Lan Printer
       Bypass Spooler: NO
   ─────────────────────Destination AppleTalk Device─
         Printer Name: LaserWriter II NT
         Printer Zone: Printer Zone
```

Figure 4.23

The Printer Information screen setting for direct printer access

```
Printer Information
    LANtastic Server: \\GATEWAY
     Server Resource: @PRINTER
      Source Network: LANtastic & AppleTalk
  Destination Device: AppleTalk
           LaserPrep: YES
        Chooser Name: Lan Printer
      Bypass Spooler: YES
                        ─────Destination AppleTalk Device─────
         Printer Name: LaserWriter II NT
         Printer Zone: Printer Zone
```

Artisoft does not recommend this configuration, because many Macintosh printers need to communicate directly with the printer in order to print properly. If your Mac users are using graphics or page layout applications, you should use a configuration that looks like the one in Figure 4.23.

Using the set-up shown in Figure 4.23 will allow Mac users the choice of printing directly to the printer or printing to the gateway and using the spooler.

Remember, all of your Macintoshes should be using the same version of the LaserWriter driver. Otherwise, the printer will have to reinitialize itself each time it receives a document from a Mac that has a different version of the LaserWriter driver than the one used to print the previous page.

File Extension Mapping

The File Extension Mapping section provides you with several options and tools for managing MS-DOS-to-Macintosh file type mapping based on the document's extension. Figure 4.24 shows the list of options available for managing the extension mapping features.

The options you have are:

- **View File Definitions By Name** From this option you can view all of the programs that have been defined. This

Figure 4.24

The File Definition Options screen

```
File Definition Options

View File Definitions By Name
View File Definitions By Extension
Update All Files With Specified Extension
Update All Files Belonging To Specified Type
Update All Extensions For All Types
```

is also the option where you create new extension definitions.

To create an new definition:

1. Select "View File Definitions by Name" and press the **Enter** key.

2. You will see a list of program names, as shown in Figure 4.25. Press the **Insert** key.

3. A dialog box will appear, and you'll be asked to enter the program's name. Type the Macintosh program name and press **Enter**.

4. Next, you will be asked to enter the program's Macintosh creator code. Enter the creator code and press **Enter**.

5. You will be asked to enter the program's type code. Enter the type code and press **Enter**.

These steps complete the initial steps for defining the program name, but the extension is not yet assigned.

To finish mapping the extension:

1. Select the name you just created and press the **Enter** key.

2. You will see a File Definition screen for the Macintosh program, as shown in Figure 4.26. To enter the DOS extension, press the **Insert** key.

Figure 4.25

The File Definitions list

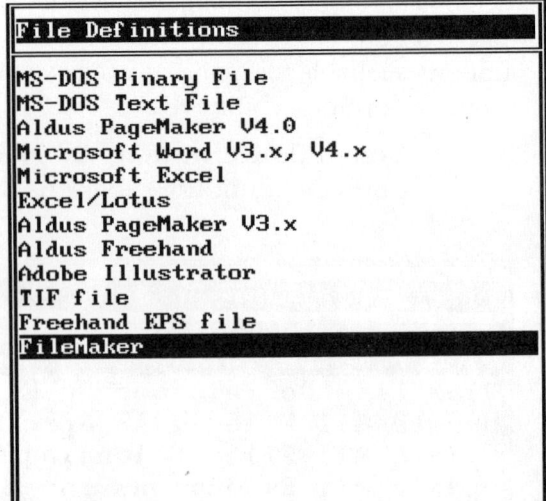

Using a LANtastic Macintosh Gateway

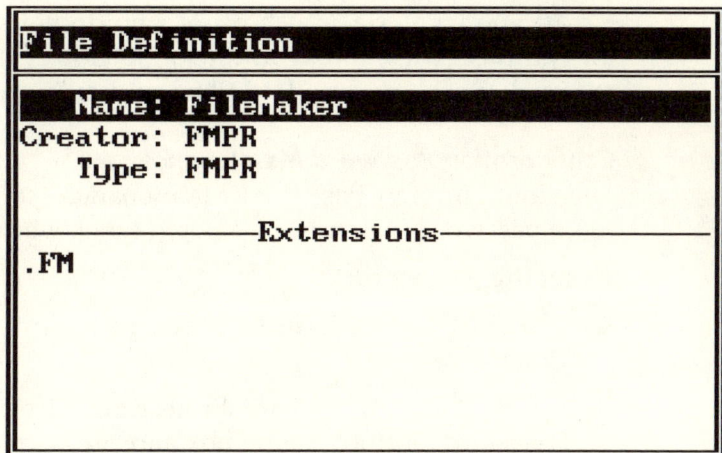

Figure 4.26

The File Definition screen for a Macintosh program

3. Enter the DOS extension in the dialog box that appears and press the **Enter** key.

4. If you want to add another extension to the same Macintosh program, repeat steps 2 and 3.

5. Press **Escape** to exit the screen.

Whenever you edit or create a new extension mapping, you will have to update the extension map for files already on the drive. This is done by using one of the Update selections listed below.

- **View File Definitions By Extension** This selection shows you all of the extensions that have been mapped, along with their corresponding Macintosh programs. From this section you can select an extension and modify it, but you cannot create a new mapping.

- **Update All Files With Specified Extension** This selection lets you update, or associate, all files with a specific extension to the corresponding Macintosh program.

- **Update All Files Belonging to a Specific Type** This selection lets you update, or associate, all Macintosh files with a specific type code to the corresponding MS-DOS extension.

- **Update All Extensions For All Types** This selection lets you update, or associate, all files to their corresponding Macintosh programs.

If you have Macintosh users who do not see the proper icons for MS-DOS files, and you know that the extensions have been mapped, you should update all of your extension mappings.

Configuration Password Maintenance

The Configuration Password Maintenance section of LMAC-MGR sets a password that must be entered whenever LMAC-MGR is run.

To set the password:

1. Select "Configuration Password Maintenance" and press **Enter**.

2. Select "Enable Password Protections" from the Configuration Password Options dialog box and press **Enter**.

3. Enter your password in the dialog box that appears and press the **Enter** key.

Your password is now set up. The other option you have is to disable the password for LMAC-MGR. To disable password protection:

1. Select "Configuration Password Maintenance" and press **Enter**.

2. Select "Disable Password Protections" from the Configuration Password Options dialog box and press **Enter**.

The password is now removed and anyone can access LMAC-MGR.

Managing Systems Files

All of the functions performed by the gateway server program LMSERVER.EXE depend on the System Configuration files, which are set up and managed by LMAC-MGR. The system files control the file names of the Macintosh files on the server, the DOS extension mappings, all user and group names, and other volume information. If one of these files becomes corrupted, LMSERVER will not run.

If these files become corrupted, you'll have to rebuild or restore the system files. If at all possible, you should restore the system files rather than rebuild them. But if you did not back them up, then you'll have to try using rebuilt files.

With the Manage Systems Files section, you also back up and restore the system files. If you have a complex gateway configuration, you'll want to back up the system files. This way, if something should happen to them, you can easily restore them without spending hours rebuilding your gateway's configuration.

To perform any of the functions available from the Manage Systems Files section:

1. Select "Manage Systems Files" and press **Enter**.
2. Select the function you want to perform and press **Enter**.

If you select Optimize System Files, the process will immediately begin, and your system files will be rebuilt and verified. Then you'll be returned to the System File Options dialog screen.

When backing up or restoring system files, you'll have to reboot the server if you've been running LANtastic. This is because the SHARE command is loaded with LANtastic, and the backup does not function if SHARE is in memory. After you restart:

1. Run LMAC-MGR.
2. Select "Manage Systems Files" and press **Enter**.
3. Select "Backup System Files."
4. Provide the path for the backup files and press **Enter**.

Since you're using a network, you might as well back up regularly to a LANtastic PC file server. This way you will not have to contend with floppies, and the files will always be accessible.

Using the Gateway

Once you have the gateway server configured and your system files backed up, you are ready to start using the gateway. The program LMSERVER.EXE is what controls the LANtastic for Macintosh gateway. It controls the access and directs all of the incoming and outgoing traffic, making sure every bit reaches its proper destination. Once you've configured your gateway server with LMAC-MGR, you're ready to fire up the gateway.

However, before starting LMSERVER, you should probably restart your gateway machine. This is because the LMAC-MGR program can be run without starting any of the network functions, even though the LANtastic PC network should be running when you use LMAC-MGR.

After you've started the STARTNET.BAT file, you need to change to the C:\LANMAC directory and run the LMSTART.BAT batch file. LMSERVER will start after the AppleTalk drivers and protocols are loaded, going through an initialization process where it reads the system files.

Once LMSERVER has started, you will see a screen like the one in Figure 4.27, which displays the gateway server's status.

There are a total of four screens that you can view from LMSERVER. They are:

- **Server** This screen (shown in Fig. 4.27) displays the LANtastic for Macintosh's status and efficiency. From the Server screen you can monitor the number of active sessions, the number of open files and how many are waiting to be opened, the read/write buffer usage, the command buffer usage, and the number of spooled print jobs. Also, the Server name is displayed, along with the date and time that the LANtastic for Macintosh server was started.

- **Volume** Displays the Macintosh volumes and their status, as shown in Figure 4.28.

- **User** The User screen shows all of the users who are logged into the gateway. It also displays the login time, the session number, the network number, and the node number for each user. Figure 4.29 shows LANtastic for Macintosh's User screen.

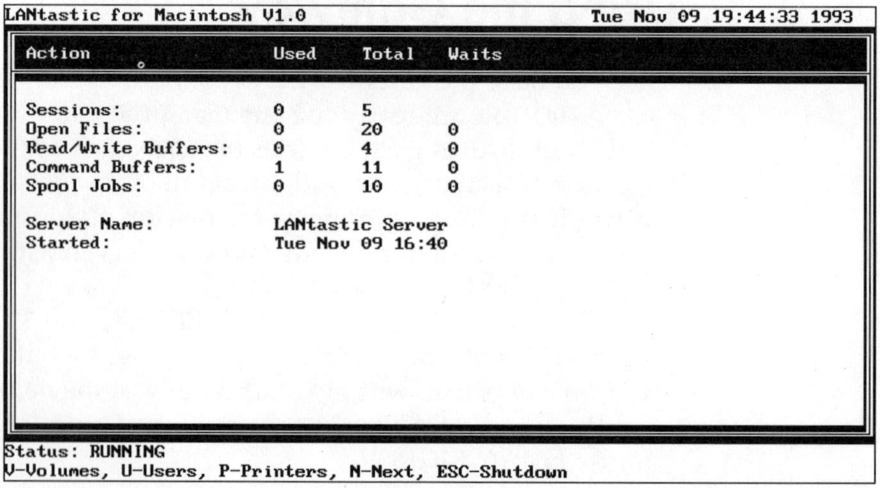

Figure 4.27
The LANtastic for Macintosh Server screen

```
LANtastic for Macintosh V1.0                    Tue Nov 09 19:44:33 1993
Action                    Used      Total     Waits

Sessions:                   0         5
Open Files:                 0        20         0
Read/Write Buffers:         0         4         0
Command Buffers:            1        11         0
Spool Jobs:                 0        10         0

Server Name:              LANtastic Server
Started:                  Tue Nov 09 16:40




Status: RUNNING
V-Volumes, U-Users, P-Printers, N-Next, ESC-Shutdown
```

USING A LANTASTIC MACINTOSH GATEWAY   163

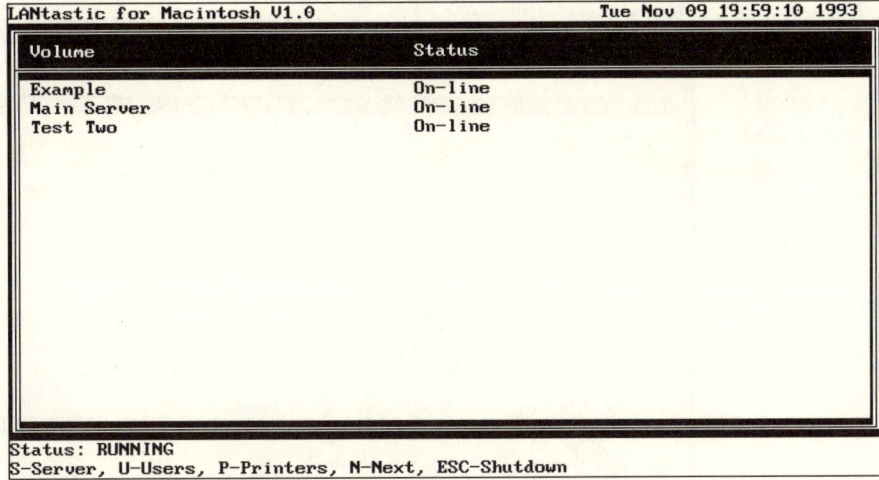

Figure 4.28
The Volume screen

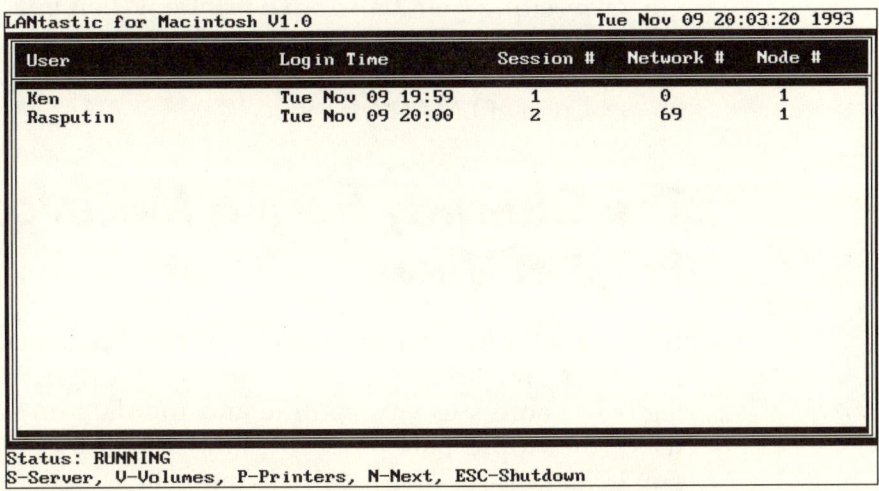

Figure 4.29
LANtastic for Macintosh's User screen

- **Printer**   From the Printer screen you can monitor and control the status of all printers routed through the gateway server. You can also see a printer's status: what type of device it is, how many documents are spooled, and how many documents are queued. Figure 4.30 shows the Printer screen for LANtastic for Macintosh. This is the only screen from which you control a server function other than shutting down the server.

The options you have for controlling a printer are stopping and starting the printer's print queue, stopping and starting print-

Figure 4.30

The Printer screen for LANtastic for Macintosh

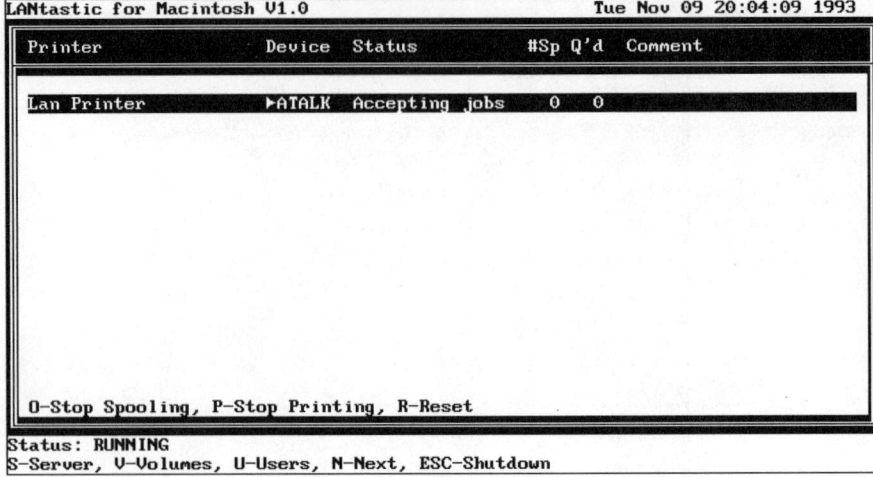

ing, or resetting (reinitializing) a printer. When you reset a printer, you will be sending the Laser Prep file to the printer, if the selected printer has the Laser Prep option set to YES in the Printer Management section of LMAC-Manager.

The Gateway from a Macintosh Point of View

LANtastic for Macintosh obeys all of the AppleShare rules except the Every and Administration privileges. A user with these privileges has access to any volume and the data on it. For all other users, the AppleShare procedures described in Chapter 3 apply to any LANtastic for Macintosh volume. The icon for a LANtastic for Macintosh volume looks like the Main Server icon in Figure 4.31.

Because LANtastic for Macintosh appears to the user as an AppleShare volume, there is no need to repeat the instructions about using the Finder's Sharing command. Instead, this section is going to concentrate on using the LAN MAC Manager program.

Figure 4.31

The LANtastic for Macintosh volume icon

Main Server

Using a LANtastic Macintosh Gateway

The LAN MAC Manager is the Macintosh administration program for LANtastic for Macintosh. The Macintosh administration program is essential, because you can perform any administration tasks on the gateway server without shutting down the server. If you had to shut down the server every time you wanted to modify a user profile, add a user or group, or set LANtastic access rights on a volume, it would rapidly become a problem. That is why we have the LAN MAC Manager.

When you start LAN MAC Manager, you will be presented with a Login dialog box. Even if you are logged into the LANtastic gateway as a user, you still have to log in as an administrator. Logging in as the administrator also counts as being an additional user.

With LAN MAC Manager, you can either get information or manipulate the following:

- Server info
- Volumes
- Users
- Groups
- File definitions
- File extensions
- Server shut-down

Figure 4.32 shows LAN MAC Manager with all of its windows open.

The File Definitions and Extensions windows do not open automatically when LAN MAC Manager is run, but all of the others do. All of LAN MAC Manager's functions can be executed from within the window for each function. The only window that is for information only is the Server Information window. In the Server Information window, you can see some of the same information that is in the LMSERVER Server Information window.

Each of the windows has buttons that enable you to perform various functions. If a button is grayed out, you need to select an item listed in the main window. Selecting an item in the list will enable the grayed-out button, and you can then perform the task specified by the button name. For the remainder of this section, I'll describe the functions that you can perform from each of the LAN MAC Manager windows, but detailed steps will be skipped.

Figure 4.32

LAN MAC Manager

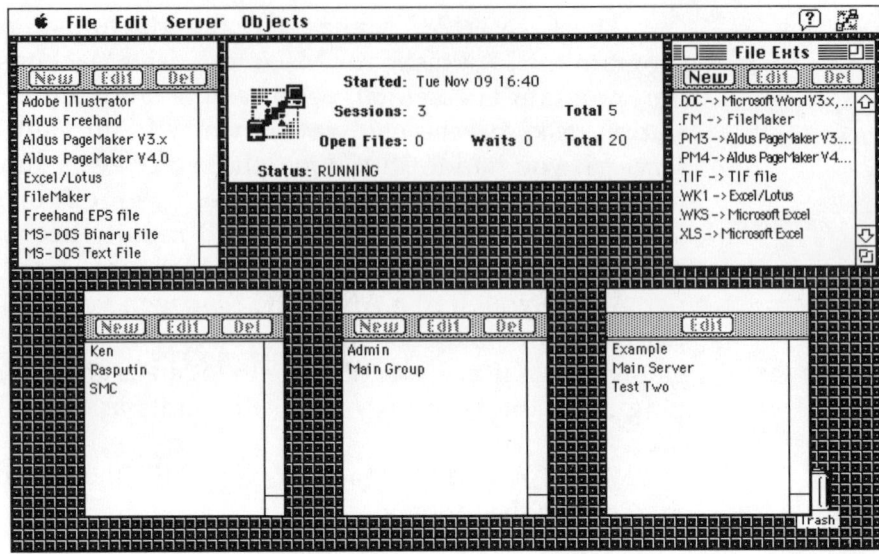

The remaining windows all let you perform some function. The windows and the functions you can perform from them are listed below:

- **Groups** From within the Groups window you can edit, add, or delete a user group. Figure 4.33 shows the Groups window and its associated Add Group and Edit Group windows.

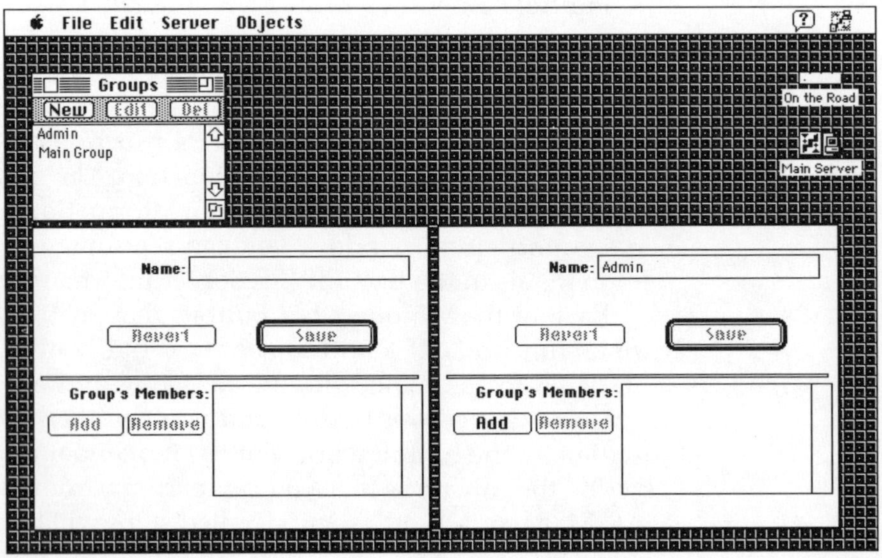

Figure 4.33

The Groups window and its associated function windows

Using a LANtastic Macintosh Gateway

The primary functions you can perform from the Groups window are to add, delete, or modify a group. When you modify or add a group, you can also add or remove users from a specific group. To add a user, click on the Add button and a list of users will appear. Double-clicking on the user will add that user. Likewise, to remove a user, all you do is select the user name and press the Delete button.

- **Users** Just like the Groups window, the Users window lets you add, edit, and delete users. In addition to these functions, you can assign the user's primary group and assign user LANtastic access privileges. The methods for modifying, adding, deleting, and assigning are the same as those described in the Groups section above. Figure 4.34 shows the Users window with its associated New User and Edit User windows.

- **Volumes** From the Volumes window, the only option you have is to edit a volume's attributes. The Edit function allows you to set the same information for a volume as you would from LMAC-MGR when you edit a volume. You can assign the owner, group, password, and access privileges. You can also lock a volume so it is read-only. Figure 4.35 shows the Volume and Edit Volume windows.

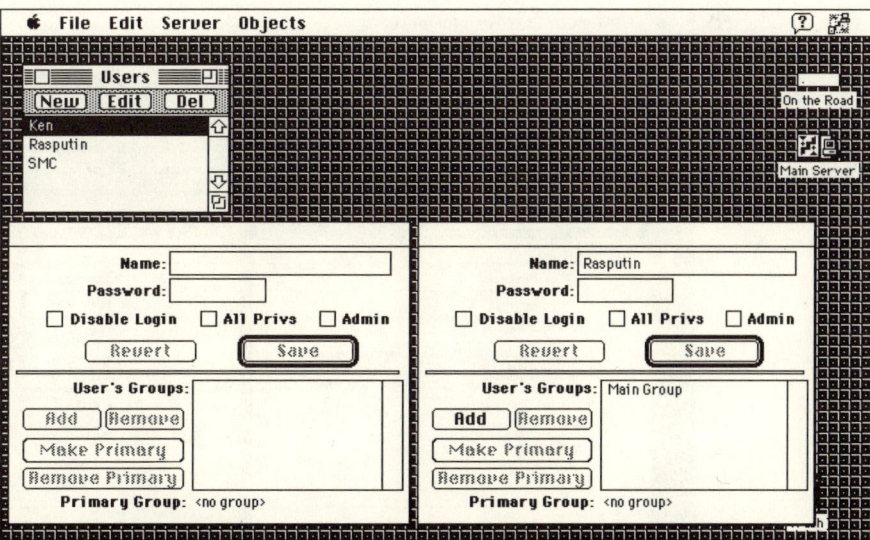

Figure 4.34
The Users window with its associated New User and Edit User windows

Figure 4.35

The Volume and Edit Volume windows

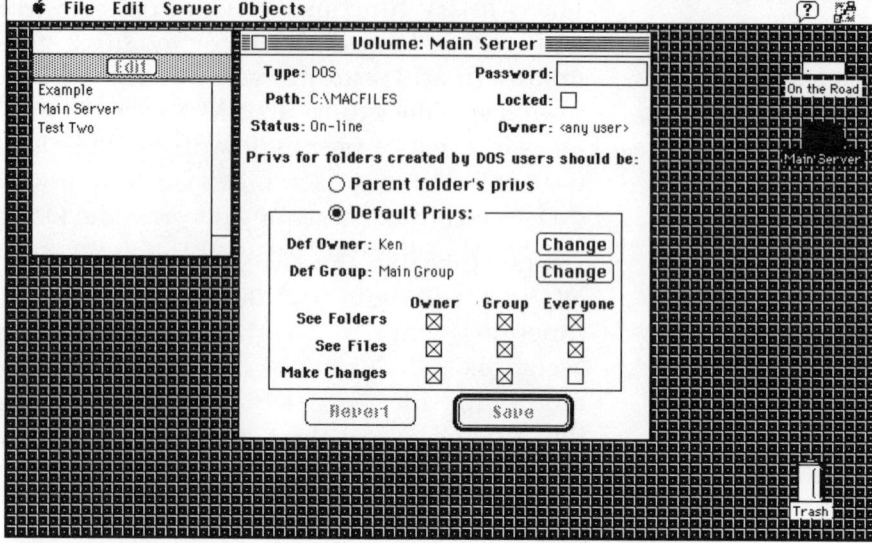

- **File Definitions** From the File Definition window you can add, edit, or delete a program's MS-DOS extension mapping. A file definition must be created before you can add an MS-DOS extension. To create the file definition, you will have to know the application's type and creator codes. Figure 4.36 shows the File Definitions window and its Add and Edit windows.

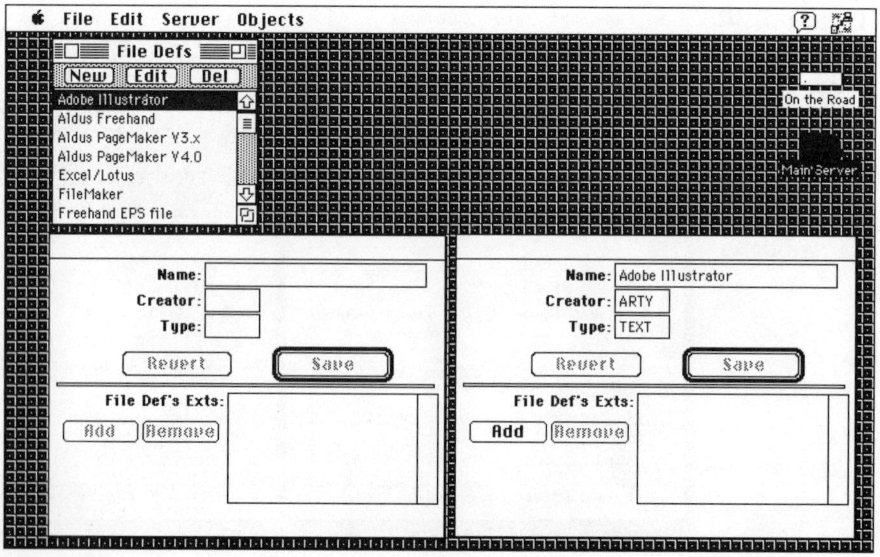

Figure 4.36

The File Definitions window and its associated windows

Using a LANtastic Macintosh Gateway

- **File Extensions** The File Extensions window lets you add, edit, or delete MS-DOS file extensions. You have to create a file definition before you can add an MS-DOS extension. Once you have a file definition created, all you have to do to add an extension is enter the extension in the Add window, then select the file definition by clicking on the Select File Def button. Figure 4.37 shows File Extensions window and its Add and Edit windows.

MAC LAN Manager is an easy program to use and a useful tool. Remember that to use it, you must log in as a user who has LANtastic administration access.

Trouble-shooting LANtastic for Macintosh

As with all software, sometimes something will not work properly. Thus, it is possible that you might have problems with LANtastic for Macintosh. Usually, any problem you'll encounter will be minor and easy to fix. In this section we'll look at some of the more common problems you might encounter. If you run into a problem that is not covered here or in the LANtastic for Macintosh manual, call Artisoft tech support.

Figure 4.37

The File Extensions window and its Add and Edit windows

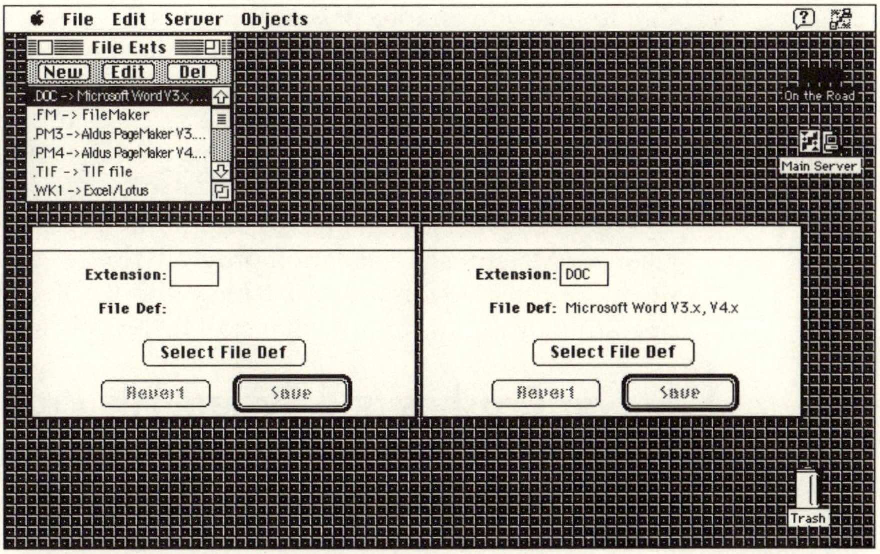

The types of problems you'll encounter will probably fall into one of the following categories:

- Configuration errors
- Server crashes
- Memory or buffer problems
- Printer problems

For each of these categories we'll discuss some of the symptoms, causes, and possible solutions.

Configuration Errors

Configuration errors occur when you first attempt to run the LMSTART.BAT file to start the server. Usually, the problem is an error in the NET.CFG file, the LMSTART.BAT, or one of the other DOS configuration files like the CONFIG.SYS or AUTOEXEC.BAT. One other problem you might have with the initial starting of the gateway is a memory error.

Any error during the initial startup will probably be accompanied by an error message from LMSERVER and displayed across the bottom of the screen. Usually, the error message will point you toward the cause of the problem or recommend a solution.

Appendix C in the LANtastic for Macintosh manual has a list of errors that you might see, and it gives recommended solutions for each error message. Although this list is not complete, it should give you an idea of where to look.

If your error message mentions AppleTalk or the network adapter card, you will have to check your manual for the adapter, the adapter's configuration, and the settings in the NET.CFG file to make sure the adapter's settings in the NET.CFG file match the card's configuration.

Usually, you will not have configuration problems. The LANtastic for Macintosh installation program does a good job of setting up these files. Also, you must have the LANtastic PC network operating properly before you install LANtastic for Macintosh.

Server Crashes and System File Problems

The one thing you can do to keep your problems to a minimum is to back up your system files. If the gateway server crashes for whatever reason, the system index files will probably be corrupted because they are always open. If the server appears to operate properly after a crash, it is probable that the index files are corrupted. So to be safe, it is better to restore the server's system files than to risk using the files on the crashed server.

Any errors dealing with system files that are missing or corrupted can be fixed by restoring the system files from a backup or by running the LMAC-MGR program. If you use the LMAC-MAC Manager program to fix a file, be sure to test the server thoroughly before you back up the system files and delete your previous backup. If you back up corrupted system files, chances are you'll overwrite a good backup with a bad one and have to reconfigure the gateway server from scratch.

Be sure to check for any error messages in the LANtastic for Macintosh manual. If the error message is in the manual, you could save yourself lots of time by following Artisoft's recommended fix.

Memory or Buffer Problems

As you use the gateway server and add users, you'll find that you will need to adjust the system buffers on the server. It is quite possible that you'll have memory problems if your server gets heavy usage. This is because the server uses conventional memory with only some of the LANtastic network software operating when loaded high. You will have to experiment to find your optimum configuration.

The error messages you receive when you're having memory problems are quite specific and will usually say something like "Error: Initializing System buffer error code -10". Most of these error messages result from insufficient base memory. Make sure you are not running any TSR programs on the server, and optimize your memory by carefully setting any system environment settings so that they use the minimum amount of memory. Doing things like setting the LASTDRIVE to K instead of Z will free a small amount of memory. Check your MS-DOS manual to get more information about optimizing the server's memory.

If you're running MS-DOS 6.0, you can try putting all of the commands from the STARTNET.BAT and LMSTART.BAT files into the AUTOEXEC.BAT file and then running MEMMAKER to let MS-DOS automatically optimize your system's memory. However, don't do this unless you are familiar with MS-DOS and know how to reverse the changes that are made automatically. Anything you can do to conserve conventional memory will help your gateway run more efficiently.

Printer Problems

The area where you may have the most problems is with the printer set-up and configuration. Most of the error messages in the LANtastic for Macintosh manual deal with one type of printer problem or another. If you're using a PostScript printer that is connected to a MS-DOS machine, make sure you can print to the printer before you set up LANtastic for Macintosh. This will probably save you a lot of time.

Sometimes a PostScript printer will hang when it tries to print a job if it has received bad data. If the server is queuing your print jobs and they are not being printed, even though you do not see any error messages you should physically restart the printer, and then (if you've set the printer resource to use the Laser Prep option) reset the printer from the gateway's console. This may be enough to kick the problem loose.

There are also times when you may have to delete the printer system files and either restore them from your backup or recreate them using LMAC-MGR. If you have to delete the printer system files, you can do so by deleting the PR_*.*, PQ_*.*, and PRN_RES.* files. This is a common fix, used for several of the error messages that deal with resource files that can't be opened or found.

On other occasions, you will have to delete queued jobs using the LANtastic NET_MGR program to clear the queue and then have your users print their jobs again. Once again, the error messages can be of great help, and if all else fails, contact Artisoft tech support.

Conclusion

LANtastic for Macintosh may seem to be a bit weak when compared to the other NOSs in this book. But for a small or medium-sized business that already has a LANtastic network installed, or one that wishes for an inexpensive and efficient network, it can be just the right solution.

Using a LANtastic Macintosh Gateway

This chapter should provide you with a solid operational knowledge of LANtastic for Macintosh, enabling you to set up and configure a gateway server. At the same time, you will know where your problems are most likely to occur and have some idea about how to fix them. Also, the information in this chapter exceeds the information in the LANtastic for Macintosh manual in almost all respects, although I have been told by Artisoft that they are rewriting their manual. Hopefully, it will be better in its next incarnation.

Connecting Your Macintosh to a Novell Server

Introduction

When you purchase NetWare for Macintosh, you receive the software necessary for networking your Novell server and your Macintoshes, plus a four-hundred-page manual. The problem is that this chapter is only about 40 pages. If you have ever tried to read the Novell manual and then set up the NetWare for Macintosh services, you will understand why Novell has Certified Novell Engineers (CNE) and Certified Novell Administrators (CNA).

    For a small office, the expense of hiring or training a CNE or a CNA to connect your Macs could be a major expense. Also, you could be a CNE or CNA and not have much hands-on experience with Macintoshes, in which case your only advantage is that you know better how to interpret the manual. Whatever your position or your need, this chapter will provide you with a concise and easy means for installing NetWare for Macintosh and setting up a Novell print server.

To accomplish this goal, this chapter discusses the following topics:

- Novell network configurations
- Preparing your server and installing the NetWare for Macintosh software
- Connecting your Mac
- Testing your network
- Making sense of the Novell AppleTalk printing services
- Accessing a Novell server with third-party software

If you are thinking about connecting a Mac to a Novell network and you do not want to install the NetWare for Macintosh software, you should read the section on Accessing a Novell Server with Third-Party Software before you buy NetWare for Macintosh. It is possible that you could save yourself some headaches and simplify your life.

Just the Facts Please (Various Server Configurations)

As we have demonstrated in Chapter 2, it is possible to configure Macintosh networks in a variety of ways. NetWare configurations can be—and in large companies, usually are—quite complex, which means that it is possible to connect your Mac(s) to your Novell network in a variety of ways. You can use AppleTalk, EtherTalk, Token Ring, and any number of router and gateway options.

This section discusses some of the different topologies you could be using, although this chapter will use a simple and straightforward Ethernet networking topology for its examples. More important than the actual topology of your network are the nuts and bolts for connecting a Macintosh to your network. Using a simple network configuration makes it easier to concentrate on Macintosh integration. Just remember that the software configurations will vary depending on your NetWare network configuration.

Macintosh Network Cards

If you are using an Ethernet, ARCnet, or Token Ring configuration for your Novell network and you want to use the same topology for your Macs, you have an almost plug-and-play solution when you use NetWare for Macintosh. All you need to do is install the card or SCSI adapter, install the card's drivers into or onto your Macs, and connect the cables. After that, you install the NetWare for Macintosh onto the NetWare server(s) that will be used with your Macs.

If you are using Ethernet, you will probably be using 10BaseT, coaxial, or ThickNet for your cabling. All of these cable types are supported by the Mac. Also, any Mac can be connected to an Ethernet network, even Macs without card slots. You can use an Ethernet card or an Ethernet SCSI adapter. If you want to add a Mac to a Token Ring or ARCnet network, you must have a Macintosh with a NuBus or PDS (Processor Direct Slot) slot; there are no SCSI Macintosh adapters for these protocols.

Because your network topology will depend on what you already have set up, it is difficult to say what Macintosh topology you should use. Figure 5.1 shows several possible network configurations combined into a single internet. You will see in the figure that there are Macs at different points within the network and they can all communicate with the servers.

This is because NetWare for Macintosh adds the AppleTalk Filing Protocol to the NetWare Network Operating System. If you use Ethernet or Token Ring adapters, your server will act as a router, and the Mac will just be another workstation on the network in whatever zone you choose. What makes using a Mac on a Novell network so nice is that you do not need to add any software to the Mac for this to work.

Once NetWare for Macintosh is installed, you can access your servers and shared printers using standard Macintosh System software. However, you need to keep in mind that even when they connect to a NetWare server, your Macs can also network with each other using System 7's peer-to-peer networking.

The Mac's native capabilities are very similar to those used by Microsoft's Windows for Workgroups: even while being connected to a Novell server, the Windows workstation can share files with another Windows for Workgroups workstation. As the sys-

Figure 5.1
A NetWare network with several Macintoshes

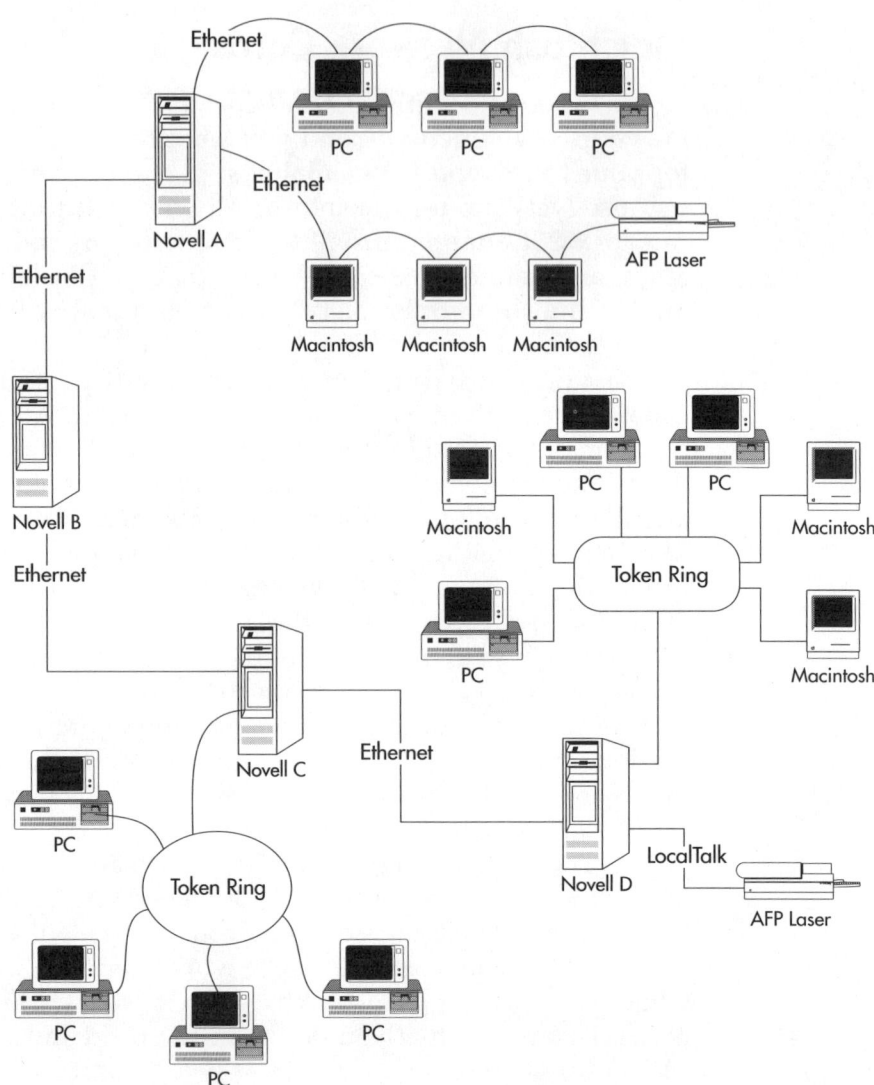

tem administrator, you need to keep this in mind, although it in no way affects how your Mac will work with the NetWare network—except possibly by adding to the overall network traffic. If your network traffic is already heavy, you may not want your users using the Mac's peer-to-peer capabilities.

Unfortunately, the Macintosh file-sharing process does not work in reverse. You cannot access a shared Macintosh volume using the Novell NOS from a MS-DOS machine unless the MS-DOS machine has the proper software installed, such as Farallon's

Connecting Your Macintosh to a Novell Server

PhoneNET PC. Farallon's PhoneNET PC will be discussed in Chapter 8.

NetWare as an AppleTalk Router

Figure 5.1 shows a Macintosh AppleTalk network where all of the Macs are connected using a star topology; one Mac is acting as a file server and an Ethernet gateway. There is another configuration you can set up that will let you use your Macs' built-in AppleTalk network, with the Novell server acting as the gateway. Figure 5.2 shows a Novell network with MS-DOS workstations using Ethernet and Macs using LocalTalk.

In Figure 5.2, the Novell server has a Dayna Communications DL2000 AppleTalk card installed. Dayna's card is the only one

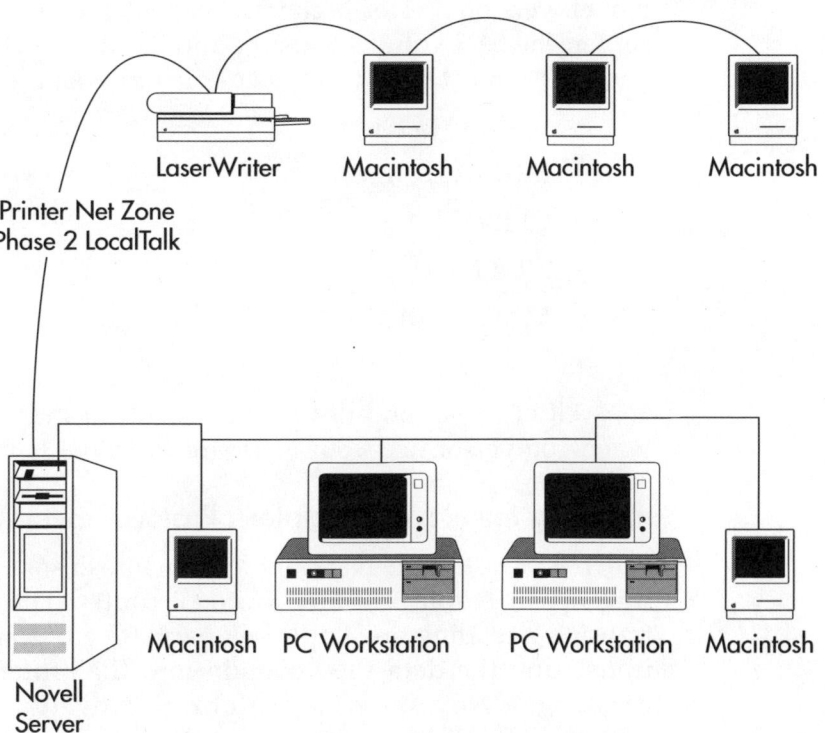

Figure 5.2
A NetWare configuration using an AppleTalk card in the server

supported by NetWare. This could be because Novell licensed its original AFP software from Dayna. In any case, this configuration will let you use the Macintosh's built-in AppleTalk hardware, eliminating the expense of the Ethernet hardware, while providing you with full access to the Novell network.

Preparing Your Novell Server for the Mac Invasion

As already stated, you must install Novell's NetWare for Macintosh before you can connect a Mac to your Novell network. (Two other ways for connecting Macs to a Novell network will be discussed the last section of this chapter.) The installation is straightforward and uses Novell's INSTALL.NLM. This section will walk you through the steps for installing NetWare for Macintosh.

Before you install NetWare for Macintosh, you must be using Novell version 3.11 or higher, DOS needs to be in memory on the server, the SYS volume must be mounted, and the following files and NLMs must be in the System directory on the volume SYS.

- STREAMS.NLM
- BRRIEVE.NLM
- CLIB.NLM
- NUT.NLM
- MAC.NAM
- V_MAC

All of these modules should been put in their proper places when you performed your NetWare version 3.11 installation.

Installing the Novell-Macintosh Protocol Layers

When you install the NetWare for Macintosh software, you are setting up an AppleTalk File Protocol router. The router acts as a translator, reading the AppleTalk packets sent from your Macs and translating the data they contain into IPX (Internetwork Packet eXchange), Novell's native protocol. Novell accomplishes this with the AFP.NLM.

It is possible to perform the entire installation by adding the NetWare for Macintosh software to your Novell server. Although there are NetWare utilities for the Macintosh, and you need them

CONNECTING YOUR MACINTOSH TO A NOVELL SERVER

to take full advantage of the Novell server, your Macs will be able to use the Novell network resources with just the Mac's standard operating system. This means that the most important aspect of setting up NetWare for Macintosh must be done at your server.

To install your NetWare for Macintosh software:

1. Check your SYS volume to make sure you have enough disk space.
2. Prepare the server volumes that will be used with Macintoshes so they can use Macintosh file names.
3. Load Novell's INSTALL.NLM and start the installation.
4. Configure NetWare for Macintosh.
5. Exit Install. (Setup for printers is explained in the next section; if you wish, you can also configure the printer before exiting Install.)

Each of these steps will be explained in detail. The examples used in the explanation will not necessarily reflect your network, but all of the basics for setting up NetWare for Macintosh are covered. You should review your manual, using these steps as a guide to get through the manual, especially if you are new to NetWare. (When I was new to NetWare, it took me quite some time to be able to figure out the installation steps. Hopefully, this section will save you some grief.)

Step 1

Check your SYS volume to make sure you have enough disk space for the Macintosh support files and printer queues. If you do not have much space on your .SYS volume, you can use a switch (-d and path name) with ATPS. This command places the print queue onto the specified volume. You must designate a directory where NetWare can create a subdirectory called PRINT, if it does not already exist. If you use this option, you will have to delete any pre-existing queues created by ATPS with the PCONSOLE utility from an MS-DOS machine.

If you are going to use your server as a print spooler for a PostScript printer, you may need to reserve up to 10M of disk space, and maybe more. You should base your decision on the types of files that will be printed and on the number of users using the print spool. Macintosh graphics files converted to PostScript can take up a lot of disk space while they are being spooled.

An example is the printing of a fax received by a Mac. A single page, when spooled, will use over 2M of disk space. In this case, to spool a four-page fax, you would need 8M. The good news is that as soon as the document is printed, the queue is cleared and the disk space is reclaimed. However, you can see that several users printing at once could cause a traffic jam, resulting in frustrated people who can't get their documents printed. (This is also a reason for letting Macs print directly to their own LaserWriter. You'll find more reasons below.)

Step 2

Prepare the server volumes that will be used with Macintoshes so they can use Macintosh file names.

The following instructions use programs that were installed during NetWare 3.11's initial setup.

1. Edit your STARTUP.NCF file to include the command lines

    ```
    LOAD MAC
    SET MINIMUM PACKET RECEIVE BUFFERS=100
    ```

2. From the server console, load the (MAC.NAM) Macintosh name space capability by typing **LOAD MAC**. If you restarted your server after completing step 1, above, you do not need to run the LOAD MAC command.

3. From the server console, type the command **ADD NAME SPACE MACINTOSH TO VOLUME [VOLUME_NAME]**. You must repeat this command for each volume that will be used by a Macintosh client. This command sets up the means for a Macintosh to store files on a server volume using normal Macintosh naming conventions. A Macintosh user will not be able to use a volume if the Macintosh name space has not been configured.

Step 3

Load Novell's INSTALL.NLM and start the installation. From your server console, you need to perform the following tasks:

1. Type **LOAD INSTALL**. This command loads the NetWare installation module.

Connecting Your Macintosh to a Novell Server

2. Select "Product Options" from the Installation Options window.
3. When the Currently Installed Products window appears, press the **Insert** key.
4. Insert your NetWare for Macintosh disk into a floppy disk drive.
5. Enter the drive letter for the diskette that contains the NetWare for Macintosh files, or the path name if you copied the files to your hard disk, and then press the **Enter** key.
6. Confirm that the proper STARTUP.NFC file is selected and press the **Enter** key.
7. Select the Install NW_MAC option to copy the NetWare for Macintosh files onto your server.

Step 4

After installing the NetWare for Macintosh files, you need to edit your AUTOEXEC.NCF file before your NetWare server will act as an AppleShare File Server.

1. When the update is complete, you will be returned to the Currently Installed Products window. In it, you will see a line that says "NW-MAC v3.01 NetWare for Macintosh." This line will automatically be selected unless you have an additional add-on product installed. Select the NetWare for Macintosh line and press the **Enter** Key.
2. Select the line "SYS;\SYSTEM\AUTOEXEC.NCF" from the Editable Configuration Files window and press the **Enter** key.
3. The following is the AUTOEXEC.CFG file from the Server Inferno. The line numbers are added for reference; your

> **Note**
>
> There are several ways to edit your AUTOEXEC.NCF file. The configuration settings from this point on will have to be made to accommodate your system. This means that you may have to go back to the manual to make sure your configuration settings are correct. The following steps are for a server and Macintoshes all running on Ethernet.

AUTOEXEC.CFG should not have line numbers. Lines 1 through 4, 8, 10, and 11 are all part of the original AUTOEXEC.CFG from before NetWare for the Mac was installed.

1. file server name INFERNO
2. ipx internal net AAA1
3. load NE2000 port=300 int=3
   frame=ETHERNET_802.3
4. bind IPX to NE2000 net=AAB1
5. **load appletlk net=55000 zone={"Zone 1"}**
6. **load ne2000 port=300 int=3
   frame=ethernet_snap name=esnap**
7. **bind appletlk esnap net 101-105
   zone={"Zone 1"}**
8. mount all
9. **load afp**
10. load remote
11. load rspx
12. **load atps**

Lines 5 through 7 and 9 are the minimum necessary for a Macintosh to access a NetWare network after NetWare for Macintosh is installed. Line 5 loads the AppleTalk module and sets the AppleTalk zones for the network, just like line 2 loads the NetWare's IPX protocol layer. Line 6 loads the LAN drivers for the Ethernet card, and line 7 binds the AppleTalk protocol to the LAN drivers and specifies which zone (from those assigned in line 5) will be used with the adapter card. Line 9 loads the AppleTalk File Protocol, and line 12 loads the AppleTalk Print Services.

Step 5

Exit Install. (Set-up for printers is explained in the next section; if you wish, you can also configure the printer before exiting Install.)

Generally speaking, the principles behind loading the AppleTalk File Protocol are the same as setting up the standard NetWare services. If you are using multiple network cards in your server, such as a Dayna Communications AppleTalk card or Token Ring cards, your CONFIG.NFC file will have to be modified to reflect the different adapters. The principal steps are:

1. Load the AppleTalk module, assign the network number, and set up the zones.

Connecting Your Macintosh to a Novell Server

2. Load the LAN drivers for your network adapters.
3. Bind AppleTalk to the LAN drivers and assign the LAN driver to a zone.
4. Load the AppleTalk File Protocol.

When you load the AppleTalk module, you have to assign both a network number and a zone. The type of network number you use must coincide with the network transport protocol. If you are going to use Phase 2 Ethernet, you need to use a network number that reflects Phase 2 network. Again, this principle applies to any of the various network cards you might use.

When assigning zones, you can either assign the zone names by specifying them on the command line that loads the AppleTalk module, or you can use the ATZONES.CFG file. With the ATZONES.CFG file, it is easier to assign zones to specific network numbers. To use the ATZONES.CFG file, you need to use the switch "-z" in place of the zone assignment on the line that loads the AppleTalk module.

NetWare then reads the contents of the ATZONES.CFG file into memory. As each bind statement is executed, NetWare reads the zone name, and then assigns the zone to the network number associated with it, as defined in the ATZONES.CFG file. The ATZONES.CFG file makes it easier to set up your server as a multi-protocol router, or to set up zones to set up multi-purpose zones. The following is a sample ATZONES.CFG file:

```
net=AAB1 zone={"Zone 1"}
net=AAB2 zone={"Zone 2"}
net=AAB3-AAB6 zone={
"Zone 3"
"Zone 4"
"Zone 5"
"Zone 6"
}
```

Although using the ATZONES.CFG file is not necessary, it can be useful, depending on your network configuration—especially if you need to set your network in Transition Mode. Transition Mode is where you have an internet that uses a several different network adapter cards. If you need more information about assigning different zones, you should refer to your NetWare manual.

A Brief Look at ATCON

ATCON is an NLM that allows you to manage your AppleTalk routers from either a server or a remote console. If you think one of your AppleTalk routers is down, if you are having network problems, or if you think you are having problems related to your AppleTalk networks, ATCON can perform a variety of diagnostics for you. The different functions you can perform with ATCON are:

- **Echo Test**   Verifies node-to-node communications.
- **Lookup Service**   Verifies what specific services are available.
- **Router Interfaces**   This function lets you view all of the AppleTalk router interfaces, both those assigned to the internal network and those assigned to different interface cards.
- **Router Options**   Lets you view the options you specified on the LOAD. APPLETALK line.
- **Router Statistics**   Lets you view detailed information about the packet traffic on a specific router.
- **Stack Interface**   Lets you view the internal network.
- **Stack Statistics**   Displays statistics on packets processed by the AppleTalk stack.
- **View the RTMP Table**   This function displays information for all AppleTalk networks accessible by a specific router.
- **View System Log**   Displays the System Log so you can check for errors.
- **Zone List**   Lists all of the AppleTalk zones processed by the AppleTalk stack.

To run ATCON, all you need to do is type **LOAD ATCON** from the server or remote console and select one of the options above. ATCON is a diagnostic tool: it will only help you locate a problem, not solve it.

Connecting Your Mac

Once your server is set up, logging into a NetWare server is very simple. All you have to do is access the server using Apple's built-in

Connecting Your Macintosh to a Novell Server

networking software, which is called AppleShare. Even though NetWare for the Mac comes with some utilities for controlling certain NetWare functions from a Mac, none of these utilities is necessary if you just want to access the server and printing services. The following sections discuss preparing and accessing a NetWare server from your Mac, plus installing and using the NetWare Macintosh utilities.

Preparing Your Mac

The only preparation you need perform on your Mac is the installation of AppleShare Workstation software. The AppleShare Workstation software is an installable option for Macintosh System versions 6.0.X and 7.X. The installation varies slightly depending on your System version. The procedure for installing and using the AppleShare software is covered in Chapter 2.

The Macintosh NetWare Utilities

The Macintosh NetWare Utilities are included with the NetWare for Macintosh 3.11 package. On the disk MAC UTILITIES v2.11 you will find the following items:

- Two Readme files
- TeachText, a text editor with which to read the Readme files
- Notify, a System extension for use with the NetWare messaging system
- NetWare Control Center, a supervisor's control and set-up utility
- NetWare DA for System 7.X
- NetWare DA for System 6.X
- NetWare UAM, NetWare User Authentication Method Macintosh software

The NetWare DAs use the following modules to give the user access to different Novell network services:

- **About**   Describes the NetWare Macintosh utilities.
- **Message**   Sends broadcast messages to other users on the network.
- **Print Queue**   Provides information on queued print jobs.

Figure 5.3

NetWare's Mac Utilities disk

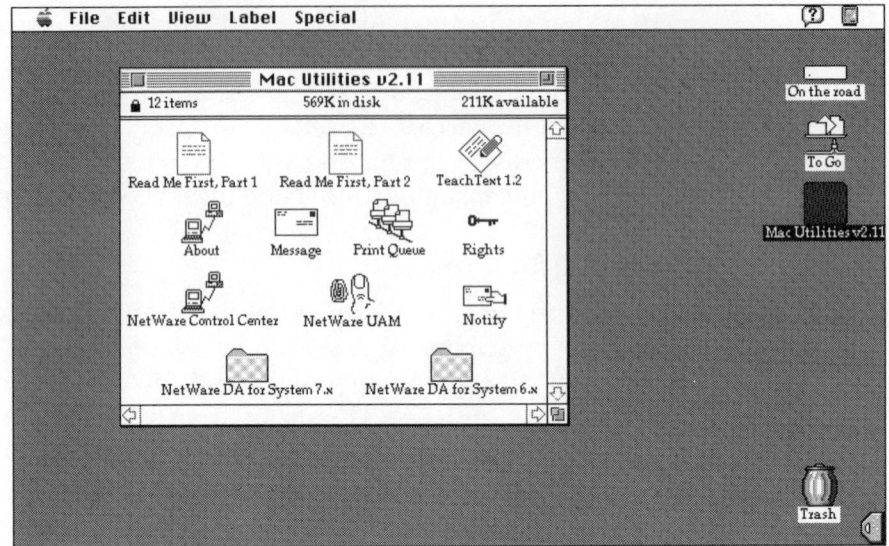

- **Rights** Provides information and some management capabilities for assigning access rights to folders and files.

Figure 5.3 shows the contents of NetWare's Mac Utilities disk.

Installing the NetWare Macintosh Utilities

How you install the Novell utilities depends on your Macintosh System version. Because System 7 is the prevalent Macintosh operating system, the installation procedures listed here are for System 7.X. The differences between a System 7 and a System 6 installation will be noted.

After you have inserted your Macintosh Utilities disk, follow the steps below to perform a complete installation.

1. Open the NetWare DA for System 7.X folder and copy the NetWare DA onto your System folder icon. The DA will automatically be copied into the Apple Menu Items folder inside the System folder. If you are installing the NetWare DA on a Mac with System 7, you will have to use Apple's Font/DA Mover. (Instructions for using the Font/DA Mover can be found in your Macintosh user's manual.)

2. Create a folder anywhere on your hard drive and call it anything you want. NetWare might be a good choice, but it really doesn't matter.

3. Copy About, Message, Print Queue, Rights, and NetWare UAM into the folder created in step 2.

4. Copy Notify into your System Folder by dragging it into your closed System folder. It will be copied into your Extensions folder. If you are using System 6.0.X, Notify will just float loose in your System folder.

5. Copy the NetWare Control Center onto your hard drive. This can be placed anywhere you wish.

6. Restart your Macintosh.

7. Open the NetWare desk accessory and click on Setup. The first time you open the NetWare DA, you will be asked to locate the NetWare Modules you placed in the "name anything you want" folder. Once you have told the NetWare DA where to locate the modules, it will remember where they are, and you will only have to relocate them if you move their folder.

8. Open the System folder and create a folder called "AppleShare folder." Copy the NetWare UAM module into the AppleShare folder. (See Fig. 5.4.) If you wish, you can also place the DA modules into this folder.

The above steps complete the Macintosh installation of the NetWare Utilities.

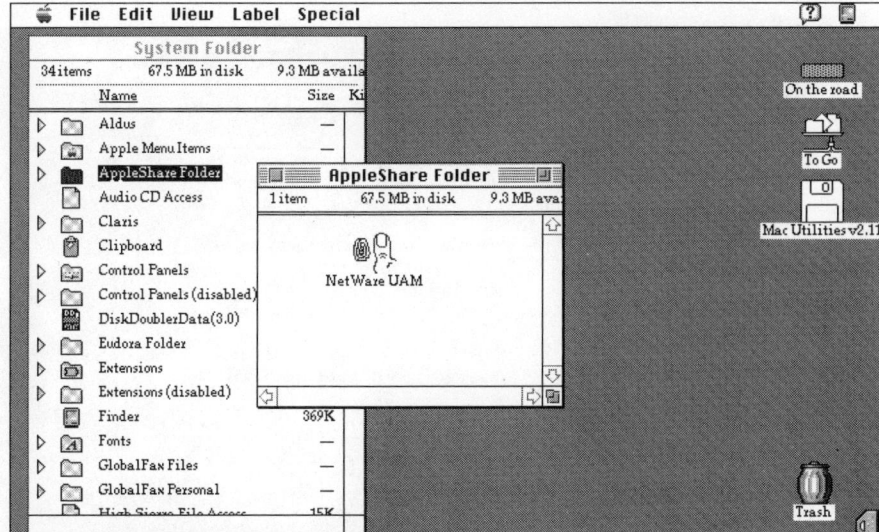

Figure 5.4

Setting up NetWare's Mac utilities

Using the NetWare Macintosh Utilities

When you open the NetWare desk accessory, you will see four different NetWare Utilities that correspond to the modules you placed in the NetWare folder. Figure 5.5 shows the NetWare DA as it appears when you first open the DA.

When the NetWare utility is launched, the About utility is automatically opened. This module gives you a brief description of each NetWare Macintosh module.

The second module is the Message module. With the Message module, you can send a message to any Macintosh, MS-DOS, or Windows user who has the NetWare Notify module installed. Message is a small chat package allowing real-time messaging with the user you select. Figure 5.6 shows the Message module after a message has been sent to the network supervisor.

The third module is Print Queue, for managing any documents you may send to a print queue. Unless you are logged into the network as a supervisor or have supervisor privileges, you will only be able to manage documents created by the Macintosh accessing the queue.

In the queue window, you will be able to see all of the print jobs and the order in which they were placed on the queue. Figure 5.7 shows two queued jobs, with one selected for manipulation.

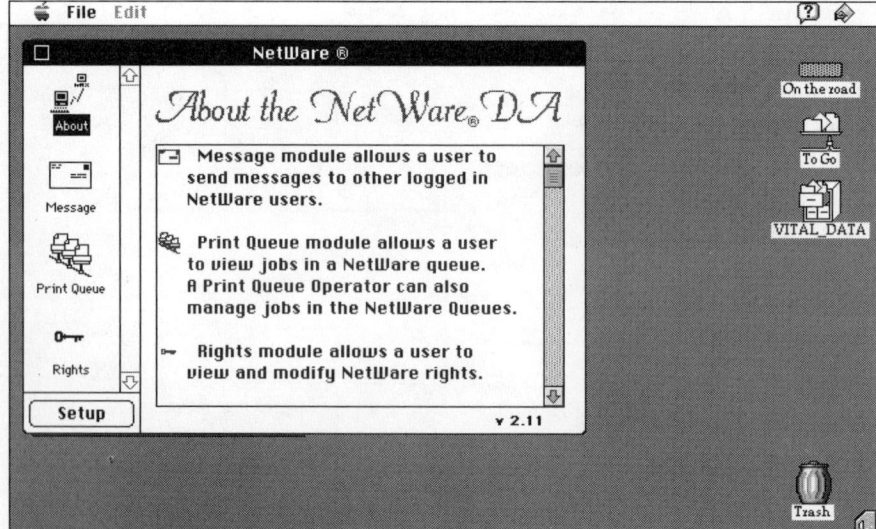

Figure 5.5
Opening NetWare's Mac utilities

Figure 5.6

NetWare's Message module

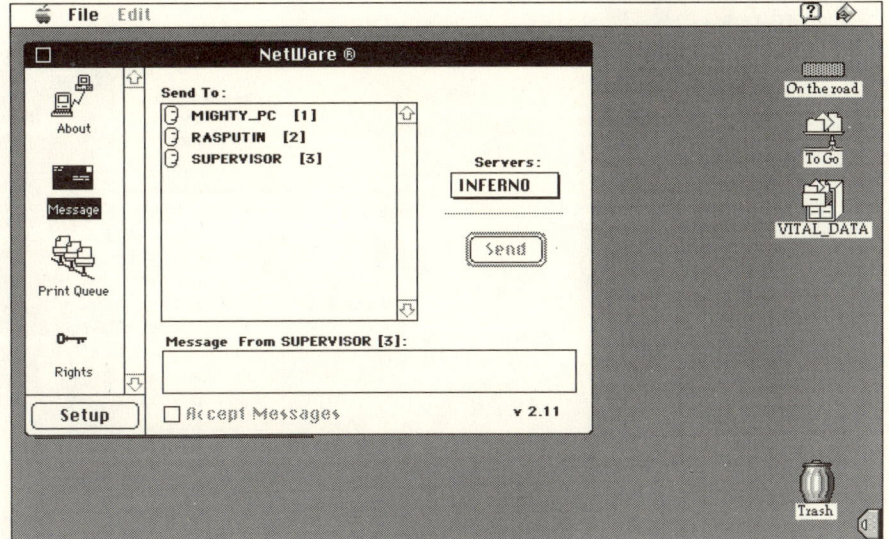

Figure 5.7

NetWare's Print Queue module

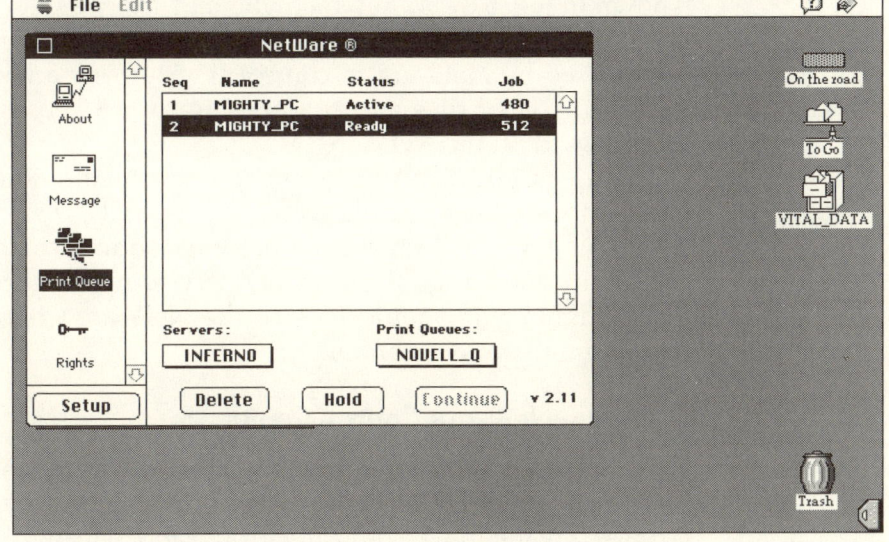

The manipulations that can be performed with Print Queue are the deletion of a queued job, holding a queued job to be printed later, and the releasing of a held item with the Continue button. If you have queue manipulation capabilities, you can manipulate any of the jobs in the queue.

The final module is called "Rights." When you click on Rights, you are presented with a Macintosh Open dialog box

Figure 5.8

NetWare's Rights module

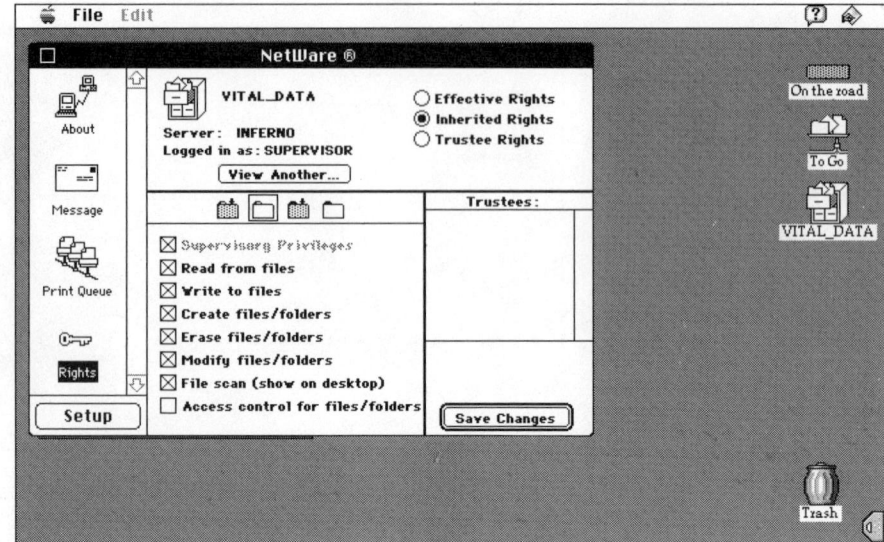

(shown in Fig. 5.8), from which you can select a folder or a file and see what rights have been assigned to it. *Rights* are the mechanisms used by NetWare to control which users a have access to a particular set of files and folders. Figure 5.8 shows the "Rights" module with in the NetWare DA.

Unless you are the network supervisor, you should not change the rights for a file or folder. Actually, you can only view the rights for a file, unless the network supervisor has given you the ability to change those rights. If you need more information about Rights, you should look in the NetWare Concepts and System Administration manuals.

Using the NetWare Control Center

The NetWare Control Center (NCC) is the Macintosh equivalent of SYSCON or USERDEF. With NCC you can create users and Groups, create and assign directories, and set the rights attributes for your server. If you are comfortable using the Mac, it is quicker and easier to use than SYSCON.

Figure 5.9 shows NCC with all of the windows open for our sample network. In Figure 5.9 you can see the User List, the Group List, the NetWare File Servers window, and the server volumes INFERNO.SYS, PRECIOUS, and VITAL_DATA. To use NCC effectively, you need to log into the server as a supervisor.

Connecting Your Macintosh to a Novell Server

Figure 5.9
NetWare's Macintosh NetWare Control Center

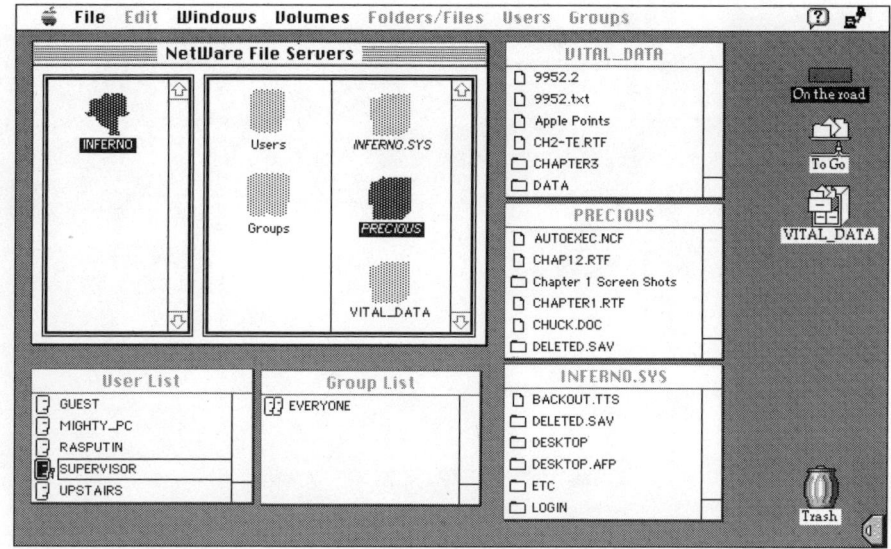

To log into the server, you have to log in from the Mac's Chooser. Or, if no NetWare volumes are mounted, NCC will search the network and let you log in if it finds a NetWare server on the network. In either case, you will need to give your user name and password.

Once you are logged in, you can then perform any of the following menu-controlled functions. Each menu section also has a corresponding figure for its associated menu.

Figure 5.10 shows the NCC File menu.

- **Select Zone**   This function allows you to select and manage a server in a zone other than Macintosh's default zone.

- **Open Server**   This is the command you use to log into a server.

- **Quit**   Quits the NCC application.

Figure 5.11 shows the NCC Windows menu.

- **Hide/Show Server Windows**   Closes the main NetWare File Server window.

- **Close Window**   Closes the active window.

- **Close All Windows**   Closes all open windows.

- **Individual Window Selection**   Selects any open window.

Figure 5.10

NCC File menu

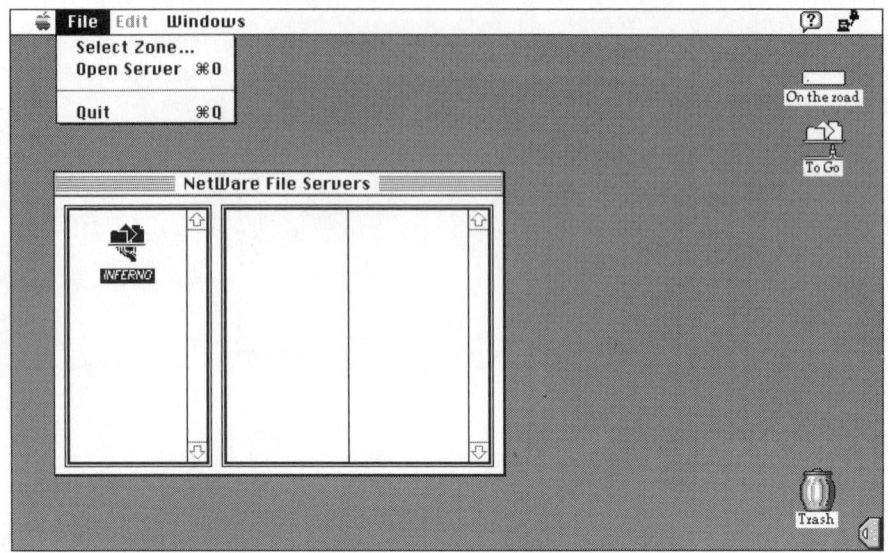

Figure 5.11

NCC Windows menu

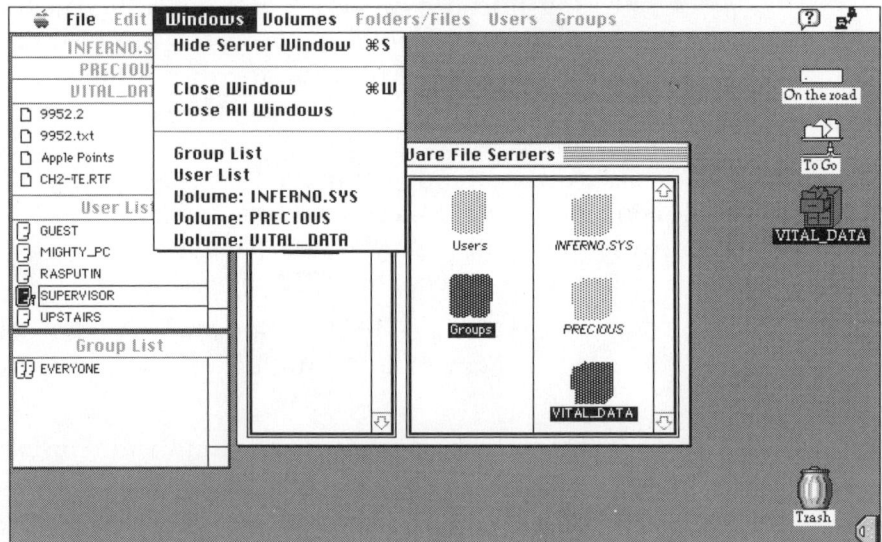

> **Note**
>
> Any of these functions, except the Hide/Show Server Window, can also be performed with the mouse, either by clicking on the window or by clicking the Close box in the upper left-hand corner.

Figure 5.12
NCC Volumes Menu

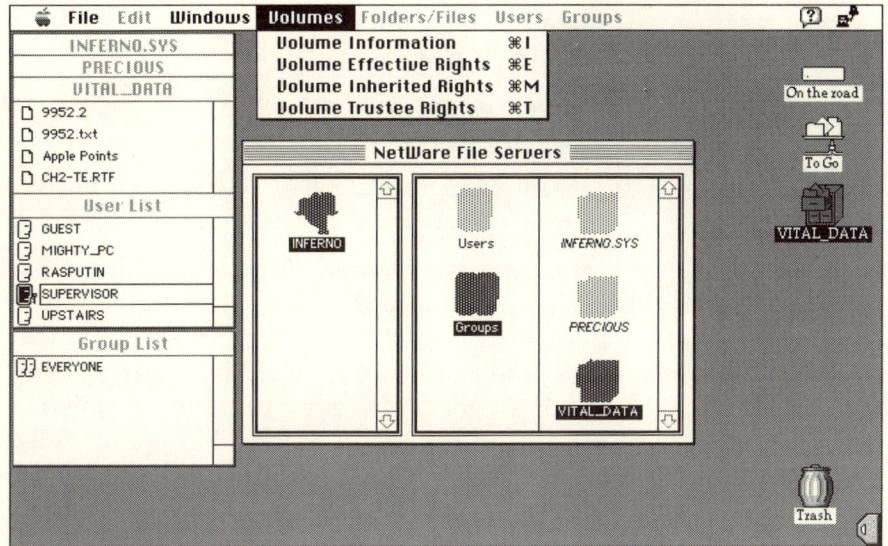

- **Volume Information**   Figure 5.12 shows a Volume Information window that displays the information for the volume INFERNO.SYS. There are no user-accessible options other than calculating the volume contents, which are displayed in the bottom of the window in Figure 5.12.

- **Volume Effective Rights**   Specifies what rights a user can invoke for a specific file or directory.

- **Volume Inherited Rights**   Specifies what rights a user can inherit for a directory on a specific volume.

- **Volume Trustee Rights**   Displays the Trustee Rights a user has over a specific volume or directory.

Rights control which users and groups can have access to specific files or directories (folders). Novell has a eight different Rights settings. With these specific rights, a user can do the following:

- **Access Control**   Modify Trustee and Inherited rights.

- **Create**   Create directories, sub-directories, and files.

- **Erase**   Delete directories, sub-directories, and files.

- **File Scan**   See files on a volume, or in a directory or sub-directory.

- **Modify**   Change attributes and rename directories, subdirectories, and files.

- **Read** Open and read a file. Operates on individual files or directories.
- **Supervisory** Change any of the access rights to a directory or file.
- **Write** Open and write to files. Operates on individual files or directories.

A *trustee* is the owner of a file or folder. Any time trustee rights are assigned to a directory, the trustee has full access to all of the files and sub-directories contained within the primary directory, unless the rights are revoked by a supervisor. The automatic rights that a trustee has over a directory are called *inherited rights*.

Each of the following Folder/File menu selections provides the same information or capabilities as the Volume Information listed above for folders or files. There is no need to repeat the explanation for each menu selection here. The information is accessed by selecting either a folder or a file from within the volume window, such as the ones in Figure 5.13.

- **Folder Information**
- **Folder Effective Rights**
- **Folder Inherited Rights**
- **Folder Trustee Rights**

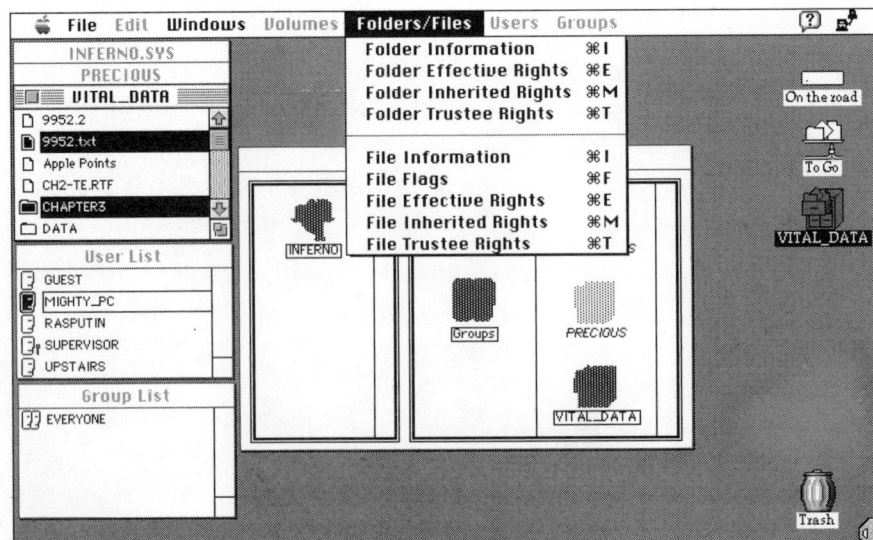

Figure 5.13

NCC Folders/Files menu

Connecting Your Macintosh to a Novell Server

- **File Information**
- **File Flags**
- **File Effective Rights**
- **File Inherited Rights**
- **File Trustee Rights**

Figure 5.14 shows the NCC Users menu.

- **User Information** The User Information window displays the user's name, ID, and full name, along with the user's primary group and the various groups of which the user is a member. Figure 5.15 shows the User Information window for GUEST.

- **Trustee Assignments** This window displays and allows you to modify the rights for a specific user as they apply to System directories and NetWare volumes. Figure 5.16 shows the Trustee Assignments window.

- **Create Home Folder** This menu option creates the user's home directory on the SYS volume. Use this option after a creating a new user.

- **Set Trustee Mode** The Set Trustee Mode is important if you want your users to have an AppleShare environment rather than a NetWare environment. Instead of using the

Figure 5.14
NCC Users menu

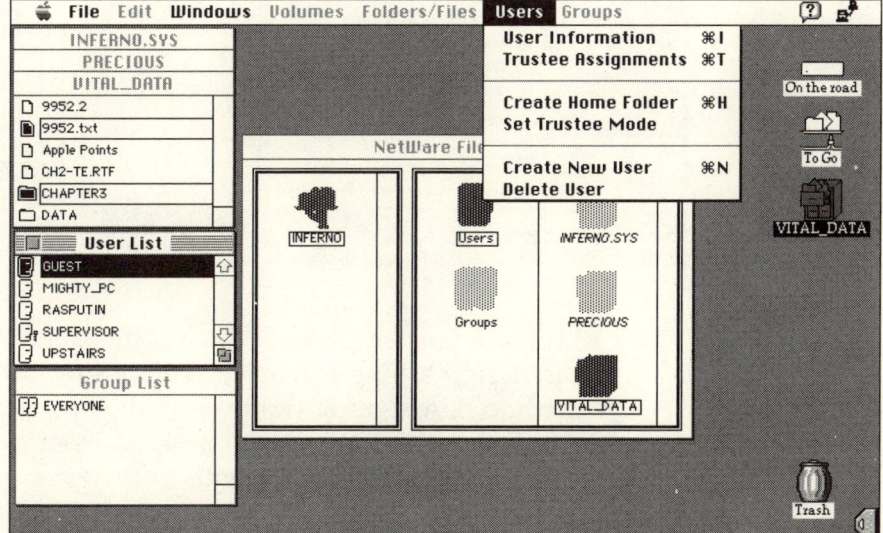

Figure 5.15
User Information window

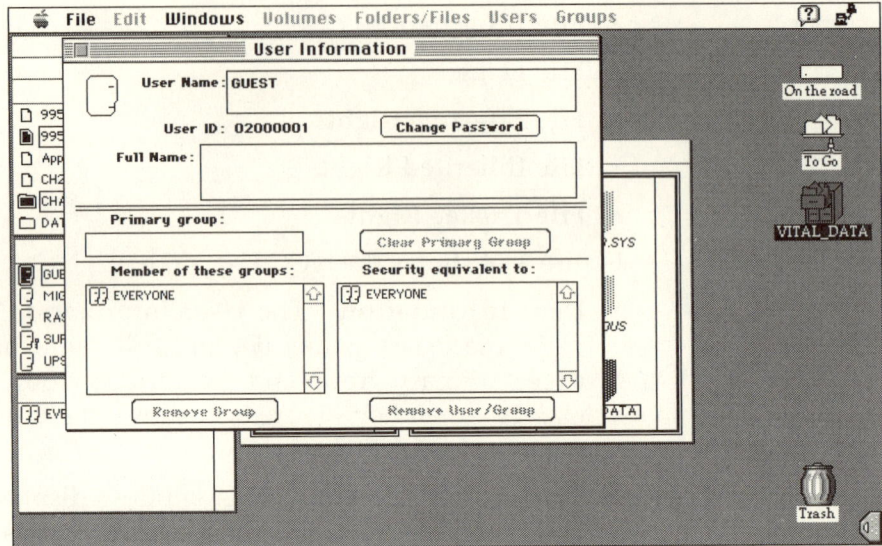

Figure 5.16
NCC's Trustee Assignments window

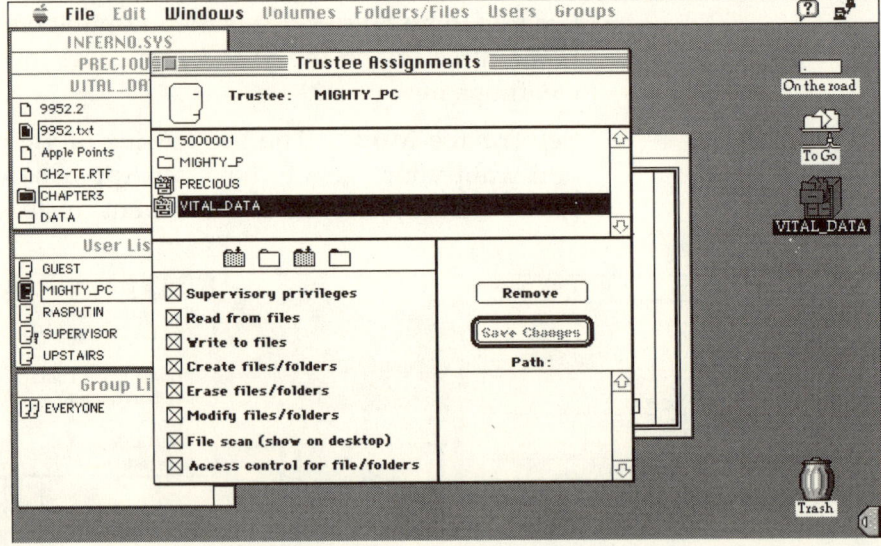

Multiple Trustees mode, which is the NetWare default, you can assign a Single Trustee. This mimics the AppleShare method of assigning rights, and allows the user to use the AppleShare Get Privileges desk accessory or the Sharing command from the File menu.

CONNECTING YOUR MACINTOSH TO A NOVELL SERVER

Figure 5.17
NCC Groups menu

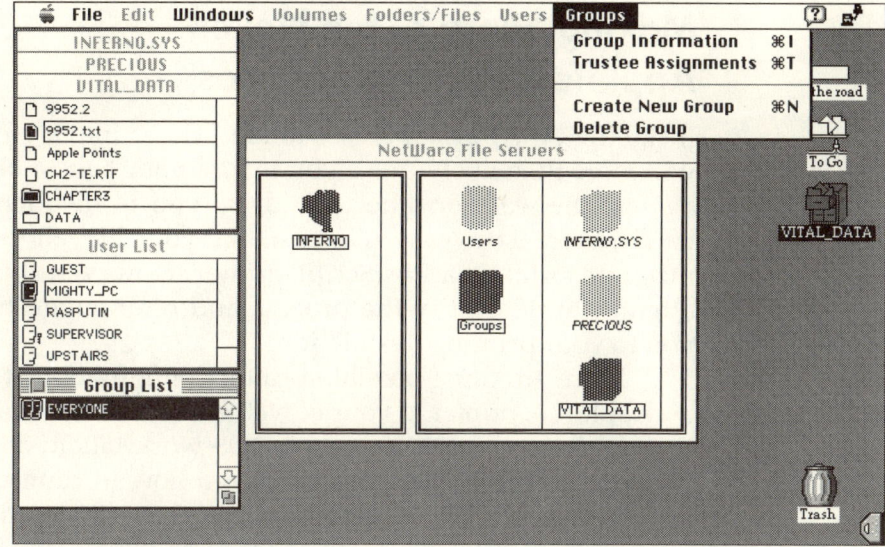

- **Create New User** Allows the System Administrator to create a new user.

- **Delete User** Allows the System Administrator to create a new group.

Figure 5.17 shows the NCC Groups menu.

- **Group Information** Provides a list of the members of a group selected from the Groups window. You can remove users from a specific group within this window.

- **Trustee Assignments** Shows the trustee assignments for a specific group as the assignments pertain to system directories of a server's volumes.

- **Create New Group** Allows the System Administrator to create a new group.

- **Delete Group** Allows the System Administrator to delete a group.

One of the nice features of NCC is the ability to drag and drop users and groups to different windows. If you want to add a user to a new group, you can drag existing users into the new group from the Users window. Anywhere you can assign users or groups, you can use the drag-and-drop technique.

Making Sense of the Novell AppleTalk Printing Services

Installing an AppleTalk-compatible printer into a Novell network will more than likely cause you to lose your hair or beat your head against the wall, or otherwise drive you to distraction. Unfortunately, there is no easy way to make your Novell network recognize and print to a PostScript printer. However, this section will attempt to demystify the process and offer suggestions to speed you to your printing destination.

There are three possible printer configurations for connecting an AppleTalk printer to your Novell environment: you can connect it to one of your Novell servers, a DOS workstation, or an AppleTalk network. In this section you will learn how to connect a PostScript laser printer to a Novell server, and how to set up printing services for a PostScript laser printer attached to your Mac via a LocalTalk network. The option of attaching the printer to a DOS workstation for Macintosh access is similar enough to attaching it to a Novell server that it will not be discussed. If you want to attach a networked printer to a DOS workstation, please refer to your Novell manual.

On the other hand, if you want to get to printing, fasten your seat belts—this could be a bumpy ride.

First Things First

Before you connect your printer to a specific computer or configure a NetWare printer for use with your Macintosh(s), you need to consider several factors. Will you be using the printer with Macintoshes and MS-DOS machines? Do you want to attach the printer to a Novell print server? Are you going to use the printer exclusively with Macs? Will you connect the printer to an AppleTalk network but still print to it from DOS and Windows machines?

If you have an extra PostScript printer kicking around (doesn't everyone?), you might want to use it exclusively with your Macs via LocalTalk and use your network for file storage and transfers. This is the easiest configuration and the one that generates the fewest headaches. However, for a small office it is unacceptable, because you are not fully utilizing an expensive piece of equipment.

Another option is to keep the printer attached to your Macs via AppleTalk and make it available to your other networked computers using the AppleTalk Printing Services available through

Connecting Your Macintosh to a Novell Server

Novell. This is the most efficient option and the configuration you should probably use. Your other option is to attach the printer to your server and use your server as a print server as well. This is the most difficult configuration to set up and manage, and it also has some drawbacks. Why this configuration is not optimum will become clear in a few paragraphs.

Figure 5.18 shows the printing options you have using Novell's NetWare.

Figure 5.18
Printing options available with NetWare

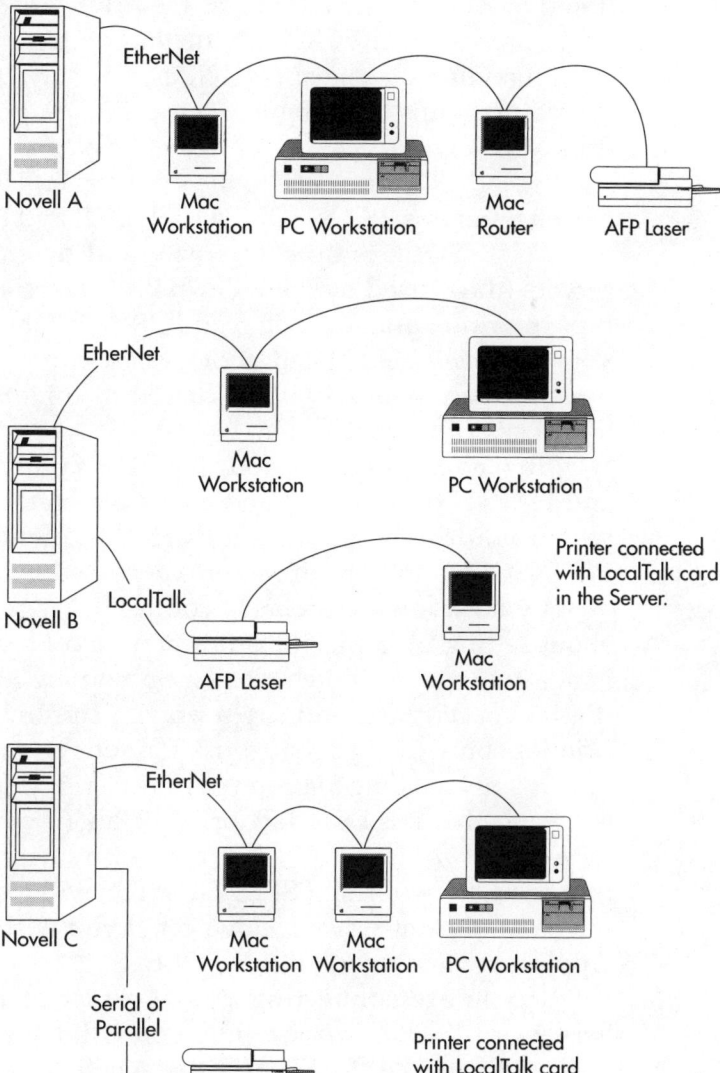

Your Novell Options

There are two primary Novell Loadable Modules (NLMs) used to control printing within the AppleTalk environment. One is the PSERVER.NLM, which controls Novell print servers and queues from within the Novell environment. The other is the ATPS.NLM (AppleTalk Print Server), which provides for AppleTalk print spooling and serving. Although Novell provides two other printing service NLMs, one for connecting a printer to a DOS workstation (PSERVER.EXE) and one as the print server for the Novell 286 environment (PSERVER.VAP), neither of these will be discussed.

In addition to the above NLMs, you have to use the following Novell programs to configure your printing options. These are used from MS-DOS machines to configure the Novell queue's print servers and to send DOS print jobs to the print server. These are the standard Novell programs: PCONSOLE, PRINTDEF, and PRINTCON.

PCONSOLE is used to create and delete queues and print servers (those used by PSERVER). PRINTDEF is used to define the type of printer you are using, and PRINTCON is used to configure your print jobs. As stated above, these are standard Novell utilities, and they will only be discussed in conjunction with printing to a PostScript laser printer.

Two more programs you should be familiar with are NPRINT and CAPTURE. NPRINT and CAPTURE are DOS programs with which you direct printing jobs to the queues you set up with PCONSOLE and to print servers controlled by PSERVER.

By now you are probably confused. There is nothing intuitive about setting up a Macintosh printer on a Novell network. And it is not going to get much clearer. So you are just going to have to dig in, concentrate, and say a prayer. I promise you will end up printing, but you'll have to work for your reward.

If you are going to keep your PostScript printer in an AppleTalk zone, whether it is LocalTalk or EtherTalk (if you are using a printer with an Ethernet option), you can get by using the ATPS module and basically ignoring PSERVER. ATPS will create your AppleTalk queues and print servers. However, if you wish, you can access the AppleTalk queues with PCONSOLE.

If you are connecting your PostScript printer to a Novell Server or MS-DOS workstation, you will have to become familiar with both the PSERVER and the ATPS NLMs. However, when deciding on how to configure the PostScript printer that will be

Connecting Your Macintosh to a Novell Server

used with Macintoshes on your network, you need to keep the following limitations of PSERVER in mind.

- The printer cannot report PostScript or printer errors to the originating workstation, regardless of whether the printer is attached via its serial or parallel port.

- You will not be able to print from a Macintosh application that outputs binary PostScript data. Binary PostScript data is a function of Adobe's PostScript Level II, and is used with some graphics programs. If your printer does not support PostScript Level II, you will not have to worry about this limitation.

- You will not be able to print banners before print jobs from Macintoshes.

- Printing speed degradation: printing can take several times longer when processed on a Novell print server.

Because of these problems, you should seriously consider using the AppleTalk Printer Services (ATPS) for connecting a PostScript printer to your Novell network if you are going to be printing to it from your Macintosh computers. If you are using a PostScript printer that has built-in Ethernet, your configuration will be even easier, although you should still use the ATPS.NLM for printing. Also, you will still be able to access the printer from DOS and Windows workstations, unless you completely forget about using the Novell print service options and rely only on the Macintosh's printing capabilities.

To use an AppleTalk laser printer attached to a Macintosh, even though you are using Ethernet or Token Ring network cards, you will need a software router such as Farallon's LocalPath or Apple's AppleTalk Internet Router to provide network access to the printer. You can find out more about Macintosh software routers in Chapters 2 and 8.

Novell's ATPS Module

The primary module for connecting a AppleTalk PostScript printer to your network is the AppleTalk Print Services (ATPS) module. In order to use the ATPS module, you have to install the NetWare for Macintosh v3.01. ATPS.NLM is installed onto the Server SYS along with the other AppleTalk modules. You will also have to load the AppleTalk module with the Load AppleTalk command. Even though ATPS creates an AppleTalk print queue, don't forget that the queue is also a NetWare queue that can be accessed by all of the Novell printing commands you are used to using.

Now you have to know how you want your printers configured. For this discussion, your choices are:

- Connecting a printer that is attached to an AppleTalk network, either via a Dayna Communications PC AppleTalk Card or from a Mac that is serving as an AppleTalk/Ethernet (or Token Ring) router.

- Connecting a printer to a Novell Server via the serial or parallel port. The examples in this book will use the serial option.

Although it is possible to connect AppleTalk ImageWriters or print from the Mac to other types of printers, this section will deal only with PostScript printers using an Apple LaserWriter II NTX. Connecting a PostScript printer is more complicated than any other option, and the principles you learn for connecting a PostScript printer can be translated to other types of AppleTalk printers.

Printing to an AppleTalk Printer

If you are using the Novell Server as an Ethernet/AppleTalk router with Dayna's AppleTalk card, you can connect the printer directly to the AppleTalk network connected to your Dayna card. The network configuration will look like Figure 5.19.

Figure 5.19
A PostScript printer connected to a Dayna AppleTalk card

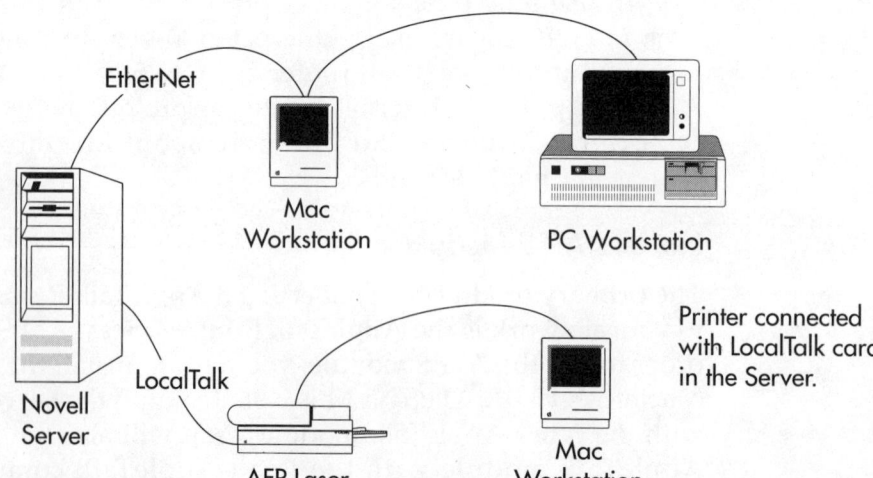

Connecting Your Macintosh to a Novell Server

With this configuration, you will be able to print directly to the printer from any Macintosh on the AppleTalk network and from any DOS or Windows machine on the Novell Network. You will also be able to print from your Macintoshes to a Novell print queue instead of directly to the printer.

If you are using Ethernet to connect your Macs to your Novell server and want to use an AppleTalk printer, you need to install an Ethernet-to-AppleTalk router. You can install a software router (Farallon's LocalPath or AppleTalk Internet Router) on one of your Macs. Figure 5.20 shows an example of a Novell network with a printer that is connected via AppleTalk to a Macintosh.

Printing to the Novell ATPS queue offers some advantages if you are not using the background printing option that is available as part of the Macintosh System software in System 7.X, or in System 6.0.X running MultiFinder. The advantage to using the queue when background printing is turned off is that your Macs don't have to wait for the printer to process the print job, which would render them unusable for the duration. Other advantages in using a Novell queue are that all print jobs are printed in the order that

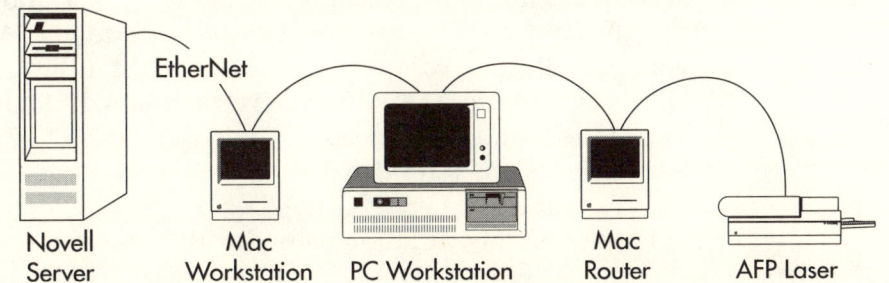

Figure 5.20
A PostScript printer connected to a Macintosh via AppleTalk

Printer connected via a software router.

Note

If you use Apple's AppleTalk Internet Router, you may want to use it on a Mac dedicated as a router or an AppleShare File Server. The Internet Router will degrade a Macintosh workstation's performance. Although the same applies to LocalPath, LocalPath does not degrade a workstation's performance to the same degree as the Internet Router.

they are received, and that if the printer is turned off, the queue will still accept jobs and wait until the printer is back on-line.

One of the disadvantages of using the Novell print queue is that the printer will not be able to send messages back to the originating Macintosh. This could be important when the printer cannot process a job because of a PostScript error, or when you want to feed a sheet of paper manually instead of using the printer's cassette. Also, PostScript downloads cannot be sent to the Novell queue: in order to download a PostScript file, you must be connected to the printer. You will have maximum printer compatibility, performance, and speed by printing to the AppleTalk printer directly from your Macs.

Using ATPS.NLM with an Ethernet/AppleTalk Router

There are several ways to use ATPS to configure your AppleTalk printer services. ATPS requires a configuration file, ATPS.CFG. ATPS.CFG supplies ATPS.NLM with all of the AppleTalk print queue parameters; you have 16 different configuration options. Rather than listing and describing each configuration parameter, this section will walk you though setting up ATPS to work with a network configuration like the one in Figure 5.20 above.

To configure ATPS, you can either edit the ATPS.CFG file with Novell's text editor or use the INSTALL utility to edit the file. How you edit the ATPS.CFG file is up to you, but edit it you must. But before you do, you need to know the name of your printer and the name of zone it resides in.

To edit the ATPS.CFG file, perform the following steps from the server or a workstation using the RCONSOLE command:

1. Type **Load Install**.
2. Select "Product Options" from the Options menu.
3. Select "NW-MAC v.3.011" from the Currently Installed Products list.
4. Select "SYS:\SYSTEM\ATPS.CFG" from the Editable Configuration Files window.

For each of the different Novell and Mac printer configurations, the command line for the ATPS.CFG file will be presented after the configuration is discussed.

Figure 5.21 shows the LaserWriter II NT, seen from the Macintosh Chooser, as residing in zone "Printer Net," which was cre-

Figure 5.21

The LaserWriter II NT shown in the Chooser as residing in the zone "Printer Net"

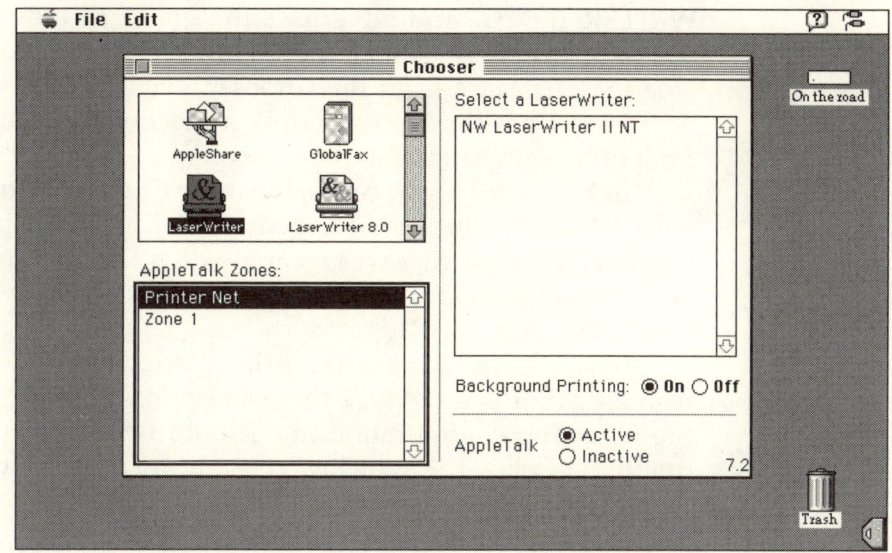

ated by Liaison (a software router from Farallon that has been discontinued). Also visible is zone "Zone 1." This zone should be familiar from the discussions on setting up your NetWare server for Macintosh access in the first part of this chapter.

ATPS.CFG syntax is "Printer_Name[:Printer_Zone]." For example, the line could look like this:

```
ATPS.CFG= "LaserWriter II NT:Printer Net"
```

If any configuration variable contains a space, the variable name must be enclosed in quotes.

The above configuration line is the standard configuration for specifying an AppleTalk printer. "Printer_Name" is the actual name of the LaserWriter as it is seen from the Chooser; it is also the name that appears on the printer's start-up page. "[:Printer_Zone]" is the name of the AppleTalk zone in which the printer resides. In the example above, the printer name is "LaserWriter II NT," and the zone is called "Printer Net." If you are using an Ethernet printer and do not need an Ethernet/AppleTalk router, you can omit the [:Printer_Zone] name, because the printer will reside in the default NetWare zone—in this configuration, Zone 1.

This configuration makes the printer available to your Macintoshes only as displayed in the Chooser configuration displayed in Figure 5.21 above. For any MS-DOS or Windows machines, Novell automatically creates a queue named "INFERNO/NW_LASER-

WRITER_II_NT," and advertises the queue to other machines in the server's default zone, Zone 1. However, this queue is not available to your Macs from the Chooser, even though you can view the queue from the NetWare desk accessory and see spooled jobs from other computers.

In Figure 5.22, you can see that the Chooser also presents you with a Novell print queue called "Novell Q." It is in Zone 1, the main Novell zone that was created when the NetWare for Macintosh was set up. However, you still have the same options as those available in Figure 5.21.

If you want to make the printer directly available to Macintosh users but want to give them an option to use a Novell queue, the following configuration line should be used. Table 5.1 below briefly describes the switches you are most likely to use with an AppleTalk queue that is set up with ATPS.

```
ATPS.CFG = -o Novell_Q -p "LaserWriter II
           NT" -z "Printer Net" -b
```

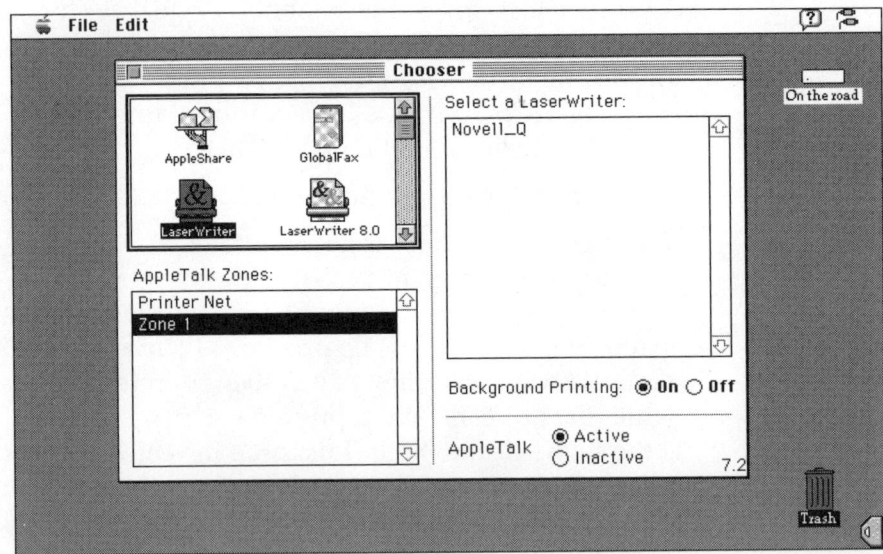

Figure 5.22
The Novell print queue called "Novell Q," shown in the Chooser as residing in "Zone 1"

> **Note**
>
> Remember, you can manipulate spooled jobs in a queue from a Macintosh if you log in as a supervisor or if you are the creator of the job.

Table 5.1 Switches used with an ATPS AppleTalk queue

	Switch	Variable	Purpose
ATPS.CFG syntax	-o	Queue_Name	Specifies names queue
	-p	Printer_Name	Specifies printer name
	-z	Zone_Name	Specifies zone name
	-b		Prints banner from Novell queue
	-h		Hides AppleTalk printer from Chooser
	-wb		Turns off the AppleTalk option so the queue will not appear in the Chooser

In the above example, you can print either to the Novell AppleTalk queue or to the printer directly. Also, each print job that is printed from the AppleTalk queue will be preceded by a print banner identifying the user, type of print job, the time and date printed, a document description, the queue from which it was printed, and the Novell server that contains the queue.

```
ATPS.CFG = -o Novell_Q -p "LaserWriter II
      NT" -z "Printer Net" -h
```

If you want to hide the printer from the Chooser (as in the following example) and force your users to print to the Novell queue, add the switch "-h." All of these switches can be used together; however, you have to be careful not to use a switch like "-h," which hides the printer from the Chooser, with the "-wb" switch, which turns off the AppleTalk print spooler (it acts as a Novell server) so that it is not visible from the Macintosh's Chooser.

```
ATPS.CFG = -o Novell_Q -p "LaserWriter II
      NT" -z "Printer Net" -wb
```

Although there are many more command switches and dozens of options available for configuring ATPS, the above will get you up and printing with a minimum of trouble.

AppleTalk and Novell's PSERVER Module

PSERVER is the Novell print server module. If you want to connect your PostScript printer (or some other type of printer) to a

Novell server or a DOS workstation and print to it from a Macintosh, you will have to use ATPS to create the AppleTalk queue and PSERVER to set up a print server, and then you will connect the ATPS queue to the print server with PCONSOLE. Figure 5.23 shows the physical configuration of the network with the printer attached to the server.

However, before we set up this configuration, we need to discuss some background information. When printing from a Macintosh to a Novell AppleTalk queue, the Mac sends the data to the AppleTalk queue as if it were a PostScript printer attached to an AppleTalk network. PSERVER then takes the data from the queue and sends it to the printer. The problem with printing through PSERVER, as mentioned earlier, is that the AppleTalk connection is actually severed when the data moves through the Novell print server. The data going from the queue to the printer is not transferred in the binary protocol used by AppleTalk.

The broken connection makes it impossible for the feedback from the printer to find the originating station like it does when attached to a Mac. The communication between the queue and the originating station are Novell printing messages only. The net effect is that the printer is lobotomized by PSERVER and cannot communicate with any Macintosh on the network.

The other problem caused by using PSERVER involves how data is moved from the queue to the printer. If you are lucky, you will be using a printer that has some external means for configuring its communications settings. Otherwise, you have to take some

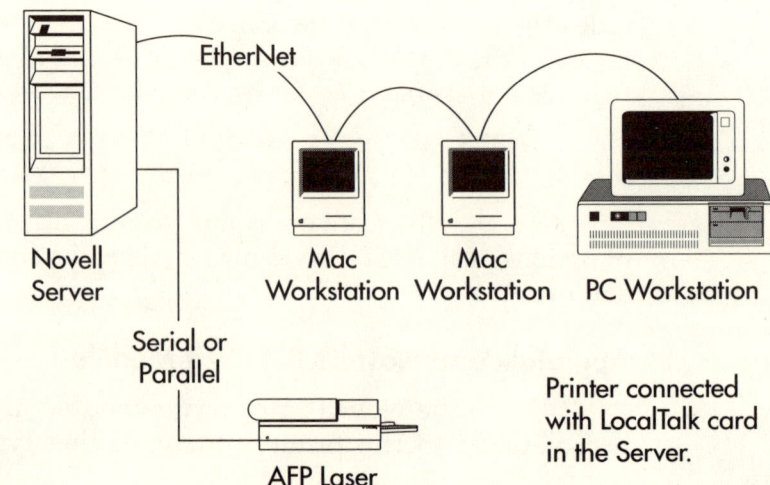

Figure 5.23
The network configuration with the printer attached to the server. This configuration requires both ATPS.NLM and PSERVER.NLM for a Macintosh to print to the printer.

extra steps to set the communications rate for maximum compatibility. Apple's LaserWriters are hardwired to accept serial data with the following communications parameters:

- 9600 baud
- No Parity
- 7 Data bits
- 1 Stop Bit
- Parity on
- X-on/X-off

To change these parameters, it is necessary to download a PostScript program to the printer that instructs the printer to communicate with the print server using the following communications settings:

- 9600 baud
- No Parity
- 8 Data bits
- 1 Stop Bit
- Parity on
- XON/XOFF

Even though PostScript is capable of using 7-bit serial data, some Macintosh programs sometimes create PostScript printer data that uses an 8-bit data structure. Macintosh data is not always compatible with the 7 bit data structure that the Apple LaserWriters defaults to when set for serial communications. This is because the Macintosh LaserWriter driver sends all of its data to a PostScript printer in a binary communications format when communicating with the printer via AppleTalk.

The 8-bit data that Macintosh programs create is called "8bitClean." Usually, the 8bitClean data is for files containing embedded graphics (usually bitmapped images like TIFF files). These files can cause problems if you do not change the communications parameters. Although graphic images are not necessarily the only applications that use the "8bitClean" category, bitmapped and graphic images almost always require a full 8 bits per byte when sent to the printer (in contrast to ASCII characters, which can easily be represented by a 7-bit character).

CHAPTER 5

Novell's PSERVER communicates with a serial printer using an Xon/Xoff error protocol; PSERVER does not use a protocol data transfer like XMODEM or ZMODEM. The result of this limitation is that some of the data (if 8-bit data is sent to the printer as 7-bit data) will be interpreted by the printer as an end-of-file marker or end-of-job command, and the print job will abort. Therefore, the communications parameters should be changed for maximum compatibility.

The rest of this section will deal with setting up a PostScript printer connected to a Novell server with AppleTalk access.

The first step is to connect your printer to the machine that will be used as a print server. The print server can be your Novell server or a DOS workstation. (If you are going to use a DOS workstation, you will have to refer to your Novell manuals for instructions on setting it up.) This example will use a Novell server as print server, as illustrated in Figure 5.23. This example also assumes that you are using an Apple LaserWriter configured to communicate through its serial port. If you are using a LaserWriter with a parallel port, the set-up is much easier.

As stated earlier, Apple LaserWriters default to the following data communication parameters: 9600 baud, No Parity, 7 Data bits, 1 Stop Bit, Parity on, X-on/X-off. The data bits parameter will have to be changed to 8 data bits before you can use the LaserWriter from the server.

The task of making this happen is not as easy as it sounds. The first thing you have to do is create the print server from an MS-DOS workstation using PCONSOLE. The print queue (this is an AppleTalk queue) will be defined by ATPS.CFG and loaded with ATPS.NLM, and the print server will be run from the Novell server with the PSERVER.NLM. If you are depending on the man-

Note

If you are using a PostScript laser printer manufactured by a company other than Apple, there is an easier way to change its communications parameters. Most PostScript laser printers come with an MS-DOS program you can use to configure the printer. If you have such a configuration progam, you can use it to change the printer's communications parameters. Also, these progams will work with an Apple LaserWriter.

CONNECTING YOUR MACINTOSH TO A NOVELL SERVER

ual from the NetWare for Macintosh to set up this configuration, you may be at your task a long time. Somehow, some pertinent steps have been left out of the process it describes.

The following steps work if you are attaching an Apple PostScript printer via the serial port. If your printer has a parallel port, use it: the parallel port simplifies the process greatly. The steps are first laid out in brief, and then each step is explained in detail.

To attach an Apple PostScript printer via a serial or parallel port:

1. Configure your print queue with ATPS by editing the ATPS.CFG file, and load the ATPS.NLM.
2. Set up the print server with PCONSOLE from a DOS workstation.
3. Unload the ATPS.NLM.
4. Load the print server from your Novell server using PSERVER.
5. Load the ATPS.NLM from your server.
6. Connect the spooler to the queue you set up with ATPS.
7. Download the SERIAL.PS file from your DOS workstation using NPRINT.
8. Unload the ATPS.NLM.
9. Unload the PSERVER.
10. Reconfigure your print server with the new data communications settings using PCONSOLE from a DOS workstation.
11. Reload the print server from your Novell server with PSERVER.
12. Reload ATPS.NLM.
13. Test the print server from your DOS, Windows, and Mac workstations. If it works properly, add the commands to your Novell AUTOEXEC.NCF file.

Step 1
Configure your print queue with ATPS by editing the ATPS.CFG file.

1. From the server, or by using RCONSOLE from a DOS workstation, load the INSTALL.NLM and select the "Product Options" menu selection.

2. Select the NW_MAC v3.01 option from the Currently Installed Products window.
3. Select the SYS:\SYSTEM\ATPS.CFG selection.
4. Enter the following in the ATPS.CFG file (ignore the brackets):

    -o [queue name] -f [font name] -wb

    For this example, the ATPS.CFG reads

    -o Novell_Q -f applwNT -wb

    The queue name can be any Novell-acceptable queue name, but it should be less than 32 characters. "-f" is the switch for the default fonts in your printer. Your choices are:

Font Name	Printer Type
APPLW.FNT	Apple LaserWriter
APPLWPLS.FNT	Apple LaserWriter Plus
APPLWNT.FNT	Apple LaserWriter NT
APPLWNTX.FNT	Apple LaserWriter NTX
HPLASER.FNT	HP Laser Jet Family

    The "-wb" switch disables the AppleTalk print server that ATPS normally sets up. If you are using a PostScript laser printer other than an Apple LaserWriter or a LaserWriter-compatible printer, you will also have to include the switch "-l" (lower-case L). The "-l" switch causes the queue to send a laser prep file with each print job sent from the Macintosh. Whether you use this switch will depend on the printer you are using.

5. Press **Escape** and save the ATPS.CFG file when asked. Then press **Escape** until you are back to the Server prompt.
6. Load the ATPS.NLM by typing **Load ATPS**. Loading the ATPS.NLM will install the Novell AppleTalk queue and make it available to PCONSOLE for the next step.

Step 2
Set up the print server with PCONSOLE from a DOS workstation.

1. Log into your server as a supervisor and run PCONSOLE from the server's system directory.
2. Select the "Print Server Information" menu selection.

Connecting Your Macintosh to a Novell Server

3. When the Print Servers window comes up, create a new print server by pressing the **Insert** key.

4. Name the print server when the "New Print Server Name:" option appears. (The print server in this example is named "Print_Server.")

5. Select the new print server from the Print Servers window.

6. Select the "Print Server Configuration" menu option from the Print Server Information.

7. Select the "Printer Configuration" menu option.

8. From the Configured Printers window, select the first available "Not Installed" selection.

9. Fill in the parameters for your printer. The following settings are the ones used in this example:

    - **Name** The printer name is user-defined and can be any name. LaserWriter_II_NT is used for this example.
    - **Type** Serial, COM1 (be sure to specifiy the correct COM port).
    - **Use interrupts** No or Yes. If you use Yes, be sure to specify the correct interrupt on the next line.
    - **IRQ** This will be blank if you do not use an interrupt setting in the line above. Otherwise, make sure you specify the correct the IRQ number. The standard IRQs are IRQ 4 for COM1 and COM3, and IRQ3 for COM2 and COM4.
    - **Buffer size in K** The default is 3.
    - **Starting from** 0
    - **Queue service mode** Change forms as needed.
    - **Baud rate** 9600
    - **Data bits** 7
    - **Stop bits** 1
    - **Parity** None
    - **Use X-on/X-off** Yes

10. Press **Escape** until you are returned to the Print Server Configuration menu. Then select the "Queues Serviced by Printer" menu selection.

11. Select the printer you just set up in the Defined Printers window and press **Enter**.
12. When the next window appears (it really does not have a name), press **Insert** to see all of your available queues.
13. Select the queue you defined using PCONSOLE, or the one created when you ran ATPS, and press **Enter**.
14. Press **Enter** again when the Priority window appears.
15. Press **Escape** until you return to the Print Server Configuration menu, and select the "Notify List for Printer" menu selection.
16. Select the printer you have been working with from the Defined Printers window.
17. Press the **Insert** key to see a list of all your users in the Notify Candidates window. Select the Job Owner and any other user you want notified in case there is a problem with printing.
18. Press **Escape** until you are returned to the system prompt.

Step 3

From the Novell server, unload the ATPS.NLM. You will either have to unload it now or unload it after the next step. PSERVER must be loaded before ATPS so the printer you have connected to the ATPS queue will work.

Step 4

Load PSERVER from the server console. PSERVER is the module that controls your printer by creating a print server. In the first example, ATPS.NLM created the queue and the print server. To load PSERVER, type **LOAD PSERVER PRINT_SERVER**. The syntax for PSERVER is always "PSERVER [Server Name]."

Step 5

Load the ATPS.NLM from your server. This makes the queue defined in the ATPS.CFG file available to your Macs and to the other workstations on the network. To load ATPS, type **LOAD ATPS** from the server terminal.

Step 6

From the Novell server, you need to use the SPOOL command to connect the Novell queue to the print spooler. If you do not connect the queue with the command line **SPOOL 0 to Novell_Q** (SPOOL [Spool number] to [Queue Name]), you will not be able to perform the next step.

Step 7
Download the SERIAL.PS file from your DOS work station using NPRINT. From a DOS workstation, change to the Public directory on your Novell server. Once there, enter the **NPRINT SERIAL.PS** (include the proper queue command if you have multiple queues) and press **Enter**. NPRINT will send a the SERIAL.PS file to your printer. The SERIAL.PS is a PostScript command file that changes your printer's communications parameters so it will operate using 8-bit data instead of 7-bit.

Once you change the communications settings for the printer, it will no longer communicate with the print server, and you will have to redefine the printer with PCONSOLE.

Step 8
Unload the ATPS.NLM. From the server terminal, type **UNLOAD ATPS**.

Step 9
Unload the PSERVER. From the server terminal, type **UNLOAD PSERVER Print_Server**. The syntax for PSERVER is always "PSERVER [Server Name]."

Step 10
Reconfigure your print server with the new data communications settings using PCONSOLE from a DOS workstation.

1. Log into your server as a supervisor and run *PCONSOLE* from the server's system directory.

2. Select the "Print Server Information" menu selection.

3. When the Print Servers window comes up, create a new print server by pressing the **Insert** key.

4. Name the print server when the "New Print Server Name:" option appears. (The print server in this example is named "Print_Server.")

5. Select the new print server from the Print Servers window.

6. Select the "Print Server Configuration" menu option from the Print Server Information.

7. Select the "Printer Configuration" menu option.

8. From the Configured Printers window, select the first available "Not Installed" selection.

9. Fill in the parameters for your printer. The following settings are the ones used in this example:

   - **Name** The printer name is user-defined and can be any name. LaserWriter_II_NT is used for this example.
   - **Type** Serial, COM1. (Be sure to specify the correct COM port.)
   - **Use interrupts** No or Yes. If you use Yes, be sure to specify the correct interrupt on the next line.
   - **IRQ** This will be blank if you do not use an interrupt setting in the line above. Otherwise, make sure you specify the correct the IRQ number. The standard IRQs are IRQ 4 for COM1 and COM3, and IRQ3 for COM2 and COM4.
   - **Buffer size in K** The default is 3.
   - **Starting from** 0
   - **Queue service mode** Change forms as needed.
   - **Baud rate** 9600
   - **Data bits** 8
   - **Stop bits** 1
   - **Parity** None
   - **Use X-on/X-off** Yes

10. Press **Escape** and save your changes, then press **Escape** until you exit PCONSOLE.

Step 11
Reload the print server from your Novell server with PSERVER. Type **LOAD PSERVER Print_Server** from the server terminal.

Step 12
Reload ATPS.NLM. Type **LOAD ATPS** from the server terminal.

Step 13
Test the print server from your DOS, Windows, and Mac workstations. If it works properly, add the commands to your Novell AUTOEXEC.NCF file.

The above steps are the quickest way to make your Apple LaserWriter work if you attach the printer to a Novell server. Every step is necessary, so if you make a mistake you may want to start over. Also, if you set up your ATPS.CFG file incorrectly and have to start over, you should run PCONSOLE and check both the print servers and queues. You may have defined a queue or server that you do not want. If you have either a queue or print server that you do not want, delete the unwanted items and then start over.

There can be a real down side to the above, depending on your printer. Some Apple printers (such as the LaserWriter II NT) retain downloaded communications settings, while others do not. If your printer does not retain downloaded communications settings, you will have to perform the above steps to download the SERIAL.PS file and then reconfigure the print server each time you turn off the printer.

Of course, your other option is to leave the printer on all the time, but this is usually not a viable alternative. Depending on your configuration, you may once again reconsider using ATPS.NLM as both a queue and print server.

Accessing a Novell Server with Third-Party Software

If you do not want to use Novell's NetWare for Macintosh, you do have a couple of options that will give your Macs access to your NetWare volumes. There is not much in the Macintosh world that will let you make the connection, but three products you can use are Dayna Communications DOSMounter Plus (which includes NetMounter) and two products made by Miramar, MacLan Gold and MacLan Novell. These products will be briefly discussed below.

NetMounter

Dayna Communications sells a product called DOS Mounter Plus that will allow a Macintosh to access a NetWare server without using Novell's NetWare for Macintosh. In addition to having all of the features listed for DOS Mounter in Chapter 3, DOS Mounter Plus installs a Chooser extension that you use like the AppleShare Chooser extension to access your NetWare server.

DOS Mounter does not provide printer support. This does not need to be a great liability, since most Mac networks have their own dedicated printers. What you would lose is the ability for a MS-DOS workstation to access a Mac printer and the ability for a Mac printer to access a MS-DOS printer. So depending on your network set-up, this could be a very viable and less expensive solution for your Novell/Macintosh networking problems.

The component of DOS Mounter that works with Novell networks is called NetMounter. Figure 5.24 shows the volumes INFERNO.SYS, INFERNO.PRECIOUS, and INFERNO.VITAL_DATA mounted with NetMounter. As you can see, the volumes are all preceded by the server name and then the volume name. This and the "NET" on the icon are the only ways to differentiate the NetMounter icons from a NetWare volume mounted with AFP under NetWare.

An important point about using NetMounter is that you have to use NetWare's LOAD MAC and the following Add Name Space command before using NetMounter:

```
ADD NAME SPACE Macintosh to volume [volume
    name]
```

Both of these commands are part of NetWare 3.11.

Figure 5.24

Novell volumes mounted with NetMounter

Novell volumes

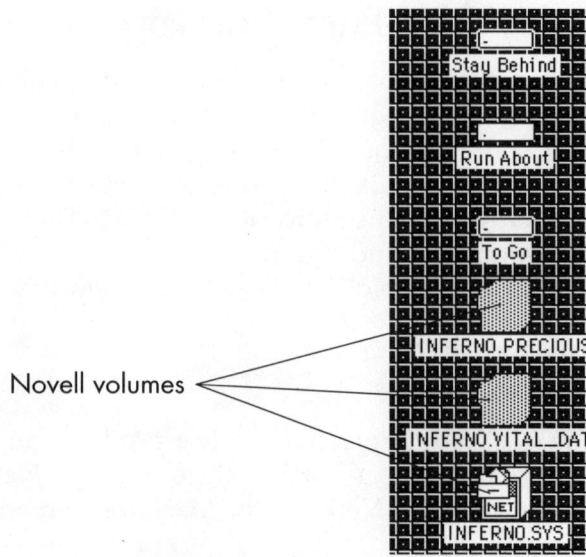

MacLan Gold and MacLan NetWare

Miramar Systems makes two products for connecting Macintoshes to Novell networks. One is MacLan Gold, and the other is MacLan NetWare. Both products allow for full network access, including printer sharing. Both of these products are gateways that require a dedicated MS-DOS 286, 386, or 486 machine. Their advantage over NetWare for Macintosh is in their cost.

MacLan Gold and NetWare both list for $696. If you have more than five Macintoshes to connect, you may want to consider either one of these products. There is no limit to the number of Macs you can connect with Miramar's products.

MacLan Gold is made to work with a variety of products, namely Novell, Vines, IBM OS/2 Lan Server, and LANtastic. You can also add to this list Microsoft's Lan Manager, since it is based on the OS/2 Lan Server. MacLan Novell is made specifically for providing Macintosh/Novell interconnectivity.

The MacLan products operate by turning the gateway MS-DOS machine into an AppleShare File Server, which is then accessible by both Macs and MS-DOS machines. Both Miramar products provide the following features:

- Print spooling for Apple LaserWriters.
- AppleTalk gateway services via AppleTalk (using an AppleTalk card), Ethernet, or Token Ring to Novell NetWare volumes or other networks.
- Router services for each of the cabling protocols above.
- AppleTalk file server services.
- File Extension Mapping. This service connects MS-DOS files with their Macintosh counterparts so you can double-click on a MS-DOS file and launch a Macintosh application.

A MacLan gateway can be administered from either the gateway machine or the Macintosh.

Conclusion

Well, there you have it: the essentials for connecting your Macs to your Novell network. There is much that was not covered, but by combining this with the information in other chapters, you should quickly be able to get your Macintosh users up and running. You can then take your time to fine-tune the network and explore some of the finer features of Novell's NetWare for Macintosh. The major topics covered in this chapter were:

- Preparing your NetWare server for Macintosh support by making it an AppleTalk router.
- Connecting an Apple LaserWriter to a NetWare server as a shared resource.
- Accessing an Apple LaserWriter from other networked machines while it is connected to an AppleTalk network using an internet router on a Mac.
- Using third-party software to access your Novell network.

This was not an easy chapter, but if you have read it carefully, you have the basics you need. And if you think that this chapter was difficult, then by all means you should read Novell's manual—then your relatives will be able to visit you in the local funny farm. For the most part, it is not as difficult as it may first appear. Connecting your Macs just takes some time, patience, and practice.

Banyan VINES

Introduction

The Banyan VINES networking system is usually described in general terms, and information is often hard to find. But it is one of the major network operating systems used in business today. VINES is a very powerful distributed network operating system.

"VINES" stands for "VIrtual NEtworking System." Machines that run DOS, OS/2, and Windows all work with the VINES networking software. Macs communicate with a VINES server using AppleTalk. VINES also offers transparent Wide Area Network (WAN) and Local Area Network (LAN) bridging with single-point administration, supporting DOS, Mac, and OS/2 environments using their native file- and document-naming formats. VINES uses UNIX for its base operating system, and its server should be a 386/33 PC or higher. It is considered to be easier to use than some of the other NOSs, and it is also found more often in large businesses.

This chapter will look specifically at installing and managing the AppleTalk option for a VINES network. It does not contain all of the information in the manuals that come with this option, but it does present the information in a different format that might be easier to understand. Unfortunately, VINES, like most of the NOSs in this book, has manuals that are sometimes difficult to plow your way through.

The first sections are going to look at VINES's requirements and terminology before discussing the actual steps for installation and set-up. After the general set-up, the next discussion will be about using Mac with VINES. After that, there will be a discussion about installing and using the VINES print server with AppleTalk PostScript printers. Then the chapter will be wrapped up with a brief trouble-shooting section that is specific to VINES.

VINES and the Macintosh

Starting with version 5.00 of VINES, Banyan implemented an AppleTalk option that lets Macintoshes access a VINES server and VINES Mail. The VINES implementation of AppleTalk is done through a UNIX kernel. It is almost a full implementation of the AFP, but not quite. There is one feature of AppleTalk that VINES does not support, and that is ADSP. If you plan the network properly, though, you can even use ADSP. Otherwise, a VINES set-up with AppleTalk will give you the same features as described in Chapter 2 for an AppleShare file server.

VINES uses AppleTalk, rather than trying to run the VINES operating system on the Mac. Your Mac users will only have a few things to be concerned with that are different from what they might be used to. However, you might have to go through some growing pains to get everything working properly. Hopefully, the information in the first few chapters will have prepared you adequately. This section will look at the capabilities you'll have with the AppleTalk option for VINES and the physical network.

AppleTalk on the VINES Server

When you install AppleTalk on the VINES server, you'll be creating an internet where the servers running the AppleTalk options are routers. With the AppleTalk implementation, the AppleTalk packet will be encapsulated inside a VINES packet, so it is possible to use intermediate VINES servers to tunnel or pass an AppleTalk packet across several hops to a server that is running AppleTalk. The consequence of this is that only the AppleTalk servers can unbundle the AppleTalk packets. This means that direct Macintosh-to-Macintosh communication across several servers is impossible. Hence, no ADSP or Apple file sharing is possible unless the

Macs are on the same physical network. Another consequence of this is that DOS/Windows machines cannot access any AppleShare file servers that are running on Macs, either through System 7 file sharing or through an AppleShare file server—unless they, too, are on the same physical network with the Macs and have AppleTalk software installed.

The only exception to the above is if you are using an AppleTalk PostScript laser printer. If the printer is accessible to the server, either directly through a DaynaTALK card installed in a VINES server or through an internet (transition) router running on a Mac connected to the server, your other users will be able to access the printer through STDA (StreetTalk Directory Services) and the VINES print services. However, a printer is the only AppleTalk device that non-Macintosh computers can access, even with the AppleTalk option installed.

The nature of VINES as a multi-server network is such that individual servers are often transparent to the user, so you might find using the Macintosh a bit awkward. This is because the Mac must log into a specific server, which may seem contrary to the resource distribution system provided by StreetTalk and STDA. Unfortunately, this is just something you'll have to live with. However, with VINES Mail for the Macintosh, you will be able to use STDA for addressing E-mail.

Also, VINES provides a one-way file extension mapping feature, where DOS files can be mapped for the Macintosh. However, VINES does not perform file extension mapping for Macintosh to DOS. So if your Mac users are going to be sharing files with DOS users, they will have to learn to use DOS file names. Otherwise, your DOS and Windows users will not know what applications created the files.

Combined Networks

The type of network physical links you are using with your Macs and VINES will have an impact on your overall network topology. You will have to assign AppleTalk zones, and if you don't plan your network properly, you will have to reconcile network address conflicts. However, before talking about the actual nuts and bolts of configuring server ports, network addresses, and zones, we're going to talk about the idiosyncrasies of the different AppleTalk physical link protocols and VINES.

If you are using EtherTalk Phase 2, your problems will be fewer than if you are using one of the other protocols available for the Macintosh. This is because you will not need additional routers if everything can be connected via Ethernet (including any AppleTalk printers).

However, chances are better than very good that you will be using a LocalTalk or PhoneNET type of network in conjunction with your Ethernet or Token Ring network. If you are using older Ethernet networks or Phase 1 Ethernet, you'll have to make accommodations for this type of network, as well. Because a VINES server can only run Phase 1 or Phase 2, you will have to decide how you are going to lay out your network with this restriction in mind.

This section will discuss router and gateways for LocalTalk and Token Ring networks and any VINES requirements associated with the routers. It will discuss Ethernet Phase 1 and 2, as well. For this section to make sense, it is critical that you read both it and the following section. The general discussions here are antecedent to the section on Mapping Your Network.

LocalTalk

The only way to connect a LocalTalk network to your server physically is with a DaynaTALK card from Dayna Communications. This may be impractical or even impossible, depending on the Mac's location in relation to your server. You'll need some type of transition router if a low-speed AppleTalk network is not physically connected to your server. When you use a full router with your VINES network, you'll find that your Macs will have full network access. The AppleTalk printer resources will also be available to your PCs.

A transition router can be a hardware or software router that routes Ethernet to LocalTalk and vice versa. If you have a Mac that is connected to the Ethernet network, you can use a software router like Farallon's LocalPath or Apple's InterNet Router. This would provide you with a topology like the one shown in Figure 6.1.

In addition to using a software router, you can also use a hardware router/gateway. However, most hardware routers are designed to provide additional network services, such as providing gateways between AppleTalk, DecNET, TCP/IP, and host of additional protocols. Depending on your needs, you can also get a hardware router that will also allow for remote access and multiple network connections. However, the more sophisticated hard-

BANYAN VINES

Figure 6.1
A network topology with a software router on a Mac

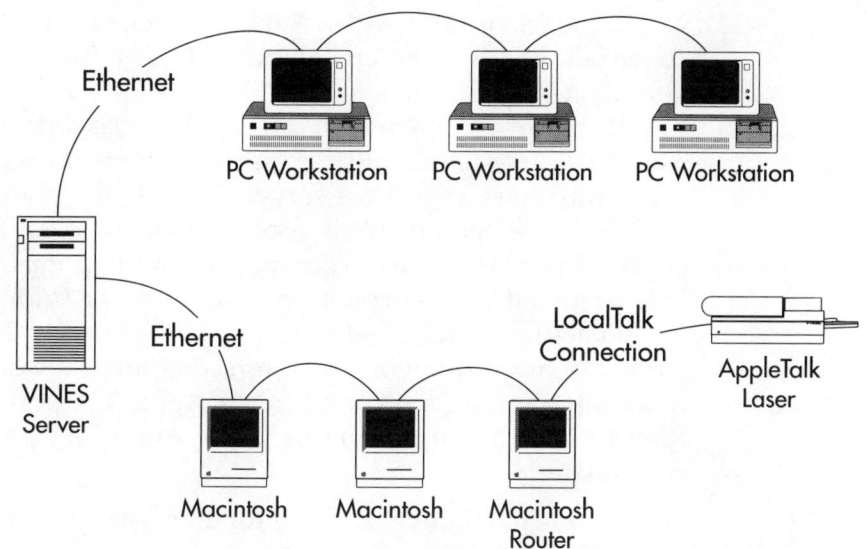

ware router/gateway solutions are expensive, and in many cases, overkill. So if you need only Ethernet to LocalTalk routing, you will want to use the less expensive software router.

As far as VINES is concerned, there are no special requirements for using one of these routers so long as it is a *seed router*, one that broadcasts its address to the network. VINES routing services will intercept and make the broadcasted zone available. However, you will have to enter the zone name when you set up the PAP printer services. On the other hand, your Macs will automatically recognize the zones, with no special configuration concerns. Also, any Mac on the LocalTalk network will see the zone name for the Ethernet network.

You should make sure that you are using AppleTalk Phase 2 whenever you use LocalTalk with your VINES Server. If you use AppleTalk Phase 1 for LocalTalk, you will have to configure the server as an AppleTalk Phase 1 server, and you will not be able to use EtherTalk Phase 2. Even though LocalTalk Phase 2 does not give you the advantages you receive from EtherTalk Phase 2, you will be able to use the server with both LocalTalk and EtherTalk Phase 2 without a problem.

TokenTalk

As mentioned in Chapter 3, you can use Token Ring adapters on the Mac for seamless integration into your current network. When you use a Token Ring with a VINES server, you will have to use a TokenTalk Phase 2 implementation: Phase 1 TokenTalk is not supported on VINES.

If you use a Macintosh Token Ring network, you'll have to use the source-level routing on the VINES server, because the Macs must have their own server. In a VINES environment without the AppleTalk option, if you are using a Token Ring network, you may or may not have source-level routing enabled, since it is only needed if you are communicating across a bridge.

Enabling source-level routing when you add a Mac to the network will mean that you have to reconfigure the adapter card setting on the server and configure an AppleTalk port for the Token Ring LAN segment. Configuring the AppleTalk port will be discussed later.

To turn on source-level routing for an existing card:

1. Select the "System Maintenance" option from the Operator menu on the Server.
2. Select "Configure/Diagnose Server."
3. From the Configure/Diagnose Server menu, select "Add Cards/Change Card Configuration."
4. Next, select "Change Card Settings."
5. Select the LAN card to be changed.
6. When a menu appears displaying the card's current settings, you will see the alternatives listed in parentheses. If you see an Enable End Node Source Routing prompt, then your card supports source-level routing. The default for this setting is "N," or No source-level routing. Change this setting to "Y."
7. Press **F10** to save your changes.

Once your Token Ring adapter is configured for source-level routing, you can configure it as an AppleTalk port.

EtherTalk

As already mentioned, Ethernet is the preferred way to connect Macs to your VINES server. But you will have to determine whether you are going to use AppleTalk Phase 1 or Phase 2, or a combination of the Phases, and how you are going to set up your zones afterward.

The most important task you will have to perform is network addressing. You can use a combination of AppleTalk Phase 1 and 2 on the same physical link, but you will lose the advantages you gain with Phase 2, because all network traffic will have to bow to the lowest common denominator—in this case, Phase 1. Therefore, we'll review each of these protocols briefly, concentrating on the VINES environment.

AppleTalk Phase 1

You should use AppleTalk Phase 1 only if you have older Macs or old Ethernet cards that will not support Phase 2. Because Phase 1 does not support extended addressing, you would be wise to place these Macs on their own network branch, then integrate them either by installing an Ethernet card in the server that will only service the Phase 1 physical link or by using a transition router and branching the Phase 1 network off of a Phase 2 network.

In either case, these Macs would have their own AppleTalk zone so that they would not impact Macs using AppleTalk Phase 2. The maximum number of machines you can have on a Phase 1 network is 254, although using this many would probably clog the bandwidth so badly that the net would be close to useless.

Since the Macs can run on the same physical link as PCs, you'll also want to be careful about dropping a Phase 1 Mac into a network that is configured for Phase 2 to service PCs. You'll be forced to change the configuration that services the PCs to Phase 1, and you'll basically mess up your network addresses. This can really cause problems on a large internet.

If you have only one AppleTalk port on the VINES server, and it is a Phase 1 port, the server will be able to act as a router, but only if you will be tunneling to another VINES server that is running AppleTalk Phase 2. Doing this will take advantage of the routing capabilities built into the VINES server.

AppleTalk Phase 2

By now, you know that the network physical link of preference when using Macs is Ethernet Phase 2. With Phase 2, you'll have the extended addressing capabilities that allow you to assign multiple zones to the network. Only an EtherTalk Phase 2 or TokenTalk physical link can support multiple zones.

It is possible that you are in the process of upgrading your network from Phase 1 to Phase 2, in which case you will still have to deal with the constraints of Phase 1, using transition routers, until you have completely converted your network.

A Phase 2 network enhances the overall performance of the network by:

- Reducing network traffic with automatic router selection for non-routing nodes (or *end nodes*).

- Reducing router traffic by sending only the routing table information that the receiving router does not already have (this technique is called a *split horizon*). The router does not send information about routers that can be reached through an intermediate router, because the recipient already has that information.

- Not constraining zones to a physical link, but assigning them as needed, so that a zone becomes a virtual location connecting separate resources from all over the internet into one logical configuration.

Mapping Your Network

Now, with the obligatory discussion of the physical link protocols out of the way, let's see how this all works. To put the general information above to use, we need a picture of a possible network. Figure 6.2 shows a VINES network with some servers and Macintosh networks connected.

In Figure 6.2, you'll see examples of all four Macintosh network protocols that work on a VINES network. What is important to notice is that the physical links are segregated according to the AppleTalk protocols they are running. Also important are the network addresses. You cannot have the same address on any two physical links of the network, because if you do, neither of the links (networks) will operate. The net effect will be that they cancel each other out. Assigning network address is done at the port level, and is discussed in the AppleTalk Ports section.

When you install Macs into your VINES network, you will have to know what AppleTalk protocol each network is using, its network address, and the zones assigned to the network. In Figure 6.2, you can see what protocol is being run on each segment. Also, you'll see individual VINES servers that are not configured for AppleTalk, but are still able to pass AppleTalk packets to another server that does have the AppleTalk option installed. This is called

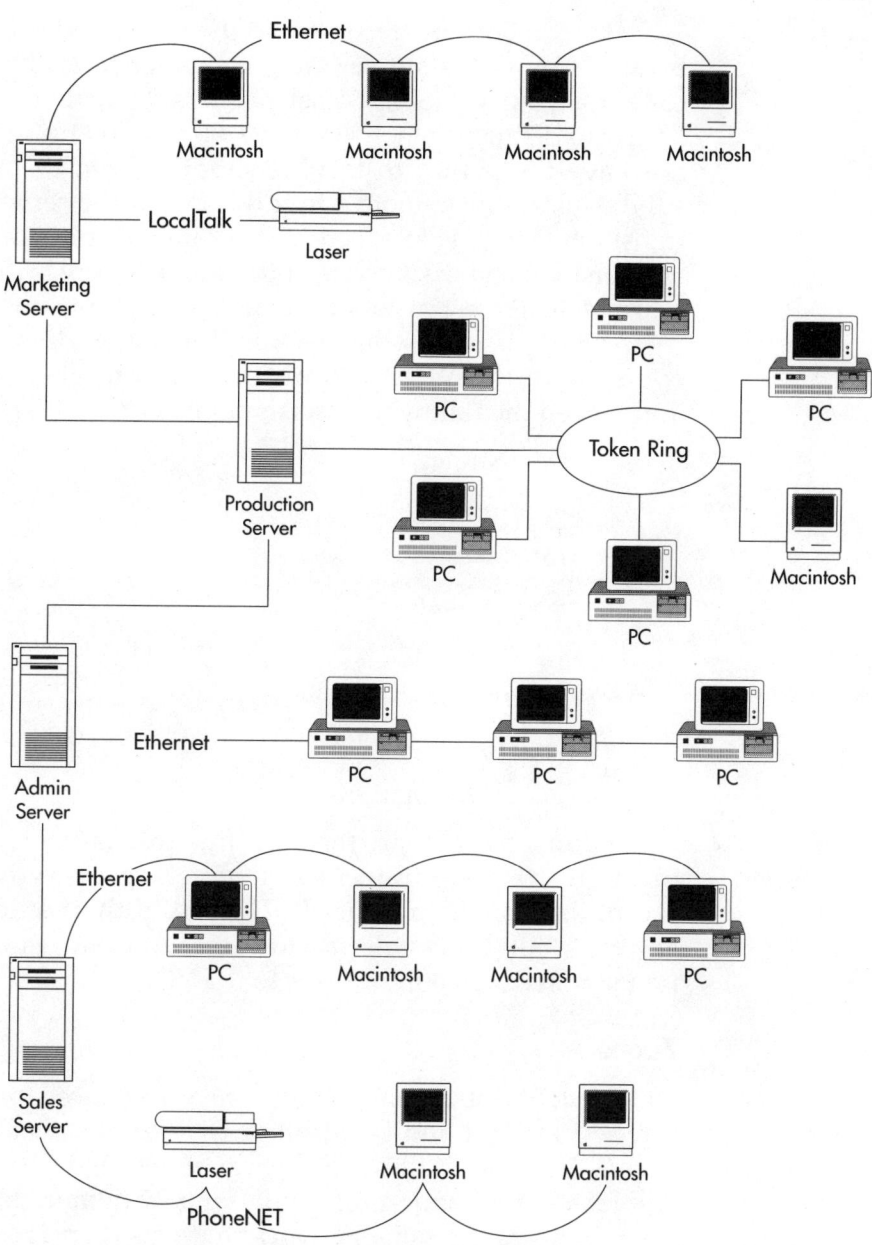

Figure 6.2
A VINES network

tunneling, and it is accomplished by using the VINES Port (discussed in the AppleTalk Ports section) to send AppleTalk packets through the network as VINES packets.

Banyan does not recommend the prolonged use of a transition bridge, so you should seriously consider installing DaynaTALK cards for your PostScript laser printers. If there is a problem, it is harder to diagnose when you have a transition bridge, and you will not have the ability to trouble-shoot it from the VINES server. VINES allows for remote administration if the server to which the transition bridge is attached is in a different physical location. But you'll have to have someone at the site reset any bridges or routers, which defeats the purpose of centralized administration.

When planning your network, you should use the chart that comes with the VINES AppleTalk option, or make your own. You'll need the following information:

- LAN Name
- Description
- Slot
- Seed status
- Network number or range number
- Default Zone
- Zone List
- Server Destinations

Filling out a chart that has this information will walk you through the planning process, covering everything you need except the actual wiring itself. The rest of this section and the one on AppleTalk Ports will provide you with the rest of the information you need to connect Macs to the VINES server.

Zones

So far, a lot has been said about zones. You know that they identify physical Phase 1 and LocalTalk networks, and that TokenTalk and EtherTalk Phase 2 allow for logical zones, as well. The zone is an AppleTalk designation for identifying or defining a network. Figure 6.3 shows the same network that was displayed in Figure 6.2, except that here you will see zone designations instead of raw network information.

When zone information is assigned to a specific physical link or network, it defines how people will be able to access data and resources. Each VINES port has a default zone to which you can add

Figure 6.3
The network with zone information

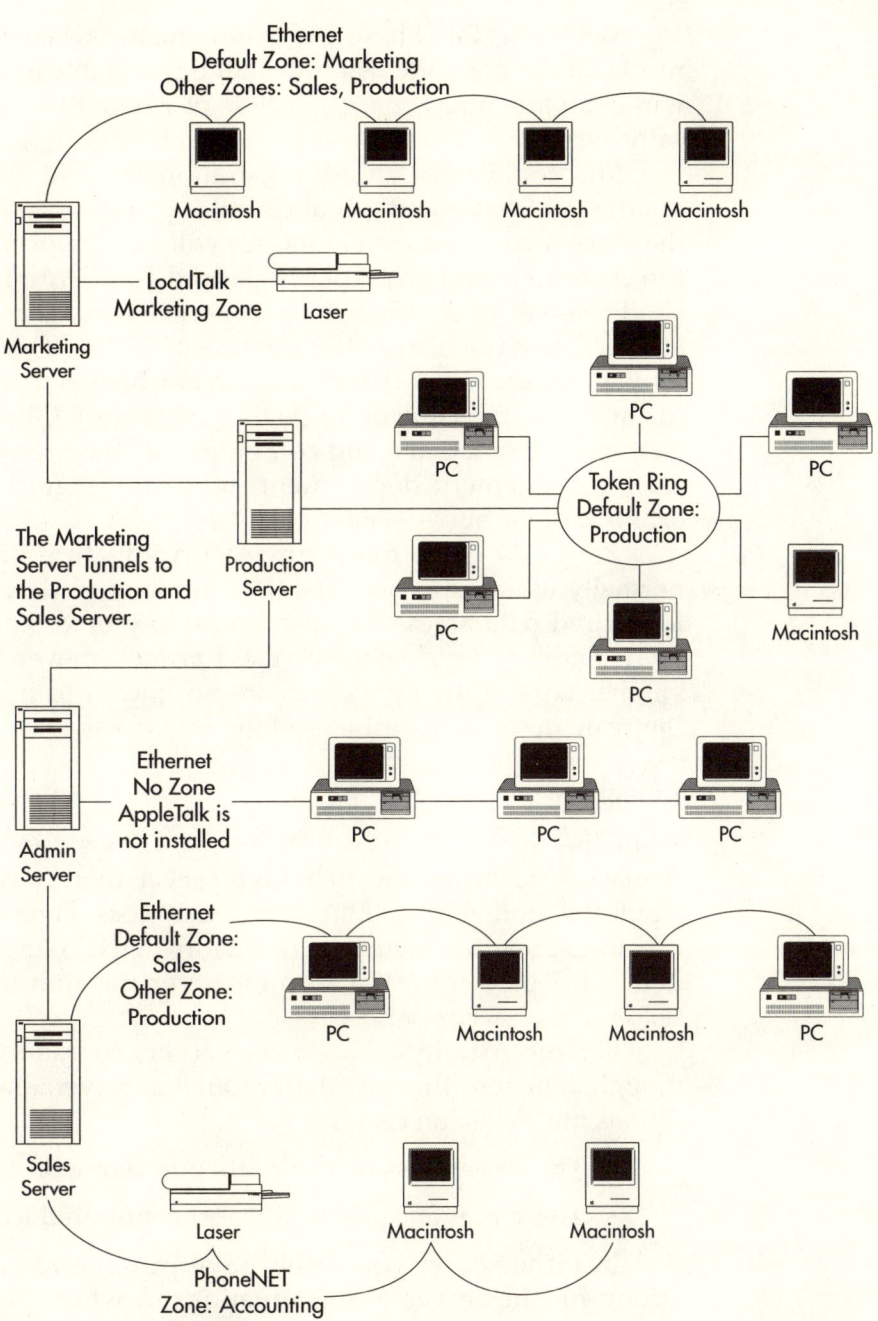

other zones. One way to look at a zone is to think of it as a tunneling mechanism that contains all of the network resources for a group.

With EtherTalk Phase 2, it doesn't matter where these resources reside on the network. They will all be available to anyone who is within a particular zone, regardless of where that person is physically located.

You could have an administration office at corporate headquarters in Seattle and a branch office in San Francisco. However, the office manager in San Francisco will need information that is in the Admin zone in Seattle. If you add the Admin zone to the VINES server in San Francisco, the office manager would then be able to access the corporate resources in Seattle. That is, it would if your network has a direct connection between the two offices (using a switched line or an ISDN connection). Likewise, the sales staff in San Francisco could communicate share resources with the sales management department in Seattle. Figure 6.4 shows an example of the above scenario.

Zones do not provide any security features. Someone who normally uses one zone—like the Admin zone described above—for shared data access can also access any other zone on the network, and can simultaneously use a printer or even a file server in another zone. Although zones are not meant to provide security, they can, in some cases, be used to limit access.

Tunneling

Tunneling is a feature of VINES that allows one server to pass AppleTalk information through a server that does not have the AppleTalk option to another server that does. Figure 6.5 shows an example scenario in which there are three VINES servers. AppleTalk data must pass from the Admin server through the Production server to the Service server.

For the Admin and Service servers to communicate, even though data goes through the Production server, one of these conditions must exist on each server.

- The server has an AppleTalk port defined.
- The server has the VINES port configured for AppleTalk.

In either case, you must have purchased the AppleTalk option for the server. Some situations in which you might need tunneling, besides needing to get data from one workgroup to another, are:

- The server that is tunneling the data is running on a version of VINES older than 5.0.

Figure 6.4

Using zones on an internet

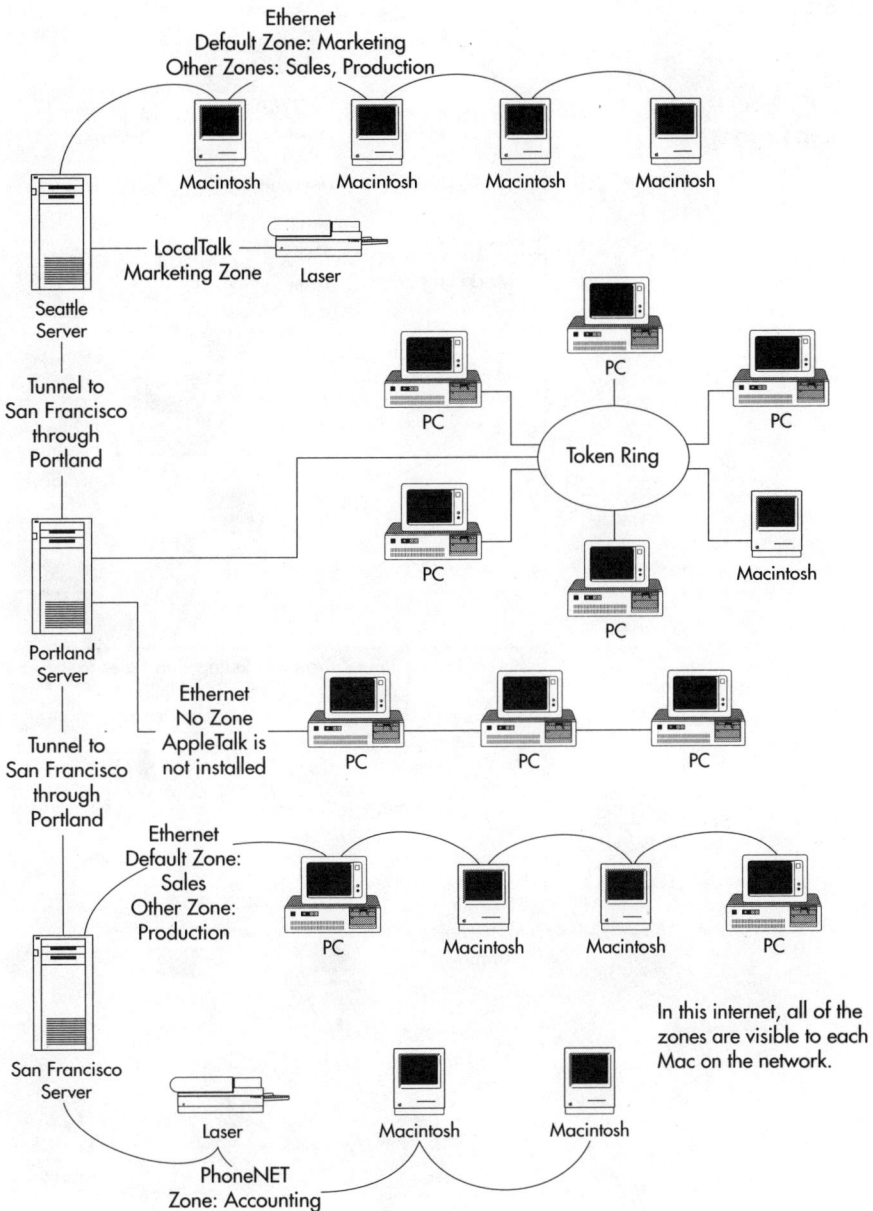

- You need to connect a server that is running AppleTalk Phase 2 to one running AppleTalk Phase 1.
- The server that is tunneling the data does not have AppleTalk installed.

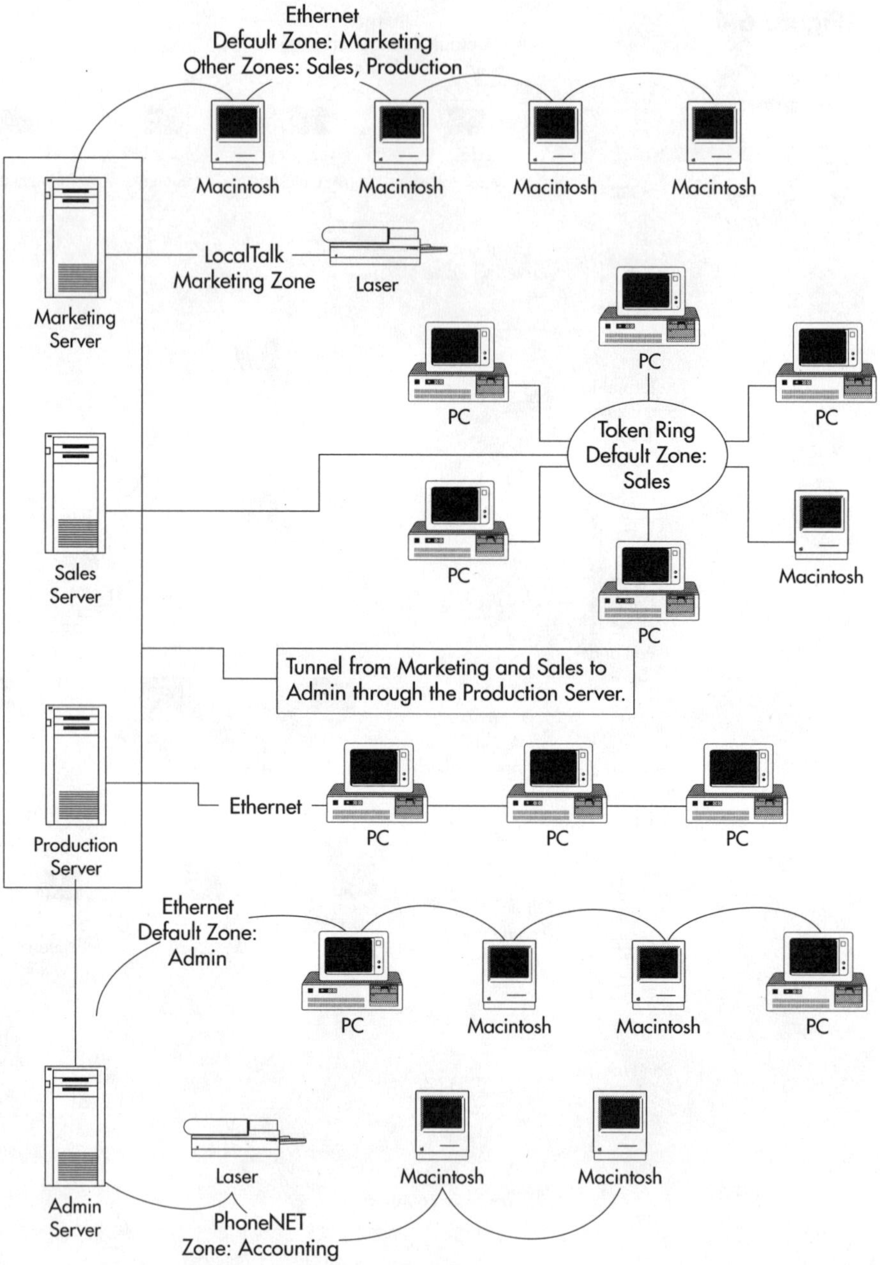

Figure 6.5

Tunneling through a VINES server

[Diagram showing a network topology with Marketing Server, Sales Server, Production Server, and Admin Server connected vertically. The Marketing Server connects to an Ethernet segment (Default Zone: Marketing, Other Zones: Sales, Production) with four Macintoshes, and a LocalTalk Marketing Zone with a Laser printer. The Sales Server connects to a Token Ring (Default Zone: Sales) with multiple PCs and a Macintosh. A note reads: "Tunnel from Marketing and Sales to Admin through the Production Server." The Production Server connects to an Ethernet with three PCs. The Admin Server connects to an Ethernet (Default Zone: Admin) with PCs and Macintoshes, and a PhoneNET Zone: Accounting with a Laser printer and two Macintoshes.]

In the introduction to this section, I mentioned that the VINES server disguises the AppleTalk packets when they are sent through the server. This is the same process that allows for tunneling. When the AppleTalk packet leaves one server, it looks like—and is—a VINES packet: VINES header information has been added to it. This way, when the packet travels through the server that does not have AppleTalk, it is assumed to be a normal VINES packet and is sent merrily on its way. When the packet reaches its destination, the receiving server strips the packet of its VINES information and sends the encapsulated AppleTalk packet to its proper destination.

One other concern you might have about tunneling is the number of hops that the data will have to travel. AppleTalk can deal with only 15 hops. So if you have a large organization with lots of servers, you will have to plan carefully how the data from one VINES AppleShare server gets to another, and keep this limitation in mind.

AppleTalk Ports

We've discussed the implications of the different AppleTalk protocols you can run on a VINES server, and this discussion has frequently mentioned ports. Although you are probably familiar with ports because you have to deal with them for your PCs, we now have to talk about all of the issues related to using AppleTalk with your ports. The port is a logical definition that determines the server's capabilities in conjunction with its network cards.

Each network card that will be connecting the VINES server to an AppleTalk network is a port, and it must be configured to accept the AppleTalk protocol. In addition to the physical network cards, a VINES server has one additional port, called a *VINES port*. The VINES port is a logical port that the Server can use for tunneling, but you should not use the VINES port for actual network connections because it cannot use AppleTalk Phase 2 addressing. You will find more information about the VINES port in the section below called The VINES Port.

This brings us to the issue of addressing, and the port's capabilities in general. The remaining sections here will deal with port-related issues, filling in the final bits of information you need before installing AppleTalk on the VINES server.

Addresses

AppleTalk depends on network addresses for getting the data from one machine to another. Each AppleTalk device on a network has a node number, a socket number, and a network number. Network numbers are a numbering system that defines the physical network itself.

In order to assign network numbers, you'll need a physical map of your network, and each port must be assigned an address. You should know what network numbers you are going to assign before you set up the VINES AppleTalk option. AppleTalk Phase 2 physical links will use network range numbers, while Phase 1 and LocalTalk ports will have single-digit network numbers. The numbers are actually arbitrary; the only limitation is that you do not assign duplicate numbers to the different ports. For your network numbers, you can choose any number between 1 and 65279. When assigning network numbers, keep the following rules in mind:

- Network range numbers for AppleTalk Phase 2 cannot overlap.
- You cannot use an address for LocalTalk or AppleTalk Phase 1 that is part of a range used by an AppleTalk Phase 2 network.
- If you are using a mixed-phase network, all Phase 2-compatible ports must have a single-digit range number, like 5 to 5.
- The range between Phase 2 address numbers should be kept small, like 6 to 10, to allow for future expansion.

The simpler you keep your network numbering strategy, the easier it will be to maintain. One way to make sure you do not have network numbering conflicts when dealing with a large internet is to assign a range of numbers that can be used for each location. For instance, in the Seattle/San Francisco example from above, you might want to assign Seattle a range of numbers of 1 to 1000, and San Francisco from 1001 to 2000. In doing this, you will prevent network number conflicts between Seattle and San Francisco, and your life will be easier.

If you are using an internet router, you will have to make sure that the network numbers for all the networks that the router is connecting are correct. Figure 6.6 shows Farallon's Liaison routing between a LocalTalk and EtherTalk Phase 2 network.

In Figure 6.6, the EtherTalk 2 network is connected to the VINES server, and the network number must be the same as the network number assigned to the server port. The network number for the LocalTalk port was assigned automatically by Liaison, but it can be changed manually to correspond to a number you want

Figure 6.6

Liaison routing between two networks

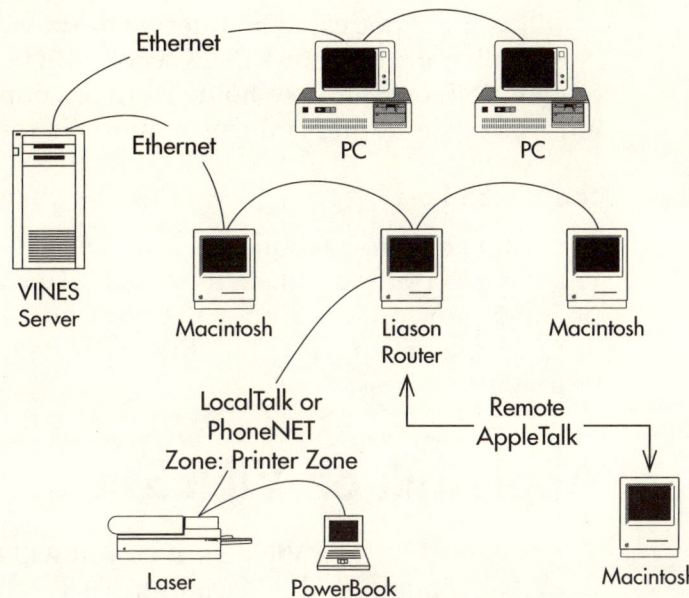

to assign. (Liaison is no longer being sold by Farallon, but it is still in wide use, and Farallon will continue to support it.) You will have to watch the network numbers assigned by routers, because they will assign their own numbers automatically unless you override that assignment with a number you've selected.

I mentioned node and socket numbers as being part of an AppleTalk network address. You shouldn't have to worry about these types of numbers, but you might want to know about them anyway. A *node number* is the number automatically assigned to an AppleTalk device on the network. *Socket numbers* are numbers assigned to a node that differentiate different AppleTalk services running on a particular Mac, such as file sharing and E-mail services.

Seed and Non-seed Ports

A *seed port* is an AppleTalk port to which you assign the zone and network information. In Figure 6.6, the EtherTalk Phase 2 port on the router is a non-seed port, because it receives its information from the VINES server, which is a seed port. But the LocalTalk port is a seed port, even though the network number was assigned automatically. On each AppleTalk network, at least one port should be a seed port. Otherwise, you stand a chance of having a network address conflict.

If you are not using an internet or transition router, all of the AppleTalk ports on your VINES server will be seed ports. The port on the VINES server does not need to be configured as a seed port if it receives its address information from a router.

The VINES Port

If you are going to be tunneling from one VINES server to another, you have to configure the VINES port. The VINES port is a seed port, so you must assign a network address. Even when the VINES server is an AppleTalk Phase 2 server, the VINES port will be a single address.

AppleTalk on VINES

To run AppleTalk on a VINES server, you will first have to purchase the VINES option for the Macintosh. This section assumes that you have the VINES option for the Macintosh, and goes through the steps of installing and configuring a VINES server so it will act as an AFP file server and provide printer services for an AppleTalk printer.

Installing the VINES Macintosh Option

If you purchased VINES with the Macintosh option, AppleTalk was loaded when you installed VINES. Otherwise, you will be adding the VINES Macintosh option.

To install the option for the Macintosh:

1. Install the Option Key that came with the software on the server's parallel port.
2. From the server console's Operator menu, shut down the server software (item 4).
3. After the server shuts down, select "System Maintenance" from the Operator menu.
4. Select "INSTALL Option Key Contents." After the server loads the Option Key contents, you will see the Manage Software Options menu. You should see all of the options installed on the server, including AppleTalk Protocol Support.
5. Press the **ESC** key or select the EXIT option, and you will be returned to the Systems Maintenance screen.

The AppleTalk Option is now loaded, but you have to rebuild the drivers before you can use it.

To rebuild the drivers:

1. Choose "Configure/Diagnose Server" from the Systems Maintenance menu.
2. From the VINES Server Configuration screen, select "Add Cards/Change Card Configuration."
3. In the Add/Change Card window, select "Save Configuration and Exit." This will cause the drivers to be rebuilt, and you will then be returned to the VINES Server Configuration menu.
4. Once the drivers are rebuilt, return to the System Maintenance screen.
5. Remove the Option Key.
6. Reboot the server.

AppleTalk will not restart until you have restarted the server. Once the server is running again, you are ready to configure the AppleTalk ports.

Configuration

In this section you will use all of the information that preceded this section. Before you start to configure your server, you should have a worksheet that looks like Figure 6.7.

On the worksheet, you should have all of the previously mentioned items filled out so you can configure the AppleTalk ports without problems or conflicts.

To configure your AppleTalk ports:

1. Start at the server console and display the Operator menu.
2. Select "Manage Communications."
3. From the Manage Communications screen, select "AppleTalk." The Manage AppleTalk screen will look like Figure 6.8.

Here, your choices will be:

- **Start/Stop AppleTalk** This option turns the AppleTalk services on or off; it is a toggle switch. If AppleTalk is stopped when you shut down the server, it will be stopped when you restart it.

Figure 6.7

Network configuration sheet

Server or LAN name:				
Description:				
Port Number & Type	Seed Status	Network number or range number	Default Zone Name	Zone List
VINES Port				

Server or LAN name:				
Description:				
Port Number & Type	Seed Status	Network number or range number	Default Zone Name	Zone List
VINES Port				

Server or LAN name:				
Description:				
Port Number & Type	Seed Status	Network number or range number	Default Zone Name	Zone List
VINES Port				

Figure 6.8

The Manage AppleTalk screen

```
                                                    +---------------------+
                                                    | Manage AppleTalk    |
                                                    +---------------------+
  Server:  SMC_Server
  Netid:   2907326
  Version: 5.50 (1)

                     A P P L E T A L K   Phase 2

                     AppleTalk Software is RUNNING

          Use arrow keys to select a choice and press <RETURN>

                    1 - Start/Stop AppleTalk
                    2 - Manage Ports
                    3 - Change AppleTalk Phase
                    4 - Manage Routing through VINES networks
                    5 - Display Port Status
                    6 - Display Routes



  ESC to exit; F1 for HELP
```

- **Manage Ports** From the Manage Ports screen you define and manage your server's AppleTalk ports.
- **Change AppleTalk Phase** This option lets you change the VINES server's AppleTalk Phase.
- **Manage Routing through VINES networks** This is the menu selection you access if you are going to use the VINES tunneling capabilities.
- **Display Port Status** The Display Port Status screen is used to diagnose problems by confirming what ports are running and the status of those ports. You can also view the port's default zone from this screen.
- **Display Routes** The AppleTalk Routes screen displays the network information that is being broadcast from the server or received by the server from another AppleTalk router.

In Figure 6.8, notice that AppleTalk is running. In order to configure your AppleTalk Ports, you will have to stop AppleTalk.

To stop AppleTalk:

1. Select "Start/Stop AppleTalk" from the Manage AppleTalk menu.
2. The screen that appears asks you whether you want to stop AppleTalk. Select YES and then press the **Return** key.
3. You will be asked if you want to give a one-minute warning to your users. At this point, you don't have any users, so it you might as well answer with NO.
4. You will be returned to the Manage AppleTalk screen, which should indicate that AppleTalk has been stopped, as shown in Figure 6.9.

Now that AppleTalk is stopped, you can configure your AppleTalk ports. You can configure any network card to be an AppleTalk port. If you anticipate that you will be adding Macs to ports that have only PCs connected to them, you might want to consider configuring them now. That way, you won't have to do it later, and when you're ready to add the Mac, all you have to do is add it to the network. This is really easy if you're using 10BaseT—all you have to do is run the cable from the Mac to your hub and turn it on.

Figure 6.9

The Manage AppleTalk screen with AppleTalk stopped

```
+--------------------------------------------------------------+
|                                              : Manage AppleTalk :
+--------------------------------------------------------------+
: Server:  SMC_Server                                          :
: Netid:   2907326                                             :
: Version: 5.52 (5)                                            :
:                                                              :
:              A P P L E T A L K   Phase 2                     :
:                                                              :
:               AppleTalk Software is STOPPED                  :
:                                                              :
:        Use arrow keys to select a choice and press <RETURN>  :
:                                                              :
:                   1 - Start/Stop AppleTalk                   :
:                   2 - Manage Ports                           :
:                   3 - Change AppleTalk Phase                 :
:                   4 - Manage Routing through VINES networks  :
:                   5 - Display Port Status                    :
:                   6 - Display Routes                         :
:                                                              :
:                                                              :
: ESC to exit; F1 for HELP                                     :
+--------------------------------------------------------------+
```

Before you configure the AppleTalk port, you should set the server's Phase. When AppleTalk is installed on the server, the default is AppleTalk Phase 2. If you're going to be using Phase 1 cards, you should change the AppleTalk Phase before you configure the ports, because the Phase setting will affect your network addresses.

Changing the Phase is a toggle, just like starting and stopping AppleTalk. Once you've set the Phase, you can configure your AppleTalk ports.

To configure the ports:

1. Select "Manage Ports" from the Manage AppleTalk screen. You will see the Manage Ports screen, which displays a configured port (see Fig. 6.10).

2. From the Manage Ports screen, you will want to ADD a port. You will have an option to add a port for each network card and the VINES port, and you will see a screen similar to Figure 6.11.

Figure 6.10

The Manage Ports screen

```
+--------------------------------------------------------------+
|                                              : Manage AppleTalk :
+                                              +---------------+
|                                              : Manage Ports  :
+--------------------------------------------------------------+
: Use arrow keys to select a command and press <RETURN>        :
:                                                              :
:       ADD a port                    DELETE port              :
:       MODIFY a port                 ENABLE/DISABLE port      :
:       MANAGE zones                                           :
:--------------------------------------------------------------:
: Server: SMC_Server                  AppleTalk Phase 2 STOPPED:
:                                                              :
: Port  St  Description      Network Range    Default Zone     :
: ----  --  -----------      -------------    ------------     :
:                                                              :
:  3    E   Primary Network    101-105        Zone 1           :
:                                                              :
:                                                              :
:                                                              :
: ESC to exit; F9 for zone details; F1 for HELP                :
+--------------------------------------------------------------+
```

BANYAN VINES | 245

Figure 6.11
The Add an AppleTalk Port screen

```
+------------------------------------------------------------+
|                                          | Manage AppleTalk |
|                                          +------------------+
|                                          | ADD an AppleTalk port |
+------------------------------------------+
|                                                            |
|   Use arrow keys to select from the list below and press <RETURN> |
|   (There are 2 possible network interfaces for AppleTalk)  |
|                                                            |
|   Interface              Slot (AppleTalk port)             |
|   ---------              ----                              |
|                                                            |
|   Novell NE1000/NE2000     3                               |
|   VINES                                                    |
|                                                            |
|                                                            |
|                                                            |
|                                                            |
| ESC to exit; F1 for HELP                                   |
+------------------------------------------------------------+
```

3. Select the interface card you want to configure and press the **Return** key.

   If you have more than one network card with the same name, you can distinguish betwqeen them by the slot number, which indicates the physical slot the card occupies in the server.

4. You will be asked if you want the port to be seed port. Select YES.

5. You will then see a Set AppleTalk Port Configuration screen like the one in Figure 6.12. As you can see, you will need to fill out the following:

   - **Description**   The description is provided for easy identification. It can be 32 characters long.

   - **Network range start**   This is the beginning range number for a Phase 2 AppleTalk port.

Figure 6.12
The AppleTalk Configuration screen

```
+------------------------------------------------------------+
|                                          | Manage AppleTalk |
|                                          +------------------+
|                                          | ADD an AppleTalk port |
|                                          +------------------+
|                                          | Set AppleTalk port configuration |
+------------------------------------------+
|                                                            |
|   For each field, type the appropriate information and press <RETURN>. |
|                                                            |
|                                                            |
|   Description:                                             |
|   Network range start:                                     |
|   Network range end:                                       |
|   Default zone:                                            |
|                                                            |
|                                                            |
| F10 when done; ESC to exit; F1 for HELP                    |
+------------------------------------------------------------+
```

- **Network range end**   This is the ending range number for a Phase 2 AppleTalk port.
- **Default zone**   This is the name of the default AppleTalk zone that will be broadcast to the Macintoshes and visible from the Chooser. A zone name can only be 32 characters long.

6. After you have filled out the port information, which should have come from your set-up sheet, press **F10** to save your changes. The AppleTalk Port Configuration screen should look something like Figure 6.13.
7. You will be returned to the "Add a port" screen, from which you can configure additional ports. You should see the port you just configured, as shown in Figure 6.14.

All of the information displayed should be familiar except the "St" column. An "E" in the "St" column means that the port is Enabled, while a "D" means that the port is Disabled.

Figure 6.13

The completed AppleTalk port configuration

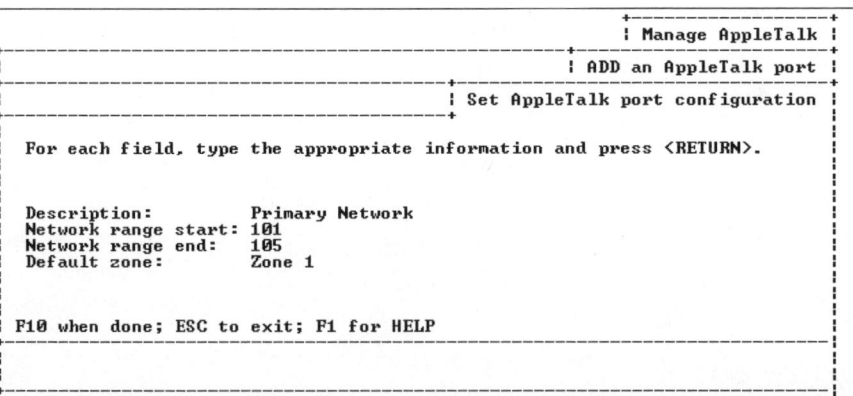

```
+------------------------------------------------+
|                               | Manage AppleTalk |
+-------------------------------+------------------+
|                               | ADD an AppleTalk port |
+-------------------------------+------------------------+
|                               | Set AppleTalk port configuration |
+-------------------------------+----------------------------------+
| For each field, type the appropriate information and press <RETURN>. |
|                                                                      |
| Description:           Primary Network                               |
| Network range start:   101                                           |
| Network range end:     105                                           |
| Default zone:          Zone 1                                        |
|                                                                      |
| F10 when done; ESC to exit; F1 for HELP                              |
+----------------------------------------------------------------------+
```

Note

If you are configuring a Phase 1 network, you will have only a single name network address number to assign. Also, remember that if you have a network running both AppleTalk Phase 1 and Phase 2, your Phase 2 beginning and ending range numbers must be the same to be compatible with the Phase 1 networks.

Figure 6.14
The AppleTalk port configured

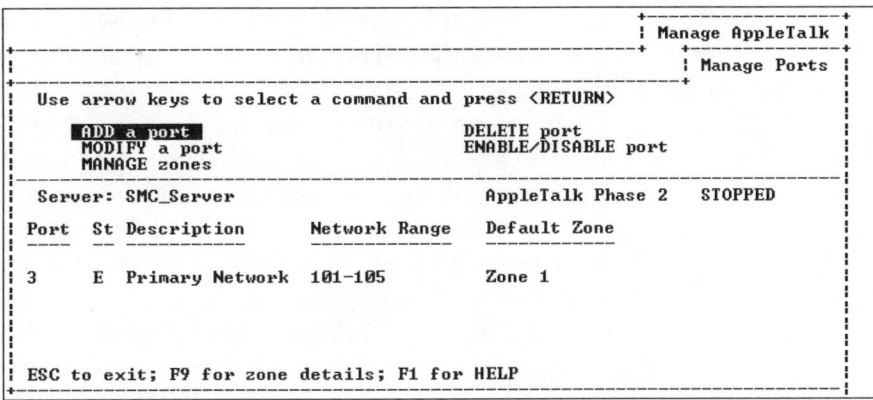

To configure more ports, you will have to repeat steps 1 through 6 for each port.

Restarting AppleTalk

After you have configured all of your ports, you need to restart AppleTalk. This is done just like stopping AppleTalk.

To restart AppleTalk:

1. Select "Start/Stop AppleTalk" from the Manage AppleTalk menu.

2. The screen that appears asks you whether you want to start AppleTalk. Select YES and then press the **Return** key.

3. You will be returned to the Manage AppleTalk screen, which should indicate that AppleTalk is running, as shown in Figure 6.15.

Figure 6.15
The Manage AppleTalk screen with AppleTalk running

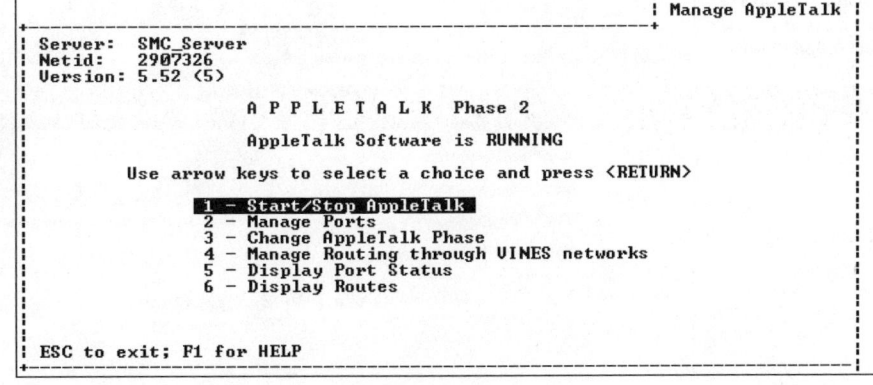

Chapter 6

Once AppleTalk has been started, the Macintoshes on the network can access the server. It will take a few minutes for the service to become available. Also, whenever you make changes to zones, add ports, or otherwise modify the AppleTalk services, there will be a period of time, called an *aging out*, that must happen before the services are available. This is much more important on a large network than on a small one, but even on a small network you need to give AppleTalk enough time to broadcast the changes to the Macs on the network.

To make sure the service is available, you will have to monitor the aging processes from the server console using the VINES Network and Systems Management software (VNSM). To see if zone information has changed, you can use the Run Network Summary.

To use the Network Management selection:

1. From the VNSM Operator menu (see Fig. 6.16), select "Run Network Management."

2. When the VINES Network Summary screen appears, select "SHOW Protocol Information."

3. Choose the server for which you want protocol information (see Fig. 6.17).

4. From the Protocol Information screen (see Fig. 6.18), select "AppleTalk Zones."

5. From the AppleTalk Zones Table Data screen, you will see the AppleTalk zones that are currently available, as shown in Figure 6.19.

Figure 6.16
The Operator menu

```
              BANYAN   SYSTEMS   INCORPORATED
              VINES: Virtual Networking System Version 5.52 (5)
                    Serial No: 2907326   Server: SMC_Server
        Copyright (c) 1984,1992 by Banyan Systems Incorporated ALL RIGHTS RESERVED
                              OPERATOR MENU

          1. Display Service Status      6. Console Security/Selection

          2. Backup/Restore              7. Manage Communications

          3. Send Messages to Users      8. Printer Control

          4. Shut Down Server Software   9. Run Network Management

          5. Restart Services           10. System Maintenance

                        Enter your choice (1-10):
```

BANYAN VINES

Figure 6.17
The VINES Network Summary screen with a server selected

```
+--------------------------------------------------------------+
|                                          : VINES Network Summary :
+--------------------------------------------------------------+
: Use arrow keys to highlight a choice and press ENTER.        :
:                                                              :
:   SHOW communications statistics    SHOW protocol information:
:   SHOW service statistics           SHOW topology information:
:   SHOW file system statistics       SHOW OS information      :
:   SHOW disk usage statistics        TRACE a route            :
:   REMOVE server from list           HELP (F1)                :
:                                                              :
:   Server-Name Revision  Load-averages   Mavg  Msgin  Msgout  Drops Swavg :
:                         1min 5min 15min                      :
:   SMC_Server  5.52 (5)  0.43 0.75 0.56  7.31  14188  20568   0     0.04  :
:                                                              :
+--------------------------------------------------------------+
```

Figure 6.18
The Protocol Information screen

```
+--------------------------------------------------------------+
|                                          : VINES Network Summary :
+--------------------------------------------------------------+
|                                          : Protocol Information :
+--------------------------------------------------------------+
: Use arrow keys to highlight a choice, then press ENTER.      :
:                                                              :
:      1 - VINES Neighbors                                     :
:      2 - VINES Routes                                        :
:      3 - VINES Source Level Routes                           :
:      4 - APPLETALK ARP entries                               :
:      5 - APPLETALK Ports                                     :
:      6 - APPLETALK Port Zones                                :
:      7 - APPLETALK Names                                     :
:      8 - APPLETALK Zones                                     :
:      9 - APPLETALK Routes                                    :
:                                                              :
: ESC to exit; F3 for main options                             :
+--------------------------------------------------------------+
```

Figure 6.19
The Table Data screen with AppleTalk zone information

```
+--------------------------------------------------------------+
|                                          : VINES Network Summary :
+--------------------------------------------------------------+
|                                          : Protocol Information :
+--------------------------------------------------------------+
|                                                   : Table data :
+--------------------------------------------------------------+
: Server: SMC_Server         Netid: 02907326   APPLETALK Zones: 2 :
:                                                              :
:   EthMulticast 0900070000a4                                  :
:   TrnMulticast c00000002000                                  :
:   ZonNam       Printer Zone                                  :
:   Netwks       48842                                         :
:                                                              :
:   EthMulticast 0900070000c2                                  :
:   TrnMulticast c00000002000                                  :
:   ZonNam       Zone 1                                        :
:   Netwks       101                                           :
:                                                              :
:   F3 for main options; F1 for HELP; ESC to exit              :
+--------------------------------------------------------------+
```

If the AppleTalk zone you've added is visible, it will be available. Likewise, if a zone was deleted and is still visible, it has not aged out. It is visible through the Macintosh's Chooser until it ages out.

This can cause a problem if someone tries to log in while you are performing maintenance, because the zone can still be selected. But once it ages out, the zone will disappear, along with all of its associated resources. As a result, the user will suddenly encounter network errors and find resources unavailable. For this reason, you should send a message to your Mac users before you perform maintenance, requesting that they log out of the network.

The steps for checking the zone information should be kept handy, because they are similar to those you will use to trouble-shoot the server for AppleTalk problem. The steps will not be repeated; you will just be asked to go to the Protocol Information screen.

StreetTalk and STDA

StreetTalk and StreetTalk Directory Assistance (STDA) are the heart of VINES user and service control. These services and systems will not be discussed except as they apply to Macintosh operations. These subjects are too broad to be covered here.

Adding Macintosh users to your access lists is the same as adding a PC user, except that the Mac user's profile can only use two commands, SETMAIL and !SETSTDA. These commands are specifically for using the VINES Intelligent Messaging Mail system.

!SETSTDA is used to select the Mac Users STDA database with Network Mail for Macintosh. This command must be included for Network Mail access. The SETMAIL command will make the mail service available to the Mac users. No other commands will work in the Mac users profile.

There are other commands that can be initiated by a Macintosh user, but these are done from the Mac using the VINES utility. The Mac user has no way to issue an equivalent of command-line commands like a PC user. This also means that a server cannot be controlled or configured from a Macintosh.

The StreetTalk issue you will have to be careful with is that the Mac user's name length can only be 31 characters, including the organization, group name, and the @ sign. If a name is longer than 31 characters, the Macintosh user will not be able to log in. This is because the Macintosh's Chooser can only display user names that are 32 or fewer characters. Also, all passwords for Macintosh users must be 8 characters or less.

You will have to educate your Mac users about their StreetTalk names. The structure of StreetTalk will be unfamiliar to the Mac users, and they will forget that they have to include their full StreetTalk name in order to log in. So when Mac users call you saying that they can't log in, you should first check to make sure they are using their full StreetTalk names.

You will also have to assign Mac users the ability to See Folders from the root level of the server directory. Otherwise, they will not be able to see their folders. You will have to use the SETARL utility from a PC, or log into the server from a Mac as the administrator and use the Macintosh VINES utility, as is discussed in the VINES on the Mac section.

STDA must be turned on in order for PCs to access a PAP printer service, the VINES designation for an AppleTalk PostScript printer. STDA is not necessary for Macs to access one of these printers. You will find more information about PAP printers in the AppleTalk PostScript Printers section.

DOS Extension Mapping

VINES allows for DOS Extension Mapping, which allows PC files with specific extensions to appear as native Macintosh files when viewed from the Mac. The Mac will not associate an application icon with a file unless the DOS extension has been mapped.

The DOS Extension Mapping must be turned on and the extensions added. You can map a total of 44 file types if you use application names that are 8 characters or less, but this is unreasonable, since many Mac applications have names that are longer than 8 characters. Therefore, figure that you will have the ability to map only 21 different file types, since this is the VINES limit when you have application names longer than 8 characters.

To map file extensions, you will have to use the VINES Operate utility:

1. From the Operate a Server screen (see Fig. 6.20), choose "AFP Services."

2. When the Control A Service screen appears, you will have to select the "Configure Service" command (see Fig. 6.21).

3. You will be presented with two options, as seen in Figure 6.22.

4. The next screen that appears is the Define Extension Mappings screen (see Fig. 6.23). From here you can add, change, or delete an extension mapping. In Figure 6.23 you will see several mappings that are already defined.

Figure 6.20

The VINES Operate utility

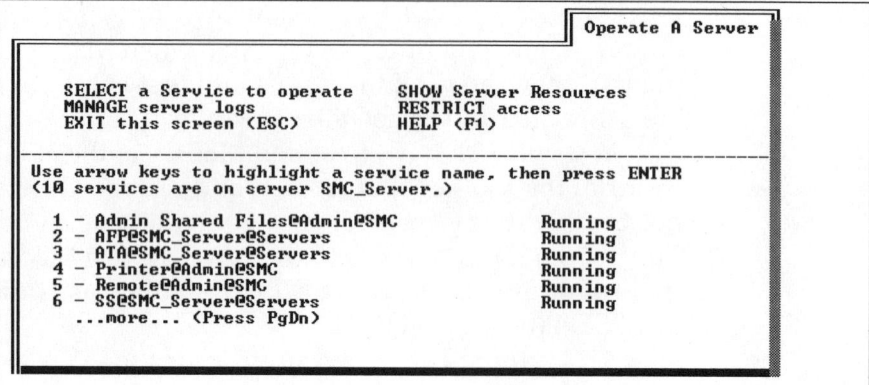

Figure 6.21

The Control A Service screen

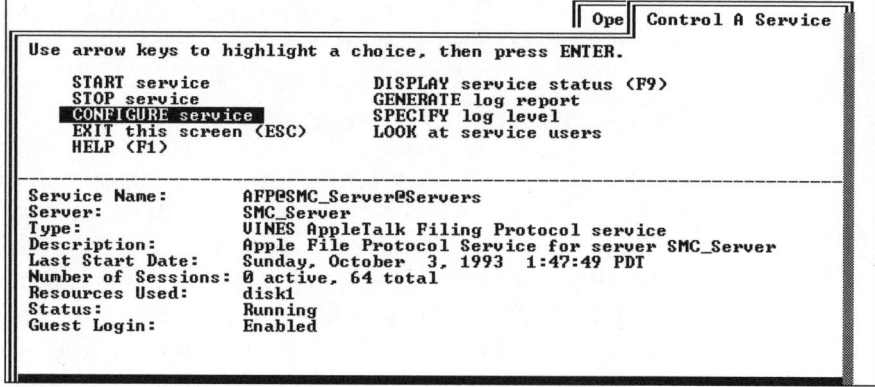

Figure 6.22

The Configure AFP Server screen

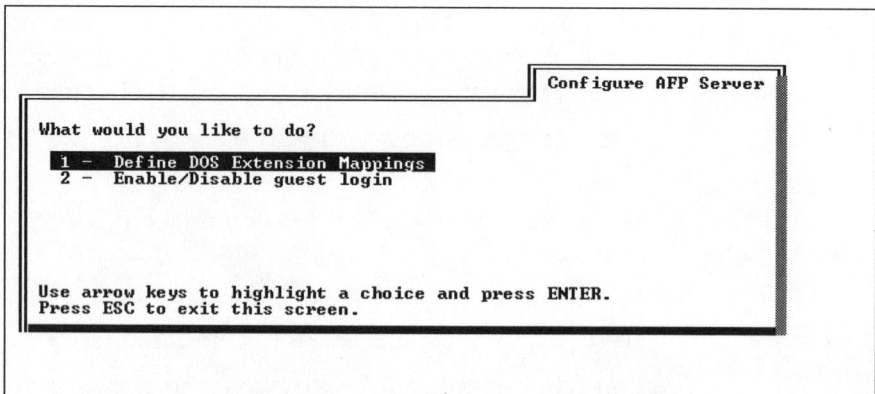

When you add an application to the extension list by selecting "Add Mapping," you can either choose a predefined application or enter the Macintosh application information manually (see Fig. 6.24).

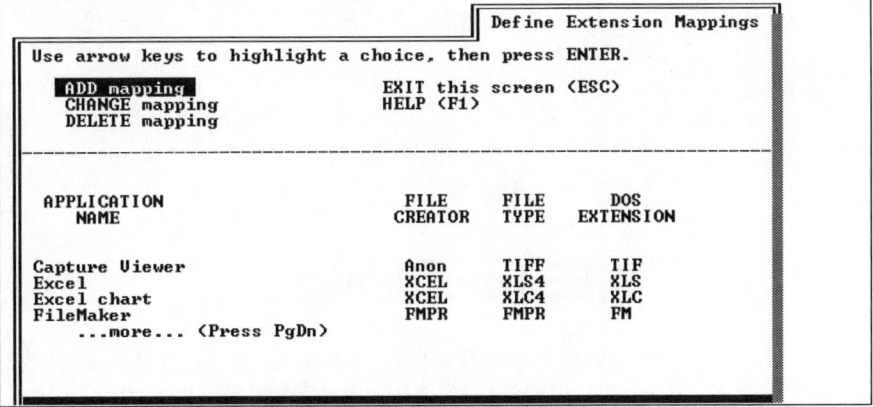

Figure 6.23
The Define Extension Mappings screen

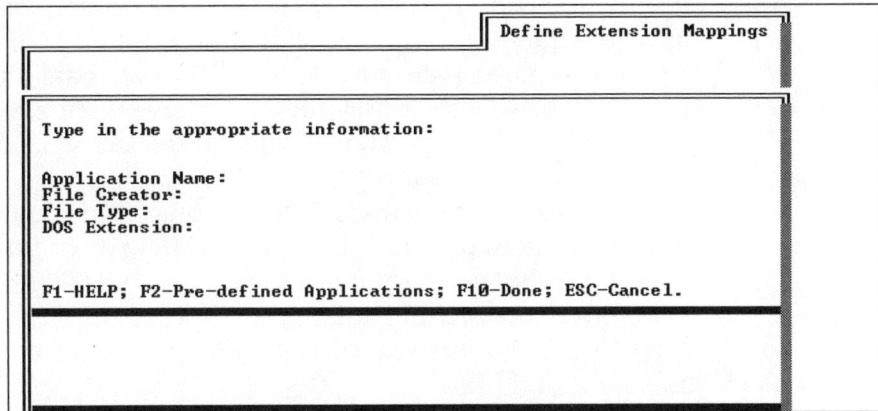

Figure 6.24
Adding a new mapping

When you enter the mapping information, you need to match the Macintosh application's file creator and type with the associated DOS extension. (For more information on file type and creator codes, see Chapter 2.) Also, you cannot enter duplicate extensions. When using this feature, you should make sure that the file formats for the mapped extensions will be translated automatically by the Macintosh, or that the files are fully cross-platform compatible. Otherwise, the Mac will not open the file.

Guest Login

The other option you have for controlling an AFP file server is whether to allow a guest login. Guest logins are a feature of all AppleShare file servers if the access privileges are set properly. With a VINES server, you either allow or disallow guest logins by enabling them in the Configure AFP Server section of the Operate application.

Figure 6.22 shows the option to enable guest logins. Since it is just a toggle switch, there is nothing else to say about this feature, except that you really have to watch your access rights if you do allow guest logins.

VINES on the Mac

Once you have the server set up so that it is visible from the Macintosh Chooser, you are ready to access the VINES server from a Mac. The Macintosh should have the AppleShare extension installed and be prepared to act as an AppleShare client. If you have any questions about how this should work, see Chapter 2.

It is not necessary for your Mac users to have the VINES software installed on their Macintoshes. However, if a Macintosh does not see the server, you should go through the steps in the Chapter 10. The trouble-shooting section in this chapter deals only with VINES-specific problems, while Chapter 10 deals primarily with Macintosh network trouble-shooting. If you are sure that everything on the server is set up properly, and the VNSM Service Monitor shows that AppleTalk server is running (as shown in Fig. 6.25), you have either a cabling or a Macintosh problem.

Testing the Connection the First Time

When you log into the server, follow the steps form Chapter 2 for logging into an AppleShare file server. Do this before installing

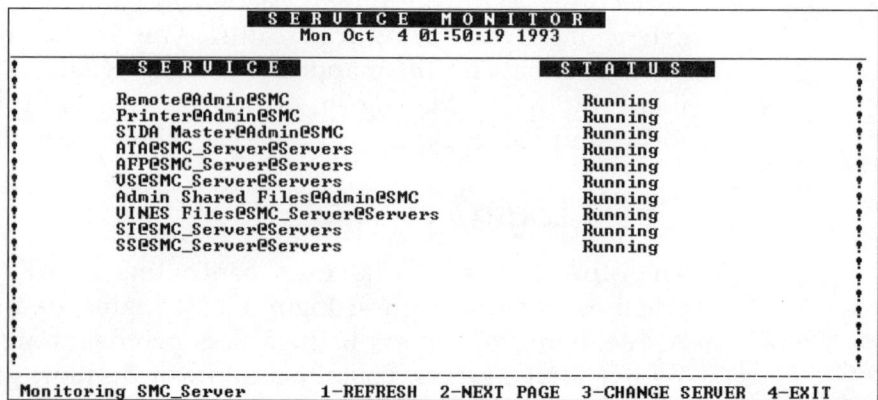

Figure 6.25
The Service Monitor

any of the VINES Macintosh software. As the administrator, as long as you haven't restricted the type of computer you can log in from, you should be able to mount the VINES server and see its folders and files.

Once you you're sure that you can access the server from a Mac, you can install the VINES Macintosh software. However, you might want to think twice before installing this software onto other people's machines. This is because the VINES Utilities are for letting people set the access rights to the VINES server. The VINES Utilities are the Macintosh version of the SETARL utility run from DOS machines. If you do not let DOS users set access rights, then you probably don't want your Mac users setting them, either.

The VINES Utilities come in two pieces. One is the VINES system extension, and the other is the VINES Utilities application. The VINES extension is a Chooser extension that lets someone log into a VINES server, but it does not mount the server volumes. Logging onto the server is a prerequisite to using the VINES Utilities or the VINES Network Mail for the Macintosh.

The VINES Extension

As mentioned above, the VINES system extension is a Chooser extension that logs the user into the VINES server. Because it is a Chooser extension, it is visible from the Chooser, just like the AppleShare extension (see Fig. 6.26).

Figure 6.26
The VINES extension as seen from the Chooser

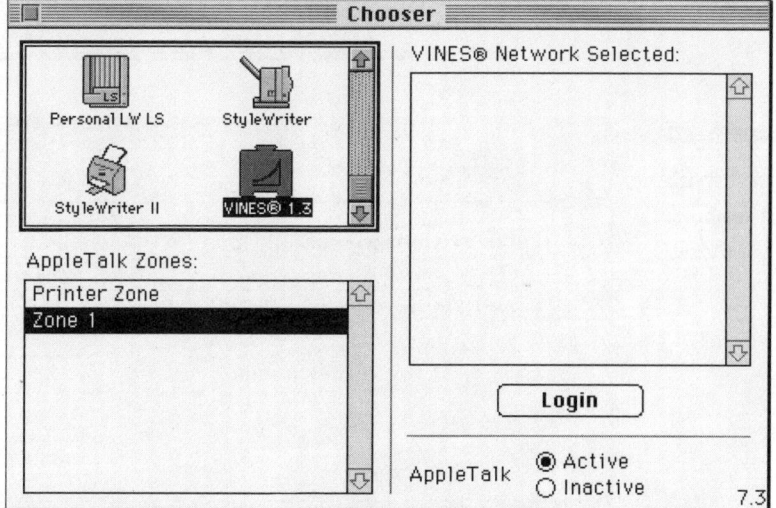

CHAPTER 6

When the VINES extension is selected, all you will see is the Login button. You cannot select a file server as you do when selecting the AppleShare system extension. When you click the Login button, you will see the VINES Network Login dialog window, as shown in Figure 6.27.

The procedure is simple. Enter your StreetTalk name and password and click on the OK button, and you're logged into the server. If you want to be logged in automatically when the Mac boots, you'll have to use the Options button and check the Login at System Startup Time check box (see Fig. 6.28).

In the Options dialog window, you can specify which zone to look in first and which server you want to log into. When setting up the auto login feature, be careful. If the Macintosh is going to

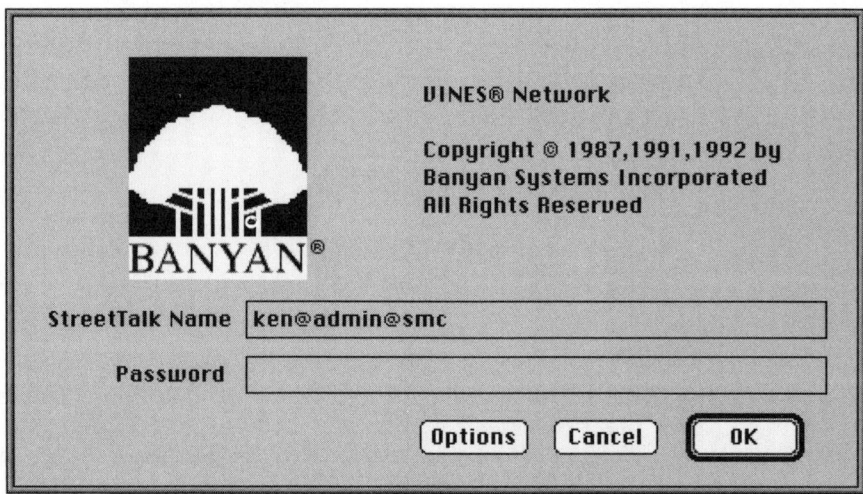

Figure 6.27
The VINES Login dialog window

Figure 6.28
The VINES Login Options dialog window

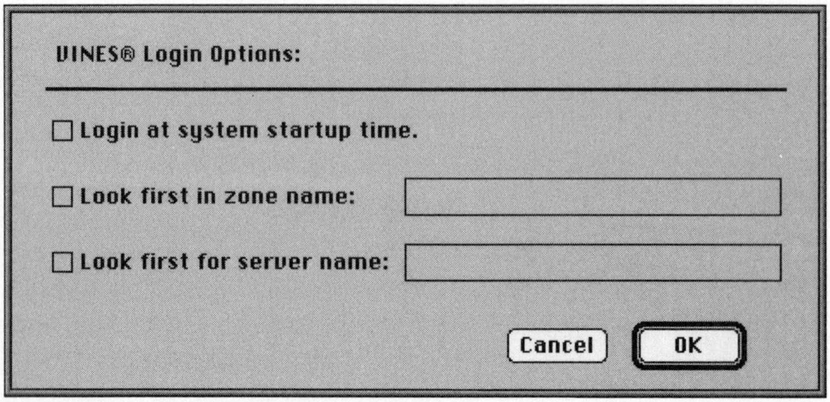

> **Note**
>
> If a Macintosh user attempts to log in using an incorrect name, the Mac will display a message that is similar to what is seen from a PC, namely that the name pair or password is incorrect.

be used by more than one person, both of whom have accounts on the server, the Mac should not be set for auto login. This is because any messages received by the VINES Utilities application for the first person who logs in will be visible to the other user, even after the first user logs out.

To prevent another user from seeing the messages for the first user, the Macintosh must be restarted. After the restart, the next user can then log in normally without accessing the messages for the first user. However, if the VINES extension is set to log a user in automatically, the messages for the predefined user will always be visible.

To log out, all the user has to do is select the VINES extension, where the Login button (as seen in Fig. 6.26) will now say Logout. This functions just like typing LOGOUT at the DOS prompt on a PC. The user is automatically logged out of the server.

What will seem strange, and even inconsistent, is that when users log out, they can remain connected to the server as users, they are just not registered through STDA as active users. It is even possible to mount a server volume with one name and log into VINES with another. This inconsistency demonstrates that the AFP services are separate from the other VINES services, and it can result in some confusion. This will be discussed in the next section.

The VINES Utilities

This section is meant as an overview of the VINES Utilities, not a complete tutorial. The *VINES User's Guide for Macintosh* has complete instructions for the Macintosh VINES Utilities program. The VINES Utilities is a small program that lets Macintosh users send and receive messages and manage access rights. It displays the information a PC user would receive with the WHOAMI.EXE program. In order to use VINES Utilities, the user must be logged into

Figure 6.29

The Utilities Selector window for VINES Utilities

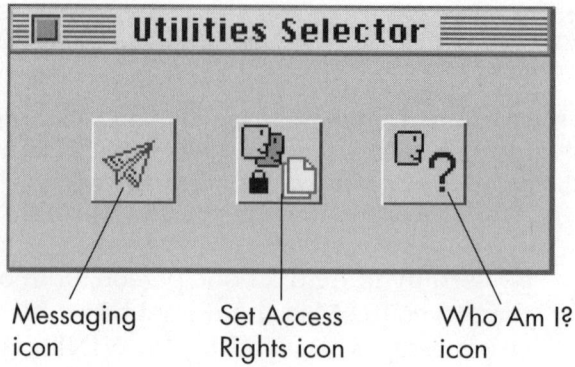

the VINES server, and the VINES system extension must be installed.

If a user is not logged in when the VINES Utilities is executed, the login dialog will appear, as shown in Figure 6.27. Once the user is logged in and the Utilities launched, the Utilities Selector window will appear, as shown in Figure 6.29.

You can access the appropriate utility by clicking on the appropriate icon or by selecting the utility from the Utilities menu. The three utilities are:

- VINES Messages
- Set Access Rights
- Who Am I?

Each of these utilities corresponds to its DOS counterpart and performs the same basic function. As a VINES administrator, you can log into VINES from a Macintosh and set both the VINES and Macintosh access rights. You may remember the discussion about access rights for AppleShare file servers in Chapter 2. That discussion also applies to the VINES implementation of AppleShare, so you might want to review that information either before continuing or immediately after reading this section.

Before discussing access rights, we're going to look at the other two utilities. The first one is the Who Am I? utility. All this utility does is display a dialog window with the login information, as shown in Figure 6.30.

This is not exciting. As you can see from Figure 6.30, all it does is display the user name, group, and organization for the current user. If you have forgotten who you are, it might be useful.

Figure 6.30

The Who Am I? utility window

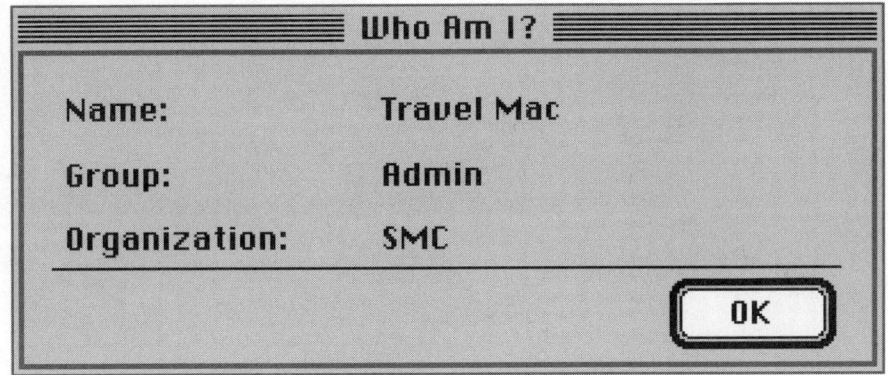

Personally, I prefer to look at my driver's license when I have a memory lapse.

The VINES Messages utility is a little more substantial. It has two windows, Read and Send, as shown in Figure 6.31.

Type your message in the Send window, and then address it by typing the recipient's StreetTalk name in the "To:" section or by selecting the recipient from the address book. To select the recipient from the address book, click on the Address Book button and select the user from the list that appears (see Fig. 6.32).

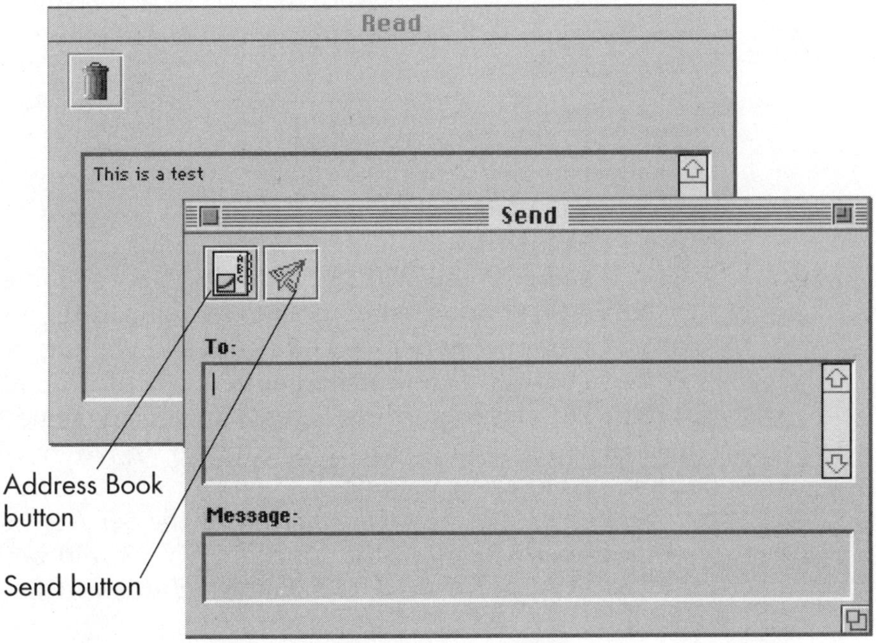

Figure 6.31

The VINES Messages utility

Figure 6.32

The address book

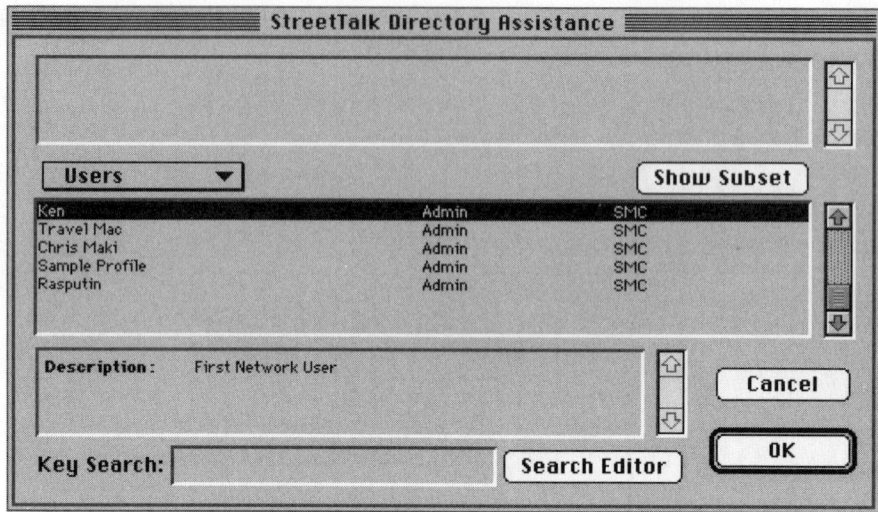

The address book is really a StreetTalk directory tool. You can search for a user's name by displaying the users in a specific list, changing lists, or displaying users by nickname. You can also search for users by pattern and description, saving the results of the search pattern. Select multiple addressees by depressing the **Shift** or **Option** key while clicking on the names in the list. Once the names are selected, all you have to do is click the Send button and the message will be sent to the selected recipients. In the Read window you will see all of your messages; they will remain until you delete them.

The final and most complex accessory is the Set Access Rights utility. To use Set Access Rights, you need to have a VINES AFP volume mounted, and it must be mounted using the same name with which you logged into the VINES server when you opened the VINES Utilities. It is possible to log into VINES from the Chooser or with the VINES Utilities, and at the same time mount a VINES AFP volume using a different name. If the VINES AFP volume is mounted with one user name and you log in as the administrator with a different name, you will not be able to use the VINES Utilities to perform access rights management. Be sure you use the same name when you log in as when you mount the VINES AFP server volume.

As I've already mentioned, with the Set Access Rights utility you can perform all of the functions you would perform with the SETARL program on a PC. The Macintosh utility is necessary because you would have a difficult time selecting folders and files that use Macintosh file names from a PC. So the VINES Set Access Rights utility gives you the means for controlling Macintosh directories.

You can use the Sharing command from the Macintosh's File menu (as described in Chapter 2) to control the Macintosh access rights, but you cannot control the VINES access rights or the list access rights with the Mac's Sharing menu. For full control, you will need to use the VINES utility.

The features of the Set Access Rights section that differ from the Mac's native ability to set access privileges are:

- Set VINES and Macintosh access rights for both MS-DOS and Macintosh volumes, directories, and files.
- Provide for access rights inheritance for volumes and directories.
- Manage lists and set access rights for the Extended List.

To use the Set Access Rights utility, you need to be logged into VINES and have a VINES volume mounted using the same user name. If you do not use the same user name, you will not have the ability to manage any of the access rights, and you'll only see information about the selected volume or directory without the ability to make changes. So the first step in using the Set Access Rights utility is to mount the VINES volume and log into VINES using the same StreetTalk name. If you are not an administrator, you will be able to control only folders that you own.

Once you are logged in and the VINES volume is mounted, use the VINES Set Access Rights utility with these steps:

1. Double-click on the Set Access Rights icon in the VINES Utility, or select "Set Access Rights" from the Utilities menu (see Fig. 6.33). Select the volume or directory using the Macintosh selection dialog box. Choosing the Volume Info button is the same as selecting the VINES volume and clicking on the Info button (see Fig. 6.34).

2. Select the volume or directory using the Macintosh selection dialog box. Choosing the Volume Info button is the same as selecting the VINES volume and clicking on the Info button (see Fig. 6.34).

Figure 6.33

Selecting "Set Access Rights"

Figure 6.34

The Open dialog window

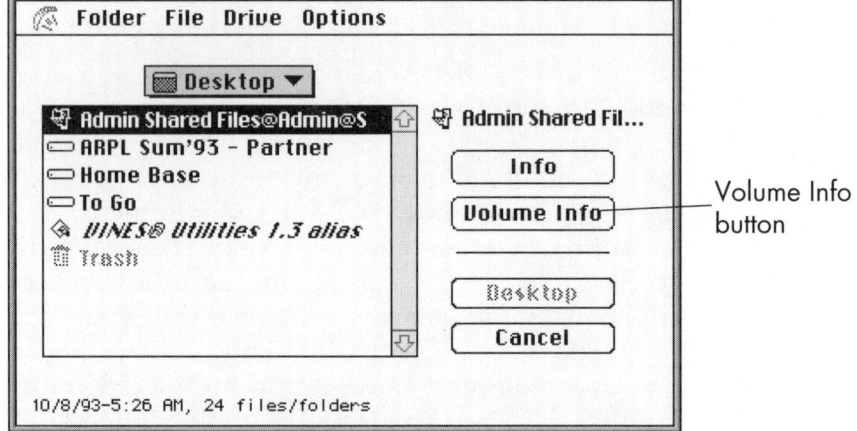

3. After selecting the volume or directory you want to manage, you will see a window like the one in Figure 6.35. Figure 6.35 is the Macintosh view, displaying the VINES Macintosh access rights, which are the same as the AppleShare access privileges described in Chapter 3. The primary difference is the ability to set inheritance rights and manage the Maximum Rights and Extended List options.

Figure 6.36 shows the Macintosh access privileges for the same volume as displayed in Figure 6.35. Notice that with the Macintosh access privileges settings, you cannot set Inheritance or Maximum Rights, and you do not have access to Extended Lists.

BANYAN VINES | 263

Figure 6.35

The Set Access Rights window for a server volume

Info

Owner and Group access

Maximum Rights and List

Options

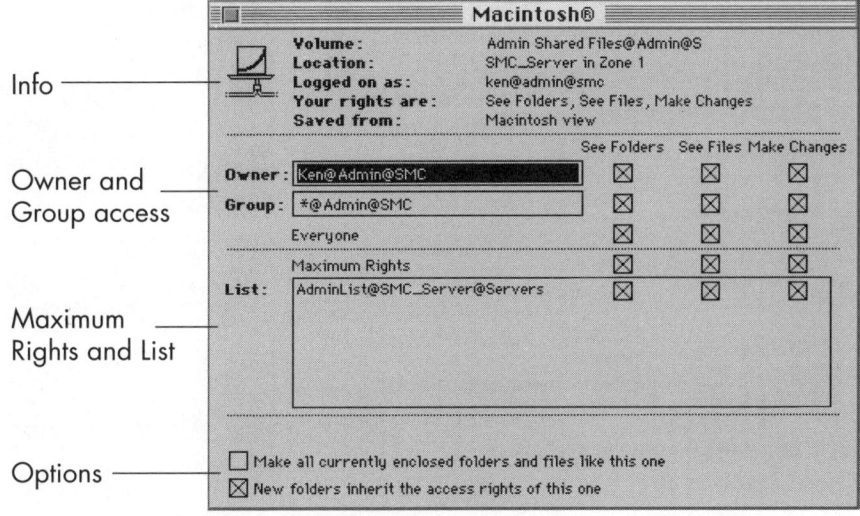

Figure 6.36

The Macintosh access privileges resulting from the Sharing command from the Finder's File menu

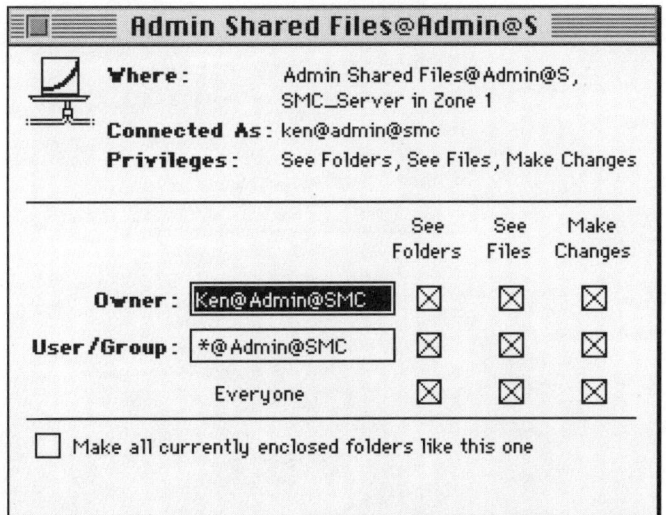

> **Note**
>
> If you are accessing a VINES volume, be careful. It is possible to make changes that will prevent others from accessing the server volume, and you can inadvertently affect MS-DOS users, as well. Do not make changes that have global effects on a volume unless you are sure you know what you are doing.

CHAPTER 6

4. Make the changes you want. Remember that volume changes will effect every directory on the volume.

5. If you want to change VINES access rights, you can select the VINES view from the Access Rights menu with the Views command, or by using the ⌘-2 keyboard sequence. Figure 6.37 shows the Access Rights menu.

6. From the VINES view, as shown in Figure 6.38, you can set any of the VINES access rights that you would normally set when using the SETARL program on a DOS machine.

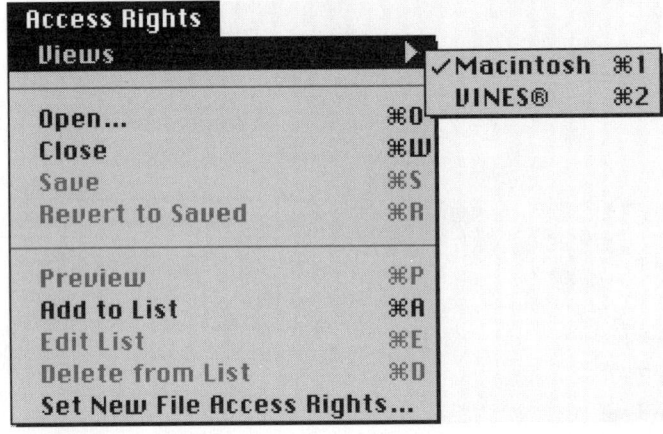

Figure 6.37
The Access Rights menu

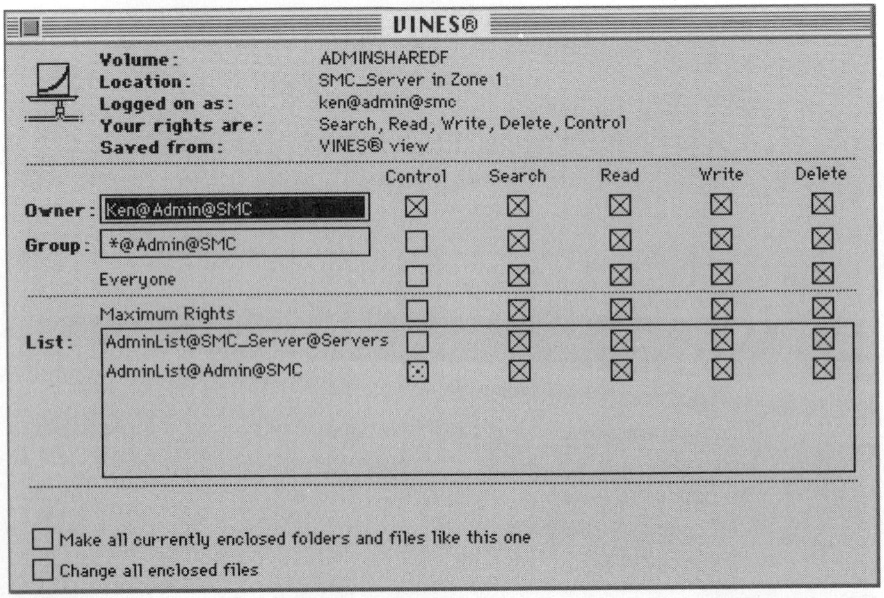

Figure 6.38
The VINES view

Banyan VINES

From either view, you can edit the VINES user list. Your options are shown in Figure 6.37, the Access Rights menu. You can add up to five names to the list, edit it, or delete a user from the list. However, if you want to add lists or add users to a list, they must already exist as StreetTalk entries. You cannot create new users or lists from the Macintosh.

The following are the generic steps you need to take to edit a list (a specific example will follow):

1. Select the list in the List section of the Macintosh or VINES view window.
2. Choose the action you want to perform from the Access Rights menu.
3. Select the list or user from the StreetTalk Directory Assistance dialog window (see Fig. 6.39).
4. Click on the OK button.

In Figure 6.38, there is only one list in the Maximum Rights section, the AdminList@SMC@Servers list.

To add another list to the Maximum Rights section:

1. Select the list.
2. Select "Add to List" from the Access Rights menu.
3. Select "Lists" from the StreetTalk Directory Assistance dialog window (see Fig. 6.40).

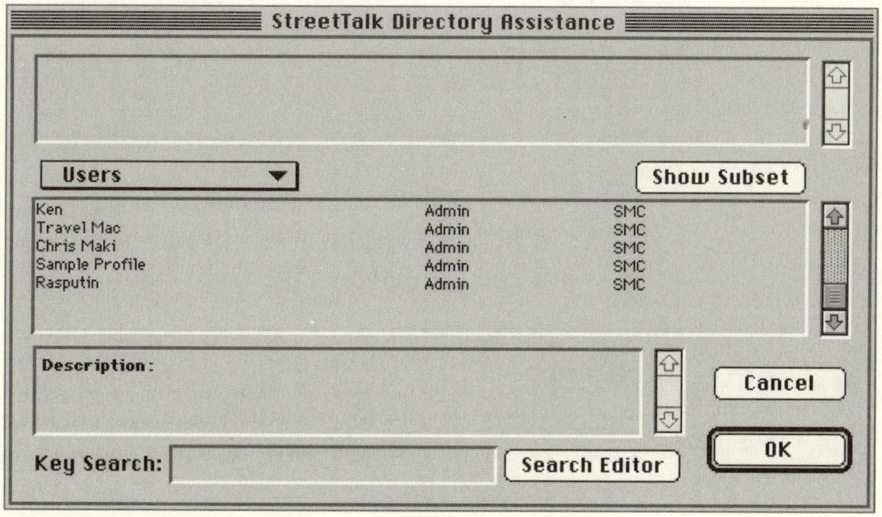

Figure 6.39
The StreetTalk Directory Assistance dialog window

Figure 6.40

Selecting a StreetTalk category

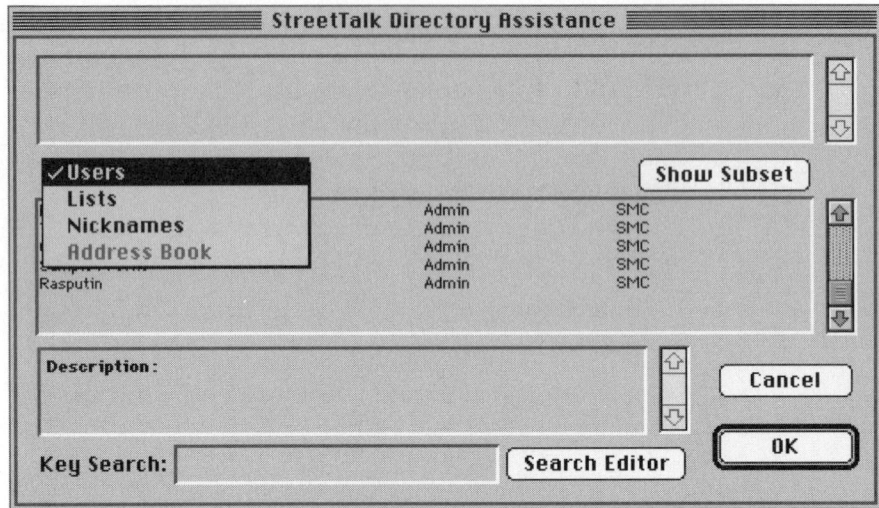

Figure 6.41

Selecting the list to add

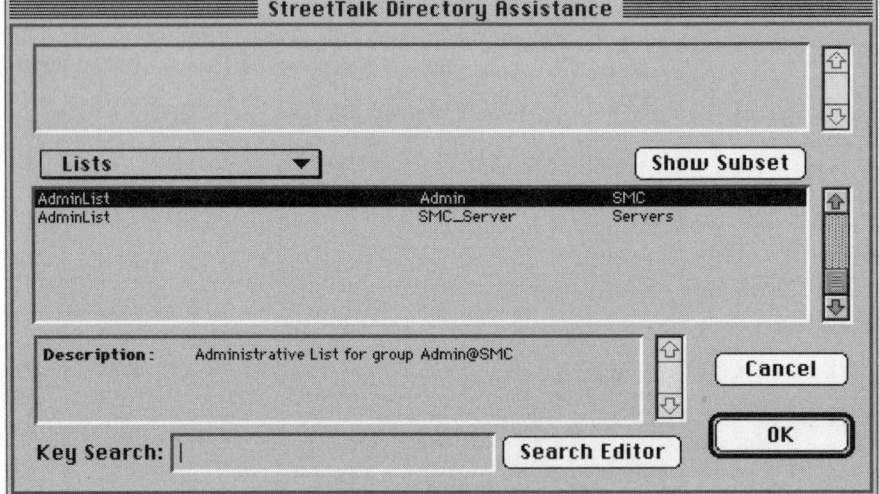

4. Select the list you want to add (see Fig. 6.41).
5. Click on the OK button. You will be returned to the view window and the list will be added, as shown in Figure 6.42.

Once the list is added, you will have to set the access rights for that list by:

1. Selecting the rights you want to assign (clicking in a box toggles it on or off). A box with an "X" in it has the rights repre-

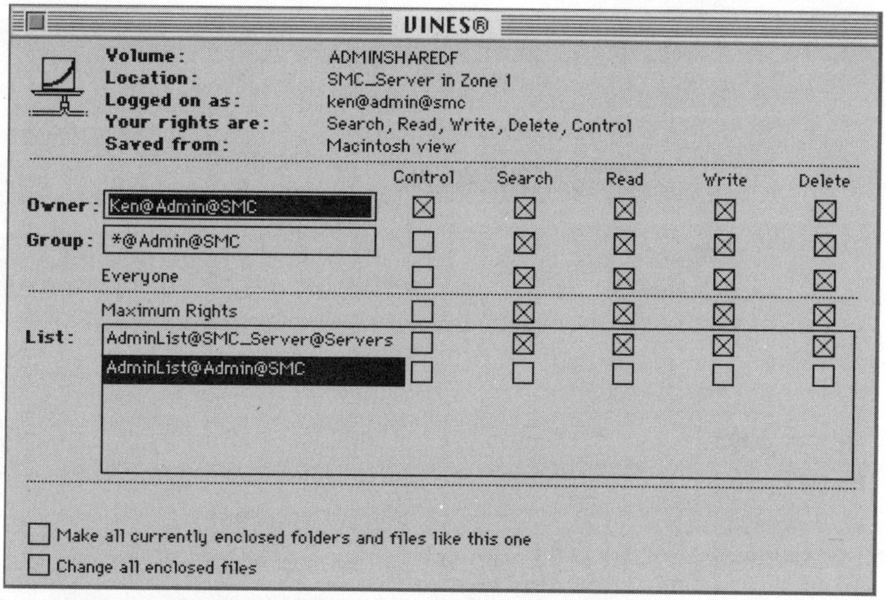

Figure 6.42

The VINES view with an added list

sented by the column heading. You can also use the Set New File Access Rights command from the Access Rights menu.

2. Checking the options you want for the new list.

3. Selecting "Save" from the Access Rights menu or closing the window. If you have changed any access rights and not saved the changes, you will be prompted to do so when you close the window.

If a user is included in more than one list, that user will have access rights that correspond to the maximum for any list. If one list allows for control and another does not, but a user is in both lists, then the user will have control access (see the note on the next page). Also, granting a user Read, Write, and Delete access in the VINES view will provide See Folders, See Files, and Make Changes access from the Macintosh view. Figure 6.43 shows the Macintosh view after the AdminList@Admin@SMC list was added.

The VINES Utility also has an on-line help facility. This is accessed by selecting the Apple menu while in the VINES Utility. Under the "About VINES Utilities..." menu option you will see a "Help..." selection. By accessing this, you can get immediate on-line help that might be able to answer your question without going to the manual.

Note

You need to be very careful about who has control access. Anyone given control access should be well trained. Otherwise, it is possible to lock everyone out of a server accidentally. Once the access rights are saved, they take effect immediately, and can impact every network user including assigned administrators. Fixing a problem where everyone has been denied access privileges is not fun. This aspect of the VINES Utilities for the Macintosh should not be overlooked or taken lightly.

Figure 6.43

The added list from the Macintosh view

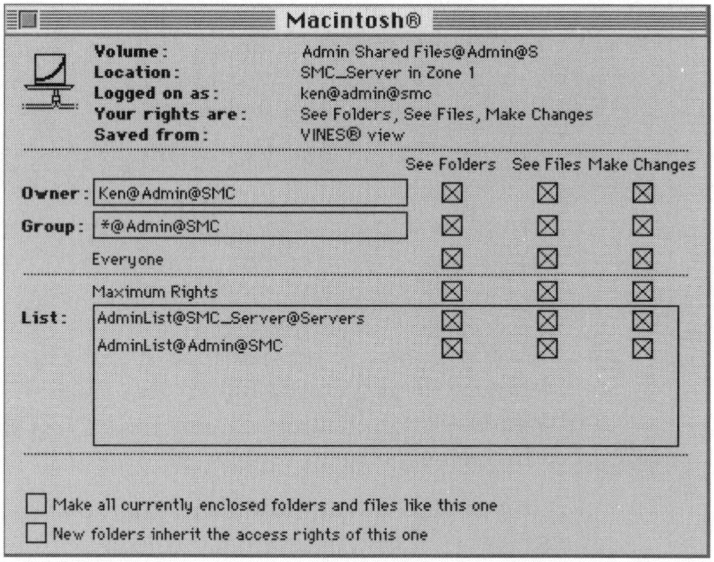

Using a Macintosh Internet Router

When you use a Macintosh internet router like Apple's InterNet Router or Farallon's LocalPath, there will be times when the router hiccups. An MS-DOS user will not be able to log into the network, yet everything will seem to be working from other workstations. The first time this happens, you will think that the user is using the wrong name or password, or that there is a hardware problem.

Don't shoot the user. It is quite possible that the router has crashed, even though everything else seems to be working. If this happens, all you have to do is reboot the Macintosh that has the router. If this solves the problem, then you're home free. Otherwise, you will have to do deeper trouble-shooting. The reason this is mentioned here is that the problem will appear to be a PC- or VINES-related problem when it is not. If you've got a large network, the Mac router will be one of the last things you check, because it makes no sense that a Mac router should affect PC logins. Just keep this tidbit in mind.

Also, another detail when using a router is making sure that your network addresses are correct. If the router is passing data between LocalTalk and Ethernet or Token Ring networks, make sure that the LocalTalk port on the router is a seed port and that it is not hidden. You will want the VINES server to see the LocalTalk network and zone name if it contains an AppleTalk PostScript printer, if that printer is going to be accessed by MS-DOS, Windows, or UNIX users.

Intelligent Messaging or VINES Mail

VINES Mail is an additional option that you can purchase for the VINES system. If you're using VINES Mail as your primary E-mail system, you will probably want to install it on your Macs. VINES Mail requires the VINES extension and the VINES Mail program. The Macintosh VINES Mail program give your Macintosh users full user status on the VINES Mail system.

For Macintoshes to have access to VINES Mail, they must have the SETMAIL command in their user profiles, and they must have mailboxes. Otherwise, the Mac users will not be able to log into the mail server. All administration for the Intelligent Messaging system must be done from the server console or a PC workstation. There are no Macintosh utilities for administering the VINES E-mail system.

AppleTalk PostScript Printers

One of the essential elements of Macintosh use is using an AppleTalk PostScript printer. Whether the printer is manufactured by Apple or a third-party manufacturer, using one in conjunction with a VINES server is the same. As long as the printer supports AppleTalk and the Macintosh uses the Apple LaserWriter driver to access the printer, the procedures for using the printer on a VINES network are the same.

You cannot connect the printer to the server via the serial or parallel port and still have Macintosh access. If the printer is connected to the server, you will have to use an AppleTalk card from Dayna Communications and VINES routing capabilities, or the Printer will have to be connected to a Macintosh. If your Macs are connected to the server using LocalTalk, you will not need an internet router for either Macintosh or PC access to the printer, since the VINES server will already be providing the routing services you need.

If, however, your Macs are connected to the network with a high-speed physical link, then you will need some type of routing service to access a LocalTalk printer. Apple's newer printers do support Ethernet connections, and one of these printers could be on the network without routing services. But there are enough non-Ethernet printers out there that you will probably be using an internet router on a Mac to provide printer access.

If you do not intend to let non-Macintosh workstations access the printer, or if you do not wish to use the VINES print-spooling capabilities, you do not need to create a VINES printer service for the Macs. The Macs can access the printer without a VINES printer service. The VINES printer service allows MS-DOS and UNIX machines to access and use the AppleTalk printer. If your Macintosh workgroup is large enough, you might want to dedicate the printer to their use only, and not even set up the VINES printer service. However, if you do want the printer controlled through VINES, this section will go through the steps of setting up the VINES PAP (Printer Access Protocol) printer service.

Creating

The process for making the AppleTalk PostScript printer accessible involves setting up the VINES print service as a server-based service (say that three time in a row!). I'm assuming that you are already familiar with VINES printer services, so I will only go into detail where there are special Macintosh considerations. Follow these steps:

1. Run MSERVICE from your administration workstation.
2. Select "Add a Server-based Service."
3. Name the service and give it a description. Remember that the name cannot be more than 32 characters long if it is going to be accessed by Macs.

BANYAN VINES

4. Select "VINES Print Service" as the service you're going to add.

5. Select the disk that will contain the service and to which the printer files will be spooled. PostScript files can be quite large, so you should select a disk that has several megabytes (20M or more) available for spooling.

6. Set the queue size by specifying the number of jobs the queue will accept.

7. Configure the Paper Formats. If you want, you can delete the Standard paper format. This format cannot be used on a PostScript printer. The PostScript format is all you need, unless you have to make allowances for legal or tabloid paper sizes.

8. Set up the Users and Operators by adding the appropriate lists. This step is only necessary for your PC users; any Macintosh user will be able to access this service once it is set up.

9. Add the users or lists to whom alert messages will go.

10. Select the type of printer destination you want to set up. In this case, it is the PAP printer, as shown in Figure 6.44.

At this point, you will have to define the printer service's destination attributes. Before you go on, there are few important things to keep in mind. One is that the PAP printer will be broadcast over the network and available in the server's default zone if the printer is being routed by a Macintosh. If the printer is connected to the server via an AppleTalk card, it will be available in the zone defined by the AppleTalk port to which it is connected.

Figure 6.44
The printer service destination

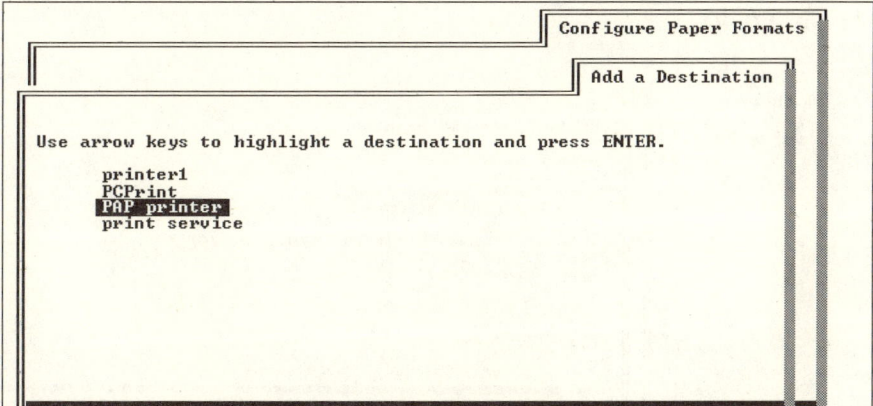

CHAPTER 6

Another point to keep in mind is that the printer name must correspond *exactly* to the name of the PostScript laser printer. Sometimes there is a space at the end of a printer's name. If you fail to include the space, the server will not access the printer, and you will have to start over by deleting the service you've just created. The easiest way to figure out the name of the printer is to access it from a Macintosh and execute a Print command. In the Print dialog window, you will see the printer's name enclosed in quotation marks.

In Figure 6.45, you can see that at the end of "LaserWriter II NT" there is a space, so the printer's name is really "LaserWriter II NTT".

After the attributes have been set, you can change every destination attribute except the printer's name. Any Macintosh workstation can access this printer service, whether or not the workstation is logged into the server. This means that there is no control over who has access to the printer if it is accessed from a Mac.

Figure 6.46 shows the Destination Attributes screen for a PAP printer.

Figure 6.45
Checking the printer's name

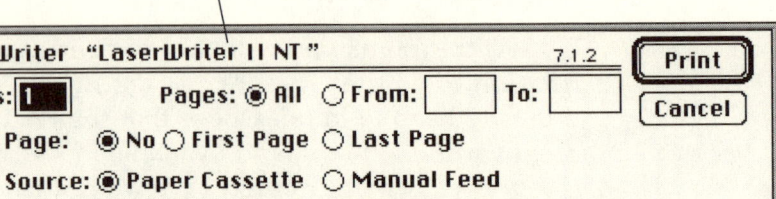

Figure 6.46
The Destination Attributes screen

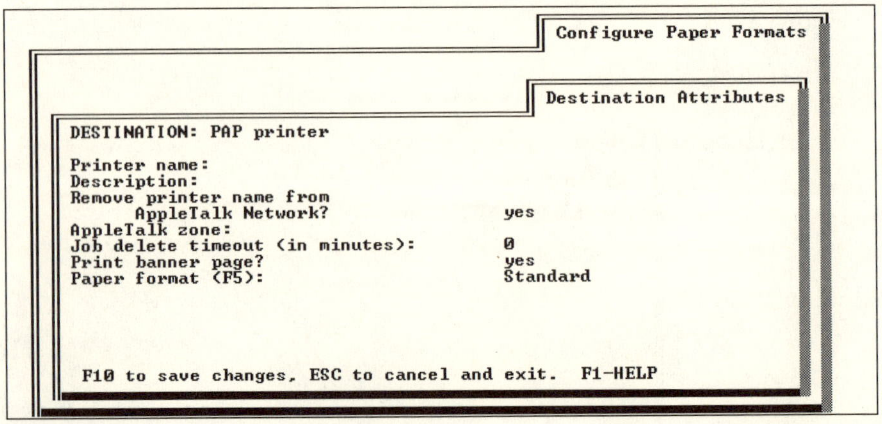

The following is a line-by-line description of this screen:

- **Printer name**   The actual name of the PostScript printer.
- **Description**   A description to help you know which printer this service is for.
- **Remove printer name from AppleTalk Network?**   A "Yes" in this section will keep the printer's name from being broadcast on the AppleTalk network. You should not let the name be broadcast, because Mac users could then bypass the server and print directly to the printer. This will eliminate competition between the Macs that are printing and the server.
- **AppleTalk zone**   This is the zone that contains the printer, not the zone where you want the printer located. If the printer is on an AppleTalk network that is being routed by a Mac, the printer service will be broadcast in the default zone of the server's AppleTalk port.
- **Job delete time-out (in minutes)**   This will determine how long the server tries to send the print job to the printer. Because some PostScript print jobs can take a very long time, you should either leave the setting at the default of 0 or set it high enough that a cued job will not get deleted if a PostScript job is taking an hour to print.
- **Print banner page**   This is entirely up to you. The banner page will print after the job is completed, but since controls are limited anyway, you may find that banner pages are a waste of paper and toner.
- **Paper format (F5)**   The paper format should be PostScript. If it is set to Standard, you will find that MS-DOS machines will not print.

Once you have the description set up, save it by pressing **F10**. It should look something like Figure 6.47.

These steps set up the basic PAP printer service. The next step is to configure the printer's filters. The filter you want to add to the printer is one that will translate DOS text files into a PostScript format. If you do not install the filter, the printer will not print text files, and will work only with applications that provide a PostScript printer driver.

CHAPTER 6

Figure 6.47
The completed Destination Attributes screen

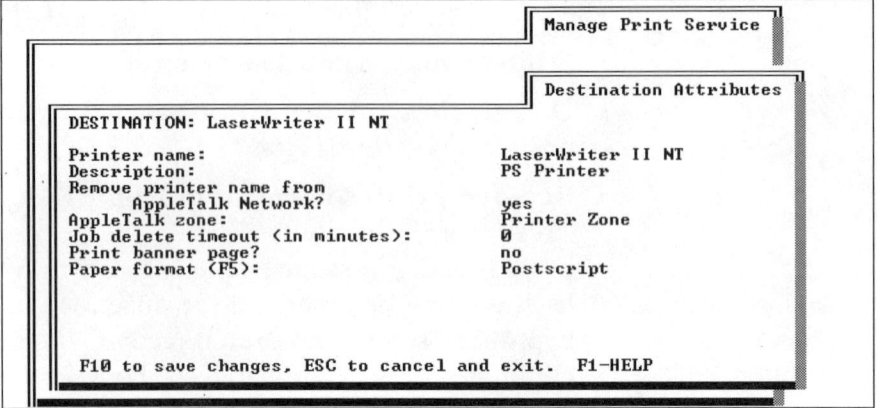

You will be prompted to add a filter during the initial set-up, or you can:

1. Access the Filter Setup screen by selecting the service.
2. Control the service.
3. Access the Configure Service option from the Control screen. Select the Configure Filters screen. The Configure Filters screen looks like Figure 6.48.

Select "Add." The next screen (see Fig. 6.49) contains the following fields:

- **Filter Name** This can be anything you want to call the filter. The name can be up to 31 characters.

- **Filter Description** The description can be up to 63 characters, and is used for your information only.

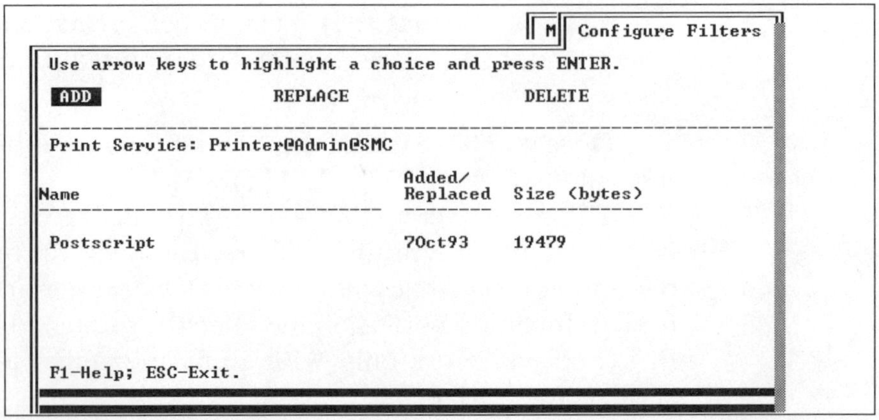

Figure 6.48
The Configure Filters screen

BANYAN VINES

Figure 6.49
The Filter Setup screen

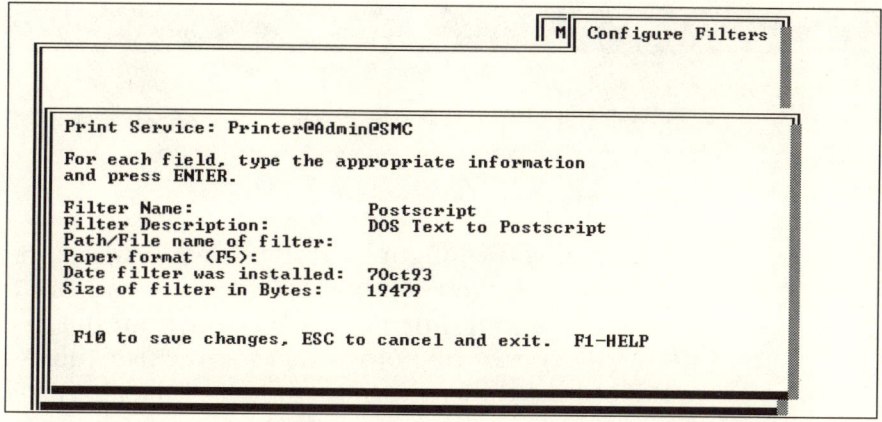

```
                                              ┌─M─┐ Configure Filters
Print Service: Printer@Admin@SMC

For each field, type the appropriate information
and press ENTER.

Filter Name:                    Postscript
Filter Description:             DOS Text to Postscript
Path/File name of filter:
Paper format (F5):
Date filter was installed:      7Oct93
Size of filter in Bytes:        19479


F10 to save changes, ESC to cancel and exit.   F1-HELP
```

- **Path/File name of filter** The two filters you can use are on the root level of the Z: (VINES) drive. The UNIX-to-DOS filter is TODOS, and the DOS-to-PostScript is POSTFILT.

- **Paper Format (F5)** Do not select a paper format if you want the filter to run on every job. Otherwise, select the paper format that will control which jobs the filter will be run on.

The POSTFILT filter will check every job if it is set up, as shown in Figure 6.49. For any job that does not conform to the Adobe 2.0 PostScript conventions, it will insert a basic PostScript text driver so the job will be printed as text. After the filter is configured, your Configure Filters screen should look like Figure 6.50.

Figure 6.50
The Configure Filters screen with a configured filter

```
                                              ┌─M─┐ Configure Filters
Use arrow keys to highlight a choice and press ENTER.
 ADD            REPLACE                  DELETE

Print Service: Printer@Admin@SMC
                                Added/
Name                            Replaced    Size (bytes)

Postscript                      7Oct93      19479




F1-Help; ESC-Exit.
```

> **Note**
>
> You can configure only one PAP destination per printer service. Each PostScript printer has to have its own printer service.

When you configure a PAP printer, it will start automatically, but it will take a few minutes for the printer service to intercept the PostScript printer's name and block it from the network. Until it does, the service will not work properly. Also, this is a good way to trouble-shoot the PAP printer. If, after it has been set up, the PostScript printer is visible from the Macintosh Chooser, then there is a problem, and you will have to reconfigure the service. (This is assuming that you removed the printer name from the network.)

Trouble-shooting

This section will look at some of the problems you might have with VINES and AppleTalk. It will not include hardware, physical link, or general Macintosh trouble-shooting. If you need information on trouble-shooting networked Macs, look in Chapter 10. This section discusses the tools that you have within the VINES system for trouble-shooting your network and some of the known problems you will encounter.

Known Problems

One of the most troublesome aspects of the VINES AppleTalk implementation has to do with access rights. If a Macintosh user creates a new folder, no-one except the creator will be able to access the files in the directory. The directory will function as a drop box for all others. The only way to fix this is to use the VINES Utilities for the Mac, or the SETARL program from a DOS workstation, and reset the access rights. This is a known problem, acknowledged by Banyan. However, if your Mac users are trained, the problem can be avoided.

To work around this problem, if others are to have access to the directory, the Mac user will have to perform the following steps:

1. Select the folder.

2. Select "Sharing..." from the Finder's File menu.
3. If the group name is correct in the window that appears, set the access privileges for the proper access (See Chapter 2 for more information). Figure 6.51 shows a folder before it is corrected as it appears in the Sharing window.
4. Check the "Make all currently enclosed folders like this one" box.
5. Close the window.
6. Save the changes when prompted.

The above procedure will give people either limited or full access, depending on the Owner and User/Group attributes selected. Banyan has said that the fix to this problem will take a while, because it is a complicated and a surface patch will only create more problems.

If you are using a version of VINES prior to 5.52(5), you should get the patch to 5.52(5). This patch contains fixes that make PAP printing work more easily, and it also fixes some AppleTalk problems that earlier versions of 5.0 had. The following are some minor problems acknowledged by Banyan:

Single Port Servers

On an AppleTalk Phase 2 server with a single LAN segment that is the only AppleTalk port and that does not have any routers, the

Figure 6.51
A folder with restricted access, before it is corrected

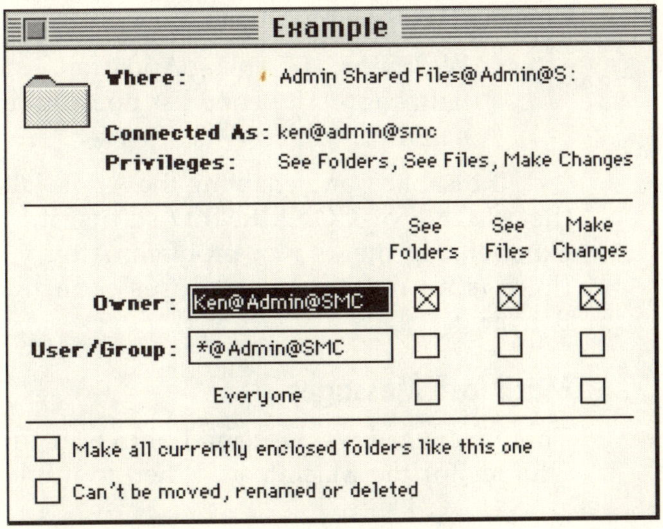

port must be configured as a seed port, or you will receive an error message during configuration requesting more information.

Changing Port Status on a Server with an AppleTalk Tunnel

If your server has an AppleTalk tunnel and your users suddenly see evidence of losing their VINES resources, such as volume icons disappearing or printer services no longer appearing in the Chooser, you could be experiencing a known problem. When you check the port status in the Display Port Status screen of the Manage AppleTalk menu at the Server Console, and the port on any server on the path to the service shows a status of CONFLICT, there is a problem.

Either you are experiencing a real conflict, or you need site-specific patch number 5.52(5)-VNS-BM-1. To confirm whether you're experiencing a real conflict, disable and then enable AppleTalk for the port with the conflict. If you receive either of the following error messages, you have a real conflict:

- WARNING: Disabling AppleTalk seed port x (range aa-bb [the range configured for the seed port]) because of network range conflicts (range dd-ee [the range in use on the attached cable])
- WARNING: Disabling AppleTalk seed port x (First [Default] Zone) during port initialization because of default zone name mismatch (Second Zone [Zone on attached cable])

The following error message may indicate that you are experiencing the known problem:

- WARNING: Disabling AppleTalk seed port x during port initialization. The zone list does not agree with the attached network.

If disabling and enabling the AppleTalk port does not result in the ALONE or CONFIRMED status, it is unlikely that you are experiencing the known problem. After you have confirmed that there is no real zone or address conflict, you should contact Banyan.

Macintosh Messages

This problem was described above in the discussion of VINES Utilities for the Macintosh. When multiple users log in using the same Mac, you need to reboot the Mac, or subsequent users will be able to read messages for the original user.

SuperLaser Spool

Macs running System 6.0.7 and using the VINES driver cannot use SuperLaser Spool.

Password Changes

With the VINES system extension 1.3, you can force a password change. However, the Mac user can re-enter the same password, in which case there will be no change.

Macintosh Mail Problems

The default word wrap length for MacMail 1.3 is 88 characters per line. In order to be compatible with DOS workstations, the word wrap needs to be reset to 79 characters per line.

In the STDA phone book, the first and last entries will not be visible if the cursor keys are used. They are visible if you use the scroll bars.

Mail sent from a Macintosh Mail client will not be received if it is sent through a SNADS Softswitch Mail gateway.

SMPT-originated mail will not show the date on the envelope for a Macintosh client. This is because VINES Macintosh Mail does not put a binary date on the envelope.

Port Status

When you have problems with AppleTalk and VINES, you should always check the Display Port Status from the AppleTalk section of the Manage Communications section at the Server Console. In order for AppleTalk to be running properly, the Port Status should be CONFIRMED, as shown in Figure 6.52.

Any other status means that there is a problem with the AppleTalk port. The first thing you should do is stop and then start AppleTalk to see if the problem goes away. If you receive an error message during the port initialization processes, you will know that there is a problem that needs to be corrected. The problem you're most likely to encounter is an address conflict. If this should occur, you will have to check the routers on your AppleTalk network and verify the addresses they are using. One of the routers

Figure 6.52

The port status

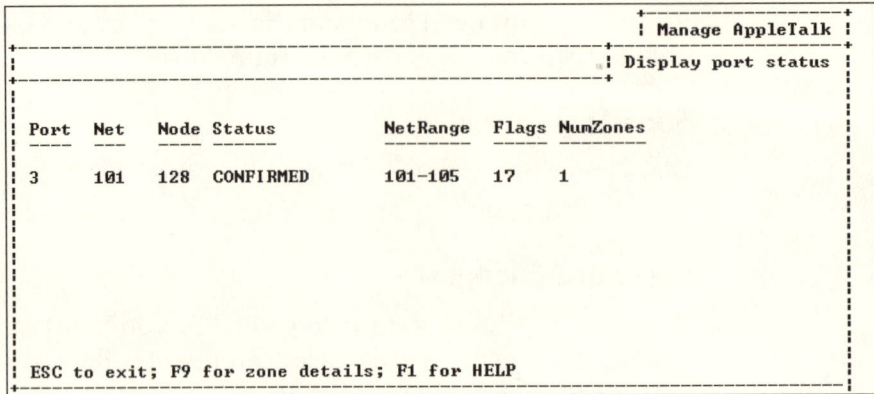

could be dynamically assigning a network number that is in conflict with your assigned numbers. For this reason alone, you should always use seeded ports.

The following are the messages you could receive for the port status:

- **Alone** This is the normal status for a seed port when there are no routers on the LAN segment. If there are routers on the LAN segment, this status means that the server cannot communicate with them.

- **Confirmed** The port is initialized and working.

- **Conflict** There is a configuration problem, most likely an address number conflict. The port is shut down automatically when a conflict occurs. More information can be obtained from the system error log.

- **Initializing** The port is in the process of starting up and confirming the LAN's configuration information. When it is done, you will see the status change to one of the other status codes.

- **Need Info** This is the normal status for a non-seed port when there are no routers on the LAN segment. If there are routers on the LAN segment, this status means that the server cannot communicate with them. If there are no routers on this port, the port should be changed to a seed port.

- **Shutdown** This is a rare message; it indicates that the OS has shut down AppleTalk. The most likely cause for this message is an overloaded communications buffer. You should enlarge the communications buffer if you get this message. Another possible cause for this message is exceeding the node limit for AppleTalk.

- **User Disabled**   The port is disabled by the user.

Another way to determine what is going on with the AppleTalk network is to check the port flag status. You will find a description for all of the codes in the *Managing AppleTalk on a VINES Network* manual. Also, you should have a Macintosh network utility, like Apple's Inter•Poll, that will check the network from a Mac's point of view. If you cannot get to the server from the Mac with Inter•Poll then you could have a cabling problem, a router could be down, or the server could be off-line.

Your trouble-shooting steps should be:

- Check the server and the status of AppleTalk, the AppleTalk ports, and the Routing Table.
- Check your routers and maybe even reboot them.
- Check the network from the Mac trying to get to the server.
- During each step of the process, check your network address numbers to ensure that there is not a conflict.
- If you have just started the AppleShare services or changed zone information, make sure you have let enough time lapse for the service to start and the zone aging to take place.

After you have done these things, your next steps will depend on what you found. I'm assuming that you know enough to fix address conflicts and know that if the server is running and the Macs can't see it, you might have a problem with the physical link. Network trouble-shooting can drive you to your wits' end. All I can do is refer you to Chapter 10 and wish you luck.

Conclusion

VINES has consistently been rated as one of the easiest networks to use. With its implementation of AppleTalk and the ability to span the world with a WAN, VINES is a network operating system that deserves serious consideration for use with the Mac. In this chapter you have the basics for installing and using VINES with the Mac for full cross-platform connectivity.

Although this chapter is not 100% complete, you have the information that is most essential for making your network Macintosh-compatible. There is little in this chapter that you can't find in the VINES manuals, but I've tried to consolidate the most helpful and essential information into the 30 or 40 pages that you have here. I apologize in advance for any omissions you might find. If you use this chapter along with the chapters that are specifically Macintosh-related, you will be able to get your VINES network up and running.

Microsoft LAN Manager

Introduction

LAN Manager is Microsoft's OS/2-based server platform for enterprise networking. If you have a shop where LAN Manager is being used and you want to provide Macintosh support, it is a fairly simple process to install and administer LAN Manager Services for Macintosh.

Of the networks discussed in this book, LAN Manager is the easiest to set up and use when installing the Macintosh Services option. The LAN Manager Services for Macintosh implementation of the AppleTalk File Protocol is very solid, and it is easy to administer. In this chapter you will find all the information you need to install and configure LAN Manager Services for Macintosh. Also included in this chapter is some of the most basic information you'll need for trouble-shooting a LAN Manager Services for Macintosh file server. Although you will not find an answer to every situation, when you are done with this chapter you will have cross-platform access between your Macs and PCs and network access to PostScript AppleTalk printers.

LAN Manager Services for the Macintosh

If you read the popular PC magazines, you'll quickly learn that LAN Manager in not always ranked as high as some of the other NOSs. However, when it comes to providing AppleTalk support, LAN Manager is one of the easier ones to set up and administer. I found LAN Manager and the LAN Manager Services for Macintosh easier to set up and configure than either Novell 3.11 or Banyan VINES.

In the process of setting up the other two networks, I had to call for technical support, and there were problems with the AFP implementation with either access rights or printer set-up. The LAN Manager Services for Macintosh set-up and configuration process went smoothly and quickly. This does not mean that LAN Manager is perfect, only that it was easier to set up and make work.

If you are dealing in an environment where you have multiple servers and need Macintosh access, LAN Manager does not provide for AppleTalk tunneling. LAN Manager's domain-based architecture is well-suited for multiple server support, but the Macintosh Services option does not participate in the domain structure. Instead, AppleTalk is strictly a server-based service that makes shared directories available as Macintosh volumes, through either seeded or non-seeded ports. You can choose which directories will be shared, choose which user group has access, and assign owners, just as you would on an AppleShare file server. For multiple server support, you will have to maintain physical link

> **Note**
>
> One of the nice features of LAN Manager that may be overlooked by network administrators is that you don't need a PC as an administration workstation. This makes LAN Manager a great alternative to AppleShare and a dedicated Macintosh server. When you figure the cost of the server machine, even a good 486, and LAN Manager, you'll end up with a better server for less money than you would if you purchased Apple's top-end server. You'll have a high-performance server that can accommodate 50 Macintosh workstations—not to mention the other benefits you'll receive, such as fault tolerance, disk mirroring, UPS (uninterrupted power supply) support, and other standard features.

integrity, where each intermediate LAN Manager server has Services for Macintosh installed so it can act as an internet router.

Figure 7.1 shows a LAN Manager internet. You will notice that in order for Mac networks to communicate with each other, the server that is part of the physical link must have LAN Manager Services for Macintosh installed.

If you want some servers on the network shown in Figure 7.1 to be regular LAN Manager servers, not participating in the AppleTalk network, you can use any physical link that will not require the passing of AppleTalk packets through the server's net-

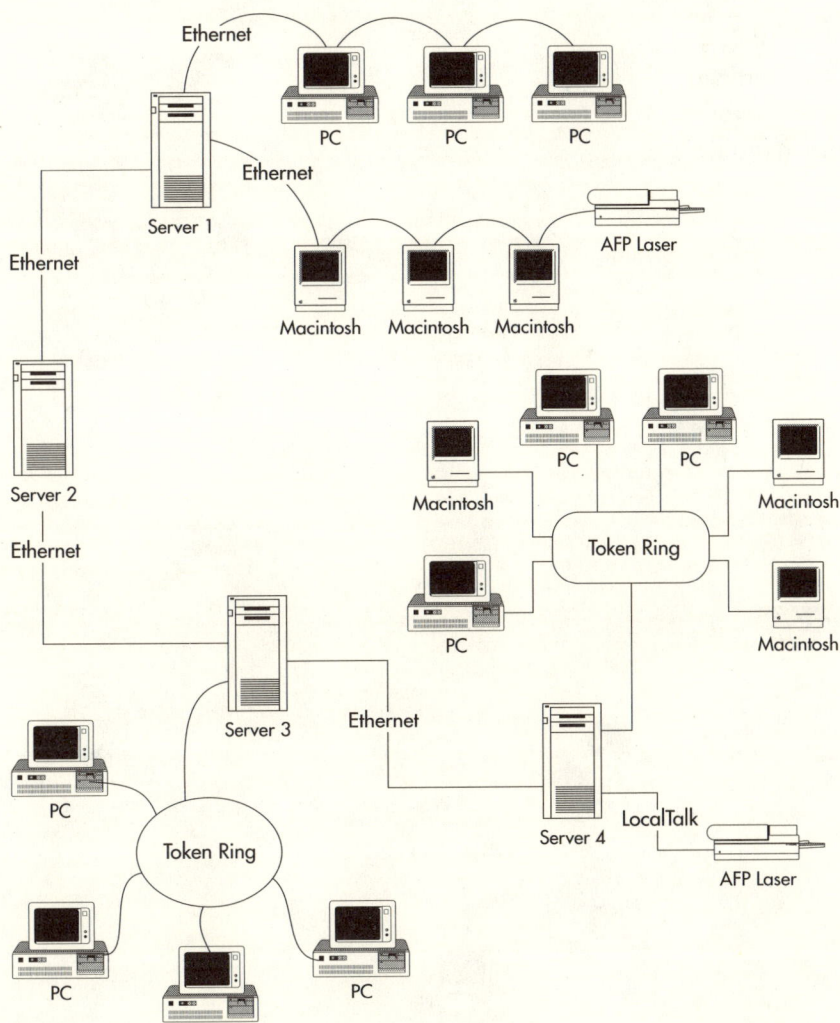

Figure 7.1

A LAN Manager internet

work adapter. This requires some type of hub architecture, such as 10BaseT or Token Ring. Your other choice would be to use a coaxial network like cheapernet.

The data packets on a LAN Manager network are not encapsulated inside another protocol. Instead, they are bound to the network adapter and sent along as AppleTalk packets. You cannot tunnel the AppleTalk packets from server to server unless AppleTalk is installed on each intermediate server. This means that any server supporting AFP connected in a WAN must be connected to another server that also supports AFP. Figure 7.2 shows

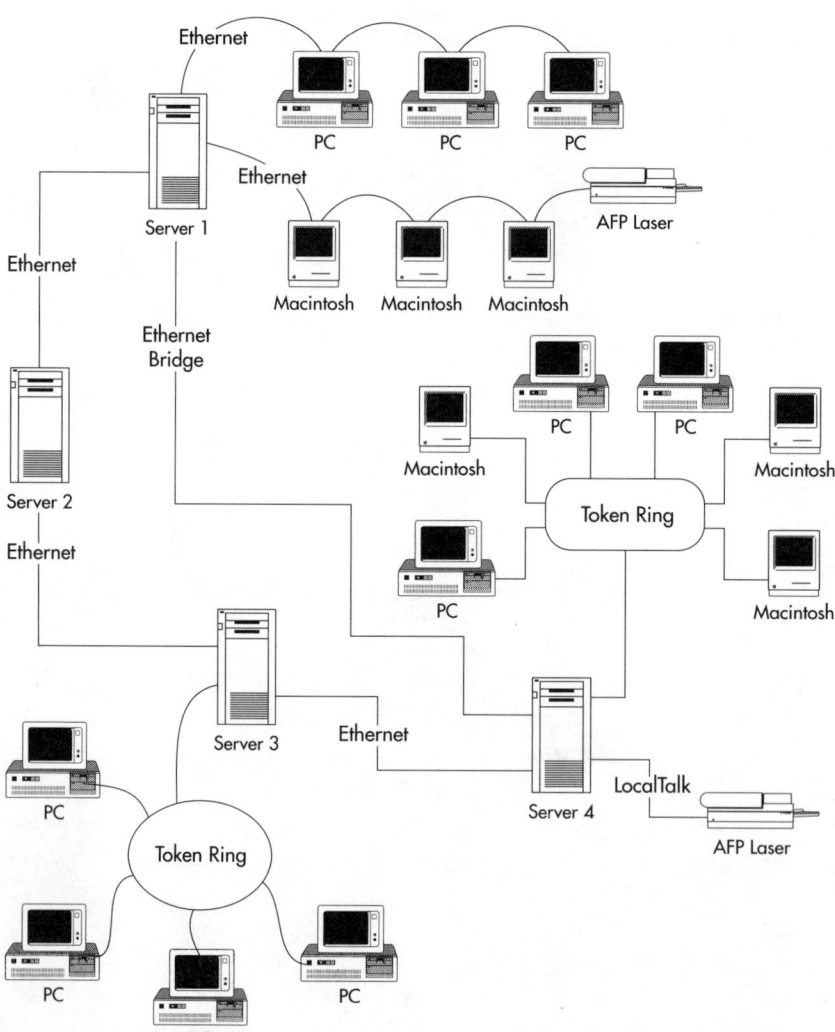

Figure 7.2
An alternate network configuration

the same network as Figure 7.1, except that servers 2 and 3 are not set up with Services for Macintosh. Instead, there is a direct physical link between Servers 1 and 4.

Otherwise, you will have to use an intelligent hardware hub that can function as a multi-protocol router, so it can bypass or route the AppleTalk packets around the non-AFP server, while directing the TCP/IP and/or NetBEUI packets to the server. This work-around is not really convenient, but it will work.

The above basically covers the major disadvantage you'll have with a LAN Manager network when connecting Macs. Otherwise, it works just like an AppleShare file server would, with the exception of running Macintosh programs that run concurrently with AppleShare, such as CE Software's QuickMail or AppleTalk Remote Access. If you have to provide either of these services (or similar ones) for the Mac network, they can implemented on a workstation that has low usage, or on an inexpensive dedicated Mac. This situation is true for any NOS that is not Macintosh-based, and it is not a criticism of LAN Manager.

Like I said at the beginning of the section, LAN Manager Services for Macintosh is easy to install, configure, and use. I find LAN Manager's logic and simplicity very appealing. Given this plug for LAN Manager, the rest of this chapter will look at setting it up for use with the Mac.

LAN Manager Services for Macintosh Installation

There are two steps required for installing LAN Manager Services for Macintosh. The first is planning your network, and the other is the actual installation. During the initial installation, you will also be given the opportunity to configure the AppleTalk services. If you do not have your network plan before you install, you could end up with problems like network number conflicts or missing zone names. This section will discuss the server's requirements, the process of planning your network, and the installation.

Your Server's Requirements

To run the Services for Macintosh, your server will require an additional megabyte of memory. This is above and beyond its current memory requirements. You'll need a minimum of 6M; 8M is the recommended minimum. Your network cards have to be NDIS (Network Driver Interface Spec)-compliant if you plan to bind the AppleTalk protocol to a card that is already bound to LAN Managers TCP/IP or NETBEUI protocols.

Otherwise, you can dedicate an Ethernet or Token Ring card to the AppleTalk binding. If you are going to be using Daystar's AppleTalk card, it will be a dedicated card for a LocalTalk network. Using the LocalTalk card will provide your server with physical link protocol routing capabilities.

Your server needs to be running LAN Manager 2.1 or later, with user-level security instead of share-level security. You can still have servers on the network that use share-level security, but they will not be AFP servers.

Once you have Services for Macintosh installed, any Macintosh running System 6.0.3 or later will be able to use the network.

You can use any of the three physical link protocols, namely Ethernet, Token Ring, or LocalTalk. "LocalTalk" includes any PhoneNET or twisted-pair wiring based on the PhoneNET system.

Planning the Network

Before you install the Macintosh option for LAN Manager, you need to do your homework. You need to know the network numbers for all of the seeded routers on your network, and have a plan from which to work as you configure your server. You'll need the following information:

- Network numbers for each network connected to the server, including all of the AppleTalk networks.
- The AppleTalk phase you are going to use.
- The router status for the server, either seeded or non-seeded.
- The zone or zone names you will assign to the router ports.

If you need more information about zones or AppleTalk networks, check Chapter 2. There you should find the information you need to finish planning your network.

Installing LAN Manager Services for Macintosh

LAN Manager Services for Macintosh must be installed after you have set up the LAN Manager server. You do not have the option

Microsoft LAN Manager

to install the software during the initial installation. The LAN Manager Services for Macintosh software comes with its own installer. After you have set up one server, you can install the Services for Macintosh over the network. Remember, you need to have a license for each server you install with the LAN Manager Services for Macintosh. The installation process binds AppleTalk to the network card. Both methods of installation will be covered in this section.

Initial Installation

To install LAN Manager Services for Macintosh:

1. Log into the server as an administrator.
2. Put the Macintosh Setup Disk into drive A:.
3. Type **a:setup** from an OS/2 command window.
4. Select "Install" when the Start Installation screen appears.

The initial installation copies all of the Services for Macintosh files to the MACNTOSH directory inside the LANMAN directory. The next step of the installation process is the automatic configuration of the Services for Macintosh. The default configuration is as follows:

- **AppleTalk Phase**   Phase 2.
- **Network adapter**   The first adapter in the PROTOCOL.INI file.
- **Media Type**   Depending on the type of network adapter found, it can be EtherTalk or TokenTalk. A LocalTalk card would not be the first one listed in the PROTOCOL.INI file
- **AppleTalk Routing**   Disabled—the default is a non-seeded AppleTalk port.

At this point, you have the choice of accepting the default configuration or configuring Services for Macintosh. To accept the default configuration, all you have to do is select the "Save" option.

If you select "Save," your configuration will be written to the CONFIG.SYS, PROTOCOL.INI, and LANMAN.INI files, and you will exit from the set-up application. The entries for these files are discussed in the section LAN Manager .INI files at the end of this chapter.

If you choose to configure Services for Macintosh, you need to select the Configure button. The instructions for manual configuration of Services for Macintosh are in the section entitled Configuring Services for Macintosh.

Installation Via the Network

To install Services for Macintosh to other servers over the network, you need to copy the Services for Macintosh files to a directory that will be shared. When copying the files, you need to use the XCOPY command.

To set up the directory:

1. Make sure you're logged into the server as an administrator.
2. Create the directory you will share, naming it something like MACINST.
3. Share the directory.
4. Copy the Services for Macintosh files with the XCOPY command from the d:\MACINST directory. The syntax should be: XCOPY a:\ c:\MACINST /s.

Be sure to use the "/s" switch, or the files will not be copied properly. Once the files are in the shared directory, you are ready to perform the network installation.

Perform the following network installation steps from the server on which the Services for Macintosh will be installed.

1. Log into the server as an administrator.
2. Connect to the shared directory with the NET USE command (NET USE d: \\Server_Name\MACINST).
3. Select the network drive you just mounted and type **setup**.

See the Initial Installation section above to set up the default configuration. Otherwise, see the next section for manually configuring the Services for Macintosh. The purpose of the network installation is to facilitate the installation of Services for Macintosh onto other LAN Manager servers within the network.

Configuring Services for Macintosh

Once you've installed the Services for Macintosh software, you will probably want to use a configuration other than the default.

Although you can change these settings whenever you want, it is always easier to get things right the first time. If you've planned your network properly, you can get the Macintosh Services installed and running immediately by using the information from your planning worksheets. These instructions are also the same ones you'd use to change your Services for Macintosh at some future date, with the exception of starting the set-up program.

If you need to reconfigure the Services for Macintosh, start the Services for Macintosh set-up program with the following steps:

1. From an OS/2 command line, set the active directory to MACNTOSH. This directory is inside the LANMAN directory.

2. Type **setup** at the "c:\lanman\macntosh" prompt. This will start the set-up program.

3. Select the Configure option.

   Once you are at this point, you can set all of your AppleTalk preferences. This includes binding the AppleTalk protocol to your networking card(s) and setting the router, AppleTalk Phase, and AppleTalk Zones. Your first task should be to select the AppleTalk Phase you are going to use with the network. If you are using Phase 2, you can skip these steps, because Phase 2 is LAN Manager's default setting. The reason for setting the AppleTalk Phase first is that the type of network adapter cards available for configuration varies depending on which AppleTalk phase you're running.

To change the AppleTalk Phase:

1. You need to unbind AppleTalk from the network. Select "Networks" from the Service for Macintosh Configuration screen.

2. The Network Adapter Configuration screen will appear with your installed network adapters.

3. Select "Remove" for each network card.

4. Select "Cancel" or press **Escape** to return to the Services for Macintosh Configuration screen.

5. Select "Change Phase."

   If you are changing from Phase 1 to Phase 2, you will see the Seed Router Settings screen for the server's internal network router. Here, you will have to assign the network number. If you have to assign the network numbers, you will have to perform this task and return to the Services for Macintosh Configuration screen. Remember, if you using an LocalTalk adapter card, you can still use AppleTalk Phase 2, even though the card will have a non-extended network number. The information for assigning network addresses follows the section about setting up your network adapters.

The next task is to bind the AppleTalk protocol to your adapter card and configure or reconfigure the card.

To bind the AppleTalk protocol to your adapter card:

1. From the Services for Macintosh Configuration screen, select the Networks button.

2. The Network Adapter Configuration screen will appear. From this screen you can:
   - Add a network adapter
   - Remove an adapter
   - Seed the network
   - Stop seeding the network

3. Select the Add button. A list of network adapter cards will appear, from which you select the type of adapter you're using. This list shows only the network cards that can be bound to AppleTalk or NDIS adapter cards.

4. Select the network card you want to bind to AppleTalk and use the Select button. This process binds the selected card to the AppleTalk protocol stack and returns you to the Network Adapter Configuration screen.

5. To bind additional cards to the AppleTalk Protocol stack, repeat steps 3 and 4 for each card.

The driver for the card you selected must already be installed. If it is not, you will see a dialog box asking you to return to the LAN Manger set-up program so you can add the network card driver.

After setting up your network cards, you will have to determine their network addresses if you are using the server as an AppleTalk router. Otherwise, you have to have seed routers on the network from which the server ports will get their network address. When you seed any of the network adapters in your server, Services for Macintosh will automatically turn on the server's routing capabilities. You can have a combination of seeded and non-seeded cards. You only need to seed one network card (port) to turn on the server's routing capabilities.

To seed a network:

1. From the Network Adapter Configuration screen, select "Seed..." Depending on the phase of the server, you will see one of two Seed Router Settings screens. You will see one screen for Phase 1 or LocalTalk cards, and the other if you're configuring a Phase 2 Ethernet or Token Ring card.

2. Set the network number. Remember that the network number for a Phase 1 network is a single number from 1 to 65534. Phase 2 network numbers are entered as range numbers; each number can be from 1 to 65279. If you have questions about AppleTalk network numbers, see Chapter 6. Range numbers are discussed in Chapter 6, but the concepts apply to all NOSs.

3. Assign the zone name(s). The default zone name is the server's LAN Manager domain name. You will probably want to change this. Once again, if you are not clear about the function of zones and zone names, read Chapter 2.

4. Add any additional zones you might need in a Phase 2 network by selecting the Add Zone button and entering the zone name.

5. Set the default zone by selecting the Set Default Zone button.

If you are using only one AppleTalk port, you will only have to set the default zone for the adapter; it will also be the default zone for the server. When using more than one AppleTalk port, you will have two defaults to set: the adapter's default zone and the default adapter. The default zone on the default network adapter becomes the server's zone, or the zone that the server will be broadcast from. So you need to have the correct adapter and select the zone, or your network will not appear where you want it.

Setting the default adapter is the same as setting the default network. Since there are several ways to talk about this, including setting the default network port, it can be a bit confusing, so be careful.

To set the default adapter or network:

1. If you're not there, return to the Services for Macintosh Configuration screen.

2. Select the network adapter you want to use as the default from the list in the AppleTalk Network section.

3. Select the Set Default Network button.

If you are changing the default network, and thereby changing the default AppleTalk zone, you will see a dialog box informing you of the change. If this is the incorrect zone, you will have to reset the card's default zone, as outlined in the steps above.

Now you should have Services for Macintosh configured. Before you exit the Services for Macintosh Configuration window, you need to save your changes. To do this, select the Save button from the Services for Macintosh Configuration window, and then select Exit Setup. The Services for Macintosh will now be running. Your next tasks will be to select the directories and printers you want to share and designate your users. These tasks are discussed in the following section.

LAN Manager Services for Macintosh Administration

Once you have configured the Services for Macintosh, you will have some administration tasks to perform. You need to designate which shared directories will be available to Mac users, who will be their owners, and which groups will have access the shared directories. Also, you need to enable guest access if you are providing this type of support. You may also want to add some applications to the extension mapping. And you'll need to know how to stop and resume AppleTalk services.

All of these functions are performed with the MACADMIN program, which is the focus of this section. These topics will be discussed in the following order:

- Sharing and modifying Macintosh volumes
- Access rights
- Allowing guest logins
- Extension mapping
- Stopping and restarting services for Macintosh
- Using the MACADMIN program from an OS/2 workstation

To access the Macintosh administration program, you have to type **MACADMIN** from an OS/2 prompt. If you run MACADMIN from a window, you will have to expand it to its full size. When MACADMIN starts, you will see the opening screen.

MACADMIN operates a lot like NET ADMIN, so it should be familiar. There are three menus in the MACADMIN program:

- **The View menu** Used to look at the Macintosh file servers and select the server you want to administer, and to control the Services for Macintosh.

- **The Configuration menu** Used to set up Macintosh volumes, set server options, and print a server report. The server options include setting the owner of the server, file extension mapping, and setting the Macintosh name that will be visible from the Macintosh Chooser.

- **The Status menu** Used to see which Macintosh users are logged in, which volumes they are using, and how long they've been logged in. You can also see which files are open and who has them open.

Most of these menus will be discussed in the following sections. However, most of the information presented will be what you need to get the server up and running. Informational sections of the MACADMIN program will not be discussed. I need to leave you with something to discover on your own.

Sharing and Modifying Macintosh Volumes

The most important task is to determine which directories will be shared and who is going to have access to them. Just installing Services for Macintosh does not automatically make any shared directory available. So you should probably have a plan before you start. Do you need to share an E-mail directory? Is each Mac user going to have a home directory/volume for data files? Are you going to share directories between workgroups? How you share the various directories will depend on your particular needs.

LAN Manager operates using shared directories, and each shared directory appears to the user as a volume. The same principle applies to Services for Macintosh. Each directory that is made available will be mounted as a individual Macintosh volume. To set up your Macintosh volumes, you must first create a shared directory using LAN Managers' NET ADMIN program. After you have created your basic shared directory structure, you can assign the directories to be accessed as Macintosh volumes.

To share directories as Macintosh volumes:

1. Start MACADMIN.
2. Select "Mac Volumes" from the Config menu.
3. You will see a screen where all of the configured Macintosh volumes are displayed. To create a new Mac volume, select "Add."
4. The Add/Modify Mac Volume window will appear. From here, you can set up or modify your Macintosh volumes and their users.
5. Fill out the Volume name. This is the name that the Macintosh user will see in the Chooser when selecting the volume to mount. This name must be less than 32 characters in length.
6. The LM Sharename is the directory name of the shared LAN Manager directory. Rather than entering this name, you can let MACADMIN enter it by selecting the Share button. This will bring up a list of the shared LAN Manager directories.

Use the following steps to select a LAN Manager volume for Macintosh access:

1. Select the directory you want to share as a Macintosh volume.
2. Click OK. This will return you to the Add/Modify Mac Volume window with the LM Sharename and Server Path fields filled out. If you choose, you can enter the data into the LM Sharename and Server Path fields manually, but it makes more sense to me to use the Share button.
3. Your next task will be to set the access rights for the shared volume. Setting the access rights will be discussed in the Access Rights section. From here, you would start at step 4 of the steps listed in the Access Rights section.

At this point, the volume will not be available until you assign its access information. But before you go on, there are a couple of things you should know. You cannot share a sub-directory of an existing volume. Also, you cannot create more than one Macintosh volume for each shared directory. Either of these actions would produce an error message.

Access Rights

The assignment of access rights is a two-step process. You may have noticed in Figure 7.14, the Add/Modify Mac Volume screen, that you can assign AppleShare access privileges. AppleShare access privileges are described in Chapter 2, so they will not discussed here. Before you set the access privileges to Macintosh volumes, you need to make sure your users and groups are defined. If they are not, you will have to set them up using the NET ADMIN program. See your LAN Manager Administrator's Guide for instructions for setting up users and groups.

To set the AppleShare privileges:

1. Run the MACADMIN program.
2. Select the "Mac Volumes..." menu selection from the Config menu.
3. Select the volume you want to change from the Mac Volumes window and use the Zoom button.
4. You will be presented with the Add/Modify Mac Volumes window. This is where you will begin if you have just set up a volume. Select the Owner button.
5. From the list of users, select the volume's owner. The selected owner will be placed in the Owner field.
6. Select the Groups button.
7. From the list of groups, select the volume's group.
8. Click OK.
9. Repeat steps 3 through 8 for each Macintosh volume you want to change.

Next, you will have to set the privileges for the volume. This is done by entering an "X" in each of the available selections for each category: Owner, Group, and Everyone. But before you do, you need to know that the owner assigned to a Macintosh volume is the owner of the volume and any directory created on the shared Macintosh volume by an MS-DOS, Windows, or OS/2 workstation, even if the users of these machines are included in the Group assigned to the shared volume.

It works this way. Say that George is a user on a workstation other than a Macintosh, and he creates a directory called "George" on a volume that is also shared as a Macintosh volume. When the directory is examined from a Macintosh, using the "Sharing..." command from the File menu, the owner of the directory will be the owner you assigned in the Add/Modify Mac Volume screen—let's say this is Susan. However, if a directory is created by a Macintosh user, Jean, then Jean will be the directory's owner. So Susan will own any directory created on the Macintosh volume, but Jean will own the directories she creates.

However, if Susan changes the privileges for the directory created by George, the changes will affect only other Macintosh users. The PC, Windows, or OS/2 users who have the appropriate access rights, as assigned to them by the administrator from LAN Manager's NET ADMIN program, will still have those same access, regardless of how they are changed by Susan. However, if Susan decides to change the rights to George's directory so that only she can access is contents, then Jean will no longer be able to rights the directory: it will be grayed out when she sees it from a dialog box, or will have the locked folder icon when viewed from the finder.

With this bit of trivia out of the way, let's look at assigning access privileges to a Macintosh volume. For each Macintosh volume you can assign an owner and a group. For each owner and group you can assign the following access privileges:

- See Folders
- See Files
- Make Changes

Also, each of these privileges can be assigned to Everyone.

When you assign an owner to a Macintosh volume, the owner should be an administrator or someone from the assigned group. The owner of the directory will be the only one who can change the access privileges to a directory or volume from a Macintosh. Also, because the owner can change a volume's privileges, you need to make sure the person who has this responsibility knows how the AppleShare privilege system works. If you allow access privileges for everyone, then the rights assigned to Everyone will supersede any restrictions made to the Owner or Group privileges. And if you have enabled guest logins, then anyone logging in as a Macintosh guest will have access to the files unless the privileges are specifically changed by the volume's owner.

You can also make private volumes, which will not be visible from the Macintosh's Chooser to anyone except the registered user. This is something that is not a usual capability for an AppleShare volume, but one that can be quite handy. If you want to set up private volumes, all you need to do is assign the Owner attributes and leave the Group and Everyone access privileges blank. The only person who can see a shared directory set up in this manner is the Owner. For others to see the volume, you would have to have at least one access privilege attribute in either the Group or Everyone sections checked.

Allowing Guest Logins

Depending on your security needs, you can either allow or disallow guest access to your Macintosh volumes. If you decide to disallow guest access, you don't need to do anything, because this is the server's default setting. If you do allow guest access, you will have to enable this capability specifically. Also, if you enable guest access, you should pay very close attention to how you assign the volume's access privileges. You may want to restrict guest access to some volumes and only enable specific privileges on others. Before you enable guest access, make sure you understand AppleShare access rights, as described in Chapter 2.

Enabling guest access is a multi-step process that requires the stopping and starting of the MacFile services on the server, the editing of the LANMAN.INI file, and the addition of the guest user. Instructions for stopping and starting the MacFile services are given in the section on Stopping and Restarting Services for Macintosh. They are not complicated, but you do need to be careful.

To enable guest logins:

1. Stop the MacFile Service from the Net Admin or MACADMIN program.

2. Add **macguest** = *username* to the [MacFile] section of the LANMAN.INI file. The user name must be the same as the user name you will assign in the next step.

3. Use the Net Admin program to create a user with the same name as the one specified in the LANMAN.INI file. The user you add must have guest accesses and no password. If you have set the server to require passwords for every user, you

must use the following OS/2 command line to add the guest account:

```
NET USER /ADD USERNAME /PASWORDREQ:NO
   /PRIVILEGE:GUEST
```

Once again, the user name is the same as the name entered into the LANMAN.INI file.

4. Restart the MacFile service.

After the MacFile service is restarted, Macintosh guest logins will be permitted. With the Macintosh guest access enabled, anyone will be able to log into the server as a guest. Remember, if you have enabled all of the access privileges for Everyone, then guests will also have full access to the server's files.

Extension Mapping

The Services for Macintosh comes with a fair number of predefined file extensions. However, it is not an exhaustive list, and you might want to modify or add a few extension definitions. The extension mapping is one-way, from the OS/2 or DOS extension to the Macintosh file type.

There is no automatic mapping from the Macintosh to OS/2 or MS-DOS. If you have files that will be created on the Mac and shared on other platforms, you will have to teach your Mac users how to use MS-DOS file names. Otherwise, it is quite likely that the translated names for the Mac documents will be incomprehensible when viewed on a MS-DOS workstation.

This does not mean that you shouldn't use Services for Macintosh's extension mapping capabilities. Adding the extensions for your Mac users will make their lives a bit easier.

To add or modify an extension mapping:

1. Start the MACADMIN program from an OS/2 prompt at the server.

2. Select "Server Options" from the Config menu.

3. The window that appears displays all of the currently mapped extensions. To add an extension, click the Add button. If you are modifying an extension, select the extension and then click the Add button.

4. The Add/Modify Extension Mapping window will open. Enter the appropriate information for the extension, file type, and file creator.

5. Click the OK button, and you will be returned to the Server Options screen. If you want to add or modify another extension, repeat steps 3 and 4. When you are finished, click OK. If you select Cancel, you will lose all of your changes.

Stopping and Restarting Services for Macintosh

Whenever you make changes to the one of LAN Manager's configuration files that affect a service, you have to stop and restart the service before the change can take effect. In some cases, you might have to restart the server, but often all you have to do is stop and restart the service. When you make changes to the Services for Macintosh configuration, you will have to stop and restart the MacFile services on the server. There are two ways to perform this action: you can use the NET ADMIN or the MACADMIN programs.

To use the NET ADMIN program:

1. Make sure all of your Macintosh users are logged out. Otherwise, they will lose their connection to the server when you stop the MacFile services.

2. Start NET ADMIN from the OS/2 prompt.

3. Choose "Control Services" from the Config menu.

4. In the LAN Manager Services window, select "MacFile."

5. Select the Stop button. This stops the MacFile services. To turn the MacFile services back on, repeat steps 2 through 4 above and select the Start button.

To stop and start the MacFile services using the MACADMIN program:

1. Make sure all of your Macintosh users are logged out. Otherwise, they will lose their connection to the server when you stop the MacFile services.

2. Start MACAMIN from the OS/2 prompt.

3. Choose "MacFile Services" from the View menu.

4. You will see the server's name and a message saying that MacFile is started in the MacFile Services window. Select the server for which you want to stop the MacFile services.

5. Select the Stop button. This stops the MacFile services. To turn the MACFILE services back on, repeat steps 2 through 4 above and select the Start button.

Using the MACADMIN Program from an OS/2 Workstation

If you have an OS/2 workstation, you can run the MACAMIN from the OS/2 workstation rather than from the server console. To do this, copy the MACAMIN screen files from the server or the distribution disks onto the workstation.

The following files need to be placed in the workstations LANMAN\NETPROG directory:

- **macadmin**
- **mac.msg**
- **mach.msg**

Then, the AFPADMIN.DDL needs to be placed in the LANMAN\NETLIB directory.

To copy these files from the server, you will have to mount the MACINSTL directory from the server and copy the files listed above to their proper directories.

Once you have the files on your OS/2 machine, all you have to do is type **MACADMIN** *servername* to administer a specific server, or just type **MACADMIN** and select from the OS/2 window the server you want to administer.

AppleTalk Printers

The LAN Manager Services for Macintosh will allow you to queue print jobs to a server's hard drive for AppleTalk PostScript printers and make the printer available to PC users at the same time. Depending on your needs, you can choose one of three configuration options when using a PostScript AppleTalk printer with Services for Macintosh. These options are:

MICROSOFT LAN MANAGER

- Networking the Macs and the printer(s) without allowing PC access.
- Connecting the printer to the network so both Macs and PCs have access (LAN Manager would serve the function of a print server).
- Connecting the printer to the server's serial or parallel port so both Macs and PCs have access.

Each of these configurations will be discussed in this section.

LAN Manager Services for Macintosh has built-in support for the following PostScript printers:

- The Apple LaserWriter Plus, II NT, and II NTX
- The QMS PS-810
- The NEC LC-890

If your printer is not on this list, you will have to make sure it can use a PPD for one of the printers listed above, or you will have to get the PPD file for your printer and install it on the server. A PPD file contains information about the printer's fonts and other PostScript information. If a PPD file didn't come with your printer, you can get one by contacting the printer's manufacturer. It may also be possible to get the PPD file from Adobe.

Macintosh Printer Access Only

Your first choice for connecting an AppleTalk PostScript printer to your Mac network is to make it accessible to the Macs only. How you do this will depend on the type of network and printer(s) you're using. In principle, you will connect the printer as if you were not using a file server, and in this scenario, the server has no function.

Figure 7.3 shows the three basic configurations you could have when connecting an AppleTalk PostScript printer.

Configuration A shows a LocalTalk network, with the Macs and printers all using the same physical link. In this situation, all you would do is connect the printer to the network and it would be accessible to any Macintosh.

Configuration B is a mixed-protocol network, with the Macs on Ethernet and the printers using LocalTalk. In this situation, either you would be using the server as an internet router or one

Figure 7.3
Three printer configurations

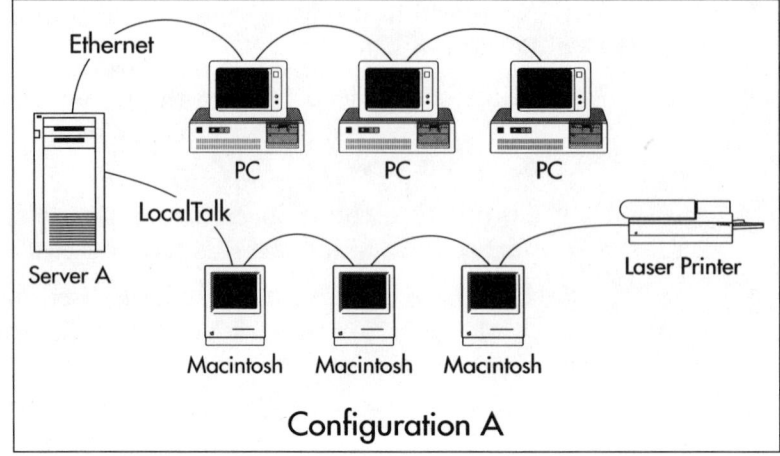
Configuration A

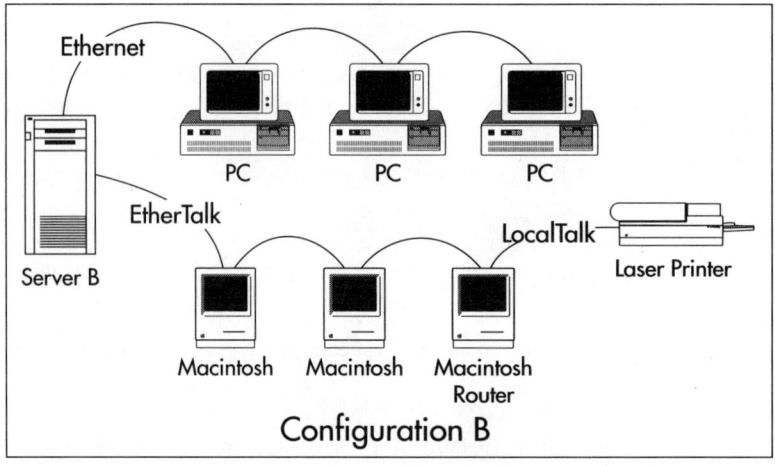
Configuration B

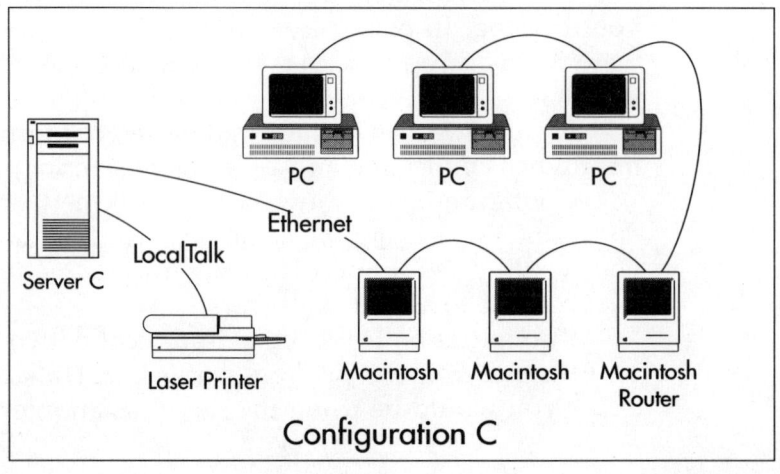
Configuration C

of the Macintosh workstations (as shown in the figure) would be the router.

Configuration C shows both the Macs and printers on the same physical link, Ethernet. This configuration is functionally the same as configuration A.

In any of these configurations, any Macintosh could access the printer by selecting it from the Chooser. With configuration B or C, you might have to select a zone other than the one that the server resides in to access the printer. But all zones are available to each Mac, so there would be no problems in accessing the printer.

Using LAN Manager as a Print Server

Using a LAN Manager server as an internet router and printer queue for a PostScript laser printer while the printer is physically part of the AppleTalk network is probably how you will want to connect your AppleTalk printer, Macs, and PCs. This is also the recommended method for connecting the printer. Figure 7.4 shows two configurations. For both configurations, the server is being used as a queue and the printers are using either LocalTalk or EtherTalk.

In both configurations, the server is functioning as a printer queue. In configuration A, the server is also a router, while configuration B uses a Macintosh with routing software. The set-up procedures are similar and allow both Macintosh and PC workstations to access the printer. Also notice in configuration B that there are two queues using the same printer as a destination. If you want, you can set up special-purpose queues (say, one that will print the spooled data at a specific time) and direct multiple queues to a single printer.

The set-up process for making a printer accessible to the Macs connected to the server is a two-part process. The first step is setting up a printer queue and destination on the server as you would for any LAN Manager printer. The second part of the process is making the printer available to the Macs. Each of these processes will be described here.

To set up the printer destination:

1. Open the OS/2 Print Manager.
2. Choose "Printers" from the Setup menu.
3. Select the Add button from the Printers dialog box.

Figure 7.4

Using LAN Manager as a print server

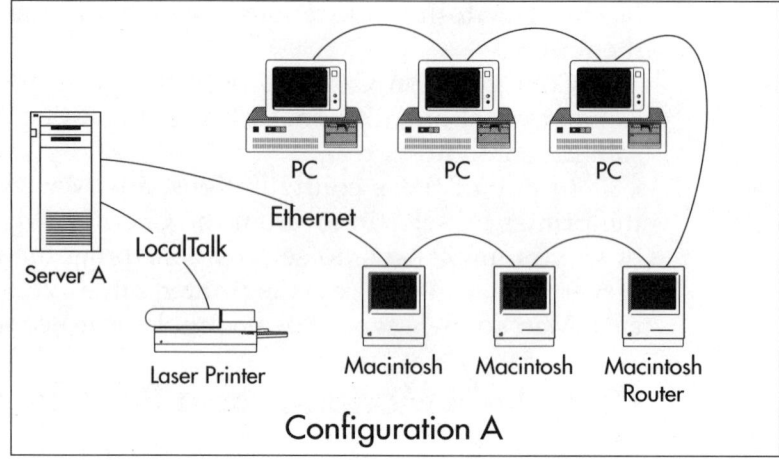
Configuration A

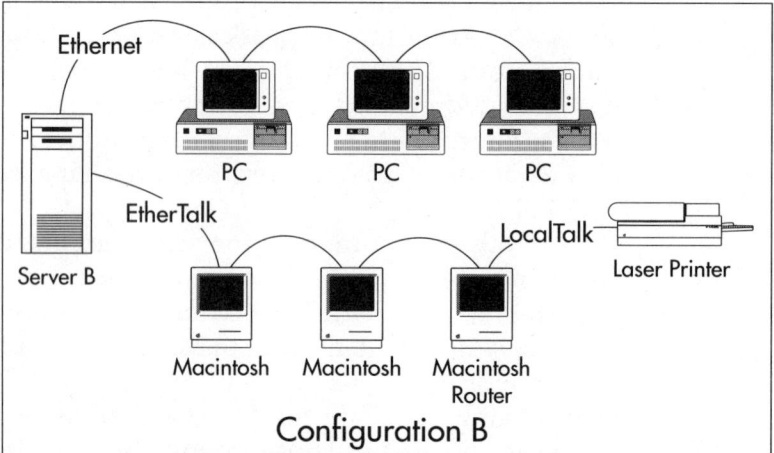
Configuration B

4. In the Add Printer window, enter the following in each of the listed fields:

- **Name** The printer's name. This name will be displayed when you set up the printer queue.

- **Description** A description of the printer for easy identification.

- **Device** Enter **None**. This is because the printer will be connected to the AppleTalk network and not to one of the server's physical ports.

- Select the printer type from the list of available printer types. If your printer is not listed, you will have to install it from the OS/2 control panel. If you need information about installing a printer type, see your LAN Manager manuals. The Change Printer window is identical to the Add Printer window.

5. Select the Add button after all of the fields are complete. You will be returned to the Printers dialog box.

6. Click the OK button to return to the Print Manager.

To create the printer queue for an AppleTalk printer:

1. Open the OS/2 Print Manager.
2. Choose "Queues" from the Setup menu.
3. Select the Add button.
4. In the Add Queue dialog box, enter the following in each of the listed fields:

    - **Name** The name for the printer queue as it will be broadcast on the PC network.
    - **Description** A description of the queue for easy identification.
    - **Queue driver** This is completed automatically.
    - **Priority** This specifies the queue's priority: 1 is the highest and 9 is the lowest. The default setting is 5.
    - **Scheduling** Complete this setting if you want the queue to print only during a specific time period.
    - **Select printer** Select the printer destination created with the steps above.
    - **Printer driver** This is automatically selected when you choose the printer destination.

    The information in the Add Queue window is the same as the Change Queue window.

5. Select the Add button. This creates the queue and returns you to the Queues dialog box.
6. Choose OK.
7. Close the Print Manager.

The above steps will have created a standard LAN Manager printer and queue for the PostScript printer, but the printer is still not accessible to the Macs. If you have not done so, you should make sure the AppleTalk printer is connected to the network.

To share the printer queue and make it available to the Macs:

1. Use the NET ADMIN program and share the queue, or type **NET SHARE** *queuename* **/print** at an OS/2 command line.

2. Stop the MacPrint services.

3. In the LANMAN.INI file, enter the following in the [AppleTalk Printers] section:

   ```
   destination = "printer name", zone name,
    nocapture
   ```

   - **destination** is the name of the printer destination created above.

   - **printer name** is the name of the printer as it would normally appear in the Chooser. This name must be entered exactly as it appears in the Macintosh's Chooser.

   - **zone name** is the physical zone in which the printer resides.

   - **nocapture** tells LAN Manager not to capture the printer name and broadcast it over the network. This entry is optional. If it is left out, the printer name will be captured and the printer name will be broadcast along with the queue name. Unless you have a specific reason for not capturing the printer's name, you should capture it. Otherwise, Macintosh print jobs will print directly to the printer and not be placed in the LAN Manager queue. An example would look like:

   ```
   Laser = "LaserWriter II NT ", Printer Zone
   ```

   The entry described in this part makes the AppleTalk printer available to MS-DOS and OS/2 workstations.

4. In the [MacQueues] section of the LANMAN.INI file, add

   ```
   queuename = "Macintosh queue name"
   ```

   - **queuename** is the name of the LAN Manager queue created above.

   - **Macintosh queue name** is the name that will be broadcast to the Macintosh users.

The entry described in this step makes the AppleTalk queue available to Macintosh users.

5. Start or restart the MacPrint service.

6. Add **macprint** to the list of services in the [server] section of the LANMAN.INI file. This will cause the MacPrint service to start automatically when the server is started.

If you want to set up the AppleTalk printer so that it is only available to the Macs, skip step 3. If you want the AppleTalk printer to be available to PCs but not to Macs, skip step 4.

Connecting the Printer to the Server

You can connect the printer to the parallel or serial port of the server and make it available to the Macs using LAN Manager, rather than placing the printer on the network. This process requires that you use LAN Manager to set up the printer and queue as if it were going to be used for MS-DOS and PS/2 workstations. This process is the same as that described in the section on Using LAN Manager as a Print Server, except that instead of connecting the device to None in the printer destination, you enter the parallel or com port for the printer.

The following steps should already be done. If not, see your LAN Manager manuals or the Using LAN Manager as a Print Server section for completing these steps:

1. Create the printer queue.
2. Create the printer destination.
3. Share the queue.

After these steps have been done, you need to

1. Stop the MacPrint service if it is on.
2. Enter **OS2queue name = "Macintosh Queue Name"** in the [MacQueues] section of the LANMAN.INI file.
3. Turn on the MacPrint service.
4. In the "srvservices" line in the [server] section of the LANMAN.INI file, add **macprint**. This will cause the MacPrint services to start automatically the next time the server is started.

The name entered as the Macintosh queue name will be broadcast over the AppleTalk network to the Macs and visible in the Chooser, while the OS/2 queue name will be what PC and OS/2 users see when they connect to the network printer.

Trouble-shooting

This section does not cover Macintosh problems except as they pertain directly to Services for Macintosh. If you are having Macintosh problems, you should look at Chapter 10. Otherwise, some of the problems you could have with LAN Manager's Services for Macintosh are listed below with the recommended fix.

Sharing a CD-ROM

This is not possible with Services for Macintosh.

User Access Problems

It is possible that your users will have problems accessing the server or a printer queue. Usually the problem will be intermittent and can be fixed by one of the following suggestions.

- Edit the "aarpretries" entry in the [AppleTalk] section of the LANMAN.INI file by increasing the number.
- There may be an insufficient number of selectors specified in the PROTOCOL.INI file. The default number is 14, but it can be adjusted upward. 14 selectors will allow about 12 Macs to be connected. To connect about 40 Macs, this number should be 35.
- Another reason that a user might have trouble connecting to the server is insufficient memory. To allocate more memory to the server for Macintosh access, you can edit the the cache size on the "HPFS386.IFS" line in the CONFIG.SYS file. Add to the "HPFS386.IFS" line a switch like "/MSFM:1024" or "/MSFM:2048".
- Check your network numbers. It is possible that you have a network number conflict.

- If you have just changed a zone name on the server, you will have to shut down any routers connected to the network you're having trouble with so the old zone names can expire.

Administrator and Server Problems

The following is a list of problems you might have while running the MACADMIN program or on the server in general.

Session and NETBEUI Problems

There are several error messages you could get, all related to an insufficient number of sessions. The number of sessions is set by a number labeled "sessions" in the protocol driver section of the PROTOCOL.INI file. These problems will affect the workstation you are using to run the MACADMIN program. The following list represents some of these problems:

- "NetBios session limit exceeded" can appear when you are viewing or selecting a server, or when you are unable to view a server.
- When configuring a new Macintosh volume, you cannot create a directory.
- Server reports do not include LANMAN.INI information.
- The error log for the workstation you're using to run the MACADMIN program contains NCB (Network Control Block) errors.

Other Administrator Errors

You could experience any of the following errors or problems while using or trying to use the MACADMIN program. There are not many errors, and most of them can easily be fixed. However, this is not a complete list.

- If you cannot access the target server, or if access is denied when you are trying to select a server, make sure you are using an account with administrator's privileges to log in.
- If the server shows an incorrect name, or if the directory or file names on a volume are incorrect, it is because of an

inconsistency in how OS/2 maps Macintosh characters. This error will occur more often if you are using a code page other than 850. There is no real fix for this problem, but you need to be aware of it in case it occurs.

- If the server does not appear in the MACADMIN Servers list, you might have to type the server's LAN Manager computer name. Also, the server can fail to appear if it is not currently running the MacFile service, if you are running MACADMIN from a domain other than the domain in which the server resides, or if you are using a protocol on the workstation (this must be an OS/2 workstation) other the server's protocol.

- Other miscellaneous errors you can experience are when the sharename is invalid or you get a message saying that the database can't be locked. In the case where the database can't be locked, try again: the MACADMIN program and the MacFile services are trying to access the same information. When you get the invalid sharename message, the corresponding LAN Manager volume is no longer being shared. To fix this, you may have to re-associate the Mac volume name to the shared directory, or you may have to reshare the directory and then re-associate the Mac volume name.

Server Excreta

There are a few server problems that really need to be addressed here. There could be a time when a letter is appended to a Macintosh volume's name. There are two causes for this problem:

- The Macintosh volume name assigned already exists on the network. When there is a duplicate server name on the network, Services for Macintosh automatically adds a letter to the server name.

- If the MacFile service has crashed, it is possible that users will see two volume names in the Chooser, the regular volume and one with a letter appended to the name like "Mac VolumeA". In cases like this, your users will probably have access to only the volume name with the appended name. To fix this problem, you'll have to restart the server.

Macintosh File Problems

Another type of problem you might experience is the loss of your Macintosh file names and/or their associated icons. Usually, even if the icons and file names are lost, the files are undamaged and usable as long as the documents can be identified and you know which application created them. This, as you might guess, can be a problem of its own. Also, fixing these problems is not so easy.

On a Macintosh disk, the information that associates icons with their programs is kept in the Desktop file. (System 6.0.X has a single Desktop file and 7.X has two Desktop files.) This same information is stored on a LAN Manager server, but it is kept in a hidden directory that cannot be accessed from a Macintosh, and the structure is a bit awkward. Each volume, directory, and sub-directory has an additional directory called ~APF.

A single volume can have a few hundred sub-directories with the ~APF label. Within each of these directories is another called ~I. The resource fork for each Macintosh file is stored in the ~APF directory on the same level as the Macintosh file and the comments entered into the file's info section (what you see when you use the Get Info command from the Finder's File menu). When you look for these directories, you will have to set the File Manager to view hidden and system files from a Windows PC or the OS/2 server.

If a PC user renames a Macintosh file and it no longer has a corresponding extension, or if an application gets renamed, the association with the file's resource fork will be lost, and the file will lose its icon. This problem can be fixed by renaming the file or application's resource fork in the ~APF directory. You can also fix some of the Macintosh data files by using a Macintosh utility that will let you edit the file's type and creator.

This will restore a data file's icon, but it will not work on a file that stores vital information in its resource fork, like an application, or a complicated Macintosh file like those created by desktop publishing programs. For applications and more complicated files, you will have to find the old file name in the ~APF directory and rename the resource fork.

If you have set the **afpinfoineas** option in the [MacFile] section of the LANMAN.INI file to "no" and you want to restore the Info comments for a file or application, you will have to edit the old file name. It is in the ~I sub-directory of the ~AFP directory for each file you need to edit.

Also contained with in the ~AFP directories are a set of files called:

- FILEINFO.AFP
- DESKTOP.AFP
- DIRID.AFP
- VOLINFO.AFP

Each of these files also has a corresponding *.BAK file.

When backing up your AppleShare volumes, you must either back them up from a Macintosh (to retain the resource fork information) or be sure to back up and restore all hidden files. Chances are that the files listed above will not be backed up because they will be open, but the *.BAK files will be.

When the files are resorted, if the Mac cannot find the *.AFP file, it will restore it from its corresponding *.BAK file. This automatic process will prevent you from having to perform this task manually.

The only time you might have to copy a *.BAK file to restore the *.AFP file is if the *.AFP is damaged. If one of these files should become damaged, you will know, because you will lose the association between the Macintosh files and their resource forks and icons all in one fell swoop. If this happens, you will have to restore the *.AFP files from their back-ups.

Conclusion

Well, that's about it. As I said at the beginning of this chapter, you have all of the information you need to set up a LAN Manager Services for Macintosh file server. Although it may seem complicated because you have to contend with OS/2, the LAN Manager administration, and the LAN Manager Macintosh administration program all at the same time, it really is not all that difficult. If you take your time and pay careful attention to each step, you'll find that LAN Manager offers a very secure and easy-to-use Macintosh file server.

If you are wondering about the Windows NT Server and Services for Macintosh, you will find that the NT Services for Macintosh are very similar to LAN Manager's. The differences are in their overall capabilities. The NT Server version is more robust than LAN Manager because it does not have the 16M memory constraint imposed by OS/2, so it is a more efficient server. Also, Services for Macintosh are fully integrated in the Windows NT server, so that both PC and Mac administration are easier. Otherwise, all of the features of LAN Manager are also available with Windows NT Services for Macintosh, and much of what is in this chapter is still applicable, as well.

Mac-centric Networks

Introduction

Until now, the primary focus of this book has been PC-based networking systems and connecting your Macs to those systems. But because each of the networks is really two networking systems, the PC NOS with AppleTalk running concurrently, you will probably want to know more about the options you have with AppleTalk. Also, you might be unaware of the Macintosh's unique qualities and capabilities.

This chapter is intended to fill you in regarding some of the Mac's network and cross-platform capabilities that are not dependent on the PC network. The topics that will be discussed include:

- Running AppleTalk on PCs
- Using the Mac as an MS-DOS machine
- Macintosh/AppleTalk network utilities
- Security on an AppleTalk network
- Remote access to AppleTalk networks

You may want to apply one, some, all, or none of these capabilities. But if you do not know about them, you cannot employ them as possible solutions in your network or cross-platform environment. This chapter will not provide the specifics for installing or using any one of these solutions, but you will find descriptions of the products and an overview of how they work, so you have a starting point for implementing any one of these solutions.

Alternatives to PC Network Operating Systems

There may be an occasion when you have an AppleTalk network and want to drop a PC into the network, or when you want to add a PC to the AppleTalk network without connecting it to an existing NOS. PC users who want direct AppleTalk access are not orphaned, but they are not desired children, either.

This is one of Apple's shortcomings. Since Windows for Workgroups has built-in networking capabilities, it would seem logical for Apple to supply a network interface for WFW machines so they could participate on an AppleTalk network without causing the network administrator great pain and suffering. Unfortunately, Apple has failed to do this, so you have to search out a third-party vendor for the AppleTalk connection.

Currently, there are four vendors who can help with this dilemma:

- Farallon
- Miramar
- CoActive
- Artisoft

Of these four, two work with LocalTalk, Ethernet, or Token Ring networks: Farallon's PhoneNET Talk and Miramar's Personal MacLAN. The CoActive solution is good, but it is only available as a LocalTalk solution.

PhoneNET Talk

PhoneNET Talk is Farallon Computing's solution for adding an MS-DOS or Windows machine to an AppleTalk network. It works by installing an appropriate adapter card—one of the AppleTalk cards or a supported Ethernet or Token Ring card—and installing the software. You can purchase a PhoneNET Talk package that contains the PhoneNET Talk LocalTalk card and software as a bundle from Farallon.

Once it is set up, you have access to any AppleShare file server and any networked laser printer or ImageWriter. However, you cannot share a hard disk on the PC, so you are restricted to using the Apple resources on the network. The biggest problem you'll encounter with PhoneNET Talk is its memory requirements. PhoneNET Talk installs a whole mess of TSRs when it is run, and they consume almost 100K of memory. Even if you load everything you can into high memory, you're still going to bump the memory ceiling, especially if you're using other TSRs—which, in turn, can cause problems with applications in DOS or Windows. If you perform memory management, it is possible to make PhoneNET Talk work and grant the PC user access to the AppleTalk network.

The PhoneNET Talk software and PhoneNET Talk adapter card were licensed from Apple by Farallon. Before Farallon got the license to the card and software, the PC LocalTalk solution was not well-known. However, since its acquisition by Farallon, the software has been improved, as has the network adapter card. Now if they could only do something about the memory limits...

Personal MacLAN

Miramar's Personal MacLAN is a software package that lets you turn a Windows or Windows for Workgroups PC into a true peer-to-peer AppleTalk workstation. With this software, you can give a PC the same type of networking capabilities found on Macintoshes using System 7.

With Personal MacLAN, your Windows PC can share its drives and printer resources on the AppleTalk network using LocalTalk, Ethernet, or Token Ring. In the Windows for Workgroups environment, you can even use the Windows for Workgroups (WFW) network on one adapter card and Personal MacLAN on another adapter card and be connected to both networks from a single PC.

Personal MacLAN also proves file mapping for its networked volumes, so a Macintosh user can double-click on a file on a shared MacLAN volume and launch the appropriate Macintosh application. And of course, it also provides the standard AppleShare security options, as described in Chapter 2.

If you are creative and have a NDIS network adapter card, you can, with the proper drivers, actually make Personal MacLAN work with a single network card. The Personal MacLAN uses ODI drivers, which normally limit each card to servicing a single protocol. But it is possible to get a driver that will let you bind the ODI driver to an NDIS card and run multiple protocols from the same card.

A primary component of Personal MacLAN is the set of PhoneNET Talk drivers that Miramar has licensed from Farallon. So this solution, which is not widely known, is implemented at your own risk. It will also work with PhoneNET Talk. However, neither Farallon nor Miramar supports this venture. If you do this, you are on your own.

The drivers you need are:

- **LSL.COM**   created on or after 11/5/92
- **ODINSUP.COM version 1.22**   created on or after 2/23/93

These drivers are Novell drivers, or available from Novell. It appears that they are in the public domain, since I have not seen any licensing restrictions regarding their use. However, Novell has published a disclaimer regarding the ODINSUP.COM driver (see the note at the bottom of this page).

If you can make it work, great. Otherwise, you'll have to find another solution. The drivers are supposedly available on CompuServe in the Novell Support section.

Novell, Inc. Disclaimer for the ODINSUP.COM Driver

Novell, Inc. makes no representations or warranties with respect to any NetWare software, and specifically disclaims any express or implied warranties of merchantability, title, or fitness for a particular purpose. Distribution of any NetWare software is forbidden without the express written consent of Novell, Inc. Further, Novell reserves the right to discontinue distribution of any NetWare software.

Novell is not responsible for lost profits or revenue, loss of use of the software, loss of data, costs of re-creating lost data, the cost of any substitute equipment or program, or claims by any party other than you. Novell strongly recommends a backup be made before any software is installed. Technical support for this software may be provided at the discretion of Novell.

To use these drivers, you will need to make modifications to your AUTOEXEC.BAT, CONFIG.SYS, NET.CFG, NET.CFG (a PhoneNET configuration file) and PROTOCOL.INI files. An example of a possible configuration should be found with the ODIN-SUP.COM file when you download it.

Personal MacLAN uses the same technology that is in its MacLAN software bridges for Novell and LANtastic Networks to provide server support for the PC drive. What it does not do is provide gateway access for drives networked via WFW. The technology used in Personal MacLAN is a marriage of Miramar's own development efforts and Farallon's PhoneNET software. Miramar has fewer memory problems than PhoneNET Talk, but it could still be considered a memory hog requiring some compromises. Personal MacLAN is a more elegant product, giving you more capabilities (e.g., true peer-to-peer file sharing) than PhoneNET Talk. However, upgrades for this product are dependent on two companies, Farallon and Miramar. You may find a time lag between the two companies when it comes to upgrades, since Farallon may want to distribute its competing product, getting the jump on Miramar.

These types of situations always make me uncomfortable, because one company (Miramar) is dependent on the other (Farallon) for its (Miramar's) product. This means that at some point in the future, Miramar could be in trouble because of a dispute with Farallon. Thankfully, these companies have maintained their working relationship and there is no reason to expect trouble, but this is a point you might want to keep in mind. We never know what tomorrow will bring.

CoActive Connector for DOS/Windows

The CoActive Connector for DOS and Windows, by CoActive, is the only parallel port AppleTalk adapter available for a PC. This makes it ideal for small LocalTalk or PhoneNET networks into which you want to place a PC. It is also useful for people who use notebook PCs and intermittently need AppleTalk network support, such as members of a sales team who work outside of the office, but who are occasionally in the office and need to access the network. The idea behind the CoActive Connector is to provide an inexpensive peer-to-peer network for MS-DOS machines that is also Macintosh-compatible. Because the AppleTalk architecture is ideally suited for small networks with fairly simple plug-and-play capabilities, CoActive decided to take a chance and develop the CoActive Connector.

The CoActive Connector is a small PhoneNET-type connector that contains a 68000 CPU for controlling network activity. All of the drivers and AppleTalk software for the LocalTalk connection and network control are built into the connector. The only software needed on a PC using a CoActive Connector is the server and file redirection software, plus a small device driver that completes the connection between the connector and the PC. The total memory requirement for a PC using a CoActive Connector is 64K of memory that can all be loaded high; this includes SHARE.EXE. This is an acceptable amount of memory for providing network and file server access.

The CoActive Connector works by connecting the parallel port adapter to your PC and loading the software. If you use a parallel printer, it can be connected to the adapter, allowing you to share the printer and to use it directly from the PC. Once the software is installed, you can make the PC's hard drive and the printer connected to the connector available as shared resources.

Any Macintosh on the network sees the CoActive Connector as if it were another Macintosh, and the shared printer as another networked printer. Likewise, any PC can see shared Macintosh resources, such as laser printers and AFP file servers. However, because the AFP drivers and protocol stacks are not controlled by the PC, you cannot use ADSP from a PC with the CoActive Connector. CoActive's AFP implementation is currently incomplete.

The implications of these shortcomings are that you cannot use QuickMail, FileMaker Pro's networking capabilities, or Farallon's Timbuktu on a PC using the CoActive Connector. Otherwise, it works. The shortcomings with the AFP implementation result in an all-or-nothing approach to file sharing. Either everyone has access to the shared PC volume, or no-one has access. You do not have the ability to assign users or groups on a CoActive server.

The only security option you have is the creation of a drop box where anyone can place a document, but only the PC user can access the directory's contents. This shortcoming in the CoActive software is being worked on, and you should see improvements in the AFP implementation in future releases of the software.

An interesting feature of the CoActive Connector is that you can connect a parallel printer to the connector, make it available as a network resource, and then shut down the computer connected to the adapter. As long as you do not turn off the power to the adapter, the printer remains available as a shared network device.

For those situations where a few PCs need access to the Mac network, or even as a networking solution in an all-PC shop, the CoActive Connector could be the answer. If you can live with the slowness of LocalTalk and the lack of security, you have a solution that will provide you with file sharing and access to AppleTalk printers from a PC running either MS-DOS or Windows. Also, when printing MS-DOS text to a PostScript printer, the CoActive Connector automatically converts the text output into PostScript so it can be printed from the laser printer.

LANtastic for Macintosh Windows Gateway

In December 1993, Artisoft released a new LANtastic for Macintosh Windows Gateway. This product is identical in function to the LANtastic for Macintosh gateway described in Chapter 7. The major differences are that it runs in Windows and it is a non-dedicated gateway.

The LANtastic for Macintosh Windows Gateway is not intended to replace LANtastic for Macintosh, because there is a performance penalty for the Windows workstation. The gateway cannot handle as many shared volumes and users while maintaining acceptable Windows performance. However, if you want to maximize resources, you can install multiple gateways rather than using the dedicated gateway.

The other difference between the Macintosh for Windows Gateway and the LANtastic for Macintosh gateway package is that Artisoft has licensing for additional native ODI drivers, so you have a wider variety of Ethernet cards to choose from.

Using Your Mac as an MS-DOS Machine

Sounds strange, doesn't it? Using your Mac as an MS-DOS machine, that is. Well, strange as it may sound, it is possible. You can indeed, through either hardware or software emulation, use a Mac as an MS-DOS or even a Windows PC. Basically, there are three ways to use your Mac as a PC. One is to install a NuBus card that is a PC into the Mac. Another is to use emulation software from

Insignia Solutions, and the third way is to connect your Mac to a PC and control the PC from the Mac with Argosy's RunPC. All three of these products provide different capabilities, and you'll have to decide what you need before you settle on the solution. This section will look briefly at all three possibilities.

A Hardware Macintosh/MS-DOS Machine

If you're using a Mac that has a NuBus slot, you can add an MS-DOS co-processor card to the Mac. At the moment, there is only one company that makes such a card, Orange Micro. But Apple has announced and demonstrated in public an MS-DOS co-processor card that is supposed to be available in the first quarter of 1994.

OrangePC

Orange Micro's OrangePC is a PC on a full-size NuBus card that comes in three flavors, so to speak. OrangePC can be a 25 Mhz 486SLC, a 25 Mhz 386SX, or a 16 Mhz 386SX. The basic configurations for these cards are listed in Table 8.1.

Each of the OrangePC cards runs independently of the Macintosh except for the hard disk and monitor. OrangePC partitions part of a Macintosh hard disk as a DOS disk, and its display is a window on the Macintosh screen. You have some expansion capability with the extra ISA slot on the card. Whether the slot is capable of using a Bus Mastering card I don't know, but if it is, you could improve the card's performance by giving it its own dedicated SCSI hard drive. Other uses for the slot are data acquisition cards, an independent monitor card, or some other special purpose card.

The OrangePC card has been criticized as an incomplete system because it does not integrate well with the Mac OS: its copying and file sharing are inadequate.[1] Also, the OrangePC's price is high enough to tempt someone to purchase a PC instead of the card. However, if you need a dual system solution and do not want a second machine cluttering up your desk, an OrangePC could be just what the doctor ordered.

Houdini Card

Apple has announced an 040 Processor Direct PC co-processor card that may come close to being the perfect solution for those

---
[1] *MacWEEK*, 14 June 1993, 47.

Table 8.1 OrangePC configurations

CPU	Speed	Memory	Ports	Slots
cx486SLC	25 Mhz	2M expandable to 16M	1 Serial, 1 Parallel	1 ISA
80386SX	25 Mhz	2M expandable to 16M	1 Serial, 1 Parallel	1 ISA
80386SX	16 Mhz	2M expandable to 16M	None	None

who need a Mac and a PC. Right now, the card is code-named Houdini. It is rumored that it will be bundled and shipped first in a Quadra 610 within the first quarter of 1994, and then as an add-on product for other Macs shortly thereafter. However, the production numbers will be limited.

Although the Houdini Card is not a real product yet, it is important enough to write about. I just hope that this does become a real product. The card is supposed to be a 25 Mhz 486SX with overdrive capabilities, which means that you could have the speed of a 50 Mhz 486DX inside a Macintosh. The card will have one 72-pin SIMMs slot and use the same type of memory as all of the new Macintosh models. The 72-pin SIMMs can use up to a 32M memory module. The card can also use up to half of the Macintosh's system memory. So if you have 16M in your Mac, you could allocate 8M for the Houdini card and 8M for the Mac. Or you can install memory on the Houdini and leave the Mac's memory alone.

There are no serial or parallel slots on the Houdini. Instead, it uses the Mac's I/O, hard disk, monitor, and floppy disks. The Houdini does have a VGA and joystick port, in case you want to connect a VGA monitor to the card instead of using the Mac's monitor.

Although the Houdini card shares hardware resources with the Mac, it runs independently. When you are using the Mac's monitor for both the Houdini and the Mac, you will switch between the two platforms with a hot switch, working in one environment or the other. If you connect an external VGA monitor to the Houdini, you will still have to switch from one platform to the other, but you will see the PC's screen at all times. Either way, both machines will (in a virtual sense) continue to run concurrently.

The Houdini card will use the Mac's hard drive, but it does not partition the drive with an MS-DOS volume on top of the Mac volume. Rather, it uses the Mac's drive and file format as if it were an MS-DOS drive. This means that all of the MS-DOS files are available to the Mac and vice versa.

If you need to network the Houdini (now remember, this is what I've been told—I haven't experienced it yet), you can use the Mac's built-in Ethernet port for your PC NOS while using the Houdini for AppleTalk from the Mac. However, there are conflicting reports about the networking. It is also said that you can access any AppleShare volume mounted on the Mac's Desktop from the MS-DOS machine. And if all of this is not enough, the Houdini is supposed to be multi-media-compatible: it is capable of using the Macintosh's built-in stereo and CD-ROM.

So if it comes to pass, it will be a dream come true for many who need both a Mac and a PC. The Houdini card will go a long way toward making the Mac a more universal machine. It will sell for about $500.00.

Emulation Software

Another way to solve the Macintosh/MS-DOS problem (if you see it as such) is to use an MS-DOS emulator on the Mac. Insignia Solutions offers several MS-DOS software emulators that create virtual PCs on the Mac. You can choose any one of the following SoftPC packages:

- Universal SoftPC
- Professional SoftPC
- SoftPC with Windows

These three products are all similar, and each has more advanced features than the previous one. Table 8.2 shows the variable SoftPC features for each of the different versions. The following features are the same for all versions of SoftPC.

- **ROM BIOS** AT-compatible
- **MS-DOS** MS-DOS 5.0
- **Hard disk drives** C: and D: size is dependent on available Macintosh hard disk space. Minimum hard disk space depends on SoftPC versions (see Table 8.3).
- **Floppy disk drive** A: uses the Macintosh's SuperDrive as a high-density 3.5-inch drive.
- **Network drive** E: through Z: assignable to Macintosh folders and disk drives.

Table 8.2 SoftPC's variable features

Feature	Universal SoftPC	Professional SoftPC	SoftPC with Windows
Processors	80286 Real Mode, 80287	80286 Protected Mode, 80287	80286 Real and Protected Mode, 80287
RAM	256K to 640K	256K to 640K, Expanded up to 32K LIM	640K, Expanded up to 32K LIM, Extended to 15M
Video	Color Graphics Adapter (CGA) or Enhanced Graphics Adapter (EGA)	Color Graphics Adapter (CGA), Enhanced Graphics Adapter (EGA) or Video Graphics Adapter (VGA)	Color Graphics Adapter (CGA), Enhanced Graphics Adapter (EGA) or Video Graphics Adapter (VGA)
Display	16 Colors or grayscales or Monochrome depending on Macintosh's capabilities	16 Colors or grayscales or Monochrome depending on Macintosh's capabilities	At least 16 Colors or grayscales or Monochrome depending on Macintosh's capabilities Windows DeskTop: Black & White, 16 or 256 Resolution: colors minimum 400 × 200 maximum 1280 × 1024

Table 8.3 Variable Macintosh requirements

Macintosh Configuration	Universal SoftPC	Professional SoftPC	SoftPC with Windows
CPU	68000 or better	68020 or better	68040
System	6.0 or later	6.0 or later	6.0.5 or latter
RAM	4M minimum, 5M recommended	8M	8M minimum, 16M recommended
Hard Disk Space	2M minimum, 4M recommended	6M	16.5M minimum, 18M recommended

- **Parallel port** LPT1:, which is redirected to the Mac's printer. Emulates an Epson LQ-2500 or PostScript.
- **Serial ports** Com1 and Com2 using Macintosh Serial ports.
- **Keyboard** AT-style 101-key keyboard. Can be supported by any Macintosh keyboard.
- **Mouse** Microsoft bus mouse
- **CD-ROM access** Microsoft CD-ROM extension
- **Network access** Novell, using Insignia's SoftNode software.

SoftPC is an emulation package, so you are constrained by the Mac's hardware. You have to choose the SoftPC package that will work best with your Macintosh, as well as a version of SoftPC that will run your MS-DOS programs. The challenge here is to balance SoftPC's capabilities with the speed of the Macintosh. When you run SoftPC, there is a speed penalty, because you are not using a real AT-class computer.

In theory, you can run SoftPC on any Macintosh. However, if you install SoftPC with Windows on a Mac with a 68030 CPU, it will run so slowly that you won't want to use it. If you install Universal SoftPC on a Macintosh Quadra (all Quadras have a 68040 CPU), you will find that it runs at a fairly decent speed.

So, pick your version carefully. Table 8.3 shows Insignia's recommendations for the type of Mac and basic hardware requirements for the different versions of SoftPC.

Note

When running SoftPC with Windows on a Quadra 660 AV, which has a 25 Mhz 68040, I found it so slow that running the Windows portion of SoftPC with Windows was unacceptable. Five minutes to boot Windows just doesn't cut it. However, running the DOS portion of SoftPC with Windows was OK. If you're planning to use SoftPC with Windows, you really need a 33 Mhz 68040 Macintosh. Anything slower will drive you to distraction. Insignia has released an upgrade for SoftPC with Windows that is supposed to improve its speed. I haven't tried it yet, but anything would be an improvement.

RunPC

Argosy's RunPC is an interesting program that lets you operate a PC from a Macintosh. With RunPC, you can run PC applications on a real PC and control them from within a window on your Macintosh. In addition to operating the PC, you can also use RunPC to perform the following tasks:

- Mount MS-DOS disks on the Mac's Desktop.
- Print to Mac or MS-DOS printers from MS-DOS applications.
- Use MS-DOS windowing or multi-tasking programs like DESQview to run multiple applications.
- Use RunPC to connect to host PCs using pcANYWHERE.

RunPC is available as a network version or as a standalone package. In the standalone package, you connect to the PC with a serial cable or via modem. The network version has all of the features of the standalone package, and it also lets you control a PC that is networked using AppleTalk.

While connecting to a PC from a Mac and taking control of it may not seem too exciting, it is satisfying to use RunPC. The program really works, and it is easy to install and use. When using RunPC, the host computer can be running MS-DOS programs at full speed, and the only speed penalty is how fast the screen information is sent to the Mac. Unfortunately, RunPC does not work with Windows or programs that use graphics modes other than CGA, but this is the only real fault that RunPC has.

To make using RunPC from the Mac easier, the interface contains buttons (see Fig. 8.1) for keyboard commands.

It you are using a Mac that does not have a numeric keypad, like a PowerBook, you can access the PC's numeric keypad through a pull-down menu. So for MS-DOS access from a Mac, RunPC can definitely be an asset.

Timbuktu

Timbuktu for Windows is a product produced by Farallon that will let you control a Windows PC remotely from a Macintosh over an AppleTalk network, or a Macintosh from a Windows PC. With Timbuktu, you can have the following capabilities:

- Controlling a Windows PC from a Macintosh.

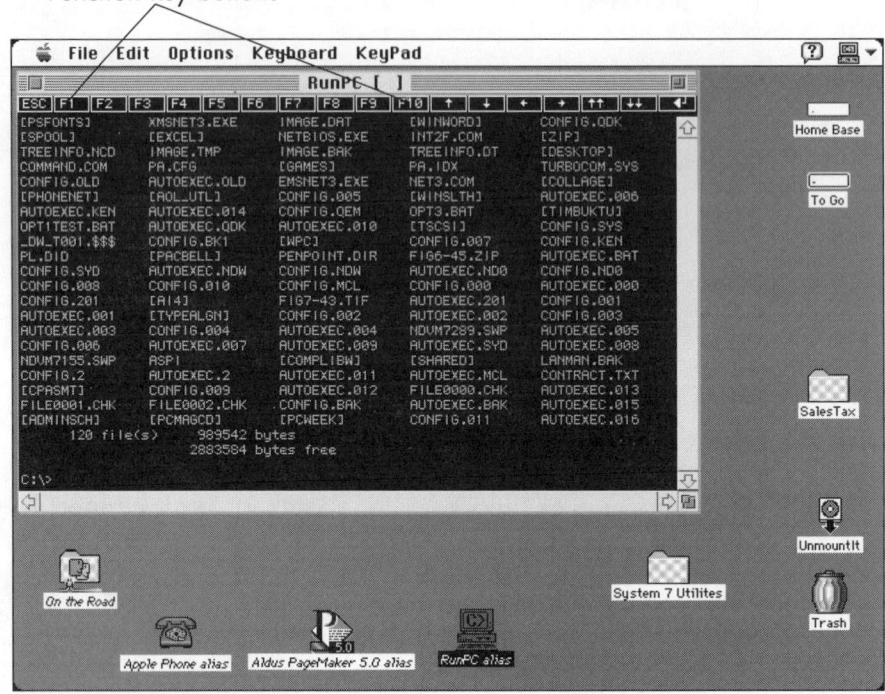

Figure 8.1 RunPC on the Mac

- Controlling a Mac from a Windows PC.
- Controlling a Windows PC from another Windows PC.
- Controlling a Macintosh from another Mac.
- Transferring files between machines connected with Timbuktu.

Timbuktu is sold as a single application, so you will have to purchase a copy for each machine you plan to control remotely, whether it is a Mac or a PC. And to use Timbuktu for Windows, the AppleTalk implementation for the MS-DOS machines must support ADSP. This means that you will have to use an AppleTalk implementation for the PC that uses Farallon's PhoneNET drivers, since that is the only one that I know of that supports ADSP. If you're not using Ethernet, you'll find that Timbuktu is rather slow. Sending screen images over the network involves passing a lot of information from one machine to another, especially if the images are in color.

Timbuktu was originally published by Farallon as a Macintosh remote control application to be used between two Macs on an AppleTalk network or two Macs connected by a modem. You can also control a Mac from a Windows PC with Timbuktu. However, you cannot access the Windows PC with a remote Macintosh unless you can log into the AppleTalk network using an AppleTalk remote connection program or an AppleTalk-compatible netmodem. (These utilities will be discussed in the Remote Connections section.) Unfortunately, you cannot use Timbuktu to run MS-DOS unless DOS is being run in a DOS Window. Otherwise, Timbuktu is a great utility for providing support, training, and even observing what is taking place on a networked machine.

Network Utilities

When dealing with a network of any size, whether it is on PCs or Macs, you'll probably want to use some of the network utilities that are designed to make your life easier. As the administrator, you'll want to use some of the utilities listed here for trouble-shooting and network administration. There are more network utilities available for the Mac than can be listed in this section, but this list of the most popular utilities will give you an idea of what is available.

I've found that utilities are rarely needed on a Macintosh network, especially if it is a LocalTalk or PhoneNET network. Usually, if you need a utility other than a network mapping utility, it is for trouble-shooting an Ethernet network, because the low-speed Macintosh networks are extremely stable and rarely have problems. Even small Ethernet networks are easy to maintain and trouble-shoot. So before you run up your budget with utility software, make sure you're going to need it.

This section discusses five types of utility software:

- Network mapping
- Traffic analyzers
- Packet analyzers
- Network management
- System and software management

> **Note**
>
> When performing networking management by scanning the network, you should install an Apple utility called Responder in the System Folder of each Mac on the network if you are using any System prior to System 7. With System 7, the Responder functions are built into the System. Responder reads the user's name from the Chooser (in System 7, this is the Macintosh name in the Sharing Setup control panel), the version of the Mac's System software, the LaserWriter driver, and the version of AppleTalk, and makes this information available to a network utility. Responder is removed.

Each section will discuss briefly how the utilities work, and then a few utilities of each type will be listed. You will find some additional discussion about using some of these utilities in Chapter 10.

Network Mapping

Network mapping utilities scan your AppleTalk network and then create a network map showing all of the AppleTalk devices found during the scan. You can use them to scan a specific branch of the network, or they can check an entire internet. They will come back with a map and list of the routers, AFP servers, individual workstations, AppleTalk printers, and any other AppleTalk device you've connected to the network.

They are used for determining the cable configuration of your network, as well as for finding nodes that are not responding. One other feature found on some of the AppleTalk network mapping software is the ability to map AppleTalk sockets.

By checking the sockets on a network, you tell which network services are running on the various workstations and servers. In a complicated network, this can help you determine why data may not be making it to its proper destination. Figure 8.2 shows a network map, which shows all of the AppleTalk devices and their sockets. The nicest network mapping software lists all of the network devices and also shows a graphic map of that information. Unfortunately, not all utilities do this.

The following is a list of AppleTalk utilities that are specifically designed for mapping an AppleTalk network.

Mac-centric Networks

> **Note**
>
> An AppleTalk socket is the network address for an AppleTalk service, usually provided by a server or workstation. An example is a file server that is running AppleShare and QuickMail. In order for network requests to be serviced properly, they have to know where they are going. All requests for file transfers contain the address for the file server's node and the socket that services AppleShare. However, all E-mail traffic is addressed to the file server's node and the QuickMail server socket. Every program that broadcasts or directly accesses AppleTalk has its own socket number. This includes applications like Quark Express, which has a network protection scheme whereby it checks intermittently with all of the Macs on a network to make sure no other copy of Quark with the same serial number is running, even though Quark's only other user for network access is printing.

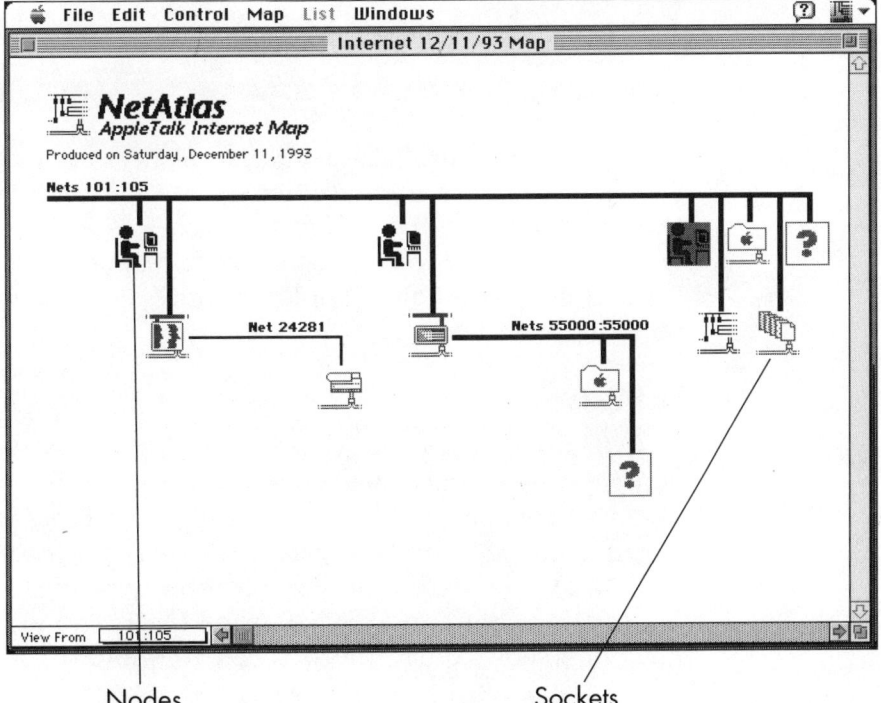

Figure 8.2 An AppleTalk network map

Inter•Poll

Inter•Poll is Apple's network management utility. It doesn't really map a network with a graphic representation of the network.

Figure 8.3

Inter•Poll's main window

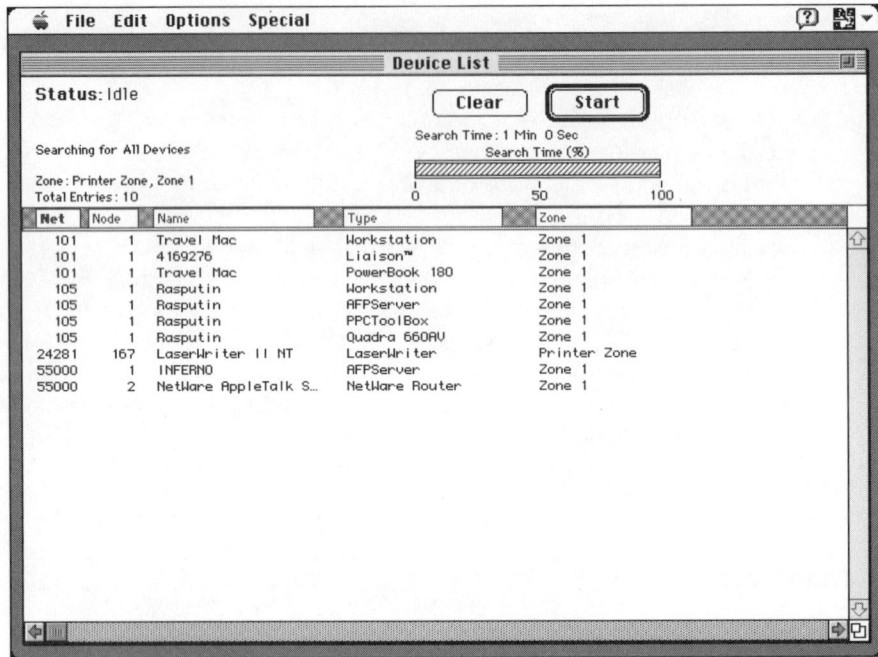

However, it does list each device on the network (see Fig. 8.3), and you can perform a limited interrogation of each network device. You can also filter the network searches to look for specific networked devices. If you want to make a real network map, you will have to do it manually. Apple provides symbols with Inter•Poll for doing so in a MacDraw format.

NetAtlas

NetAtlas is Farallon's network mapping utility. With NetAtlas, you get a list of each device on the network and a graphic map. The map contains symbols for the different types of devices that NetAtlas can identify. If a specific device is not listed, you can add it to NetAtlas's definition list. NetAtlas provides the same basic information about any device, using the Responder or System 7. Figure 8.4 shows the results of a NetAtlas internet scan.

LANsurveyor

LANsurveyor is another network mapping utility, published by Neon Software. Neon Software is a small software company that specializes in Macintosh network utilities. LANsurveyor is a little

Figure 8.4

A NetAtlas map and device list

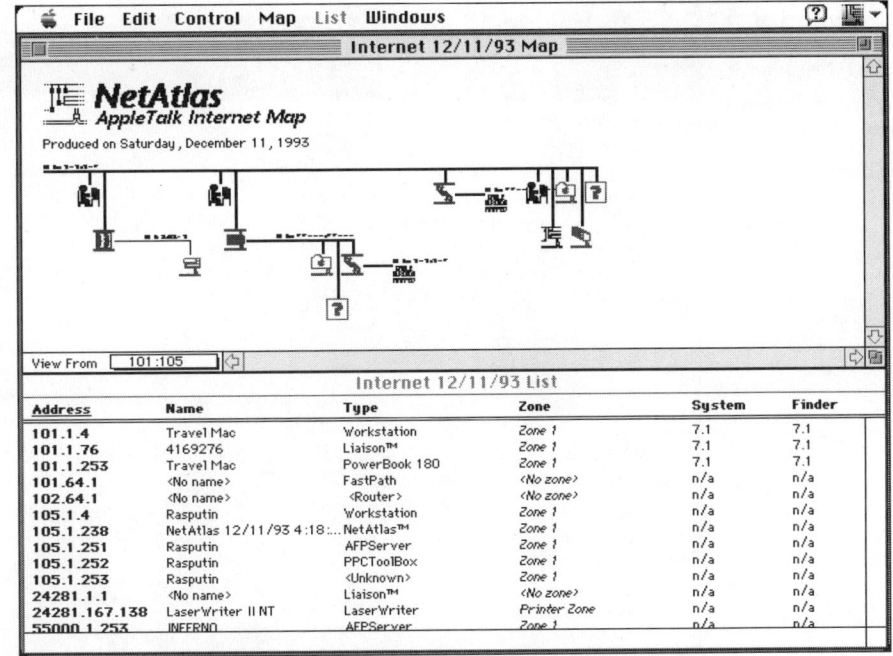

more powerful than the others because it can also map SNMP data if the AppleTalk network is using SNMP, but it is not as intuitive or easy to use as NetAtlas. It also allows you to poll various devices on the network and to monitor network traffic. Figure 8.5 shows a LANsurveyor map.

Network Supervisor LANscape

Network Supervisor LANscape is written by Management Science Associates. Like the other network utilities, it draws a map, and you can get Responder-type information from the other devices on the network. Network Supervisor LANscape also comes with its own Responder-type extension that can be used instead of System 7's or System 6.0.X's Responder.

Traffic Analyzers

Once you get a number of devices all using a network, there will be times when you need to analyze the traffic on the network. If you suspect that the network speed is too slow, or if you just monitor the network's traffic to maintain its efficiency, you will need a utility that allows you to see what is happening on the network.

Figure 8.5

A LANsurveyor map

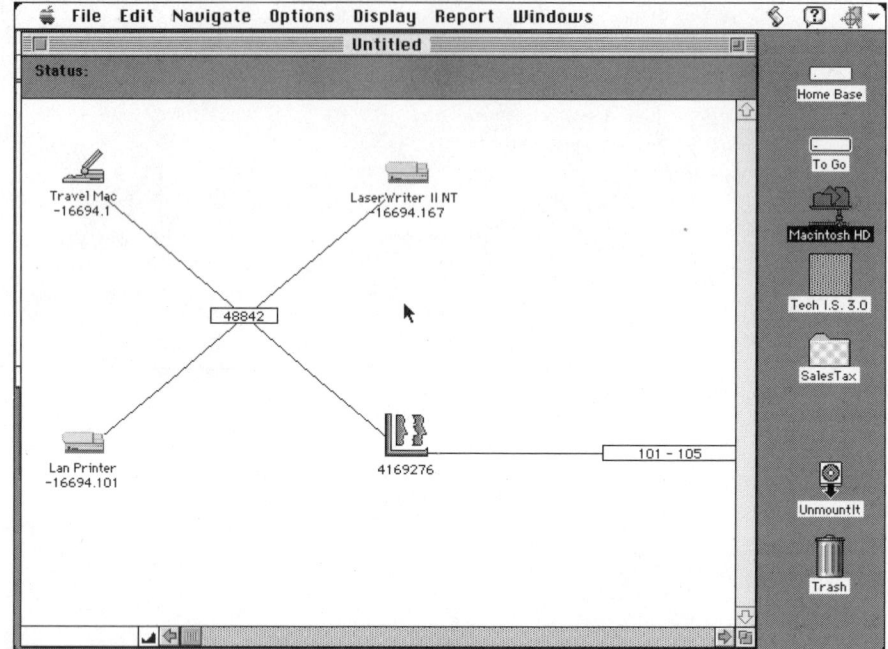

This information includes which nodes are communicating, how much traffic is passing between them, and which nodes are generating traffic. Traffic analyzers should let you monitor, in real time, bandwidth efficiency, data packets, error information, and general network efficiency. Once you've gathered all of this information, you can then analyze it and use it improve network efficiency.

There are several types of network traffic analyzers available. Some will work only on AppleTalk networks, while others will work on almost any type of network. Other traffic analyzers can check data in multiple zones, routers, and bridges. All of them have the ability to filter what type of network traffic you're watching. There are other analyzers that work in conjunction with hubs or gateways; usually, these are provided by the hardware's manufacture. Before you go out and buy a network traffic analyzer, you will need to do some research and decide what type of analyzer you want.

The traffic analyzers that work only on AppleTalk networks are less expensive than those that can analyze larger internets with multiple protocols. You will have to make the choice of what type you want to use. Traffic analyzers are needed only for larger net-

> **Note**
>
> An example of a network analyzer and management software that you can get with a 10BaseT hub is the AsantéView software, which you can use in conjunction with the AsantéHub 1012. The AsantéView software is a complete network management system for SNMP networks. The only task it does not perform is packet analysis. You can use it to create a network map, control the hub, or monitor traffic. You can have it page you if a predefined set of conditions occur, get slot information on the cards installed in your Macs, and even perform software management. The AsantéView software is one of the most complete management packages you can get, but you also need to be using the Asanté 1012 hub.
>
> AsantéView works using SNMP and TCP/IP, and it is also available as a Windows package. This is a high-end product and is not needed for a small network. If you have a larger network and use TCP/IP with LAN Manager, Novell, or some other NOS, then with an AsantéHub and their network management software you can have total control of the network and up to eight hubs. If you have a problem with the hub, you can connect to it via a serial cable and correct whatever is wrong.

works. If you're using a small network, you really don't need a traffic analyzer. If you want a utility for a small network, you should use a mapping utility that has some traffic analyzing capabilities, like LANsurveyor. Anything more powerful is probably a waste.

This section discusses several traffic analyzers, but it will not go into great detail on any of them. Some traffic analyzers that work on multi-protocol networks are also included in the list. The one common denominator that all of these packages share is their ability to work with AppleTalk networks.

TrafficWatch

Traffic Watch was Farallon Computing's network traffic analyzer, but it is now sold by Neon Software. It has all of the capabilities listed above, but it can only monitor one network at a time. You can use TrafficWatch on an Ethernet network or a LocalTalk network, but not both at the same time. Traffic Watch is a basic traffic analysis program and is not meant to monitor routers or gateways. Primarily, it is for use within a single AppleTalk zone. Analysis of network traffic is done with a spreadsheet application, and Traffic Watch comes with an Excel template for this purpose.

Net Watchman

Net Watchman is published by the AG Group, another company that specializes in Macintosh network utilities. Net Watchman can be used to monitor multiple zones, bridges, routers, and other network services. In addition to watching traffic patterns, it can be used to monitor selected network services and warn the network administrator when predefined conditions are met. Net Watchman can also page the network administrator when things go awry. Net Watchman has many network management features as well as traffic management.

TalkStat and TalkSpy

TalkStat and TalkSpy are a set of utilities published by Distributed Technologies. With these two utilities, you can gather statistics on protocol, network utilization, packet error and size, and bandwidth utilization. This utility has the same basic features as Traffic Watch, and analysis is performed in the same way using a spreadsheet.

RouterCheck

RouterCheck is another Neon Software package. RouterCheck is a full network and internet management utility, similar to Net Watchman. You can monitor multiple AppleTalk zones, check traffic flow, and set alarms for user-defined conditions. It, too, has the ability to page the network administrator with an alphanumeric pager, or it can send alerts to the administrator's Macintosh. It can monitor traffic across routers and bridges, displaying the network's routing table. This application is more than just a traffic analyzer.

Packet Analyzers

A packet analyzer lets you gather and look at the contents of the network packet. Packet analyzers are primarily trouble-shooting utilities. Because different types of physical links use different packets, you'll need a packet analyzer for each of the different network types.

An example of when you might need a packet analyzer is if you have a laser printer that works most of the time, but on some types of jobs, or when you are printing from a specific machine, the printer seems to malfunction. By analyzing the data packets received by the printer, you might be able to figure out what is wrong with the data that is received by the printer. Maybe you have a router that is not repackaging the packets as they are transferred from Ethernet to LocalTalk.

Packet analyzers let you specify what type of data you're going to look at by allowing you to select to the data's protocols, nodes, and type. In the example above, you could isolate PostScript printer data sent by the suspect computer to the router, and then from the router to the printer, and compare the contents. Analyzing the packets is a tedious process, but if you're a good detective, you will be able to see if the data is getting corrupted en route to its destination.

There are only a couple of packet analyzers for each AppleTalk protocol on the market—literally, two each for Ethernet and LocalTalk. Two of the packages, NetMinder LocalTalk and NetMinder Ethernet, are published by Neon Software. The other two, EtherPeek and LocalPeek, are manufactured by the AG Group. The AG Group also produces a package called TokenPeek for capturing packet data from a Token Ring network.

Whenever you're collecting packets and trying to isolate a problem, you'll be dealing with massive amounts of data, so in addition to collecting packet data for analysis, all of these packages include analysis tools to help you narrow your search. They also have automated data collection features. Although packet analyzers are not full-fledged network management packages, you can also use them to collect other network statistics, like bandwidth for the packet capture session. Figure 8.6 shows the results of a packet collection session from NetMinder LocalTalk.

Network Management

All of the utilities discussed in this section are network management utilities of one type or another. But there are some packages

> **Note**
>
> The AG Group has a package called NetPatrol Pack, which includes Net Watchman, EtherPeek, and LocalPeek. This collection of utilities will provide you with a complete network management system for your AppleTalk network.

Figure 8.6

NetMinder after a packet collection session

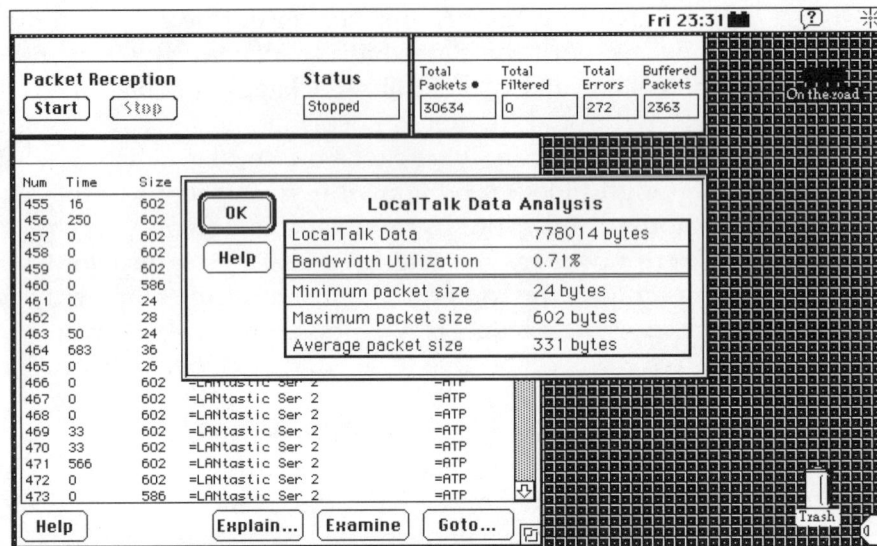

that combine network mapping and traffic management, or that are of a more general nature, performing a task that does not fit in the other categories. Packages that can be included in this category, discussed in the Traffic Analyzers section, are Net Watchman and Router Check. This section will look briefly at two more general-purpose network management utilities that were not discussed in the Traffic Analysis section.

Network Vital Signs

Network Vital Signs, published by Dayna Communications, is a network monitoring and warning system. With it you can monitor network devices such as printers and file servers. You can also have Network Vital Signs monitor the network's performance and notify the network administrator or manager when network performance slows down or a fault occurs.

NetWORKS and NetWORKS, Jr.

NetWORKS is published by Caravelle Networks. Caravelle calls Net-WORKS a network monitoring/warning system. NetWORKS monitors all of an AppleTalk network's devices and warns the network administrator when problems occur. You can also test any device on the network with NetWORKS. NetWORKS monitors free disk space on servers, routers, bridges, and printers. Notification can take place via QuickMail, Microsoft Mail, or a pager. NetWORKS, Jr. is a version of NetWORKS that can monitor 20 network devices.

System and Software Management

In general, system and software management packages allow you to control the Macintoshes on a network by configuring their Systems, performing software updates and installations, and monitoring usage of installed software to control software licenses.

The packages described in this section perform some or all of the tasks listed above. Depending your needs and the complexity of your network, you'll find life a lot easier if you can standardize the Macs on your network without having to run from Mac to Mac making sure they are configured properly or upgrading the software on each machine. You'll want to use one of these utilities to keep control of your Macs. This section will look briefly at several packages that all fall into the category of software or system management.

GraceLAN and GraceLAN Network Manager

GraceLAN Network Manager, by Technology Works, is one of the most complete network software management systems available. It can be used on Macs, PCs, and Macs using A/UX (Apple's version of UNIX) over the network. GraceLAN lets you generate an inventory of network software, hardware, and System configurations. You can also synchronize the clocks on the networked machines and have routine status reports collected at specific intervals. Updates are performed by distributing the upgrade files to the users' machines. GraceLAN collects and analyzes information selected from your Mac; it does not have the management capabilities of GraceLAN Network Manager.

KeyServer

KeyServer is a software license control system published by Sassafras Software. KeyServer is installed onto local or client Macs within the computing environment so you have control over both individual Macs and networked machines. With the remote administrator you can monitor application usage, gather information for reports, and install programs remotely.

Likewise

Likewise is an Apple program that is used to standardize the system settings of Macs on your network. With it you can synchronize the time and system environment settings and control the names of the Macs on your network.

NetDistributor Pro

NetDistributor Pro, published by Trik, is a network software distribution program. It enables you to install software, including system software and applications in use, from a central Macintosh. With NetDistributor, you can perform most system maintenance over the network.

Quota

Quota is a server-based software license controller published by Proteus Technology. It controls the number of an application's concurrent launches, allowing only the licensed number of simultaneous application runs. Quota also audits the application's activity, queues users for software when it is unavailable, and prevents the copying of software from the server. It also has a checkout feature that lets an authorized user take software from the server for use off-site for a limited amount of time.

Skyline

Skyline, published by the AG Group, is a network utility for the purpose of monitoring multi-protocol networks. It derives its name from the chart it produces to show network activity by network or node, which can look like a city skyline. By selecting one of the bars in the chart, you can see the network activity represented by the bar.

Status*Mac

Status*Mac, published by ON Technology, is a management tool that lets you get the configuration information from the Macs on your network. Status*Mac is not a real-time program, and its primary purpose is to provide a complete inventory of the software and system configuration of your client Macintoshes. However, you can also use it to install software onto client Macs by transferring files and folders using ADSP.

Version Territory

Version Territory is published by SoftWriters. It is a utility that enables you to install software on client machines. When you install the software on one machine, the rest of the machines on the network are upgraded. The upgrade operation takes place in the background, and Version Territory provides you with a report of its activities.

Security

It is often the case that one of a network administrator's major concerns is network and data security. Security precautions range from letting only registered users on the network to encrypting sensitive company trade secrets. Security techniques can include, but are not restricted to, limiting access to network resources, controlling remote access, and auditing user access.

Another use of security software is to keep track of hardware. There are a couple of security programs that will check the network's hardware configurations periodically to make sure none of your hardware has gone on a stroll. So there are different types of security software, and all of the security software packages have different capabilities.

Of course, what type of security precautions you'll take and the type of software you need will depend on your network requirements; which you undoubtedly know better than I do. So rather than boring you with all of the possibilities, this section will look at some of the security software you can use on an AppleTalk network.

File Guard

File Guard is a security application produced by ASD Software. It is one of the most comprehensive security programs available, providing network and individual machine security. You can use it to create encrypted directories, set access rights to volumes for specified users and groups, and even specify which printers will be visible from specific machines. FileGuard's advanced features include an auditing log, copy protecting software and files, and locking of system folders, to name a few. In order for this utility to be effective, it must be installed on every Macintosh on the network.

Security Force

Published by Globus Software, Security Force is a network hardware security system. Once Security Force is installed, the Macs on the network will be forced to check in with another Mac at predefined intervals. The software will notify the administrator if a Mac is disconnected from the network, and it will also monitor all SCSI devices connected to the network's Macs.

Nok Nok A/S

Nok Nok A/S is also another utility published by Trik. It works with AppleShare 4.0 servers. It records and logs all user activity, and can be configured to disconnect users if they are idle or have been logged in too long. Nok Nok is also available for individual Macs using System 7 file sharing.

Silver Cloud

Silver Cloud, published by the AG Group, is a utility for making the user's interaction with a large AppleTalk network easier. It allows the network administrator to control which zones, servers, and other network resources a user can access. The administrator also has the ability to order the internet's zones.

netSecure

netSecure, a utility for limiting access to AFP servers, and goes beyond the standard AppleShare access privileges. netSecure is published by usrEZ Software. It gives a user or the network administrator the ability to encrypt and password-protect folders on the server.

Remote Connections

One of the capabilities that is becoming increasingly important is the ability to log into a network from a remote location. It is probable that in the near future, most business networks will have to provide remote access capabilities to their networks. At the simplest level, the remote access capabilities will consist of the ability to log in and check and send E-mail. However, more complex connections are likely to be the order of the day.

As a matter of fact, most NOSs already address this issue in one way or another, but you may need to find your own solution to provide Macintosh access. An example is VINES: with VINES, you can set up a server to provide remote access for PCs, but Macs cannot use this service. To provide Macintosh access, you will have to use one of the solutions listed in this section.

Before launching into the list of products, I would like to point out that a couple of the products already discussed in this chapter can also be used for remote access to AppleTalk networks.

One of them is Timbuktu, by Farallon. With Timbuktu and a modem, you can call another Macintosh computer and operate the computer remotely. If you use Timbuktu to dial into an AppleTalk network, you can take control of any machine on the network that has Timbuktu installed.

Also mentioned was RunPC, by Argosy Software. RunPC can be used to connect remotely to a PC from a Mac by dialing in with a modem and connecting to the PC. Like Timbuktu, you can use RunPC over a remote network if you log into an AppleShare network and connect using the network version of RunPC.

The products discussed in this section are both software and hardware products. Usually, you will need some type of hardware to connect remotely to an AppleTalk network. You will have to use a network modem and a remote access server of some type, in addition to the remote software.

The products listed in this section will be discussed as complete remote access solutions. This way, you do not have to try to put together some type of jigsaw puzzle for your solution. It is important to remember is that modem connections can be slow, so the faster the modem, the more efficient your remote connection.

Apple Remote Access

Apple has tried very hard to make remote connections to an AppleTalk network as easy and efficient as possible. The first product they released, in conjunction with the first PowerBook Macs, was AppleTalk Remote Access (ARA). They have now upgraded ARA so that it is a family of products designed to meet different needs, depending on the number of users who will be accessing the network remotely.

The new family of ARA products consists of Apple Remote Access Client, Apple Remote Access Personal Server, and Apple Remote Access MultiPort Server. With these products, Apple has created a remote access system that is hard to beat. The only major flaw that it has is the lack of an MS-DOS or Windows client software.

Apple Remote Access Client

The Apple Remote Access Client software is the Macintosh software needed by any remote Mac that will be logging into an ARA personal or multiport server, or any Mac acting as a server with Apple's older version of ARA, Apple Remote Access 1.0. ARA Client has been optimized with intelligent phone dialing technology to make remote connections as easy as possible, so connecting is easy even if you are trying to connect from a foreign country. The new dialing technology is called DialAssist.

With ARA Client, you can dial into any ARA-compatible server. The types of connections supported by ARA Client are standard telephone, X.25, ISDN, and Cellular. (The x.25 and ISDN connections require additional software.) The client software requires a modem and a Macintosh running System 7.

When a remote user logs into an ARA Server, the user becomes just another computer on the network. All network operations are the same as if the Mac were connected locally to the server, except that the remote user will have access only to the network resources allowed by the ARA server software.

Apple Remote Access Personal Server

ARA Personal Server is designed for individual and small workgroup connections using a single modem and a Mac with ARA Personal Server installed. ARA Personal Server supports standard telephone, ISDN, and cellular connections. However, for the X.25 and ISDN connections, you'll need additional software.

The Macintosh that will act as a server requires a Mac running System 7 and a modem. ARA Personal Server will work with the network physical link used by the server Mac, whether it is LocalTalk, Ethernet, or Token Ring. The security features in ARA Personal Server include the standard AppleShare passwords, dial back security, selectable connect time, activity logs (for up to 100 users), and automatic account disabling.

Apple Remote Access MultiPort Server

The ARA MultiPort Server is Apple's solution for multiple remote connections. It is sold as a 4-port server that uses the Apple Remote Access Serial card, and you can purchase additional 4-port expansion kits for a maximum of 16 ports per server. The Apple Remote Access Serial card is a NuBus card and requires a Mac with one or more NuBus slots. You will need a modem for each of the ports on the ARA MultiPort Server card(s).

The ARA MultiPort Server is basically the same as the ARA Personal Server, except that it also supports X.25 (with additional software). Another difference is that the MultiPort Server can support up to 8,192 users. A feature is its ability to monitor the MultiPort Server using SNMP from a SNMP network administration station.

Shiva Products

Shiva has been making Macintosh remote access products for quite a while. The company has expanded its product line to include remote access products for Novell's NetWare using MS-DOS, Windows, or Windows for Workgroups. Since we're talking about remote AppleTalk connections, this section will look at Shiva's products that connect Macs to your AppleTalk network.

LanRover/E 2.0 and LanRover/L for AppleTalk Remote Access

The LanRover is a dial-in AppleTalk Remote Access server using ARA 1.0. It is an alternative to using a dedicated Macintosh for remote access. The LanRover/E is a 4- or 8-port Ethernet-based router. The LanRover/L is a single port LocalTalk-compatible server. Both of the LanRovers require modems running at 2400 bps or greater.

The LanRover/E can also be used as an AppleTalk to TCP/IP dial-in gateway. Other features found on the LanRovers include password and dial-back security, zone and device filtering, and activity logging. Operationally, the LanRover enables the dial-in user to access the AppleTalk network as if it were locally connected to the network. At the same time, it allows locally connected users to access the modems as shared network resources.

NetModem/E

The NetModem/E is a high-speed network modem that supports both dial-out and dial-in access on an Ethernet network. It supports both AppleTalk and Novell networks, as well as MS-DOS, Windows, and Macintosh clients. All of the software you need for a remote connection is included, as well as the software needed for machines on the network to dial out.

When dialing into a NetModem with a Macintosh, you use the NetModem dial-in software, which is a Chooser device driver, and log into the AppleTalk network as a client on the network. Security is determined by user name, password, and dial-back. Once you have logged in through the NetModem, you will still have to log into any additional network resources you might want to use.

The NetModem is an excellent alternative to ARA. By using multiple NetModems, you can expand your network's ability to service remote users. There is a separate NetModem/E for Windows for Workgroups.

Liaison

If you are using Farallon's Liaison as an Ethernet- or Token Ring-to-LocalTalk router, you also have the ability to use it as a telebridge. Liaison can support one modem connected to the Macintosh it is running on, and provide dial-in AppleTalk network access. Access is controlled by user name, password, and dial-back, if you wish, and it is similar to the Shiva NetModem when providing remote dial-in access.

The remote user installs a non-routing version of Liaison, Personal Liaison, included in every Liaison package. The Personal version is a Chooser device driver that dials the modem and negotiates the connection with the Liaison router, then maintains the network connection. The user dials into the Liaison router, logs into the network, and then accesses the network resources needed. Unfortunately, Farallon has discontinued Liaison. However, it is still an alternative if it will run on your Mac.

GatorLink

The GatorLink is a three-port remote access router manufactured by Cayman Systems. It allows up to three users to dial into an AppleTalk Ethernet network using ARA. To use the GatorLink, you will have to add up to three modems for remote access. The GatorLink has the standard security capabilities, including user name and password verification with dial-back capabilities, shielding to limit access to network resources, and time limits for logged in users. Functionally, it is similar to Shiva's LanRover.

Conclusion

By the time you finish this chapter, you will have a good idea of the alternative networking capabilities if you do not want to use one of the other NOSs discussed in this book. You will also know which tools you can use to manage an AppleTalk network, and all of these tools will work as long as you're using an AFP-compliant system. You will also know what you need to provide remote Macintosh users with remote access to your network.

Although this chapter is an overview and not a detailed step-by-step tutorial regarding these products, none of them is very complicated, except for some of the more sophisticated network management tools and the packet analyzers. But I figure that if you're even thinking about using one of these utilities, you already know what you're doing, or you're willing to invest the time necessary to learn how to use them. They are really too complicated to describe without devoting a chapter to each software package.

So with this road map in hand, you should be ready to go forth and take control of your network, add AppleTalk PC users, and provide access to your remote Macintosh users. And if nothing else, you know what is possible and where to get the tools if you need them.

Cross-Platform Applications

Introduction

The emphasis of this chapter is on programs that share file formats between Macintosh, MS-DOS, and Windows machines. In some cases, the file formats are not seamlessly compatible, and require some type of translation. But these packages are compatible to the point where Macintosh and MS-DOS or Windows applications can access the data files created by the same application on either platform.

The purpose of looking at these applications is to familiarize you with the programs that work in a cross-platform environment. We will discuss these programs only in a general sense, because any real in-depth analysis would require a book of its own. But you will need to know what programs you can use in both environments. We'll look at software in these categories:

- E-mail
- Word processing
- Spreadsheets
- Desktop publishing and desktop presentation

- Graphics
- Databases
- Workgroup packages
- Integrated packages

As you can see, this is quite a list, and there are many packages in each category. Unfortunately, due to the number of available cross-platform packages, some will be missed in this chapter. However, every attempt has been made to make sure the major applications are discussed. Because there are so many applications that work in cross-platform environments, I want to reiterate that this chapter is an overview. You will find only a synopsis of each package.

Cross-Platform Software

The purpose of cross-platform software is to provide you with the tools needed for the exchange of data from one computing platform to another. The most numerous cross-platform programs are those that operate between the Microsoft Windows environment and the Mac, but there are several that span MS-DOS, Windows, and the Mac.

The trend in the computing industry is to reconcile file formats and the applications' version numbers. Each major software vendor is releasing Macintosh, Windows, and DOS versions of its products. In general, it is safe to assume that if the version numbers for a particular program are the same for the Mac and Windows versions, then the files generated by the program, regardless of the platform, will be seamlessly interchangeable.

If an application's file format is not the same, each program (regardless of platform) can usually read files created by its sister program from another platform. Programs like word processing applications can usually read documents created by competing companies' programs. For instance, a WordPerfect document created on a Macintosh can be read on a PC by Microsoft Word. So you do not have to have the same programs running on each platform, but life is easier if you do.

When you're looking for cross-platform applications, one of the features you'll want to check out is what types of documents the application can read. This is a good idea even if you're using the same applications throughout your organization. Chances are that you will have to deal with data created outside of your organization that uses different file formats. This data could come from clients, vendors, or even employees working at home. So you need to be prepared to deal with all kinds of data. You'll find some suggestions regarding data conversions in Chapter 2.

E-mail

When adding Macintoshes to an existing network, you may be adding the Mac users to your existing E-mail system, or you may be planning to install a cross-platform E-mail system. Whatever you're doing, one of your concerns will be making sure that the MS-DOS, Windows, and Macintosh computers can all use the same mail system, preferably without needing a gateway.

Gateways, while allowing you to connect different types of mail systems, have a tendency to add expense and complications to the administration of your network. Large companies often have a person just for E-mail support, but that is only when there are hundreds to thousands of users. If you're a small company, you will end up wearing the mail administrator's hat in addition to the network administrator's. Anything you can do to simplify your support problems could end up as a quality-of-life proposition.

Since our goal here is to connect Macintoshes and PCs on the same network, you'll have to choose how everyone is going to get their mail. One choice is to use an E-mail system that supports the different platforms (Macintosh, MS-DOS, and Windows); however, you might also have a few UNIX workstations to worry about. Your other choice is to use a gateway. As I said above, you should try to avoid using a gateway, but do not dismiss using one if it will solve your particular problem. With the right options, the E-mail packages in this section can connect to other E-mail systems with gateways using one of the following protocols:

- X.500
- Simple Mail Transfer Protocol (SMTP)
- Novell's Message Handling Service (MHS)

The above list is only a sampling of the most common transfer protocols. There are over a dozen to choose from, and the E-mail packages discussed here can support almost all of them. Although

E-mail gateways will not be discussed, I wanted to make sure you were aware of the possibilities they offer. The biggest disadvantage you'll encounter with gateways has to do with file transfers. When you attach a file to a mail message and send it over the gateway from a Macintosh to another mail system and platform (or vice-versa), it is possible that some files will not make the transfer.

Some E-mail gateways translate the file when it goes across the gateway, and may not deal well with Macintosh-specific information, like the separate resource and data forks. Also, the file packet might need to be translated from 8-bit to 7-bit data. Either of these restrictions can result in the need to perform extra steps to access the file once it reaches its destination. And as we all know, anything that results in extra steps is synonymous with problems. So think twice about the gateway and check out all of the details regarding its installation, administration, and use before you buy one. Get the one that will get the mail to its destination with as few extra steps as possible.

With these preliminaries out of the way, we'll look at some different E-mail packages that work on both Macintosh and PC platforms. These packages represent the most popular, full-featured E-mail packages available that also provide seamless cross-platform support. The packages are:

- **QuickMail**—CE Software
- **cc:Mail**—Lotus
- **DaVinci eMail**—DaVinci Systems
- **Microsoft Mail**—Microsoft

E-mail systems require either a dedicated computer to act as a server or hard disk space on a shared volume from which everyone can access the E-mail files. What you'll need depends on the com-

> **Note**
>
> Although it is not listed here, you should look at Banyan VINES Intelligent Messaging if you have a VINES network. Intelligent Messaging meets all of the criteria specified above for a business E-mail system, and it also takes advantage of Banyan's StreetTalk Directory Services. For a VINES network, it will work more seamlessly than any other package because it integrates with the NOS.

plexity of the system you're setting up. Since this section is not about installing or using these E-mail packages, you won't find any instructions. The purpose of this section is to provide you with the basic information you'll need to start the decision-making process.

All of the E-mail packages discussed in this section are full-featured packages intended for use in business. These packages all offer a basic set of features that represent what could considered the essential capabilities of E-mail. These capabilities are:

- The ability to send and receive messages.
- Transferring files from one user to another by attaching them to E-mail messages.
- Sending files and mail to multiple recipients.
- Launching the program for an attached file from within the E-mail application.
- Notification of a message's status (whether it was delivered or read by the recipient).
- Gateway support for communicating with other E-mail systems (from different manufacturers) in local and wide area networks, as well as with commercial E-mail services such as AT&T EasyLink or MCI Mail.
- Remote access for users who telecommute, vendor or customer communications, and any mobile work force that needs to stay in contact with the office.
- Cross-platform support.

Depending on your needs, you may think of a couple of extra items to add to this list. On the other hand, you might not need all of these capabilities. In any case, all of the E-mail packages discussed in this section have the features in the list. Some have additional features that you can purchase to add functionality to your mail system, such as the ability to use the E-mail system as a fax server. The features in the list above may not all be part of the E-mail package as it comes out of the box, but these features and more are available either from the publisher or from a third-party vendor.

QuickMail

QuickMail started life as (and really is) a Macintosh E-mail system with MS-DOS and Windows support, as long as the PCs are networked with the Macs using AppleTalk. If you're using another network protocol for the PCs, you will have to use a gateway to use the QuickMail system. Because QuickMail uses the AppleTalk protocol, the networks discussed in this book will not all allow for PC access to QuickMail. None of them uses the AppleTalk protocol for PC communications. If your network provides AppleTalk support to your PCs—Farallon's PhoneNET Talk does this—you can use QuickMail from your MS-DOS and Windows machines. The MS-DOS and Windows software is included with the basic QuickMail package.

QuickMail requires its own Macintosh as the mail server. You can use a Macintosh workstation as the mail server, but you're better off using a dedicated Mac or a Mac that is also an AppleShare file server. QuickMail is one way to capitalize on a dedicated AppleShare file server, using the same machine to provide more than one network service. Of course, you'll have to watch the amount of network traffic for both the file and mail servers. If there is too much traffic on the same Mac, you may have to perform some resource management, like sharing the network resources between a couple of Macs.

If you need to access other mail systems, gateway support for QuickMail is available from CE Software or other third-party sources. QuickMail can communicate with all of the major E-mail systems. This includes every mail system described in this section, plus others like PROFS, VMSmail, the Internet, UNIX Mail, USENET, and more. So if you do decide to service your Macs with QuickMail and need to communicate with an installed PC mail system, you have plenty of support.

For each of the gateway options, there are usually two or more vendors proving similar tools. If you have a question regarding the E-mail system you want to communicate with, check with CE Software; they can provide you with a list of the supported systems and the vendors that provide the support.

In addition to gateways, QuickMail supports remote access from any computer with a terminal emulator and a modem. QuickMail links to MCI, AT&T Easy Link, AppleLink, and other commercial on-line systems. CE Software also provides support for System 7 Pro with its AEOC system-level messaging features. For a full Macintosh-compliant mail system that will integrate with any existing mail system, you should seriously consider QuickMail.

The primary advantage QuickMail offers is that it has always been a Macintosh E-mail system. This means that QuickMail can capitalize on all of the interface features that make a Mac unique. Other E-mail systems do not have all the features that are Macintosh-specific, nor are the ones they do have implemented as elegantly as QuickMail's. QuickMail is one package that could justify getting a gateway.

When you purchase QuickMail, you receive all of the software you need to set up the mail server, the mailboxes (for 5, 10, 50, or 100 users), a telebridge, a remote dial-in, and the MS-DOS and Windows access software. Also, there are several gateways provided with a package primarily for commercial E-mail services like MCI Mail, AppleLink, GEnie and CompuServe.

cc:Mail

cc:Mail by Lotus is one of the top rated[1] E-mail packages available. It supports Macintosh, Windows, DOS, UNIX, and OS/2. cc:Mail will operate on any network physical link, and on all of the NOSs discussed in this book. As long as the drive containing the cc:Mail files can be mounted as a local drive, and your NOS supports file and record locking, you can access cc:Mail.

cc:Mail is a full-featured E-mail system. You can get gateway support for commercial E-mail services and other LAN-based E-mail systems from Lotus Development or through third-party sources. It supports dial-in access from MS-DOS, Windows, and Macintosh users. It also has a host of other features, such as fax gateway support and a bulletin board or public access service. (Other E-mail systems have some or all of these features, as well.)

cc:Mail is first and foremost an MS-DOS package. It is administered from an MS-DOS workstation, and its files reside on an MS-DOS networked server. When using a Macintosh, you need the cc:Mail for Macintosh package (an option) and Macintosh network access to the drive that contains the cc:Mail data files. Any network operating system that provides AppleTalk access to the volume or directory containing the cc:Mail files will work. You can use any of the AppleTalk physical link protocols (LocalTalk, EtherTalk, or TokenTalk).

Just because cc:Mail can access the post office from a Mac does not mean that it also acts as an AppleTalk to Other(NET) Network router. It does not. cc:Mail uses the AppleTalk Filing Protocol for

---

[1] *Info World*, 18 October 1993.

Macintosh communications, but the shared volume with the post office functions as a gateway. When a file is sent to a Windows or MS-DOS user, there is no conversion; the post office holds the mail and file until the intended recipient accesses the file. When the file is opened, the recipient has to use a program that can read the file's format, or has to use a utility to translate the file into a format that can be accessed. cc:Mail also integrates seamlessly with Lotus Notes (see the Groupware section) and provides you with a single E-mail solution for almost all of the platforms you might be using.

cc:Mail is sold in modular chunks. When you purchase it, you get the software necessary to set up the mail server and software for MS-DOS and Windows in a group pack, or you can purchase the software for an individual platform. For each additional platform, and for any gateways, you'll have to buy the software modules you need. This can make cc:Mail a bit more expensive than other mail systems. When you purchase the Macintosh Platform Pack, you will have the user E-mail and administration software, plus the ability to access your existing mail server without using a gateway. Other packages or modules you can add include the Lotus Organizer. The Lotus cc:Mail Router is used to connect multiple post offices.

DaVinci eMail

DaVinci eMail, published by DaVinci Systems, is another of the leading E-mail systems available that provides cross-platform support for MS-DOS, Windows, Macintosh, and UNIX. DaVinci eMail supports all of the network operating systems we've discussed in this book, and works by keeping all post office files on a shared network volume.

When you purchase DaVinci eMail, you will have to purchase the DaVinci eMail package, which runs with MS-DOS, and then add the packages you need for additional platform support. Any gateways you need will have to be purchased from DaVinci or third-party vendors.

The Macintosh E-mail software is called DaVinci MacAccess. It is optimized from Novell's MHS messaging system. It should work with any network, as long as the server volume with the post office files can be mounted by the Mac. However, if you're using the DaVinci CaLANdar or Coordinator software, you will have to wait for the Macintosh versions. Another feature that DaVinci eMail is missing is Macintosh remote access software.

Other than the above limitations, DaVinci eMail will provide your Macs with basic E-mail support over the network. If you need remote access, you can use a Shiva NetModem, log into the Macintosh network, and still access the network and the mail server. So even the lack of a Macintosh remote access program is only a minor inconvenience.

Microsoft Mail

Microsoft Mail comes in two flavors. One is a Macintosh version, Microsoft Mail for AppleTalk and Compatible Networks, which requires a Macintosh mail server similar to QuickMail's. The other is an MS-DOS and Windows version called Microsoft Mail for PC-Compatible Networks, where the mail files reside on a PC server. The Macintosh version of Microsoft Mail is really intended for Macintosh networks. It uses ADSP for client/server communications, so you do not need to mount the drive containing the post office.

However, the MS-DOS/Windows software cannot access a Macintosh Microsoft Mail server. And herein lies the rub. If you are using the Macintosh version of Microsoft Mail, you can also use the Macintosh version of Scheduler, which is an individual and workgroup scheduling tool like the Scheduler that ships with Microsoft Windows for WorkGroups. If you are using the MS-DOS/Windows version of Microsoft Mail, you can have Macintosh access and E-mail capabilities, but the Macintosh version of Scheduler will not work with the MS-DOS version of Microsoft Mail. The situation is also true in reverse, if you have AppleTalk running on a PC and try to access the Macintosh version's post office from a PC.

All of this leads to the quagmire. If you want to use the Macintosh and Windows Schedulers, you will have to have two post offices, one on a Macintosh and the other on the network file server. The two versions of the Scheduler program are incompatible, so they can only be used on their respective networks. Microsoft does not have any current plans to remedy this situation.

If you just want to have E-mail access and send mail and files between your users, and you can live without the Macintosh version of Scheduler, you can use the Microsoft Mail version that operates from a networked file server for the post office files, then mount that volume on all of the machines (including the Macs) that will be using Microsoft Mail. This is the standard configuration for all of the PC-based E-mail packages. The PC version of Microsoft mail is full-featured from the MS-DOS and Windows users' point of view, but its Macintosh implementation is weak.

The standard PC network version of Microsoft Mail is not as elegant or full-featured from the Macintosh, but you have all of the basic features you need—that is, the ability to send and receive mail and files. Microsoft Mail for PC Networks comes with the Macintosh E-mail software. However, to have it all—the clean Macintosh interface with features like conferencing, mail forwarding, and the ability to create forms—you'll need to use both versions of Microsoft Mail.

If you use both versions of Microsoft Mail, you will need a product called the Microsoft Mail Connection to link the AppleTalk post office to the PC post office. The Microsoft Mail Connection is a couple of gateways and requires two dedicated PCs, each with 512K memory and a hard drive. One runs the Microsoft Mail Connection, and the other runs the External Mail program that comes with Microsoft Mail. The External Mail program is what allows one Microsoft Mail post office to communicate with another Microsoft Mail post office. As you can begin to see, Microsoft Mail can provide a solution, but it is not the most elegant nor the simplest cross-platform solution. But if you already have Microsoft Mail, you might want to take the extra steps necessary to provide your Mac users with Microsoft Mail for AppleTalk and use the gateway for seamless integration, or just use the Mac Microsoft Mail program with its limited features.

Word Processing

Chances are that the most important software your organization will be using is word processing software. When you add Macintoshes to your network, you will have to be able to exchange word processing files between the Macs and the PCs on your network. If you wish, you can use different word processors on each platform and exchange the files by saving the files in a format that the Mac, MS-DOS, and Windows machines can all read.

To this end, you probably want to use RTF, or Rich Text Format, for all of your files. However, since the RTF format is not the native format of most word processors, saving files in this format would quickly become a pain in the neck. You would have to train your users to save the files in the alternative format, and even then, you would always be encountering situations where someone is trying to access a file that was not saved in the cross-platform format.

So rather than adding one more problem to your support duties, you should really use a word processing program that provides you with a cross-platform-compatible format from the beginning. The word processors discussed in this section all have versions that run on the Mac, Windows, and MS-DOS platforms. If you use one of these word processors, you will not have to worry too much about translation problems, since the word processor can read files created by its counterpart on the other platforms. However, with each of these packages, you'll have to take some extra steps to ensure file compatibility between the different versions.

In the word processing arena, there are not many programs that run on Mac, MS-DOS, and Windows environments. Even though there are numerous word processors available for any single platform, there are only two that cross all three. The two packages are Microsoft Word and WordPerfect.

This section will look at both Word and WordPerfect and discuss them with their cross-platform capabilities in mind. After looking at these programs, you will also find a section that will help you if you plan to use different word processors on the various platforms. The section on using different word processors is included so that you will be familiar with the programs when your users ask you if they can use word processor XYZ.

Microsoft Word

Microsoft Word for the Macintosh is probably the Macintosh's oldest word processor. Word has advanced quite a bit since then, and so has the rest of the word processing industry. There are now versions of Word for MS-DOS and Windows, as well. However, exchanging files between all three versions of Word is not completely seamless. (This discussion pertains to Word for Macintosh version 5.1a.) Word for Windows and Word for the Mac can exchange files in an almost seamless manner, but neither of them can create Word for DOS files without the extra step of saving the files in the Word for DOS format. However, Word for Windows or for the Mac can open the Word for DOS files, as long as each program has the proper filters installed.

When you need to create a Word for DOS file from either Word for Windows or the Mac, you have to select the Word for DOS format option from the Save As dialog box. Figure 9.1 shows the Save As dialog box from Word for Windows.

When you are using files created by Word for Windows with Word for Macintosh, the program will automatically convert the files and retain all formatting. But the document will be converted and opened as an untitled document on the Macintosh. Once it is open, you'll have to save it as a Word for Macintosh file to save your changes. If the file will be going back to a Word for Windows user, the Mac user can save it as a Word for Windows document instead.

By now, you're probably wondering what in the world makes Microsoft Word cross-platform besides the existence of a version for each of the different platforms. Basically, it is because you can use the same file format for all of the different platforms by taking a couple of extra steps. In a sense, you'll have to use the file format that represents the lowest common denominator, which is Word for MS-DOS. Although you cannot choose a default file format in

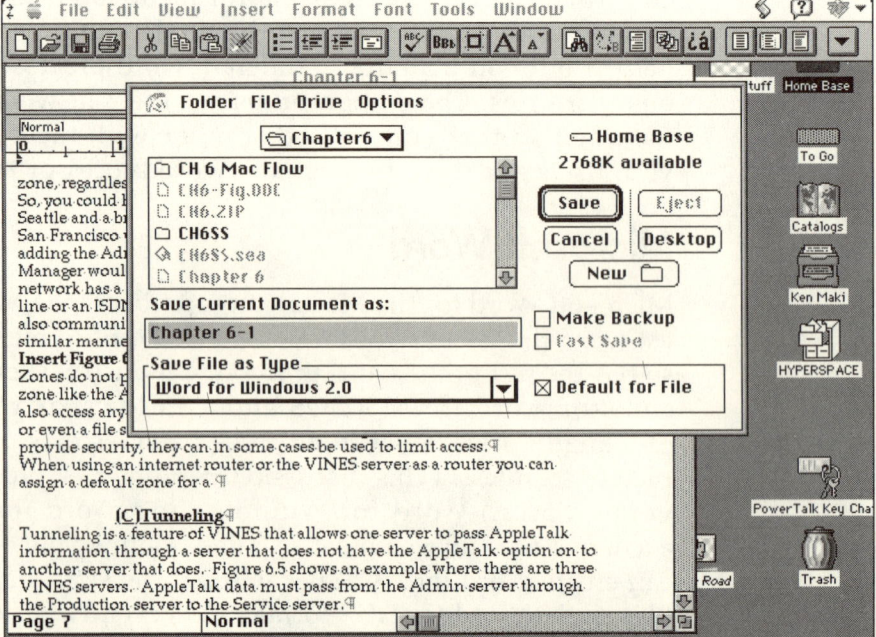

Figure 9.1
Word for Macintosh's Save As dialog box

the Mac version of Word, you can set it for each file you work with when you save it initially.

When you save a file, you can use the Default for File option. Using this option will allow you to continue using the file with the selected file format when you use the Save command (in the File menu), so you will not be asked to resave the file with the Macintosh's native file format. Also, the Mac will remember the file's format, so when it is re-opened you can continue to use the, as it were, foreign format.

To assign the file's format:

1. Select "Save as..." from the File menu. This will open the Save As dialog box.

2. Choose the file format you want to use. Figure 9.2 shows the file format selection list from the Mac's Save As dialog box.

3. Check the Default for File check box.

4. Click on the OK button after choosing the file's destination.

Figure 9.2
The file format selection list and file default check box

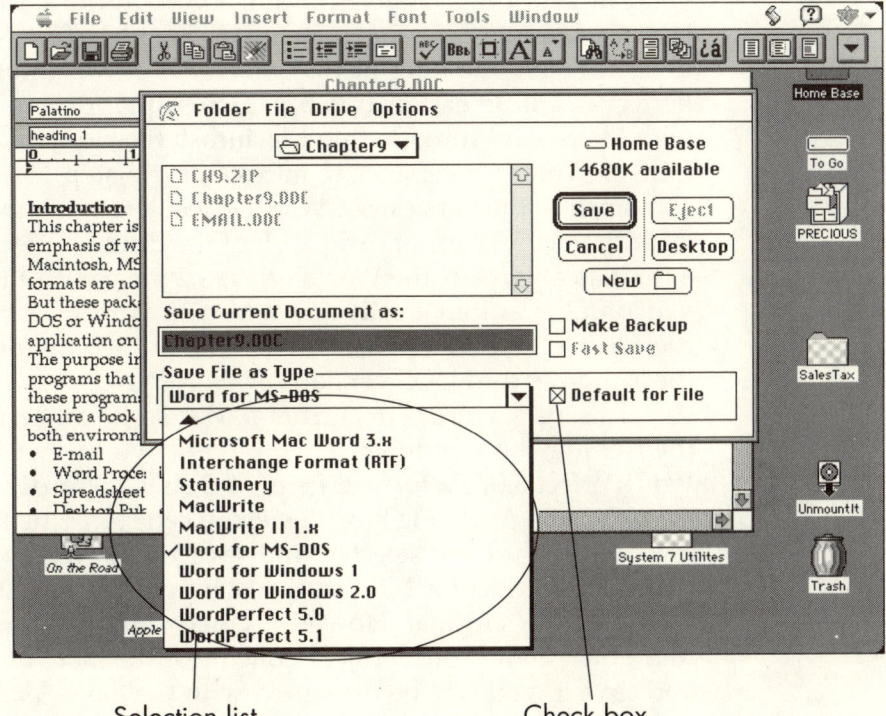

Selection list   Check box

These steps will save the file with the selected file format, and will allow you to continue to use the format while the document is open. There is a drawback to this method of saving a document. Each time you save the document, you will be presented with the Save As dialog box, and will have to rename the document. The advantage is that the Mac remembers which format you're using, so you do not have to reselect the format.

Sometime in the near future, Microsoft will be releasing Word 6.0 for the Macintosh. When it does, all three versions of Word will be identical in how they work and in their file formats. They will be so similar that all three versions (Mac, Windows, and MS-DOS) will all have the same manual. Currently, Word for Windows and Word for MS-DOS 6.0 are virtually the same, and both are on the market. The new version of Word for Macintosh is taking a bit longer to bring to market, but Microsoft has included references to Word for Macintosh in its new Manuals for Word 6.0.

WordPerfect

WordPerfect is the other cross-platform word processing program you can get. It is available in MS-DOS, Windows, Macintosh, and UNIX versions. The first version of WordPerfect for Macintosh does not have the long history of Word for Macintosh, but Word-Perfect is a little easier to use as a cross-platform solution. But as with Microsoft Word, getting Macintosh files to work with the MS-DOS or Windows versions requires an extra step.

Each of the versions of WordPerfect lets you save your files in WordPerfect 5.2 format. And each of the different versions of Word automatically reads the WordPerfect 5.2 format. But the Macintosh version (2.1) automatically saves files in WordPerfect's Macintosh file format. The Macintosh file format is incompatible with both the Windows and DOS versions of WordPerfect.

To save a WordPerfect from a Mac so it can be read by either the DOS or the Windows version, you have to save the file in the WordPerfect 5.0/5.2 format. Figure 9.3 shows WordPerfect for Macintosh's Save As dialog box where you can select the file format.

Once you have selected and saved a file with a format other than WordPerfect for Macintosh, each time you save the file, it will retain the file's format. However, when you open a file with a format other than WordPerfect's Macintosh format for the first time and save it, you will be presented with the Save As dialog box. At

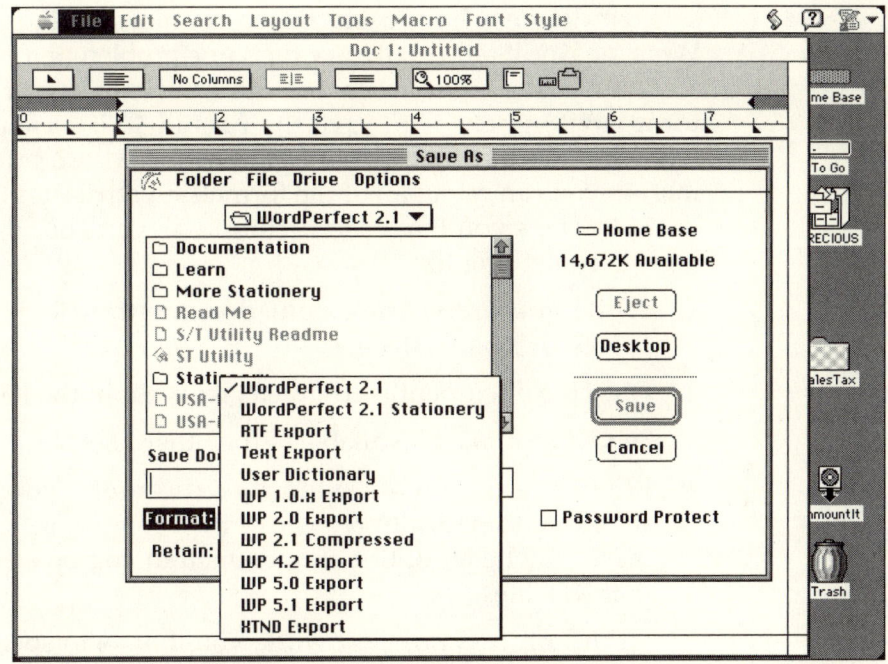

Figure 9.3
Word Perfect for the Macintosh's Save As dialog box

that time, you will have to save the file with the desired format, which will probably be WordPerfect 5.2. From this point on, any time you save the file, it will be saved with the selected format.

There is one other problem with WordPerfect that could affect its cross-platform usage. If you are using a utility to mount MS-DOS formatted floppies on a Macintosh, you cannot save a WordPerfect file directly to the floppy disk. You will have to save the file to your hard disk and then copy it to the floppy disk from the Mac's Finder.

WordPerfect has just released WordPerfect Macintosh version 3.0. However, at this moment, WordPerfect 6.0 Windows and WordPerfect 6.0 for MS-DOS cannot read a WordPerfect Macintosh 3.0 file in its native Macintosh format.

Using Other Macintosh Word Processors

When you use a Macintosh word processor that does not have a counterpart on another platform, such as Nisus, WriteNow, or MacWrite, you'll have a problem with file formats. Each of these has a native Macintosh format that cannot be read by word processors on the PC. Likewise, if you're using a PC or Windows word processor that does not have a Macintosh counterpart, like AMI Pro, XY Write, or WordStar, you'll have the same problem in reverse.

The easiest way to ensure file compatibility in a cross-platform environment is to save the files in RTF format. Almost all word processors, regardless of platform, can read a Rich Text Format, so you can retain all of the formatting attributes for your files.

The steps you'll have to perform will vary, but they will probably go something like this:

1. While you are writing your document, save it in the word processor's native format.
2. Once the document is complete, resave it in the RTF format.
3. Send it or make it available to the other users.
4. When the recipients open the file, their word processors should automatically recognize the file format. If they do not, there may be an option in the Open dialog box that will interpret RTF files.

If this process does not work, you'll have to spend some time experimenting with different file formats to see if there is one that will work.

Spreadsheets

This section will talk about cross-platform spreadsheet applications. Next to word processors, there is probably no other application that is as important to today's business world. In some cases, it is the most important application a business uses. So when you add Macintoshes to your network, you'll want to be sure that you can use all of the spreadsheet data you've accumulated. And likewise, you will probably want to generate spreadsheets from the Mac that can be used on the PCs.

Since we've been talking about three primary environments—MS-DOS, Windows, and the Mac—this discussion will be restricted to these platforms. There is only one spreadsheet package that spans all three: Lotus 123. There are two spreadsheet packages that can be used only in the Macintosh and Windows environments. They are Microsoft Excel and WingZ. Of these two packages, Microsoft Excel is the most popular. It seems that WingZ is the least popular of the programs. At one time, Informix was pushing the WingZ for Macintosh product, but there has been no press or marketing effort by Informix for a couple of years, even though the product is still for sale. Within the MS-DOS environment, chances are that you use 123. If you are using another DOS spreadsheet, we'll also talk about getting data from other spreadsheet applications to the Mac in the last part of this section, Using Other Spreadsheets.

Within the Macintosh world, Microsoft Excel is probably the most common spreadsheet. Besides WingZ and Lotus 123, there is only one other Macintosh spreadsheet, Claris Resolve. This spreadsheet is not very popular, and it is rumored that future development for Claris Resolve has been discontinued, even though the program is still supported. Resolve uses the same core technology as WingZ, and the two spreadsheets are similar. The discussion in Using Other Spreadsheets will also apply to any Macintosh spreadsheet that does not have a DOS or Windows counterpart.

Microsoft Excel

Microsoft Excel is one of the best examples of a cross-platform application. Excel for Macintosh and Excel for Windows are both in version 4.0. The same manual is used for both versions, the files are seamlessly compatible, and the program has almost the same interface on the Mac as in Windows.

Microsoft Excel can read all of the standard file formats discussed in the Using Other Spreadsheets section, and it is compatible with Lotus 123 if you save your documents in the Lotus 123 format. Excel for Windows will even let you use Lotus 123 command equivalents if you specify this option when it is installed.

As a matter of fact, these two programs are so compatible that there is nothing more to say, except that you should still watch your file names. The Mac users should use MS-DOS names when exchanging files with their Windows counterparts. Microsoft Word 6.0 for the Macintosh will have the same type of cross-platform compatibility when the Macintosh version is released.

Lotus 123

Although Lotus 123 is available for all three platforms, in the Mac world it has a long way to go to catch up with Excel, both in the number of users and in cross-platform capabilities.

123 works very well when sharing files created by the MS-DOS or Windows versions with the other platforms. Where you will have problems is with files created on a Macintosh.

Files created by the Macintosh version of 123 cannot be opened by either the MS-DOS version or the Windows version unless you specifically save the 123 file using the Lotus 123 MS-DOS format. When working with 123 files on the Macintosh, you'll have to create your file and then purposely save it with the MS-DOS version's format when you're ready to send it to a user with a PC.

Since the Macintosh can read 123's MS-DOS formats, you'll have no trouble reading the files from your cross-platform counterparts. Just remember that you'll have to be careful when sending files in the other direction.

WingZ

As mentioned above, WingZ is the odd program out. Although it is still sold and supported by Informix, it is not promoted. WingZ is a cross-platform spreadsheet that runs on the Mac, Windows, and UNIX. I believe that it was created as a support tool to complement Informix's 4GL family of products. It will be of interest primarily to those who use Informix databases.

WingZ will read Lotus 123 versions 1a and 2, DIF, SYLK, and its own file formats. The files created on a machine in the native WingZ format can be read with no problems by any other machine running WingZ. The WingZ interface is exactly the same from one platform to the next. There are no differences unless they are interface-specific. You will see a slight difference between the Macintosh and Windows dialog boxes. The script files will work on all platforms.

WingZ has everything you need in a spreadsheet. Although it is may appear to be lacking some of the features the other programs have, such as Excel's workbooks and assist features, WingZ is a very fast and efficient spreadsheet with a very powerful scripting language. (This is not meant to diminish the scripting capabilities of 123 or Excel.)

Using Other Spreadsheets

There is enough compatibility between spreadsheets from different manufacturers that you can use spreadsheet programs from different manufacturers and still exchange files across platforms. Every spreadsheet program can save and read files in either SYLK or DIF file formats. Both of these formats retain the original spreadsheet's formatting, including the cell formulas. Also, in addition to the SYLK and DIF formats, most programs will read one or more of the early Lotus 123 file formats, such as 123 1.a or 2 files.

Because spreadsheets are so important to business, programs from different publishers will always be able to use a common format to exchange data. If you have different spreadsheet programs on your network and need to share your files, all you have to do is settle on one of the common file formats for your cross-platform files. Whenever a file is going to a different type of machine, use this format, and you'll have no problems.

With some of the spreadsheet programs, such as Excel, you will be able to open the file in your cross-platform format and continue to save changes to the file without changing the file's format. Others require that you work in the program's native format and then save the file in the shared network format after you've finished with the project. Whatever your program's idiosyncrasies, you will always have the ability to exchange data with machines on different platforms.

Desktop Publishing and Graphics

The Macintosh is best known for its graphic capabilities. It is quite possible that your reason for adding a Mac to your network is that it will be used as a graphics workstation. Some will argue that the Mac is losing its edge in this arena of the computer world because many of the programs that made the Mac such a great graphics machine are now available for the Windows platform.

In some shops, this is the case. But even if a graphics program is identical on a Mac and a Windows machine, chances are that the Mac will still win out over the PC. One of the reasons is that the Mac is more easily configured than the Windows machine. When you start adding hard drives and high-resolution monitors, the cost differences between the two platforms quickly diminish.

There are often support programs, sold as extras for some of these graphics packages, that are not available for the Windows versions of the same applications. PageMaker, Quark Express, and Photoshop all have such support programs. And finally, most of the really skilled graphic artists who use these programs were trained on the Macintosh.

The real purpose of this section is to talk about the various graphics programs that are cross-platform compatible. There are quite a few, so this section will cover the programs by manufacturer rather than by the type of program. In almost all cases, the files created on the Mac are compatible with the same program in the Windows platform. And if they are not, it is only a matter of time before the files will be seamlessly compatible.

In this section, you'll find short discussions about the programs from:

- Aldus
- Altsys
- Adobe
- Quark
- Frame Technologies
- Microsoft
- Deneba

Each of these companies makes at least one graphics-type package that runs under Windows and on the Mac. A "graphics" package, for our purposes, is a drawing, painting, page layout, or presentation package.

Aldus

Aldus was one of the first Macintosh software manufacturers to release versions of its programs for Microsoft Windows. Like Microsoft, Aldus is attempting to make all of its Macintosh and Windows packages identical. The user's manual for PageMaker is the same manual for either platform. Not all of Aldus's programs are at this stage yet, but they will be.

Each of the part titles in this section has the name of the Macintosh program. The Windows package is the same name with "for Windows" added to it. So Freehand is a Macintosh program, and Freehand for Windows is the corresponding Windows program.

Freehand

Freehand is a high-end drawing and illustration package. Aldus calls it a design and illustration package. Its competing package on the Macintosh is Adobe Illustrator, and many graphic artists use both packages because each has features the other doesn't. In the Windows world, I consider CorelDRAW and Harvard Graphics as competition for Freehand, but I doubt that I could find many Mac graphic artists to agree with me.

For the Macintosh, Freehand version 4.0 is the latest available, while the Windows version is currently 3.1. Right now, the files from the Mac version do not integrate seamlessly with the Windows version. When Freehand 4.0 for Windows is released, the files will be seamlessly interchangeable. Until then, you'll just have to save Macintosh files in the Windows 3.1 format. But the wait should not be long.

PageMaker

PageMaker is Aldus's desktop publishing package. Its primary competition comes from Quark Express, and you will find a real love-hate relationship between these two packages. Each time one is upgraded, it seems to have features the other doesn't, and the competition between them is a see-saw of features. There is no way to recommend one over the other. Graphic designers who do page layout will usually be experts in one or the other; you rarely find someone who is professional with both packages.

PageMaker's files can be seamlessly exchanged between our two platforms. You will find that PageMaker's features and operation are the same whether you're using a Mac or a Windows PC. So like Excel, there is not much to say about PageMaker from a cross-platform perspective.

Persuasion

Persuasion is Aldus's desktop presentation package. It competes with PowerPoint from Microsoft. The current version number for both Macintosh and Windows is 3.0.

The files from the Mac and Windows versions of Persuasion are basically cross-platform-compatible. Because the desktop presentations tap into interface specific elements, such as dialog boxes, buttons, and so on, the file formats of Persuasion and Persuasion for Windows are not compatible on a binary level. Therefore, when a presentation or slide show is being prepared on one platform to be used on the other, the files will have to be exported and modifications made to any interface-specific elements.

IntelliDraw

IntelliDraw is similar to Freehand, but it is intended for drafting-oriented applications. It is more like a CAD (computer aided design) package than an illustration program. The current version of IntelliDraw is the same on both the Mac and Windows, version 2.0, and the file format between the two platforms is exactly the same. If the files need to be exported or imported, you can use PICT, EPS, TIFF, and ASCII text formats.

Altsys

Fontographer

Altsys began life by creating tools for the Macintosh to manipulate and create PostScript fonts. Its primary package is Fontographer, which has been around for a long time on the Mac. With the advent of Windows and the need for PostScript and TrueType fonts in the Windows environment, Altsys created a Windows version of Fontographer. Fontographer is also used for logo creation.

Because the file formats for fonts and their implementation between the Mac and Windows are different, the files created in Fontographer on different platforms are not directly compatible with each other. However, you can design a font on one platform and then use the same files after they have been exported to the other. Fontographer can use elements of Freehand and Illustrator files to aid in the creation of fonts and logos, as well.

Adobe

Adobe is the company that created the PostScript page description language. All printers that employ PostScript either license it from Adobe or use a PostScript clone. Because Adobe created PostScript, it continues to set the standards for this part of the industry. Most applications and printers that employ PostScript will soon, if they don't already, employ PostScript Level 2, soon to be the new standard version of PostScript.

Besides creating PostScript, Adobe has also developed several applications for the Mac and for Windows PCs. All of these programs in some way take advantage of PostScript, and all are cross-platform-compatible.

Illustrator

Adobe Illustrator is one of the oldest and most advanced illustration packages available for the Mac, and now you can use it on a Windows PC. For many Macintosh graphic artists, Illustrator is the only illustration package.

The current Macintosh version is 5.0, while the current Windows version is 4.0. So until the Windows version catches up with the Macintosh version, which was just upgraded, you'll have to save the Macintosh files in version 3 if you want them to be seamlessly compatible with the Windows 4.0 version.

When you save an Illustrator file from the Mac for use on a Windows PC, it is a good idea to use the IBM PC Preview. The preview is an EPS (Encapsulated PostScript) file that is optimized for the platform that will be using the file. For Windows machines, the EPS format is a special Aldus/Altsys/Adobe EPS format for IBM PC products. On a Mac, an EPS file can be edited using a text editor, but the IBM PC preview cannot.

The other alternative is to save the file without an EPS preview. If this format is used, the file can only be opened by Illustrator, which means that the file cannot be placed in a page layout program like PageMaker. Illustrator files do often end up in PageMaker; they can also used in Photoshop, Quark Express, and Fontographer. So the preview is important if the files are going to be used in another application.

Photoshop

Photoshop is a digital photo editing package. You can edit scanned photos and images with it, or you can use it to edit files—Illustrator files, TIFF, PCX, BMP, and GIF files, to name a few. Photoshop is also a cross-platform application. The current Macintosh version is 2.5.1, and the Windows version is also 2.5.

File compatibility between the programs is seamless. The major difference you'll find between the two programs is not in how they operate but in the add-on programs that are available. Photoshop uses plug-in modules for additional functionality. You'll find that most of the third-party Photoshop plug-in modules are made for the Macintosh; the Windows versions take second priority in the development cycle.

Premiere

Premiere is a multi-media video editing and presentation package that lets you create videos using Apple's QuickTime movie format. Even though the Windows version is 1.0 and the Macintosh version is 3.0, the files are compatible between the packages. The major difference is that the Windows package can also use the AVI (Audio Visual Interleaved, a Windows multimedia video format) format.

If you are using Premiere on both a Mac and a Windows PC, you should use the QuickTime format. If you are using a the AVI format on a Windows machine and intend to use the file on a Mac, you will have to convert the file to QuickTime format before you use it on the Mac.

Streamline

Streamline is Adobe's image tracing package. It is used to convert scanned images and other graphics files into EPS files. The EPS files can then be edited in Illustrator or used with a page layout program. The current version for the Macintosh is 3.0, and Windows is 3.01. Streamline creates images in EPS, PICT, or DXF (AutoCAD 2-D graphics file format). Streamline creates files with the same format on either platform.

Adobe Type Manager

Adobe Type Manager, or ATM, is an application that images PostScript fonts on the computer's monitor and automatically scales the fonts regardless of the display size. ATM is required by both Illustrator and Photoshop; it is also available as a standalone package. There are separate versions of ATM for the Mac and Windows, since each platform uses fonts differently, but their functions are the same.

TypeAlign

TypeAlign is a program that allows you to manipulate type. Its capabilities include skewing. rotating, and colorizing. TypeAlign requires ATM because it manipulates outline PostScript images. The altered type can then be used in page layout packages, some word processors, and other programs that can embed EPS files.

The Windows version of TypeAlign is 2.1, and the Macintosh version is 1.0.4. However, files created by either package can be used on the other platform if they are saved using the proper EPS format. The technology employed is very similar to that of Adobe Illustrator.

Typeface Library

Adobe is one of the major publishers of PostScript type faces. There are 220 fonts currently available from Adobe, and more than 1000 typefaces. The number of typefaces keeps increasing, and Adobe is not the only manufacturer. Each typeface available for the Mac is also available for Windows machines.

Typefaces are important, because if your Macs are being used for graphics design work and the files are then sent to someone using a Windows PC, the recipient will have to have all of the typefaces used in the document. Otherwise, the file will not look right when viewed, and it won't print. Remember that you will have to purchase versions of the same font for each platform—they are not interchangeable.

Quark

QuarkXPress

Quark is the publisher of the QuarkXPress, a page layout or desktop publishing package. It is considered to be the best page layout package available, with more features than PageMaker. But this ends up being a point of contention with graphic artists: some religiously use PageMaker, and others, QuarkXPress. Regardless of which is best, QuarkXPress is your other cross-platform page layout option.

Quark will shortly be releasing version 3.3 for both Windows and the Macintosh. The current Macintosh version is 3.2, with the Windows version at 3.12. With the current versions, the files are cross-platform-compatible, but not seamless. The Mac version has no problem reading the Windows version, but the Windows version cannot read the Mac version without some difficulty.

Frame Technologies

FrameMaker

FrameMaker is probably better known in the Windows world than in the Macintosh world. But if you're using FrameMaker in a Windows environment, there is no reason not to use it in on the Mac. FrameMaker is used primarily for business and technical publishing, but it is also considered a page layout package.

The current version for FrameMaker is 4.0 for all platforms, including most UNIX operating systems, Windows, and the Macintosh. FrameMaker is designed as a multi-user, cross-platform desktop publishing package. FrameMaker's files can be used seamlessly on all platforms.

Microsoft

PowerPoint

PowerPoint is Microsoft's desktop presentation package. It is available as part of the Microsoft Office package or as an individual package, and it is available for both the Mac and Windows platforms.

The current version of PowerPoint is 3.0 on both platforms, and the files created on the Macintosh are seamlessly compatible with a Windows PC. However, because of the differences between the computer platforms, you might have to do some tweaking when the files are used on different platforms. Any modifications that might be required are minor; otherwise, the files are seamless.

Deneba Systems

Canvas

Canvas is a hybrid drawing, painting, and illustration package. It has many years' experience on the Macintosh, and was recently introduced for Windows. Because of its popularity on the Mac, there is little doubt that Canvas will quickly find its way onto many Windows machines. The current version for both platforms is 3.0. The files are cross-platform-compatible without alteration.

Using Other Graphic Packages

If you're using a package like CorelDRAW or Harvard Graphics on the PC, you probably want to use the files on the Mac, especially if you're using Macs for desktop publishing or other graphics work. However, the file formats from these packages—and from others like Windows PaintBrush (PCX and BMP)—are truly foreign to the Mac. Only a few of the packages above will automatically read these files on the Mac. If you do not have a cross-platform Macintosh program like MacPaint or MacDraw, you'll be faced with similar problems when moving files from the Mac to the Windows platform.

To overcome these problems, you can use a utility like MacLink Plus from DataViz, or a Windows or Mac program that can read the foreign formats. Your best bet is to use MacLink. This program can convert almost any Windows/PC file into a Macintosh-compatible format, or vice versa. In the absence of MacLink, the programs you will find most useful in reading most of these file formats are Canvas and Photoshop.

You can also make the process easier by using file formats that are common to both platforms, such as TIFF and PICT. These are almost universal across platforms. Another file format that can be used across platforms is the GIF format. However, to use this format on the Mac, you will have to use a converter—a special GIF reader—and then convert the file to a PICT or a TIFF file.

Unfortunately, there are no hard and fast rules for dealing with file formats that do not translate directly, so you might have to experiment before you get the process right. The biggest problem you'll have will be in training your users, if they have to go through any series of complicated steps to convert the files. So once you have the steps figured out, be sure to train your users.

Databases

In a multi-platform environment, it is likely that you will have a need for a multi-user and cross-platform database at some point. You might use the database for your accounting system, the application you use for taking orders, document tracking, or any one of a hundred other uses. And if you're using the Macintosh and Windows machines in your shop, you'll probably need to access the database using both platforms.

To help you accomplish this end, there are several database programs that you can use to access data and to create applications that are usable in a cross-platform environment. Each of the cross-platform-compatible database applications can read the same database files. FoxBase can read all FoxBase files, whether the creating machine is DOS, Windows, or Macintosh. The same applies to any application list in this section. Almost all of these applications run on the Windows and Macintosh platform. There are very few that also run under DOS.

If you are using an SQL (Standard Query Language) database running on a platform other than a PC or Mac, there are also several ways to access this data. One way to access an SQL database is to use Microsoft Excel. Another method is to use Oracle, which is available for DOS, Windows, or the Mac. Also, most companies that provide SQL databases provide access tools for cross-platform access. Other than mentioning that it is possible, SQL access exceeds the scope of this section. The remainder of this section will concentrate on other database programs that can be accessed from Windows and the Mac. Also, included in this section will be some development platforms that use a database backend.

Microsoft Corporation

FoxBase

FoxBase, now published by Microsoft, is one of the few database packages, if not the only one, that runs on all three platforms. With FoxBase, you can develop an application for one platform, and then modify the application with nominal changes so it will run on all of the others and still access the same data files. If you're in the planning stages for developing a database application that will be accessed by Macs in addition to Windows and DOS machines, FoxBase is a development platform you should consider.

FoxBase is a fully relational database, not meant for the fainthearted when it comes to development. It is complex and time-consuming to create an application, and there are consultants and programmers who make their living providing FoxBase development services. However, if you want to take the time to learn FoxBase, or have a simple application which will be run on multiple platforms, you should consider FoxBase. Another advantage of using FoxBase is that the files are Dbase-compatible, and can therefore be accessed by other programs that can read the Dbase file format.

Blyth Software

Omnis 7

Omnis 7 is a high-end database development system. Applications developed in Omnis can be run on both Windows and Macintosh platforms with no changes to the programming code, regardless of which platform was used to develop the application. Like FoxBase, Omnis is a complete development platform that is not meant to be used for casual database applications, and it is not easy to learn. Professionals often use the Omnis platform for development.

The data files created by an Omnis application are accessible by SQL access tools or by an Omnis application, and are fully relational. Like the programming code, they are the same on either platform. Otherwise, the files are have their own format and cannot be casually browsed. Omnis provides efficient and fast database applications for workgroups and mission-critical applications.

Claris Corporation

FileMaker Pro

FileMaker Pro is a database application that works on Macintosh and Windows machines. FileMaker Pro is probably the best-selling flat-file database for the Macintosh, with its closest competitor lagging behind at a distant second. FileMaker Pro is the only database program that provides cross-platform access between Windows and the Mac, other than its high-end cousins.

FileMaker is easily accessible to the user, and the complexity of the database depends on the user's skill and devotion to the application. The closest equivalent that FileMaker has in the DOS world is Q&A by Symantec, and maybe if Symantec ever completes the Mac version of Q&A, FileMaker will have some competition. But until that day, 90% of a business's database needs can be fulfilled by FileMaker.

As a cross-platform application, FileMaker can be run in a multi-user mode from any number of Macs and Windows machines. How you access a FileMaker file depends on the type of network you're using. If all of your machines are networked with AppleTalk, you can run the FileMaker application on one machine and connect to it with ADSP. The other way to access the files is to place them on a common file server, where they can be opened by any machine that has access to the server. Each machine that will access the shared files must have its own copy of FileMaker.

Novell

AppBuilder

AppBuilder used to be Serius Workshop, and prior to that it was Serius Programmer. Serius Programmer started as an object-oriented application tool for the Macintosh, and was ported to the

Windows environment when it became Serius Workshop. Now, as AppBuilder and as a Novell product, it uses the same object-oriented concept.

AppBuilder is a development application with a database backend that allows you to create and compile either Macintosh or Windows applications. AppBuilder's data files are cross-platform-compatible; the code written for the Mac can be transferred to a Windows machine and compiled by the Windows version of AppBuilder. In this fashion, you can create an application that uses a custom database that is exactly the same on either a Windows PC or a Macintosh, while at the same time providing multi-user access.

Because AppBuilder is now published by Novell, it will be optimized for a Novell network and eventually have the ability to either use or augment NLMs (NetWare Loadable Modules). Novell wants to use AppBuilder as a means for providing Macintosh functionality for its network, bringing the Macintosh into the Novell environment as an equal client rather than as an afterthought.

Workgroup Applications

Currently, there are two main workgroup applications: Lotus Notes and WordPerfect Office. Both of these are server-based applications that allow for the structuring of the data flow within a network. In a sense, the workgroup applications are E-mail applications on steroids. Rather than just sending a message or a file to a single recipient, a workgroup application can send a document from the creator to a supervisor for approval, then automatically forward it to someone else for additional input, and so on.

In addition to smart E-mail, the workgroup applications have a shared scheduler where other workgroup members' schedules can be viewed and modified, so the boss can schedule a staff meeting for everyone and know that it is on each of their schedules. However, there are some real differences between the different workgroup applications and how they function. This section will look at Lotus Notes, WordPerfect Office, and Microsoft Office.

Whatever system is used, there is one vision that inspires all of these packages and indicates the direction they're moving. This vision is the ability to share data regardless of the computing platform, to organize that data so as to enable a collaborative network environment, and to group people together regardless of their locations. The cautionary note here is that groupware is still an emerging software category. Before you buy, research each product carefully to make sure you're getting what you need.

Lotus Notes

Lotus Notes is a server-based workgroup management system that allows you to set up a structure for data flow using a database and a department/group structure. Included in this structure are electronic mail and the proper and automatic routing of reports and documents.

It is probably easier to describe a scenario where Notes could be applied. Let's say you have to administer the computers for an advertising agency. In the agency you have five basic divisions: the account executives, the creative department, the production department, the media department, and administration. Within each of these departments you have people who have to share a great deal of information, and there is also a need to track projects and documents going from one department to another. Also, because of the size of the organization, some of the people use Windows PCs and others have Macs.

The data has to flow from the account executive to the creative department, so the account executive can tell the creative department what products need to be advertised. The creative department then works up the advertising copy for the client's approval, so the concepts and roughs have to go back to the account executive. After the client approves the concepts, they are sent to media and production for cost estimates. After that, the account executive secures approval from the client, and the creative department is given the go-ahead to create the ad. Finally, the finished ad is presented to the client, and the media department schedules it for publication in the proper magazines. After the process is completed, and sometimes while it is in progress, time sheets and material charges are passed to the administration department for billing.

With Lotus Notes, this process can be streamlined to move the necessary files efficiently from one department to another in the proper order, so that everyone concerned knows the status of any project at a given time. Also, Notes can help make sure everyone gets the proper documents at the right time—the administration can receive the proper documentation for billing purposes, the media department can let the creative department know what deadlines have to be met, and the CEO can check the exact status of any client's project.

None of this happens by magic, but it is possible when you use Notes to organize your company. The beauty of it is that it works with both Windows and Macintosh computers. Notes is the first groupware product, and as such, offers a glimpse of what computing environments will become. Although Lotus Notes has been criticized for not working well with applications other than Lotus products, it handles the routing of Macintosh applications more efficiently.

WordPerfect Office

WordPerfect Office is the WordPerfect corporation's attempt to add order to an organization. It is server-based and cross-platform-compatible between Macs and Windows PCs. However, it does not have the overall features of Lotus Notes. It is really an extended E-mail package, with shared calendaring and scheduling applications. It does have automatic routing capabilities, but it does not have the ability to create a computing environment that automates tasks and data flow within an organization. WordPerfect Office can be used to schedule resources like meeting rooms, equipment, and people's time.

In a sense, WordPerfect Office is the beginning of an environment that will be developed to control an entire organization, but it has a way to go. One of the advantages that WordPerfect has over Lotus Notes is that it is available for more platforms. Office works not only on Windows and the Mac, but also with DOS, OS/2, and UNIX platforms.

WordPerfect Office runs off an OS/2 or NetWare server, and requires gateways for access from different platforms.

Microsoft Office

The other workgroup application listed in this section is Microsoft Office. Microsoft Office is not a WorkGroup application like WordPerfect Office or Lotus Notes, but a collection of applications to provide a common set of tools for all of the users on a network. Microsoft Office provides you with copies of:

- Microsoft Word   (Windows and Macintosh)
- Microsoft Excel   (Windows and Macintosh)

- Microsoft PowerPoint   (Windows and Macintosh)
- Microsoft Mail   (Windows and Macintosh)
- Microsoft Access   (Windows only)

By using Microsoft Office, you ensure that everyone is using the same applications with the same features, and that they have the ability to communicate via E-mail. It is a start toward workgroup and office integration, but Microsoft Office does not provide the scheduling or data flow features found in WordPerfect Office or Lotus Notes.

Integrated Applications

For small offices, where you may not need the full power offered by the standalone applications listed above, you might consider using an integrated application. An integrated application is one that provides at least the following capabilities:

- Word processing
- Spreadsheet
- Database
- Communications
- Limited graphics

There are two integrated applications available that work on the Macintosh and Windows platforms: Claris Works and Microsoft Works. Microsoft Works is also available in an MS-DOS version. WordPerfect Works comes in Macintosh and MS-DOS versions, but does not have a Windows version.

From a cross-platform perspective, Microsoft Works is the product that will provide you with the fullest cross-platform support. If you have only a Macintosh and Windows shop, then you can use Claris Works. WordPerfect Works will be suitable only if you're using Macintosh and MS-DOS, but not Windows.

Microsoft Works

Microsoft Works is available for all three platforms: the Mac, Windows, and MS-DOS. Works contains a word processor, spreadsheet, communications, and database package in all three versions.

The Macintosh and Windows versions also have a simple graphics package that has drawing and painting capabilities.

The files created by Microsoft Works on one platform can be read by Works on any other platform, with the exception of the graphics files, which can't be read by the MS-DOS version. Other than the lack of the graphics package in the MS-DOS version, Works provides you with all of the tools you need for a small office. If you have to exchange files between different types of machines and have Microsoft Works on each one, you'll have no problems.

WordPerfect Works

Like Microsoft Works, WordPerfect Works provides you with all of the applications listed in the introduction to this section, including a graphics package for the MS-DOS version. However, at the moment, WordPerfect Works is limited by the lack of a Windows version. If you're only using MS-DOS and Macintosh machines, though, you can get by just fine with WordPerfect Works. The Macintosh version uses the Claris XTND translators for reading different types of files, and you can use the files from the MS-DOS version on the Mac.

ClarisWorks

Of the integrated packages listed here, ClarisWorks is the one that most reviewers prefer in the Macintosh world. In the PC world, however, ClarisWorks has been largely ignored. But if you like Claris products and want cross-platform compatibility for your integrated package, you will not get fired if you recommend ClarisWorks.

Besides having all of the integrated functions listed in the introduction, ClarisWorks implements its integration of the different modules more cleanly and intuitively than the other two packages. Of course, the data files created on one platform are seamlessly compatible with the others.

Conclusion

As I look back over this chapter, I'm almost afraid it will read like advertising copy. There are so many programs that work in cross-platform environments, it was just not possible to do more than give a brief description of each program and mention any problems you might have when transferring files from the Mac to a PC or from a PC to the Mac. You do now have the essential facts regarding these programs.

However, I need to caution you. Do not rely entirely on this section as your guide for purchasing or deciding on what program to use. Contact the program's manufacturer, read reviews, and make sure you have all of the information you need before you buy. This chapter does not contain enough information about any single program to make a decision.

What it does do is narrow down your search. It lists almost every cross-platform package available for the Macintosh, Windows, and MS-DOS platforms currently published. And as is the fate of all lists, by the time this book is published, there will be more programs to add to the list. So even as I write this, it is going out of date.

Network Trouble-shooting

Introduction

Ah, trouble-shooting. Trouble-shooting may be the bane of your existence, the challenge you thrive on, or just another part of your job as the systems administrator. Regardless of how you feel about the task, you are going to faced with problems with your Macs and your Macintosh network.

Chances are good that you are familiar with and know how to trouble-shoot your PC network, your MS-DOS and Windows networking problems, and your NOS. However, it is quite likely that Macintoshes are not your forte. And to make things worse, each NOS uses AppleTalk to communicate with the Macs, so not only do you have to know the PC NOS, you have to learn the ins and outs of AppleTalk.

Hopefully, you'll find this chapter helpful. It is designed to help you during those times when your Macs misbehave and cause network problems. For problems you might have with your NOS and its Macintosh implementation, you need to look at the chapter that covers your NOS; there is a brief trouble-shooting section at the end of each NOS chapter. Also, be sure to check the manuals that came with your NOS—they contain additional information that could not be put into this book.

Prerequisite to any trouble-shooting, you need to be familiar with Chapter 2, which explains AppleTalk and the Macintosh networking environment. Also included in Chapter 2 is a quick tour of the Macintosh System and the networking elements of the System folder. The other chapter you should skim is Chapter 8, where you will find descriptions of Macintosh networking utilities that you might need for trouble-shooting your network.

Once you are familiar with this information, you'll be ready to start trouble-shooting your Macintosh network. This chapter is divided into the following sections:

- Troubleshooting overview
- Physical link problems
- Application problems
- Support resources

Because this is only one chapter, it can only be valuable to you if you're somewhat experienced in the trouble-shooting process already. It is just not possible to cover all of the problems you can have with a Macintosh in one chapter, so you'll have to rely on your own experiences, as well. Although this chapter will not be able to solve every problem you might have with your Macintosh/PC network, you will find enough information to get you started. If you don't find what you need, the Support Resources section can help you find other answers.

Trouble-shooting Overview

This first section is intended to help you decide what is wrong with your Mac(s) or your network and how to proceed in the trouble-shooting process. Under normal circumstances, the Macintosh is a stable computing environment. But when things start going wrong, your first task will be to determine whether it is the Mac or your network that is the problem. The emphasis of the chapter and this section will be network-related.

In this section you'll find descriptions of the possible symptoms and basic Macintosh trouble-shooting techniques. The information in this section will help you determine whether the problems you're having are caused by the Macintosh, the physical link, or some other network resource. Then, once you've made your diagnosis, you will be directed on where to find the information you need to fix the problem. This section and the chapter in general assume that the troubleshooting process is one of identification, isolation, and resolution. *Identification* is the process of determining that a problem exists and identifying the problem's symptoms. *Isolation* is the process of specifying the problem's cause. Once the problem is identified and isolated, the final step is one of *resolution*, or fixing the problem.

Using this process as our model, you will find this section divided into the following sub-sections:

- Tools you'll need
- Identifying the symptoms
- Isolating the problem

The final step in the trouble-shooting process, resolution, will be discussed in the sections following this one.

Tools You'll Need

Before you even start to look for the problem, you should have some tools that will help you in the trouble-shooting processes. There are some tools you absolutely have to have, or you won't be able to work effectively on any Mac. Other tools will be helpful because they can speed the process along, helping you identify the problem more quickly.

There two categories of tools: software and hardware. Software tools can go a long way toward identifying and isolating a problem. However, there will be occasions when software won't be able to tell you what's wrong, and you'll have to resort to hardware tools like line checkers. Take a look at the products listed here and decide what you want to use. This section is divided into three parts:

- Essential tools
- Software tools
- Hardware tools

Although you will not find instructions on using the items listed here, there are some tips included within each section that will help you in the trouble-shooting process. Read the section on

Essential Tools, even if you're prone to just skimming sections. Otherwise, you might miss a suggestion or technique that will save you time and trouble.

Essential Tools

There are several things you will need as you set forth on the trouble-shooting venture. In order to get the information you need, you should have the following items. If you are missing some of these tools, your troubleshooting attempts will be hampered, at best, if not entirely thwarted.

System Software

You should have complete sets of the Macintosh operating system for each version of the Macintosh System being used on your network. You do not want to depend on the users for having the software you need. They probably will not know where it is, and more than likely they will not have it at all. So you should keep copies of each version of the Macintosh System. A complete set of System disks is composed of:

Disk Tools This disk is a bootable floppy disk that contains the Mac's hard disk formatter (as long as the hard drive is an Apple drive) and a hard disk repair utility. The formatter is called Apple HD SC Setup, and the current version number is 7.2.2 (current as this is being written). Apple's hard disk repair utility is called Disk First Aid, and its current version number is 7.2.

The System Installer and all accompanying disks Each Macintosh System version seems to have a different number of disks. You will have to know how many disks are included in the basic set of System disks for the version of the System you're working on. Right now, System 7.1 has the following disks:

- Install
- Install 2
- Tidbits
- Fonts
- Printing
- Install Me First

Install Me First is a disk that is included with any Macintosh that uses a System Enabler. The System Enabler is a special system element that is required for a particular Macintosh to run. The System Enabler is different for each Mac that uses one. Also, the System Enabler is included on the Disk Tools disk that came with a particular Macintosh, if the Mac needs a System Enabler to run. System Enablers are often updated, so you will want to check periodically to make sure you have the latest System Enablers for your various Macs.

Macintosh Systems that are purchased with an Apple CD-ROM drive internally installed come with the System Software on a CD disk. If you have any Macs that came with a CD rather than floppies, make a set of System disks from the CD. Even though the CD will boot the Mac, if there is a SCSI problem, you won't be able to use it.

System Updates In addition to the System disks, you should also keep up to date on any System Software updates. The latest version of the System Update is 2.0.1. Apple releases these System Updates periodically. They contain bug fixes and improved system elements, such as control panels and extensions. The System Update is not essential, but it can be helpful.

Network Software Installer Like the System Updates, Apple periodically releases new versions of AppleTalk software. The latest version of the Network Software Installer is 1.3.3 (but this will probably change by the time this book is published). The updates are on a disk called the Network Software Installer. If you are using an AppleShare file server, you received a Network Software Installer with the AppleShare disks. This disk is important if your network has Macs with different System versions. By keeping up to date with the Network Software and making sure each Mac is using the same version of AppleTalk, you can avoid problems.

System 7 Tune-Up If you have Macs running System 7 and not System 7.1, you should have the System 7 Tune-Up disk. This disk installs resources into the System to correct some bugs that were discovered in System 7.0 and System 7.0.1.

The System Update, the Network Software Installer, the System Enablers, and the System 7 Tune Up can all be found on on-line services like AppleLink, America Online, and CompuServe. They should also be available from your Apple Dealer.

Virus Checkers

Unfortunately, a virus-checking utility is a necessary fact of computing life. And just like the MS-DOS world, where viruses seem to spawn viruses, the Macintosh world has a few, also. So you should have a virus checker installed on every Macintosh for which you are responsible. This also means that you will have to keep up to date on new viruses and update the virus checkers as well.

Viruses can cause all types of problems, ranging from erratic Macintosh operations to difficulty in printing. At the current time, there are very few Macintosh viruses that cause damage to or destroy hard drives, but there are a couple of them kicking around. So you should implement the same types of policies and controls for your Macs as you have in place for your MS-DOS machines.

If this means that you do not let people install software on their PCs, then they should not install software on their Macs, either. For just like the PCs, the most common method for transmitting a virus is via floppy disk. The problem with Mac viruses is that they can be transmitted just by mounting a floppy disk. The following is a list of Macintosh virus utilities.

- **Symantec AntiVirus for the Macintosh**—Symantec
- **Virex**—DataWatch
- **Central Point Anti-Virus**—Central Point Software
- **VFind**—CyberSoft
- **AntiToxin**—MainStay

Hard Disk Recovery and Repair Utility

There are times when mysterious and not-so-mysterious Macintosh problems are caused by hard disk damage. The problem is that you can only detect the damage with a special utility, and Apple's Disk First Aid detects only a few basic hard disk problems. You are often left scratching your head and none the wiser, so you will have to use a more powerful utility. There are currently three hard disk utilities packages that can diagnose and repair hard disk problems:

- **MacTools**—Central Point Software

Network Trouble-shooting 393

- **Norton Utilities for Macintosh**—Symantec
- **Public Utilities**—Fifth Generation Systems

Network Mapping Utility

You really should have a network mapping utility to trouble-shoot a Macintosh network. It can tell you quickly and easily which network resources are available at a specific time. By using a mapping utility, you can save yourself a lot of running around. If a LaserWriter is turned off or down, you can save a lot of time by checking the network and going directly to the offending device. A list of network mapping utilities can be found in Chapter 8. Personally, I like NetAtlas, which is published by Farallon.

Real Tools

The section title is Real Tools, because this section is about tools that are not software. They are real tools that you should have on hand. There are not many essential tools in this category, but there are some. The following is a list of the tools you should have on hand:

Wire crimper(s)   You should have a crimper for making RJ-11 cable if you're using a PhoneNET or PhoneNET type network, or an RJ-45 crimper if you have 10BaseT Ethernet. You should have a crimper for making ThinNet cables if you network is using cheapernet.

Wire Testers   You can buy wire testers that check the integrity of any type of cabling you're using. Although the cables can sometimes be checked with a volt/continuity meter, a wire tester made specifically for the type of cable you're using is much more convenient.

Volt Meter   A volt meter can be used instead of a wire tester, especially if you're working with standard Ethernet, 10BaseT, LocalTalk, or twisted-pair wire for PhoneNET. If you are using any of these cabling types and don't have a wire tester, you should at least have a volt meter that is capable of checking continuity. Also, you will probably have to check the voltage on your network cabling from time to time.

Any of these tools can be purchased from a local electronics supply house. What you get will depend on the size of your network. Chances are that you already have most of the cable testing equipment you need, but if you don't, start with the above as your shopping list.

Software Tools

The software listed in this section is additional software you might want to have for Macintosh trouble-shooting. It is not critical that you have any of this software, but if you have more than a couple of Macs, you'll want one or two of these items just because they'll make your life easier. The types of software listed in this section are:

- Hardware diagnostics
- Software diagnostics
- System utilities

As I said, none of this software is essential. Well, actually, that is a matter of opinion—I do consider some of this software to be close to essential, even though you can live without it. I wouldn't want to work without many of these tools. The hardware and software diagnostic tools are really for those of you who do not have much experience in Macintosh trouble-shooting. In a sense, they are more useful as training tools than for correcting real problems. This is because the hardware diagnostic tools only work with a functioning Mac, and the software diagnostics are not 100% accurate. But both can be used to point you in the right direction.

Hardware Diagnostics

Hardware diagnostic software is software that will check the Macintosh's hardware for problems and malfunctions. All of the packages listed here will perform diagnostic checks of the Mac's hardware and generate result reports. The biggest drawback most of these packages have is that the Mac must be functioning well enough to boot in order for the software to work. Only one package provides for a completely non-functioning Mac, but that Mac must have a NuBus slot for the diagnostic card.

Another thing to keep in mind is that none of these packages is perfect. It is possible for any one of the them to report erroneous errors. Just remember the cautions above.

MacCheck

MacCheck is Apple's diagnostic software for checking Macintosh hardware. It does an adequate job of checking the Mac's hardware, but it does not perform as thorough a check as some of the other software. This software is free and can be obtained from on-line services like CompuServe, America Online, or AppleLink.

Snooper

Maxa's Snooper performs a complete check of all the Macintosh's components, including the hard drives, where it can perform low-level surface checks. In addition to its software, Snooper can be purchased with a NuBus card to diagnose a Mac that has completely failed. The only limitation is that the Mac must have a NuBus slot.

MacEKG

MacEKG, by MicroMAT, is another hardware diagnostic package. It is supposed to access the Mac's hardware directly, while the others use system calls to the hardware (like Snooper), or a combination of system and hardware calls (like Peace of Mind). MacEKG has the ability to benchmark a Mac's performance over time by checking a Mac automatically once a day or once a week.

Peace of Mind

Peace of Mind is put out by Polybus Systems. Like Snooper and MacEKG, it will check all of the Mac's hardware. It actually has more tests than either Snooper or MacEKG. As with the others, the Mac must be bootable in order for the software to be usable.

Software Diagnostics

Software Diagnostics check the Macintosh System software and installed applications. The idea behind this software is that it will identify software and System element incompatibilities. The problem with this type of software is that there are so many variations and software changes that it is very difficult to keep track of all the incompatibilities. But as a learning aid, to help you become familiar with the problems that do occur, this software can be a great help. And who knows, it just might pinpoint the cause of your problem, as well.

Alert

Put out by the Maxa Corporation, Alert looks for such things as software that is incompatible with the Macintosh's System, based on the version number of both the software and the System. It checks for system extension and control panel conflicts, as well. For network administrators, Alert can be used to check client Macintoshes over the AppleTalk network, using its own network responder as a background application.

Help!

Help! is a software/system checker by Teknosys that looks for software incompatibilities, duplicate files, and damaged files. It also checks things like disk space. Help! works over a network, so a network administrator can check other Macs with having to go from Mac to Mac. It is updated on a quarterly basis through a subscription service, and uses a database with over 3000 entries.

System Utilities

This section is about system utilities that are commercial utilities, or available as shareware or freeware, and can be obtained from on-line services. The utilities I want to discuss here are a couple of tools that will help you manage system extension and control panel conflicts, and as well as checking the status and types of devices on your SCSI bus.

Also useful in trouble-shooting is a hard disk formatter other than Apple's. This is because Apple's formatter works only on Apple hard drives and has limited options for formatting a Mac hard disk. There are some third-party formatters that are very comprehensive and give you maximum control over the formatting of your Mac hard disks. Sometimes, all you need to do to fix a Mac hard drive is reinstall the drivers. (Use this ability with caution.) On other occasions, you'll have to recover and reformat the drive. For serious disk problems, get Norton Utilities or MacTools.

System Extension Managers

Extension managers let you turn on and off Macintosh system extensions and control panels, either while the Mac is starting up or from a control panel. These utilities can be essential in hunting down a system extension or control panel conflict that causes the Mac to crash. If you do not have an extension manager of some type and your Mac's System software is version 7.0 or greater, you can always disable all of the extensions and control panels by holding down the **Shift** key while the Mac boots. If the Mac boots, you probably have a problem with one of the extensions or control panels. The problem is then finding the offending device, which means that you have to remove all of the extensions and control panels, loading them back into the system folder one by one and restarting the Mac each time until the problem device is found. This is definitely a tedious process, simplified by one of the following utilities.

Extensions Manager 2.0.1 This is a simple extensions control utility, made but unsupported by Apple. It is not easy to find, because special licensing is required to place it on on-line services. But it is available for distribution by individuals, and it will be on some BBSs and on-line services. As a simple trouble-shooting utility it is a great tool.

Now Utilities 4.0.1 Now Utilities is a commercial product by Now Software. It contains a utility called StartUp Manager that is worth the price of the utilities package by itself. One of the features of the StartUp Manager is the ability to create start-up sets, which let you specify various combinations of extensions and control panels for customized start-up configurations.

Conflict Catcher II This is Casaday & Greene's basic manager for controlling your Mac's start-up environment. This includes extension and control panel management, memory management, and a Windows Accelerator.

INIT Manager INIT Manager, by Baseline Publishing, is another extension manager. It allows you to create multiple start-up sets, and also has the option of disabling extensions and control panels that cause conflicts and system crashes at start-up. (This is a feature of StartUp Manager, as well.)

SCSI Utilities

SCSI utilities are those tools that allow you to check the SCSI bus and to format a Macintosh hard drive. As mentioned above, a formatter can be used in the trouble-shooting process, and sometimes to recover a crashed drive. As much as I would like to go into hard disk trouble-shooting, I cannot. There is just not enough room to cover it here. Just remember that you will, at some point in time, have a problem with a Mac hard disk, and of course your safest course of action is to always have a backup.

SCSIProbe SCSIProbe, by Robert Polic, is an old stand-by. It is a control panel device that shows the devices connected to Macintosh's SCSI bus and lets you mount hard disks that are not currently mounted. It is useful in detecting SCSI ID conflicts and determining what type of devices you have connected to a Mac's SCSI bus. SCSIProbe is on most on-lines services and many BBSs.

Hard Disk Tool Kit Hard Disk Tool Kit, by FWB, is a complete hard-disk formatting, testing, and utility package. It includes a performance checker, a SCSIProbe-like control panel, and one of the best formatters you can find for Macintosh hard drives. With the formatter, you can even modify some hard drives' SCSI parameters, if you know what you are doing. Also, the manual thoroughly explains Macintosh hard drive operations.

RapidTrak RapidTrak, by Insignia Solutions, is a hard disk formatter that can be used to enhance and optimize your Macintosh hard disks. You can also format MS-DOS removable media disks and use them on your Mac if you also have AccessPC, Insignia's Macintosh MS-DOS disk-mounting utility.

Identifying the Symptoms

You come in one morning and find a note taped to your computer's monitor. Betsy in Graphics is having a problem with her Macintosh. She can't print. So you go to her Mac and the day has started. There are several possible causes for her problem, or there may be no problem at all. All you know is that she thinks that she cannot print.

At this point, you don't even know if she can't print. All you know is that she thinks she cannot print, and that in and of itself is problem enough. As of yet, you do not know if she cannot print from a specific application or if she can't print at all. So you have to start by checking all of the possibilities. The problem could be as simple as the printer not being selected from the Macintosh's Chooser.

Betsy's printing problem is only one of a number of problems you'll run across, so rather than creating a narrative for every possible problem (which would result in a few books), this section will list the various problems someone might be having, at the same time providing you with suggestions of where to look for the causes.

As mentioned above, the emphasis will be on Macintosh problems that are network-related. However, out of necessity, there will be some general Macintosh problems listed, as well. With that said, the rest of this section will first look at initial strategies, or things you should do before you even get to the Mac to check it out, and those things you should do when first looking at the Mac. After the initial checks, you will find a list of symptoms, their possible causes, and strategies to find the problem's cause.

First Things First

So that you don't go off on a wild goose chase, you should probably make sure you perform a couple of tasks before you even go to the Macintosh workstation that is experiencing problems. This is especially true if there is even a remote possibility of the problem being network-related. The first task is to run a network-mapping utility. This way, you know before you go the Macintosh workstation with the problem whether the Mac—or, as in our example from above, the LaserWriter—is on the network and communicating. If the Mac and the LaserWriter are visible in the map, chances are that the problem is with your Mac. Also, you will be able to tell if all of your network zones are up and running. If one of your zones is missing, you should check your routers. When a zone disappears, it is probable that you have a router that is down.

By performing this simple task before looking at the problem Mac, you will eliminate many of the possible problems you could be having.

The Symptom List

The symptom list is broken down into categories. Within each category, you will find a list of symptoms that are related to the category. If a symptom is listed in more than one category, it means that the problems could be related. With each symptom, you'll find a short explanation of the possible cause.

Basic Macintosh and Start-up Problems

There are five basic problems that the Mac can have outside of actual hardware problems. The list of problems in this section is progressive, meaning that one will not occur before the other, and the basic problems are listed in order.

1. **The Mac will not start.** The reasons for a Mac is not starting can be numerous. If you do not hear the start-up sound (the Mac's start-up chime), the Mac is probably not receiving power. Other possibilities are a blown power supply or other hardware problem.

2. **The Mac does not complete the boot process.** There are a series of possibilities at this stage. I am assuming that the Mac provides you with the start-up chime. At this point, you could be receiving what is called the "Sad Mac," where the screen goes blank, and instead of the smiling Mac icon that means the boot process is starting, you get a Mac icon that is in reverse video with X's for eyes and a frown.

   The appearance of the Sad Mac means one of two things. Either you have a hard disk with a bad driver or some other hardware problem.

   If you receive the blinking, smiling Mac, but the Mac will proceed no further in the boot process, you may have a SCSI ID conflict. It is also possible that the Mac cannot find a start-up disk. A start-up disk is a hard disk or floppy disk with valid boot blocks and a system file.

   If the Mac displays the Smiling Mac icon and then cycles back to the blinking Mac icon repeatedly, the Mac has found a disk with valid boot blocks but it cannot find a Macintosh System file.

   Finally, the Mac may start the boot process but crash during the start-up process with a Macintosh error code. If this happens, then you are probably experiencing a system extension or control panel conflict.

3. **The Mac crashes after it starts up, while you are in the Finder.** If the Mac crashes as soon as the Desktop appears or shortly thereafter, you could have a corrupted System or Finder file. Other possible causes of this type of problem are low-level corruption of the Macintosh Desktop file and directory or low-level volume information file problems in the hard drive.

4. **The Mac crashes when you try to launch an application.** If the Mac consistently crashes when you try to launch an application, you'll have to rely on context to determine the problem.

Network Trouble-shooting

If this is an occurrence that is new, and the System has not been recently upgraded, then the problem is probably in the Macintosh System file. If the System has just been upgraded, then you could be having a problem because the application is incompatible with the new System.

Also, application-specific problems can sometimes be caused by system extensions or control panels that are incompatible with the application.

5. **The Mac seems to run properly, but you have random system errors.** Random system errors are the hardest to track down. They can be caused by a corrupted system, low-level hard disk problems, incompatible hard disk drivers, or an application that is only somewhat incompatible with the System or system element. Sometimes you have to live with the random system error until the problem becomes more localized.

Chooser Problems

This group of problems are called Chooser Problems because they are all related to the Macintosh's Chooser. The cause of the problem is not the Chooser, unless AppleTalk is inactive, in which case any of these problems could occur. With AppleTalk inactive, none of the Mac's networking functions will work. If you are having network problems, you should always check the Chooser first and make sure AppleTalk is active. (See Fig. 10.1.)

- Cannot see the file server.
- Cannot see the laser printer.
- Zones are not visible.

One possible cause for any of these problems is that the network, a router, or the file server is down. The other possible cause for any of these problems, especially the third one, is that the network selection is set improperly. If you have an Ethernet network and LocalTalk is selected in the Network control panel, you will not see any of your zones or other network resources. Figure 10.2 shows the Network control panel.

Printer Problems

Printer problems are one of the biggest headaches you'll have with your network. This is because every time you have a printer prob-

Figure 10.1

The Macintosh Chooser

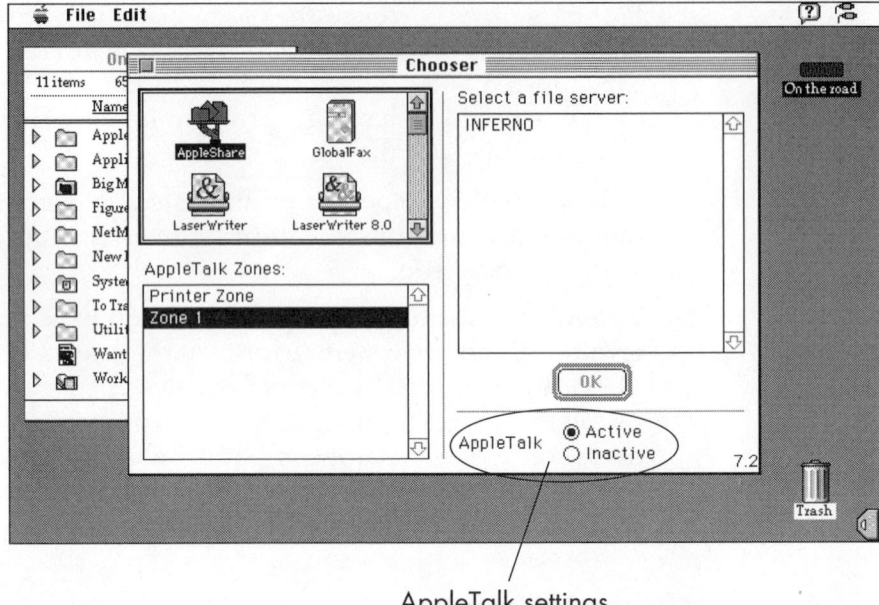

AppleTalk settings

Figure 10.2

The Network control panel

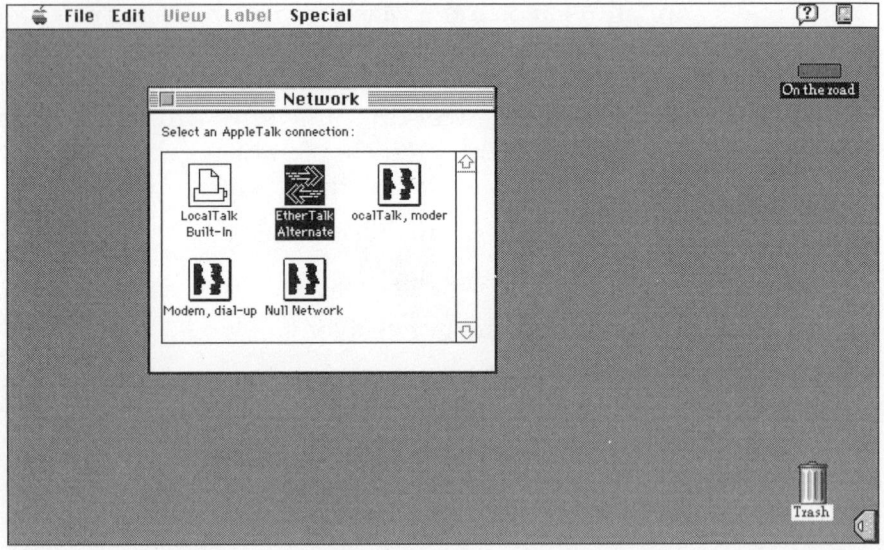

lem it will in some way be network-related, even if the problem is actually a Mac problem. The Macintosh printers you're going to be using are all network-based.

1. **Printer keeps being reinitialized.** You probably have different versions of the LaserWriter driver installed on your Macin-

toshes. All of the Macs should have the same version of the LaserWriter driver. The LaserWriter driver 8.0 can coexist with the LaserWriter driver that comes with System 7.

2. **Printer consistently fails to finish the print job.** If you are printing to a server-based printer queue, the problem could be that the application needs to communicate directly with the laser printer. Also, the file you're trying to print could be corrupted. This is a problem that sometimes occurs with high-end graphics and page layout applications. Usually, if the problem is a corrupted file, you'll have to remake the file from scratch or remove elements from the document until you find what is causing the problem. Try restarting the printer first.

3. **Using a server-based print spooler and queue.** When you're using a server-based print spooler, you can have problems when the printer malfunctions and needs to be restarted. The queue will back up, and your users will not know that there has been a malfunction until they fail to receive their output. If a file that is queued is causing the problem, you'll have to use the server's queue management software and delete the file that would not print, then inform the user that the file didn't print.

Basic Techniques

There is a series of steps you can take to help isolate and fix a problem. The steps listed here are a general set of techniques that you might use if you come across a Mac that is having problems booting, random system errors, or general system problems. Of course, the most important thing to do when trouble-shooting the Mac is to follow a consistent set of procedures.

This section will list techniques you can use when trouble-shooting. These procedures or techniques are listed in an order that you might want to use, but you will have to decide which ones to use based on your circumstances. At this point, there are no set rules. As mentioned in the Identifying the Symptoms section, you should always check the integrity of your network first. Then proceed with the relevant steps.

Basic Macintosh and Start-up Problems

If you're having start-up problems, the first thing you should do is check your cables and make sure your SCSI ID numbers are all correct. It is usually best to disconnect the cables and check the ID numbers visually. Also, make sure your drives are properly terminated—that is, the first and last SCSI devices need to be terminated. Once you have eliminated the possibility of SCSI ID conflicts and cabling problems, you can proceed with other testing procedures.

It the Mac is not completely starting up, you should:

1. Start the Mac and hold down the **Shift** key as soon as you see the Smiling Mac icon. This procedure disables all extensions and any control panels that load into the Mac's memory during the start-up process. If this works, then you can be fairly sure your problems are caused by a system extension conflict.

2. Boot with the Macintosh Disk Tools disk. By booting the Macintosh Disk Tools disk, you are not using the hard drive, so any problems related to the hard drive will be avoided.

3. Boot with the Macintosh Disk Tools disk while holding down the ⌘, **Option**, **Shift**, and **Delete (Backspace)** keys simultaneously. This procedure causes the Macintosh to boot from the Disk Tools disk, ignoring the Macintosh's hard drive. Use this technique if you get the Sad Mac while trying to boot. If the Mac starts, you will have to re-install the hard disk's driver.

4. Just before the Desktop appears, hold down the ⌘ and **Option** keys simultaneously. You will be asked if you want to rebuild the hard drive's Desktop, just before the hard disk would normally mount. Answer Yes to the question. Rebuilding the Desktop will re-associate the Mac's files to their applications, and can sometimes fix random system error problems.

    If the Desktop does not rebuild, you will have to delete the Desktop files and restart the Mac. To delete the Desktop files, you will have to use a utility that deletes these files, or one that will let you make the Desktop DB and Desktop DF files visible (use a utility like DiskTop from PrairieSoft).

    If you make these files visible, you can move them to an empty folder (they cannot be deleted until after you reboot and recreate them) and reboot the Mac. The Mac should recreate the files when you reboot. If the files do not get recreated, you probably have serious disk problems, and the drive should be reformatted.

5. Disconnect any external SCSI devices. If you cannot boot even with the Disk Tools disk, try disconnecting all external SCSI

devices. If the Mac boots, you can isolate the offending device by reconnecting them one at a time until you find the one that is causing the problem.

6. Zap the PRAM. The PRAM (Parameter RAM) contains all of the Mac's default system settings. These include the printer, network, and other System attribute settings. Zapping the PRAM will reset these settings to the factory defaults, so you will have to reset them once they have been zapped. To zap the PRAM settings, shut down the Mac and restart it while holding down the ⌘, **Option**, **P**, and **R** keys simultaneously (this is for System 7). You will hear the Mac repeat the start-up chime when the PRAM is zapped. Once the PRAM is zapped, you can release the keys and let the Mac start. If you are using System 6, hold down the **Option** key while selecting the Control Panels desk accessory, then restart the Mac.

7. Reinstall the System software. If everything works when you boot from the Disk Tools disk, but not when you boot from the hard disk (even with the system extensions turned off), then you should re-install the Mac's System software. The best thing to do is perform a clean installation by booting from the Disk Tools disk and then removing the System and Finder on the hard drive. After they have been deleted, shut down the Mac, restart with the Installer or Install Me First disk, and install the System. If you are asked to replace newer System elements, replace them.

Chooser Problems

When dealing with problems that are centered around the Chooser or the Network control panel, you might try some of the following techniques:

1. Make sure the proper network is selected in the Network control panel. If you cannot change the network selection, you should check the Chooser—AppleTalk is probably turned off.

2. Always check the Chooser and turn AppleTalk on.

3. Reinstall the Apple Network Software. If you are having problems with the Network control panel or the Chooser, re-install the networking software.

4. Reinstall the System Software. The only way to make sure the Chooser is not corrupted is to re-install the System software, as described in the Basic Macintosh and Start-up section.

5. Zap the PRAM. This is also described in the Basic Macintosh and Start-up Problems section.

Printer Problems

Printer problems are usually straightforward. If you are having a problem with printing, try the following:

1. Try to print a window from the Finder. If you can print a directory from the Finder, then your printing problems are not network- or System-related. The printing problem is application-related, or the file you are trying to print is corrupted. If you cannot print a directory window, you should re-install the printing software.

2. Restart the laser printer. One of the first things you should do is restart the laser printer. From time to time, a printer will hang and not print. So before reinstalling printer software, make sure the printer is functioning properly.

3. Print to a different printer. If you can print to one printer but not another, then the problem may be the printer, not the Mac.

4. Re-install the Mac's printing software. If you problems are due to a corrupted printer driver, you can re-install the printing software from the Printing disk that is part of your System disks.

5. Print directly to the printer. If you are having a problem and you are printing to a server queue, try printing directly to the printer, rather than using the queue.

Physical Link and Network Problems

I'm not going to tell you how to trouble-shoot your internet. I'm assuming that you already have experience tracking down cable problems, stalled hubs, and the like. Someone bumping a cable and knocking it loose will have the same result on a Macintosh network as it will on a PC network: the network will go down.

Rather than boring you with such things, this section will look at some of the network-specific problems you might have with a Macintosh. In a sense, it is a hodge-podge section, where you will find bits and pieces of information that are not found elsewhere in the book. The problems you're most likely to have, besides those already mentioned, are routers going down. It is possible to be using a software router like Liaison and have everything appear to be working properly, but have intermittent problems that may not even affect the Macs.

One thing to look out for is when a PC suddenly fails to log into the server and everything, even the network mapping utility, indicates that there is no problem. Still, that one pesky PC won't log in. If this happens to you, you are having one of two problems: either you have a hub with a port that is down, or your router is malfunctioning at a very low level. The fix is to reboot the router.

Along the same line but on a different note, if you have an Ethernet network, you should make sure your Macs have the Network control panel 3.0.2 or greater installed. It can be found on the latest version of Apple's Network Software Installer. The earlier versions of the Network control panel had a tendency to forget the router set-up and not display the zones properly. The latest network installer also contains improvements for the built-in Ethernet for the Macintosh LC and Quadra computers, as well as improved SNMP error reporting.

Another thing that can affect your Macintosh operations is the built-in Ethernet adapters on the newer Macintosh Centris and Quadra machines. The on-board Ethernet does interact well with Ethernet packet analyzers. The on-board hardware combines all of the components normally found on a Ethernet card into a single chip, and the packet analyzing software cannot access the network from these Macs. Other than these few anomalies, there is not a lot that needs to be discussed. Just make sure you have good cables and tight connections.

Application Problems

Application problems are rare. Usually, there are only three problems you will encounter with mainstream Macintosh software. The fixes for these problems are fairly easy. The first will happen after you perform a major system upgrade, such as upgrading from System 6.0.X to 7.X. When you perform a major system upgrade, you should expect some of your old software to break, unless of course you've kept current on all of your software upgrading it as the upgrades become available. As mentioned above, if you just upgraded the System and your software does not run, you'll probably have to get an upgrade from the publisher.

Another problem you'll encounter is when the application needs more memory to function properly. If you receive messages like "Application XXXX unexpectedly quit," the program could be having a memory problem.

To allocate more memory to an application:

1. Make sure the application is not running.

2. Select the Applications icon from the Finder.

3. Perform a Get Info command from the Finder's File menu (or with the ⌘-I keyboard command).

4. Enter the new memory value in the Get Info window that appears for the application (see Fig. 10.3).

5. Close the Get Info window and restart the application.

If, after increasing the application's size, it still doesn't work, you should reboot the Macintosh. Turn off all of the extensions as

Figure 10.3

An application's Get Info window

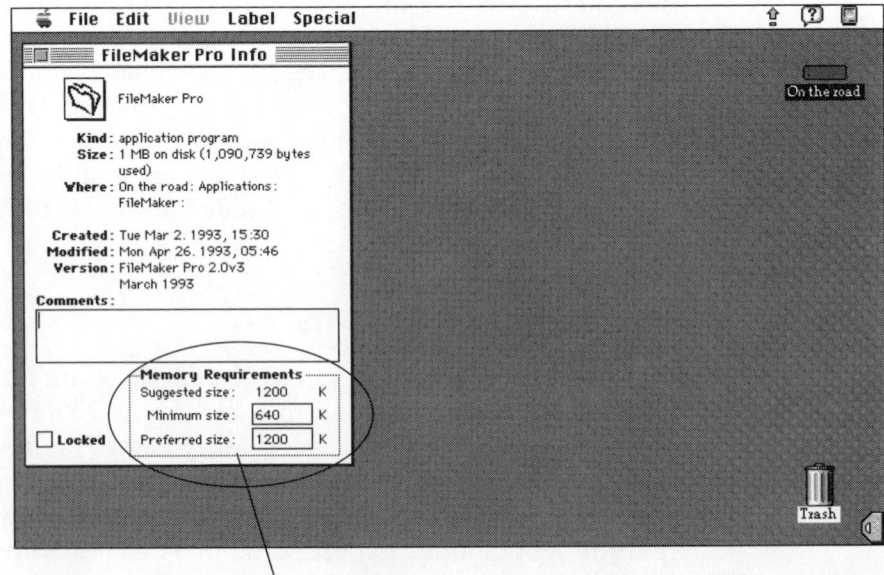

Memory size fields

the Mac boots by holding down the **Shift** key. You should see the message "Extensions off" under the "Welcome to Macintosh." Once the Mac is running without its system extensions, launch the problem application. If it runs, then the problem is one of your system extensions or control panels, and you will have find the problem device and remove it.

On the other hand, if the application does not run, and your other applications are behaving properly, you should re-install the problem program. Either throw away the program that is misbehaving and then install the new one, or re-install the application to a new folder. After the new or re-installation, try running it again.

If it fails this time, you might start thinking about re-installing your System software. However, before going that last step, call the publisher's tech support department and see if they can help. Otherwise, you're on your own. I would recommend that you re-install the system.

Whenever you are having weird problems, you should get a hard disk utility like Norton Utilities for the Macintosh or MacTools and check your hard drive. If the hard disk utility reports errors with the directory, the partition map, or b-tree, the hard disk is seriously ill and should be reformatted, even if the disk utility says it is repaired.

Support Resources

When you're responsible for making sure your Macs and network are operating properly, you will want your systems to be down for the shortest possible time. Actually, you need to appear as if you can solve any computing problem, and this chapter is really a just quick and dirty trouble-shooting guide.

It is possible that the information you need is missing. If you find yourself in a situation where you've tried the suggestions in this chapter and need more information, you can get help from the following sources:

1. The manufacturer of your NOS. If your problem involves your network and the Mac's interaction with the servers or printers on the network, you should give the NOS's manufacturer a call. The manufacturer for each of the network operating systems discussed in this book has employees who are experts regarding Macintosh integration for their NOS. Quite often, the problem will be something simple that you have over-

looked, and a few minutes on the phone with one of these experts will put you on the right path.

The biggest drawback in using the tech support department is that it will probably cost money. The only NOS manufacturer in this book that does not charge for tech support, unless you want priority tech support, is Artisoft. This means that you need to do your homework before you call, or you'll waste time and money on issues that do not need attention. You may what to check out the on-line support services each of these companies maintain before placing the call.

Banyan has a BBS that is used for tech support. Novell offers support on CompuServe, as do Microsoft and Artisoft. Artisoft has its own BBS, as well. If you do not have a critical problem, the on-line resources these companies offer can be used to save you time and money.

2. The manufacturer of your network adapter cards or transceivers. There are times when you might have a problem with the physical aspect of your network and need suggestions for hunting it down. Most manufacturers of network adapters have competent tech support departments and have seen every problem you could possibly have, so they are a great resource. However, before you call, make sure your cabling meets their specifications. Otherwise, you'll be told that your problem is due to improper cabling, and you'll have a heck of a time getting past this minor problem.

3. The publisher of the application that is causing trouble. When you have problems with Macintosh programs, you can get support from the application's publisher, even if the problem is System-related. If you've bumped into an application's shortcoming, the publisher will want to know. And once again, their tech support department has seen many problems. They may have an answer for you that would take you hours to figure out.

4. Apple computer at 800-SOS-APPL or 800-767-2775. If you think you have a hardware or system problem with a Macintosh, Apple has a tech support line that you should use. Apple's tech support lines are always busy, but their technicians are good and know about the machines they support. Your biggest problem will be the wait to get through. If you're

calling Apple, you can end up being on hold for 20 minutes, sometimes more. The length of time you'll have to wait depends on the Mac you're calling about. Figure you'll be on hold for at least 10 minutes.

5. The dealer from whom you purchased your equipment. In today's marketplace, it is often difficult to get service from the dealer, but any Macintosh dealer is supposed to be your first line of support. So you should definitely call your dealer. In some cases, your company will have a service contract with the dealer.

    Also, most dealers who sell networking solutions are certified by the NOS's manufacturer with support resources that you will not have. Do not overlook this source of support.

6. Apple Technical Information Source CD. Apple publishes a CD called the Technical Information Source CD. This CD contains copies of all System software through System 7.0.1, utilities, application upgrades, and technical information about all aspects of the Mac. It is a great resource, and it is also inexpensive. If you are responsible for Macintosh support, you should definitely consider having this CD. It can save you time, and may have the answer you need.

7. Your local Macintosh users' group. Do not forget to become acquainted with your local Macintosh users' group. They are a group of people who know the Mac, and they have resources (or know of resources) for dealing with almost all things Macintosh. Of course, some users' groups are better than others, but a good users' group is truly an asset.

Conclusion

Trouble-shooting is always a pain in the neck. There is enough information in this chapter to point you in the direction you need to go when dealing with the Macintosh. You won't find disk recovery procedures, the Macintosh error codes, or other more esoteric information in this chapter. For those needs, you should pick up a book that deals specifically with the Mac.

With the information that is in this chapter, you should be able to solve 80 to 90% of your Macintosh System, printing, and application problems. Just remember that the suggestions in this chapter are not offered in a step-by-step manner, so to use this information effectively you will need to think about what the Mac is doing, then combine that information with what you already know about computers. Do not let the Mac's graphic user interface fool you: it is a computer, and everything you know about computers does apply. Good-bye and good luck.

Index

A

A (Administration) privilege, 147
AccessPC, 93, 97, 103–106
AccessPC icons, 104, 105
Access privileges
    descriptions of, 76
    security for, 67–76
Access Privileges window, 68
Access rights, assigning, 297–299
Access Rights menu, 264
Account management, 146–150
Adapter cards
    AppleTalk network, 128
        binding AppleTalk protocol to, 292
    LocalTalk, 80
    NDIS network, 320
Adapters, 80–85
Add Extension dialog window, 109
Add Group window, 166
Add on AppleTalk port screen, 245
Address book, 259–260
Addresses, AppleTalk and, 237–239
Administrator problems, 311–312
Adobe Illustrator, 371, 373
Adobe Photoshop, 373
Adobe Premiere, 374
Adobe Streamline, 374

Adobe TypeAlign, 374–375
Adobe Typeface Library, 375
Adobe Type Manager (ATM), 374
Advanced Options, 144, 144–145
AFP-compliant server, 15
"Aging out," 248
Aldus Freehand, 370–371
Aldus IntelliDraw, 372
Aldus PageMaker, 371
Aldus Persuasion, 371
Alert, 396
Altsys Fontographer, 372
AntiToxin, 50, 392
~APF directory, 313–314
Apple File Exchange utility, 93–94
    translating MS-DOS files with, 95–97
Apple HD SC Setup, 390
Apple Internet Router, 18. *See also*
    Internet Router
Apple Menu Items folder, 40–41
Apple Remote Access Client, 346
Apple Remote Access MultiPort Server,
    346–347
Apple Remote Access Personal Server,
    346
AppleShare, 3–4, 6, 187
AppleShare extension, 55

AppleShare file server, 15–18
  accessing, 65–67
AppleShare icon, 65
AppleShare Prep file, 57
AppleShare privileges, setting, 297–299
AppleShare Workstation software,
  installing, 187
AppleTalk, 2, 3–4, 5, 6
  adapters and topologies in, 83
  checking the version of, 63
  restarting, 247–250
  stopping, 243
  on the VINES server, 224–225, 240–254
AppleTalk connection file, 13
AppleTalk Data Stream Protocol
  (ADSP), 11
AppleTalkEcho Protocol (AEP), 12
AppleTalk File Protocol (AFP), 3, 5, 11
AppleTalk File Protocol router, 180
AppleTalk ImageWriters, 204
AppleTalk LaserWriters, 18–19, 211
AppleTalk network adapter card, 128
AppleTalk Phase, changing, 291
AppleTalk Phase 1, 6
  connecting to a server, 229
AppleTalk Phase 2, 7, 130
  connecting to a server, 229–230
AppleTalk Port Configuration screen,
  245, 246
AppleTalk ports, 237–240
  configuring, 241
AppleTalk PostScript printers, VINES
  and, 269–276
AppleTalk printers, 302–310. *See also*
  Printers; Printing
  creating printer queue for, 307–308
  printing to, 204–206
AppleTalk Printer Services (ATPS), 181,
  200–219
  configuring print queue with,
    213–214

AppleTalk protocol, binding to the
  adapter card, 292
AppleTalk Remote Access (ARA), 7,
  287, 345–348
AppleTalk router, NetWare as an,
  179–185
AppleTalk Session Protocol (ASP), 11
AppleTalk setting, 77–78
AppleTalk socket, 332, 333
AppleTalk System Architecture, 9–13
AppleTalk Transaction Protocol (ATP), 12
AppleTalk tunnel, changing port status
  on a server with, 278. *See also*
  Tunneling
Apple Technical Information Source
  CD, 411
Apple technical support lines, 410–411
Apple Utilities folder, 93
Application problems, trouble-
  shooting, 407–409
Applications
  allocating more memory to, 408
  assigning extensions to, 109–116
  cross-platform, 351–384
  database, 377–380
  integrated, 383–384
  running, 22–24
  workgroup, 380–383
A/Rose extension, 55
Artisoft technical support, 169
AsantéView software, 337
Assign Application dialog window, 110
ATCON, 186–221
ATPS. *See* AppleTalk Printer Services
  (ATPS)
ATPS.CFG file, 206–207, 212
  editing, 213–214
ATPS.NLM, 202
  loading, 216
  using with an Ethernet/AppleTalk
    router, 206–209

Index

ATPS AppleTalk queue, switches used with, 209
ATPS module, 203–209
AT&T EasyLink, 355
ATZONES.CFG file, 185
Audit Trail option, 143
AUTOEXEC.CFG file, 183–184
AUTOEXEC.NCF file, 183, 219
Auto-mount option, 66–67

B

*.BAK files, 314
Banyan VINES networking system, 19, 223–281. *See also* VINES
    AppleTalk on, 240–254
    AppleTalk PostScript printers and, 269–276
    Macintosh and, 224–240, 254–269
    trouble-shooting, 276–281
BIOS upgrade, 92
Blyth Omnis 7, 378–379
Boot volume list, 57
Branch, defined, 81
Buffer problems, trouble-shooting, 171–172

C

Cabling, 80–85
    Artisoft supported, 129
    standards for, 85
CAPTURE program, 202
cc:Mail, 22, 354, 357–358
Cdevs, 38–39, 97
Central Point Anti-Virus, 50, 392
Certified Novell Administrators (CNA), 175
Certified Novell Engineers (CNE), 175
Change AppleTalk Phase option, 243
Chooser, 23, 57–58
    problems with, 401
    techniques for solving problems with, 405–406
Chooser Device, 55
Chooser extension, 220, 255
Chooser Name setting, 155
Chooser setting, 77–78
Claris FileMaker Pro, 379
Claris Resolve, 367
ClarisWorks, 383, 384
Claris XTND translation system, 118, 384
CoActive Connector for DOS and Windows, 321–323
Command Buffers setting, 146
CONFIG.SYS file, 135
Configuration errors, trouble-shooting, 170
Configuration files, 31
Configuration menu, in the MACADMIN program, 295
Configuration Password Maintenance, 160
Configure AFP Server screen, 252
Configure Filters screen, 274, 275
Conflict Catcher II, 397
Control A Service screen, 252
Control panels, 56–57
Control Panels folder, 38–39
Conversion utilities, 52
CorelDraw, 371, 376
Creator code, 51
Cross-platform applications, 351–384
Cross-platform compatibility, 20
Cross-platform software, 352–353
Custom installation screen, 60
CUSTOM setting, 152

D

Database applications, 380
DataClub, 63
Datagram Delivery Protocol (DDP), 12
Data security, 23–24. *See also* Security

DaVinci eMail, 22, 354, 358–359
DaVinci MacAccess, 358
Dayna Communications AppleTalk
    card, 179–180, 184, 270
  connecting a PostScript printer to, 204
DaynaTALK card, 225, 226, 232
Dbase file format, 378
Dbase files, 119
DCA-RFT to MacWrite option, 95, 96
Debugger program, 32
Default adapter, setting, 293–294
Define Extension Mappings screen,
    251, 253
Deneba Systems Canvas, 376
Desk Accessories, 40
Desktop, 34
Desktop files, 313
Desktop icon, 99, 100
Desktop mounting utilities, 97–109
Desktop publishing packages, 369–377
Destination Attributes screen, 272–274
Destination Device option, 154
DialAssist, 346
DIF file format, 368–369
Disk drives, 46–47
Disk First Aid, 390, 392
Disks, exchanging, 88–120
Disk space requirements, 45–46
Disk Tools disk, 45, 47, 390, 391
  booting with, 404
DiskTop, 52–53
DiskTopInfo window, 53
Disk utility software, 49
Display Port Status option, 243
Display Routes option, 243
.DOC extension, 101, 106, 111
Document icon, 73, 74, 75
DOS
  CoActive Connector for, 321–323
  MacDisk for, 116
DOS directory, 31

DOS Extension Mapping, 251–253
DOS Mounter, 93, 97
DOS Mounter icons, 102
DOS Mounter Plus, 101–103, 219
DOS naming conventions, 21
DOS-to-Mac option, 115
Drag-and-drop technique, 199
Drives
  adding, 89–90
  attaching to the SCSI bus, 90–91
Drop box, 72

E

E (Every) privilege, 147
Easy Install screen, 59
Edit Group window, 166
Edit Volume window, 167–168
8bitClean data, 211
E-mail, 21–22, 353–360
Emulation software, 326–328
End nodes, 230
EPS (Encapsulated PostScript) file, 373
Ethernet, adapters and cabling for, 83–84
Ethernet-to-AppleTalk router, 205
  using ATPS.NLM with, 206–209
Ethernet-to-SCSI adapter, 83
EtherPeek, 339
EtherTalk, 6
  connecting to a server, 228–230
EtherTalk extension, 55
EtherTalk Link Access Protocol, 13
EtherTalk Phase 2, 226
EtherTalk Phase 2 extension, 55
EtherTalk Prep extension, 55
Extension and Application Mapping
    dialog window, 110
Extension managers, 396–397
Extension mapping, 20–21
  adding or modifying, 300–301
Extensions, assigning to Macintosh
    applications, 109–116

Index

Extensions folder, 36–37
Extensions Manager 2.0.1, 397
External Mail program, 360

F

Failed Login Retries option, 143–144
FastBack Plus, 119–120
File Definition screen, 159
File Definitions list, 1258
File Definitions Options screen, 157
File Definition window, 168
File exchanges, 19–21
File Extension Mapping, 157–160, 251
File Extensions window, 169
File Guard, 343
FileMaker, 119
FileMaker Pro, 11
File servers, 17. *See also* Server
  accessing, 65–67
  AppleShare, 15–18
File sharing, 20
File Sharing extension, 55–56
File Sharing Folder, 57
File Sharing Monitor control panel, 56
File structures, 50–54
Filter Setup screen, 275
Finder, 29, 30, 34–35
Find File Desk Accessory, 45
Floppy disk drives, 89
Floppy disks, exchanging, 88–120
Folders/SubDirs window, 151
Font/DA Mover, 40, 43, 188
Font File option, 155
Fonts folder, 41–43
Font suitcases, 42–43
FormatterOne, 48
Formatting software, 47–49
FoxBase, 119
Fragmentation, checking for, 49
FrameMaker, 375–376
FWB Company, 48

G

Gateways. *See* LANtastic Macintosh Gateways
GatorLink, 348
Get Info, performing, 34
Get Info window, 408
G/Net, 85
GraceLAN, 341
GraceLAN Network Manager, 341
Graphic interface, 31
Graphics packages, 369–377
  using, 376–377
Graphic User Interface, 32
Group Account Information dialog box, 148
Group account management, 147–150
Groups window, 166–167
Groupware, 24–25
Guest account feature, 7
Guest logins, 253–254
  on Macintosh volumes, 299–300
Guest Logins option, 143

H

Hard disk, recovery and repair utility for, 392–393
Hard Disk Toolkit, 48, 398
Hard disk utility software, 47–49
Hardware diagnostic software, 394–395
Hardware platforms, 129
Harvard Graphics, 371, 376
HDMount button, 106
Help!, 396
Houdini card, 324–326

I

Individual account management, 146–147
Inheritance rights, 76–77, 196
INIT Manager, 397

Inits, 37
Inside Macintosh series, 10, 33, 50
Insignia Solutions, 103
INSTALL.NLM, 180
Installation
   of AppleShare Workstation software, 187
   customizing, 60–61
   of LAN Manager Services for Macintosh, 288–294
   of LANtastic for Macintosh software, 136–161
   of Macintosh cards, 84–85
   of Macintosh NetWare Utilities, 188–189
   of NetWare for Macintosh software, 181–185
   of networking software, 63
   of the Novell-Macintosh protocol layers, 180–185
   of 3.5-inch drives, 91–92
   of translators, 96
   of the VINES Macintosh option, 240–241
Installation set-up screen, 137
Installed software, removing, 62–63
Installer, 58–60, 61
Installer Welcome screen, 59
Install Me First disk, 391
Integrated applications, 383–384
Intelligent Messaging, 269, 354
Internet, using zones on an, 235
Internet address, 12
Internet Router, 86, 126, 205, 226, 238
   using, 268–269
Inter•Poll, 281, 333–334
In-use sectors, 49
"Invisible" files folder, access privilege settings for, 74

K

KeyServer, 341

L

L (Login) privilege, 147
LAN (Local Area Network), 2
LANMAC directory, 137, 141
LAN MAC Manager, 124, 142, 165
LANMAN.INI file, 299–300, 309
LAN Manager, 283–314
   using as a print server, 305–309
   using to set up the printer and queue, 309–310
LAN Manager for Macintosh, 294–302
LAN Manager internet, 285
LAN Manager Services for Macintosh
   AppleTalk printers and, 302–310
   configuring, 290–294
   installing, 288–294
   Macintosh installation and, 287–294
   stopping and restarting, 301–302
   trouble-shooting, 310–314
LANMAN directory, 289, 291
LanProtect, 50
LanRover/E, 347
LanRover/L, 347
LANsurveyor, 334–335
LANtastic for Macintosh networks, 125
LANtastic for Macintosh, 124–127
   configuring, 138–161
   trouble-shooting, 169–172
LANtastic for Macintosh gateway server, 127–130
LANtastic for Macintosh software, 127
LANtastic for Macintosh Windows Gateway, 323
LANtastic Macintosh Gateways, 123–172
   basic requirements for, 127–133
   setting up, 133–136
   software installation for, 136–161
   using, 161–164
LANtastic PC network software, configuring, 134–136

Index

LANtastic Server option, 154
LapLink, 117
LapLink Mac, 118–119
Laser Prep option, 155, 164, 172
LaserWriter driver, 63–64, 157
LaserWriters, 18–19, 211
Liaison, 348
Liaison routing, 238–239
Likewise, 342
Link Access Protocol, 13
Link Drivers, 139, 140
Link Support, 139, 140
LMAC-MGR.EXE program, 138, 139
   running, 141–161
LMSERVER program, 141, 142, 146, 160, 161
LMSERVER Server Information window, 165
LMSTART.BAT file, 140–141, 162
   configuration problems and, 170
Load AppleTalk command, 203
LOAD MAC command, 220
Local Area Network (LAN), 223
LocalPath, 18, 86, 226
LocalPeek, 339
LocalTalk, 7, 80–83
   connecting to a server, 226–227
   topology for, 83
LocalTalk adapter cards, 80
LocalTalk Link Access Protocol (LLAP), 13
"Locked out" folder, 71
   access privileges settings for, 71
Lotus 123, 366, 367–368
Lotus Notes, 25, 358, 381–382

M

MACADMIN program, 294–302, 301–302
   problems with, 311–312
   using from an OS/2 workstation, 302
Mac App button, 109
MacCheck, 395
MacDisk, 116
MacEKG, 395
.MAC extension, 115
MacFile services, 301–302, 312
Macintosh
   Banyan VINES networking system and, 224–240
   connecting to a Novell server, 175–221
   file structures in, 50–54
   identifying problems with, 399–401
   networking options in, 13–19
   networking software in, 54–64
   protocols and terminology in, 4–9
   support resources for, 409–411
   techniques for solving problems with, 403–405
   using as an MS-DOS machine, 323–331
   VINES on the, 254–269
   ways to use, 19–25
Macintosh access rights, 132
Macintosh applications, assigning extensions to, 109–116. *See also* Applications
Macintosh cards, installing, 84–85
Macintosh disk drives, 46–47
Macintosh file problems, 313–314
Macintosh internet, 9
Macintosh internet router, 268–269. *See also* Internet Router
Macintosh messages, problems with, 278–279
Macintosh NetWare Utilities, 187–189
   installing, 188–189
   using, 190–199
Macintosh network cards, 177–179
Macintosh networks, 79–86. *See also* Networking; Networks

Macintosh operating system, 28–54
    disk basics in, 46–50
    file structures in, 50–54
    System folder, 29–46
Macintosh Platform Pack, 358
Macintosh printer access, 303–305
Macintosh Sharing dialog box, 153
Macintosh System 6.0.X, 63–64
Macintosh System 7.X, 63–64
Macintosh users' groups, 411
Macintosh virus utilities, 392
Macintosh volumes
    defining, 150–151
    guest logins on, 299–300
    sharing and modifying, 295–296
Macintosh word processors, 365–366
MacLan Gold, 219, 221
MacLan NetWare, 221
MacLan Novell, 219
MacLink Plus, 52, 96, 117–118, 377
MacMail, problems with, 279
MAC Manager, 124
MACNTOSH directory, 289
Mac Plus, 89
MacPrint services, 309
Mac-to-DOS utility, 111–116
Mac-to-MS-DOS utility programs, 116–119
MacTools, 49, 50, 392
MAC UTILITIES v2.11 disk, 187
Main Group option, 147
Main Server icon, 164
Manage AppleTalk screen, 242, 244, 247
Manage Ports option, 243
Manage Ports screen, 244
Manage Routing through VINES Networks option, 243
Manage Systems Files section, 160–161
Managing AppleTalk on a VINES Network manual, 281
Mapping, 230–237

Maximum Byte Range Locks setting, 145
Maximum Files setting, 144
Maximum Sessions setting, 144
MCI Mail, 355
Media Formatter, 107–108
MEMMAKER, 171
Memory management, 32
Memory problems, trouble-shooting, 171–172
Menus, in the MACADMIN program, 295
Message Handling Service (MHS), 353
Message module, 190, 191
Messaging, intelligent, 269, 354
Microsoft Excel, 366, 367
Microsoft FoxBase, 378
Microsoft LAN Manager. *See* LAN Manager
Microsoft Mail, 22, 354, 359–360
Microsoft Mail Connection, 360
Microsoft Mail & Schedule, 25
Microsoft Office, 382–383
Microsoft PowerPoint, 376
Microsoft Word, 361–364
Microsoft Word for the Macintosh, 52
Microsoft Works, 383–384
MILD (Multiple Interface Link Driver), 140
Minimum Password Length option, 144
MS-DOS co-processor card, 324
MS-DOS disk, reading and transfering files from, 93–94
MS-DOS emulators, 103, 326–328
MS-DOS files
    opening, 51–52
    translating with Apple File Exchange, 95–97
MS-DOS machine, using a Macintosh as, 323–331

MS-DOS-to-Mac utility programs, 116–119
MULTI-DRIVER, 104, 106–109
MULTI-DRIVER icon, 107
Multiple System folders, 44–45

N

Name-Binding Protocol (NBP), 12–13
NDIS (Network Driver Interface Spec), 288
NDIS network adapter card, 320
NET.CFG file, 139–140
   configuration problems and, 170
NET ADMIN program, 295, 297, 298
   using, 301
NetAtlas, 334
NetDistributor Pro, 342
NET_MGR program, 136, 172
NetMinder Ethernet, 339
NetMinder LocalTalk, 339
NetModem/E, 347–348
NetMounter, 219–220
NetPatrol Pack, 339
NET QUEUE HALT command, 136
netSecure, 344
NetWare, as an AppleTalk router, 179–185
NetWare Control Center (NCC), 192–199
NetWare Control Center (NCC) File menu, 193, 194
NetWare Control Center (NCC) Folders/Files menu, 196
NetWare Control Center (NCC) Groups menu, 199
NetWare Control Center (NCC) Trustee Assignments window, 198
NetWare Control Center (NCC) Users menu, 197–198
NetWare Control Center (NCC) Volumes menu, 195
NetWare Control Center (NCC) Windows menu, 193, 194
NetWare DAs, 187–188
NetWare for Macintosh, 177
   installing, 176
NetWare for Macintosh software, installing, 181–185
NetWare Loadable Modules (NLMs), 14, 23, 202
NetWare network, 178
NetWare printing options, 201–203
NetWare server, logging into, 186–187
NetWare Utilities, 187–189
   installing, 188–189
   using, 190–199
Net Watchman, 338
Network access privileges settings, 70
Network addressing, 229
Network cards, 177–179
   AppleTalk-compatible, 128
Network configurations, 129
Network configuration sheet, 242
Network control panel, 56
Network extension, 56
Networking, 27–86
   basics of, 3–13
   Macintosh operating system and, 28–54
   Macintosh software and, 54–64
   Macintosh-specific concepts in, 64–79
Networking Control Panels, 38, 56–57
Networking extensions, 54–56
Networking options, 13–19
Networking preferences files, 57
Networking software, 54–64
   installing, 63
Network Management selection, using, 248
Network management utilities, 339–341
Network mapping, 134, 332–335

Network mapping utility, 393, 399
Network operating system (NOS), 3, 20
   security for, 67–76
Network problems, trouble-shooting, 406–407
Networks
   cabling and adapters for, 80–85
   combined, 225–230
   default, 293–294
   Macintosh, 79–86
   mapping, 230–237
   planning, 130–133, 288
   seeding, 293
   support resources for, 409–411
   trouble-shooting, 77–79, 387–411
NetWORKS, 340–341
NetWORKS, Jr., 340–341
Network settings, reconfiguring, 78–79
Network Software Installer, 391, 407
Network Supervisor LANscape, 335
Network utilities, 331–348
Network Vital Signs, 340
Node number, 239
Nok Nok A/S, 344
Non-seed ports, 239–240
Norton Utilities, 49
Norton Utilities for Macintosh, 393
NOS routers, 85–86
NOS software, 54
Novell AppBuilder, 379–380
Novell-Macintosh protocol layers, installing, 180–185
Novell Network Loadable Modules (NLMs), 14, 23, 202
"Novell Q" print queue, 208
Novell server
   accessing with third-party software, 219–221
   connecting a Macintosh to, 175–221
   preparing, 180–185
Now Utilities 4.0.1, 397
NPRINT program, 202
NuBus card, 323
NuBus FDDI boards, 85
NuBus SCSI adapter, 47

O

ODI (Open Data-Link Interface, 140
ODI drivers, 320, 323
ODINSUP.COM driver, 320–321
OmniNet, 85
Open dialog window, 262
Operating system. *See* Macintosh operating system
Operator menu, 248
OrangePC, 324
OrangePC configurations, 325
OS/2 workstation, using MACADMIN program from, 302
Output Devices choice list, 155

P

Packet analyzers, 338–339
PAP printers, 251, 271, 272
   configuring, 276
PARENT setting, 152
Password changes, 279
Password Expiration option, 144
Password Save option, 144
pcAnywhere, 118
PC disks, software for reading, 92–93
PC Exchange utility, 93, 97, 99–101, 118
PC Exchange control panel, 101
PC Exchange icon, 100
PC network operating systems, alternatives to, 318–323
PCONSOLE, 181, 202
   setting up the print server with, 214–216
Peace of Mind, 395
Peer-to-peer networking, 14

Index

Pencil icon, 72, 75
Performance option, 145
Personal MacLAN, 319–321
PhoneNET, 8, 80–83
　topologies for, 82, 83
PhoneNET Talk, 318–319
Physical links, problems with, 406–407
PICT file format, 377
"Plug and play" connections, 1
Ports
　AppleTalk, 237–240
　configuring, 244–247
　seed and non-seed, 239–240
　VINES, 240
Port servers, single, 277–278
Port status
　changing, 278
　problems with, 279–281
POSTFILT filter, 275
PostScript, 372
PostScript fonts, 43
PostScript laser printer, 225
PostScript Level II, 203
PostScript printers, 81, 153, 172
　attaching via serial or parallel port, 213
PPD file, 303
PRAM, zapping, 78, 79, 405, 406
PRAM settings, 38
Preferences folder, 39, 40
PRINTCON program, 202
PRINTDEF program, 202
Printer access, configuring, 155–157
Printer configurations, 200–201, 304
Printer destination, setting, 305–307
Printer Information screen, 154, 156–157
Printer Information window, 156
Printer Management, 153–157
Printer Name setting, 156
Printer problems, 401–403
　techniques for solving, 406
　trouble-shooting, 172
Printer queue
　creating, 307–308
　sharing, 308–309
Printers. *See also* PAP printers
　AppleTalk, 302–310
　AppleTalk PostScript, 269–276
　connecting to a server, 309–310
　defining, 154–155
Printer screen, 163
Printer service destination, 271
Printer Zone setting, 156
Printing
　to an AppleTalk printer, 204–206
　Novell Loadable Modules (NLMs) for, 202
Printing options, 201–203
Printing services, AppleTalk, 200–219
PrintMonitor Documents folder, 43
Print Queue, 190
Print Queue module, 191
Print server
　reconfiguring, 217–218
　setting up with PCONSOLE, 214–216
　using LAN Manager as a, 305–309
PRINT subdirectory, 181
Privileges settings, 152
Program linking, 56
PROTOCOL.INI file, 289, 310
Protocol AppleTalk, 139, 140
Protocol Information screen, 249
PSERVER, 209–219
　loading, 216
　printing through, 210, 212
PSERVER.NLM, 202
Public Utilities, 393

Q

Q&A, 379
QuarkXPress, 375

QuickMail, 22, 287, 354, 355–357
QuickTime movie format, 374
Quota, 342

R

RapidTrak, 48, 398
Rasputin, 17
RCONSOLE command, 206
Rdev, 55
Read-only files access privilege settings, 75
Read-only folder access privilege settings, 73, 74
Read-Only Memory, 32
Read/Write Buffers setting, 145–146
Registered users, 8
Remote connections, 344–345
Remove option, 62
Resource configuration, 137
Resources, 58
Responder utility, 332, 334
Rights module, 192
ROM BIOS, 92
RouterCheck, 338
Routers, 85–86
Routing Table Maintenance Protocol (RTMP), 13
RTF (Rich Text Format), 360, 366
RTMP Stub, 13
RunPC, 117, 118, 324, 329, 345

S

"Sad Mac" icon, 400
Save As dialog box, 362–365
Scheduler, 359
Screen Saver Timeout option, 144
SCSI (Small Computer Standard Interface), 32, 89, 90
SCSI bus, attaching drives to, 90–91
SCSI Director, 48
SCSI port, attaching a drive to, 90–91
SCSIProbe, 398
SCSI-to-Ethernet adapter, 83
SCSI Utilities, 397–398
Search utilities, 45
Security
  for access privileges, 67–76
  for data, 23–24
Security Force, 344
Security software, 343–344
Seed ports (routers), 8, 227, 239–240
Select File Def button, 169
SERIAL.PS file, 217, 219
Serius Workshop, 379–380
Server. *See also* File servers; Novell server; Print server
  configuring, 176–179, 241–247
  connecting EtherTalk to, 228–230
  connecting LocalTalk to, 226–227
  connecting the printer to, 309–310
  connecting TokenTalk to, 227–228
  problems with, 311–312
  requirements for LAN Manager Services for Macintosh, 287–288
Server crashes, trouble-shooting, 170–171
Server Name option, 143
Server Parameters dialog box, 145
Server Parameters screen, 143
Server Resource option, 154
Server screen, 162
Server Startup Parameters, 143–146
Service Monitor, 254
Session number, problems related to, 311
Set Access Rights utility, 258, 260–261
Set Access Rights window, 263
SETARL program, 251, 276
SETMAIL command, 250, 269
!SETSTDA command, 250
SHARE.EXE, 322

SHARE command, 161
Sharing command, 261
Sharing Setup control panel, 56
Shiva Products, 347
Shutdown Password option, 144
Silver Cloud, 344
Simple Mail Transfer Protocol (SMTP), 353
Single port servers, 277–278
Skyline, 342
SMC_Server, 17
"SneakerNet," 88
SNMP data, 335, 337
Snooper, 395
Socket numbers, 239
SoftPC, 326–328
  variable features of, 327
SoftPC emulators, 103
Software
  AppleShare Workstation, 187
  cross-platform, 352–353
  emulation, 326–328
  formatting, 47–49
  hard disk utility, 47–49
  hardware diagnostic, 394–395
  installing, 58–63
  LANtastic for Macintosh, 136–161
  networking, 54–64
  policy for installing, 37
  for reading PC disks, 92–93
  security, 343–344
  system, 390–392
  word processing, 360–366
Software diagnostics, 395–396
Software management utilities, 341–343
Software tools, for trouble-shooting, 394
Source-level routing, turning on, 228
Source Network option, 154
Split horizon, 230

SPMount button, 106
SPOOL command, 216–217
Spreadsheet packages, 366–369
SQL (Standard Query Language), 378
Star controller, 81
STARTNET.BAT file, 135–136, 162
Start/Stop AppleTalk option, 241
STARTUP.NCF file, 182
Startup Disk Control Panel, 45
Startup Items folder, 39
StartUp Manager utility, 397
Start-up problems
  symptoms of, 399–401
  techniques for, 403–405
Status*Mac, 342
Status menu, in the MACADMIN program, 295
StreetTalk, 250–251
StreetTalk Directory Assistance (STDA), 225, 250–251
STDA dialog window, 265
Stuffit Deluxe, 120
SuperDrive, 88, 89, 93, 100
SuperLaser Spool, 279
Support resources, 409–411
Switches, used with ATPS AppleTalk queue, 209
SYLK file format, 368–369
Symantec AntiVirus for Macintosh, 50, 392
SyQuest, 119, 120
System 7.X
  file sharing in, 14–15
  installing, 59–59
System 7 Reference Manual, 28
System 7 Tune-Up disk, 391–392
System Buffers setting, 146
System disk space requirements, 45–46
System elements, 32–33
System Enabler, 35, 391
System extension managers, 396–397

System features, selecting, 61
System folder icon, 29
System folders, 29–46
　multiple, 44–45
System Installer, 390–391
System management utilities, 341–343
System networking elements, 54–58
System Sectors setting, 146
Systems files, 29, 30, 33
　managing, 160–161
　problems with, 170–171
Systems Management Server, 17
System software, for trouble-shooting, 390–392
System Software updates, 391
System startup documents, 37
System support folders, automatic creation of, 45
System utilities, 396–398
System versions, differences in, 63–64

T

Table Data screen, 249
Tagged file, 114
TalkSpy, 338
TalkStat, 338
Third-party software, 63, 176
3.5-inch drives, installing, 91–92
Tidbits disk, 93
TIFF file format, 377
Timbuktu, 345
Timbuktu for Windows, 329–331
TokenPeek, 339
Token Ring, 6, 9
　adapters and cabling for, 84
TokenTalk, 6
　connecting to a server, 227–228
TokenTalk Extension, 56
TokenTalk Link Access Protocol, 13
TokenTalk Prep extension, 56
Tops for the Macintosh, 63

Traffic analyzers, 335–338
TrafficWatch, 337
Transaction-based protocol, 12
Translators, installing, 96
Trouble-shooting
　basic techniques for, 403–406
　identifying symptoms in, 398–403
　for LANtastic for Macintosh, 169–172
　network, 77–79, 387–411
　for Services for Macintosh, 310–314
　tools for, 389–398
　for VINES, 276–281
Trustee, defined, 196
TSR (Terminate and Stay Resident) programs, 116, 135, 319
Tunneling, 230–231, 234–237
Type code, 51

U

Update All Extensions For All Types option, 159
Update All Files Belonging to a Specific Type option, 159
Update All Files With Specified Extension option, 159
Upper Memory Block (UMB), 127, 135
User access problems, 310–311
User Account Information screen, 148
User screen, 162
Users & Groups control panel, 57
Users & Groups data file, 57
Users window, 167
Utilities Selector window, 258

V

Version Territory, 343
VFind, 392
View File Definitions By Extension option, 159
View File Definitions By Name option, 157–158

View menu, in the MACADMIN program, 295
VINES, 123, 231. *See also* Banyan VINES networking system
VINES extension, 255–257
VINES Login dialog window, 256
VINES Login Options dialog window, 256
VINES Macintosh option, installing, 240–241
VINES Mail, 269
VINES Messages utility, 258, 259
VINES Network and Systems Management software (VNSM), 248
VINES networking operating system, 66
VINES Network Summary screen, 249
VINES Operate utility, 251–252
VINES port, 237, 240
VINES printer service, 270
VINES server
   AppleTalk on the, 224–225
   tunneling through, 236–237
VINES User's Guide for Macintosh, 257
VINES Utilities, 255, 257–268, 276
VINES view, 264, 267
Virex, 50, 392
Virus checkers, 392
Viruses, 50
VNSM Service Monitor, 254
Volt meter, 393–394
Volume (Directory) Management, 150–153
Volume icon, 164
Volume Information dialog box, 151
Volumes, mounted, 17–18. *See also* Macintosh volumes
Volume screen, 162
Volumes window, 167–168

W

Who Am I? utility, 258
Who Am I? utility window, 259
Wide Area Network (WAN), 223
Windows
   CoActive Connector for, 321–323
   MacDisk for, 116
Windows for Workgroups (WFW) network, 319
WingZ, 366, 368
Wires, crimping and testing, 393
Word 6.0 for the Macintosh, 364
WordPerfect, 364–365
WordPerfect Office, 22, 24–25, 382
WordPerfect Works, 384
Word processing software, 360–366
Word Text icon, 111
Workgroup applications, 380–383
Workgroup servers, 16

X

X.500 protocol, 353
XCOPY command, 290

Z

Zapping the PRAM, 78, 79, 405, 406
ZMODEM, 119
Zone Information Protocol (ZIP), 13
Zones, 9, 232–234